Silverlight 4 Data and Services Cookbook

Over 85 practical recipes for creating rich, data-driven business applications in Silverlight

Gill Cleeren

Kevin Dockx

BIRMINGHAM - MUMBAI

Silverlight 4 Data and Services Cookbook

First published: April 2010

Production Reference: 1200410

Published by Packt Publishing Ltd.
32 Lincoln Road
Olton
Birmingham, B27 6PA, UK.

ISBN 978-1-847199-84-3

www.packtpub.com

Cover Image by Sandeep (sandyjb@gmail.com)

Credits

About the authors

Gill Cleeren is Microsoft's Regional Director, MVP ASP.NET, INETA speaker bureau member, and Silverlight Insider. He lives in Belgium, where he works as a .NET architect. Since its introduction, Gill has been a .NET enthusiast. For the first few years of his career, he developed ASP.NET applications. The very day that Silverlight was introduced to the world, back in 2007, he started working with the technology. Since then, he has given many training sessions and developed several applications, both with Silverlight and WPF.

As MVP and Regional Director, Gill is also very active in the Belgian and international community as a speaker and user group leader for Visug, the Belgian .NET user group. His blog on .NET, ASP.NET, and Silverlight can be found at www.snowball.be.

For me, writing a book about the things I like to do has always been a dream. For some time now, Silverlight has been my hobby and passion. I spend hours in front of my laptop, both during and after working hours, staring at some Silverlight project. When James Lumsden of Packt Publishing offered me the possibility to write a book on Silverlight, I was immediately carried away by the idea. Packt brought me in touch with Kevin Dockx, also from Belgium, who agreed on co-authoring this book. Days after that, we sat together and started working on the book you're holding in your hands now. During the writing period, the people of Packt have been most helpful in every way. I really want to thank Kerry George, Neha Patwari, and Zainab Bagasrawala for replying to the countless mails we have exchanged! I also want to thank the review team: Kevin DeRudder, Mike Hanley, Tarkan Karadayi, and Kris Van Der Mast. And of course, a very big thank you to both my mother and my lovely girlfriend Lindsey, for the patience during the days I spent more time writing than being with you.

Kevin Dockx lives in Belgium and works at RealDolmen, one of Belgium's biggest ICT companies, where he is a technical specialist/project leader on .NET web applications, mainly Silverlight, and a solution manager for Rich Applications (Silverlight, WPF, Surface).His main focus lies on all things Silverlight, but he still keeps an eye on the new developments concerning other products from the Microsoft .NET (Web) Stack. As a Silverlight enthusiast, he's a regular speaker on various national and international events, like Microsoft DevDays in The Netherlands or on BESUG events (the Belgian Silverlight User Group). His blog, which contains various tidbits on Silverlight, .NET, and the occasional rambling, can be found at http://blog.kevindockx.com.

I'd like to thank anyone who helped me out with this book, especially Maarten Balliauw, who pointed me in the right direction for the Windows Azure recipes. Besides that, I'd also like to thank my friends for sticking around while I was busy spending my time writing this book instead of socializing. :-)

About the reviewers

Kevin DeRudder is a .NET trainer and consultant at U2U, mainly focusing on the WEB. In the last years, Kevin was involved in lots of Silverlight and ASP.NET projects for a variety of clients and projects.

Mike Hanley is the VP of Engineering at Vertigo Software, Inc. (http://www.vertigo.com). He has worked as a Software Engineer, specializing on the Microsoft Platform for over 10 years. Recently, Mike has spent a great deal of time working on Silverlight applications for clients ranging from Hard Rock International to the Democratic National Committee. Most recently, Mike has worked on several live video events using IIS Smooth Streaming. Mike is a Certified Scrum Master and graduated from Harvey Mudd College with a B.S. in Computer Science. You can learn more about Mike on his blog: http://www.michaelhanley.org. During his spare time, Mike enjoys spending time with his wife Tylar and his first son Max. Mike also has an identical twin brother Kevin.

Tarkan Karadayi has been writing code since the age of 14. He has a Masters in Computer Science and is currently working as a Lead Developer.

> I would like to thank my wife Anna, my parents, and my three sons Taran, Kyle, and Ryan for their love and support.

Kris van der Mast, an active and dedicated moderator at the official Microsoft ASP.NET forums, has reserved himself a place among the Most Valuable Professionals since 2007 and in 2009 earned the ASP Insider title. He's also a known member of several of the Belgian user groups.

Kris works for Ordina Belgium, a consultancy company working for large corporates in Belgium and abroad, as a senior .NET developer and architect. He also provides courses to clients in his specialization and technical interests, being web technologies.

Table of Contents

Preface

This practical cookbook teaches you how to build data-rich business applications with Silverlight that draw on multiple sources of data. Most of the features covered work both in Silverlight 3 and 4. However, we cover some that are specific to Silverlight 4, which will therefore not work with Silverlight 3. Where this is the case, it will be clearly indicated.

Packed with reusable, real-world recipes, the book begins by introducing you to general principles when programming Silverlight. It then dives deep into the world of data services, covering all the options available to access data and communicate with services to make the most out of data in your Silverlight business applications, whilst at the same time providing a rich user experience. Chapters cover data binding, data controls, concepts of talking to services, communicating with WCF, ASMX, and REST services and much more.

By following the practical recipes in this book, which are of varying difficulty levels, you will learn concepts for creating data-rich business applications—from the creation of a Silverlight application, to displaying data in the Silverlight application and upgrading your existing applications to use Silverlight. Each recipe will cover a data services topic, going from the description of the problem, over a conceptual solution and a solution containing sample code.

What this book covers

Chapter 1, Learning the Nuts and Bolts of Silverlight 4 will get you up and running with Silverlight. While this book is aimed at developers who already have a basic knowledge of Silverlight, this chapter can act as a refresher. We'll also look at getting your environment correctly set up so that you enjoy developing Silverlight applications.

Chapter 2, An Introduction to Data Binding will explore how data binding works. We'll start by building a small data-driven application that contains the most important data binding features, to get a grasp of the general concepts. We'll also see that data binding isn't tied to just binding single objects to an interface; binding an entire collection of objects is supported as well. We'll also be looking at the binding modes. They allow us to specify how the data will flow (from source to target, target to source, or both). We'll finish this chapter by looking at the support that Blend 4 provides to build applications that use data binding features. In the next chapter, we'll be looking at the more advanced concepts of data binding.

Chapter 3, Advanced Data Binding teaches you advanced data binding concepts that can be used for customization, validations, and applying templates to data bound controls. We also have a look at converters, that are obvious hooks in data binding and their possibilities.

Chapter 4, The Data Grid covers recipes on how to work with the `DataGrid`. This is an essential control for applications that rely on (collections of) data.

Chapter 5, The DataForm covers recipes on how to work with the `DataForm`, which is an essential control for the applications that rely on (collections of) data.

Chapter 6, Talking to Services talks about the rich set of options that Silverlight provides to communicate with services.

Chapter 7, Talking to WCF and ASMX Services discovers Silverlights' built-in support for communicating with Windows Communication Foundation (WCF) and classic ASMX web services. Perform unidirectional as well as bidirectional communication with much better performance using `net.tcp` binding in WCF using the recipes in this chapter.

Chapter 8, Talking to REST and ADO.NET Data Services takes advantage of REST, which can be significant in the case of Silverlight. We will also look at how we can work with ADO.NET Data Services. You will abstract away a lot of plumbing code with the use of the client-side library that is available for use with Silverlight.

Chapter 9, Talking to WCF RIA Services discovers a new, free framework developed by Microsoft-WCF RIA Services- to simplify Line of Business RIA development. This chapter will teach you to easily design and develop rich data-driven applications by simplifying the access to the validation of and the authentication of services, service methods, and entities.

Chapter 10, Converting Your Existing Applications to Use Silverlight, integrates Silverlight into existing web applications and performs a step-by-step migration where Silverlight starts to become part of a system. This chapter is all about techniques to leverage your existing knowledge, applications, and business requirements to Silverlight. This chapter contains a recipe that shows how to enable WCF RIA Services for existing applications.

Appendix talks about creating a REST service from WCF, installing a SQL Server database, and working with Fiddler and Silverlight control toolkit

What you need for this book

To work with the recipes in this book, it's required that you have Visual Studio installed. This book targets Silverlight 4, which works only with Visual Studio 2010. Many of the recipes in the book will also work in Silverlight 3, so for these recipes, you have the choice of Visual Studio 2008 or 2010. We do recommend using Visual Studio 2010, as it features a lot of enhancements for developing with Silverlight. In both cases, you'll of course need to install the Silverlight Tools, which will update your Visual Studio instance to work with Silverlight. Some recipes also require Blend 4 to be installed on your machine (again, if working with Silverlight 3, Blend 3 will suffice here as well).

The first recipe of Chapter 1, *Getting our environment ready to start developing Silverlight applications*, explains in detail how to get these tools and how to install them.

Who this book is for

If you are a .NET developer who wants to build professional data-driven applications with Silverlight, then this book is for you. Basic Silverlight experience and familiarity with accessing data using ADO.NET in regular .NET applications is required.

Conventions

In this book, you will find a number of styles of text that distinguish between different kinds of information. Here are some examples of these styles, and an explanation of their meaning.

Code words in text are shown as follows: "Finally, the `DataReader` and connection are closed and the `StoreDTO` object is returned."

A block of code will be set as follows:

```
<TextBlock x:Name="AmountTextBlock"
           Text="{Binding ElementName=AmountSlider, Path=Value}">
</TextBlock>
```

New terms and **important words** are shown in bold. Words that you see on the screen, in menus or dialog boxes for example, appear in our text like this: "Do this by right-clicking, selecting **Add New Item**, and then selecting **LINQ TO SQL Classes**.".

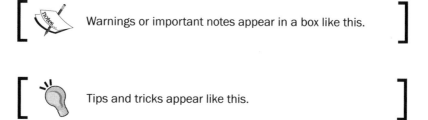

Warnings or important notes appear in a box like this.

Tips and tricks appear like this.

Reader feedback

Feedback from our readers is always welcome. Let us know what you think about this book—what you liked or may have disliked. Reader feedback is important for us to develop titles that you really get the most out of.

To send us general feedback, simply drop an email to feedback@packtpub.com, and mention the book title in the subject of your message.

If there is a book that you need and would like to see us publish, please send us a note in the **SUGGEST A TITLE** form on www.packtpub.com or email to suggest@packtpub.com.

If there is a topic that you have expertise in and you are interested in either writing or contributing to a book, see our author guide on www.packtpub.com/authors.

Customer support

Now that you are the proud owner of a Packt book, we have a number of things to help you to get the most from your purchase.

Downloading the example code for the book

Visit http://www.packtpub.com/files/code/9843_Code.zip to directly download the example code.

The downloadable files contain instructions on how to use them.

Errata

Although we have taken every care to ensure the accuracy of our contents, mistakes do happen. If you find a mistake in one of our books—maybe a mistake in text or code—we would be grateful if you would report this to us. By doing so, you can save other readers from frustration, and help us to improve subsequent versions of this book. If you find any errata, please report them by visiting http://www.packtpub.com/support, selecting your book, clicking on the **let us know** link, and entering the details of your errata. Once your errata are verified, your submission will be accepted and the errata will be uploaded on our website, or added to any list of existing errata, under the Errata section of that title. Any existing errata can be viewed by selecting your title from http://www.packtpub.com/support.

Piracy

Piracy of copyright material on the Internet is an ongoing problem across all media. At Packt, we take the protection of our copyright and licenses very seriously. If you come across any illegal copies of our works in any form on the Internet, please provide us with the location address or website name immediately so that we can pursue a remedy.

Please contact us at copyright@packtpub.com with a link to the suspected pirated material.

We appreciate your help in protecting our authors, and our ability to bring you valuable content.

Questions

You can contact us at questions@packtpub.com if you are having a problem with any aspect of the book, and we will do our best to address it.

1

Learning the Nuts and Bolts of Silverlight 4

In this chapter, we will cover the following topics:

- ► Getting our environment ready to start developing Silverlight applications
- ► Creating our first service-enabled and data-driven Silverlight 4 application using Visual Studio 2010
- ► Using the workflow between Visual Studio 2010 and Blend 4
- ► Using source control in Visual Studio 2010 and Blend 4
- ► Deploying a Silverlight application on the server

Introduction

While we assume some basic knowledge of Silverlight for this book, we also know that developers have very little time to grasp all the new technologies that keep coming out. Therefore, this first chapter contains all that we need to know to get going with Silverlight. We'll also guide you through the required tools and installations for a perfect Silverlight development environment.

Silverlight was released in the first half of 2007, and since then, it has created a lot of buzz. While ASP.NET is a server-side development platform, with the arrival of Silverlight, the focus has shifted to the **client side** again. A Silverlight application runs in **the browser** of the client and on a specific version of the **Common Language Runtime (CLR)**.

A big benefit for developers is that Silverlight uses .NET from version 2 onwards. It has a trimmed-down version of the **Base Class Library** (**BCL**) that is impressively extended considering the size of the Silverlight plugin (less than 5 MB). Because of the similarities, many skills achieved from developing applications in the full .NET framework can be leveraged for the creation of Silverlight applications.

Silverlight itself can be considered as a trimmed-down version of its desktop counterpart, **Windows Presentation Foundation** (**WPF**). Between Silverlight 4 and WPF 4, there are still some differences. Some features are included in WPF 4, but aren't in Silverlight 4 and vice versa. It's possible to reuse code written for one technology in the other. However, upfront planning is required to ensure a smooth transition between the two technologies. Microsoft has released a whitepaper based on this aspect that provides more information on how to write applications that target both Silverlight and WPF. This document can be found at `http://wpfslguidance.codeplex.com`.

With the release of Silverlight 2, Microsoft made it clear that Silverlight is aimed at both creating rich and interactive applications, and next-level enterprise applications in the browser. The latter can be easily seen with the addition of a rich control set, support for many types of services and platform features such as data binding.

Due to its client-side characteristics, Silverlight applications need to perform particular tasks to get data. It doesn't support client-side databases—not even in version 4. The way to retrieve data is through services. Silverlight 3 brought some interesting features to the platform in this area such as support for binary XML, the WCF RIA services, and simplified duplex service communication. Silverlight 4 continued in the same manner, with improvements in data binding, support for `net.tcp` communication, cross-domain access to services by means of Trusted Silverlight applications, and much more. All these added features are a proof of the commitment Microsoft is making to position Silverlight as a platform for building enterprise applications.

In this chapter, we'll get you up and running with Silverlight. While this book is aimed at developers who already have a basic knowledge of Silverlight, this chapter can act as a refresher. We'll also look at getting your environment correctly set up so that you enjoy developing Silverlight applications.

Getting our environment ready to start developing Silverlight applications

In this recipe, we'll look at what we need to install to start developing Silverlight applications. We'll learn about the basic tools that we need as a developer and also take a look at the designer tools that can come in handy for developers as well.

How to do it...

To start developing Silverlight applications, we'll need to install the necessary tools and SDKs. Carry out the following steps in order to get started:

1. We need to make sure we install Visual Web Developer Express 2010 (available for free at `http://www.microsoft.com/express/downloads/`) or Visual Studio 2010 (trial version available at `http://www.microsoft.com/visualstudio/en-us/download`).

2. Go to `http://www.silverlight.net/getstarted/` to download and install the Silverlight 4 Tools for Visual Studio 2010. Open Visual Studio 2010 after installation. Visual Studio 2010 ships with Silverlight 3 templates installed out of the box, the tools add support for version 4.

3. Go to `http://www.microsoft.com/expression/` to download and install Blend 4.

How it works...

For Silverlight development, the minimum that we need are the developer tools. These will integrate with Visual Studio 2008 (if you're using Silverlight 3) or 2010. In Visual Studio 2010, a nice, visual designer is added for editing our XAML code. In the 2008 version, this designer doesn't exist. When installing the developer tools for Silverlight 4, the following components are automatically downloaded and installed:

- Silverlight 4 developer runtime
- Silverlight 4 software development kit and Visual Studio project support
- WCF RIA services

We can write XAML code using Visual Studio. However, if you're serious about designing, you might want to consider using Microsoft Expression Blend. This tool, primarily aimed at designers, should be seen as an application that generates XAML for us by means of a rich number of options and an easy-to-use interface. It also integrates nicely with Visual Studio and source control software integration is available as well.

See also

After having installed all the necessary tools, it might be worth taking a look at the *Creating our first service-enabled and data-driven Silverlight 4 application using Visual Studio 2010* recipe as well as the *Using the workflow between Visual Studio 2010 and Blend 4* recipe. In these recipes, we create an entire application in Visual Studio 2010 and Blend 4 respectively.

Creating our first service-enabled and data-driven Silverlight 4 application using Visual Studio 2010

In this recipe, we'll build a very simple Silverlight application that uses techniques that are explained in much more detail later on in the book. We'll be using **data binding**, which is a technique to easily connect data to the **user interface** (**UI**) and connect to a **Windows Communication Foundation** (**WCF**) service.

However, the main goal is to get a grip on the basics of Silverlight by trying to answer questions such as how a Silverlight application is built, what the project structure looks like, what files are created, and what is their use.

Getting ready

To get started with Silverlight application development, make sure that you have installed Visual Studio along with the necessary tools and libraries as outlined in the previous recipe.

We are building this application from the ground up. However, the finished product can be found in the `Chapter01/SilverlightHotelBrowser` folder in the code bundle that is available on the Packt website.

How to do it...

Our first Silverlight application allows the user to view the details of a hotel that is selected in a `ComboBox` control. The hotel information is retrieved over a service and is used for filling the `ComboBox` and the details shown in several `TextBlock` controls that are placed in a grid.

The following screenshot shows the interface of the application:

To start building any Silverlight application, we'll need to perform the following steps:

1. Open Visual Studio 2010 with the Silverlight 4 tools installed. Once inside the **Integrated Development Environment** (**IDE**), go to **File | New | Project...**. In the **New Project** dialog that appears, select the **Silverlight** node under **Visual C#** and select **Silverlight Application**. Name the application as **SilverlightHotelBrowser** and click the **OK** button. In the dialog that appears as shown in the next screenshot, select **ASP.NET Web Application Project** as the type of web project that will be used to host the Silverlight application. Also, make sure that **Silverlight 4** is selected as the target version of Silverlight 4.

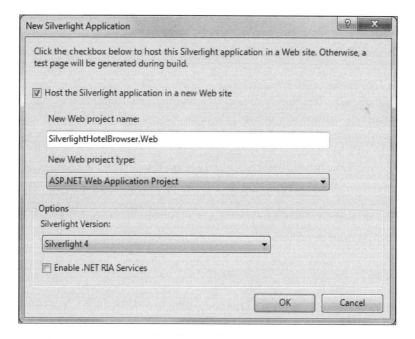

2. After Visual Studio has finished executing the project template, two projects are created in the solution: the Silverlight project and a web application project that is responsible for hosting the Silverlight content. The created solution structure can be seen in the following screenshot:

3. Our service will return the hotel information. A hotel can be represented by an instance of the `Hotel` class. This class should be included in the web project—`SilverlightHotelBrowser.Web`.

   There are a few things to note about this class:

   ❑ This class has a `DataContract` attribute attached to it. This attribute is required to specify that this class can be serialized when sent over the wire to the client application.

   ❑ Each property is attributed with the `DataMember` attribute. When adding this attribute to a property, we specify that this property is a part of the contract and that it should be included in the serialized response that will be sent to the client.

   The following code defines this class:

```
[DataContract]
public class Hotel
{
    [DataMember]
    public string Name { get; set; }
    [DataMember]
    public string Location { get; set; }
    [DataMember]
    public string Country { get; set; }
```

```
  [DataMember]
  public double Price { get; set; }
}
```

4. We'll now add a WCF service to the web project as well. Right-click on `SilverlightHotelBrowser.Web` and select **Add | New Item…**. Add a **Silverlight-enabled WCF Service** by selecting the **Silverlight** node under **Visual C#** and name it as **HotelService**. Click the **Add** button. Two files are added, namely, `HotelService.svc` and `HotelService.svc.cs`.

5. In this service class, we can now add a method that returns a hardcoded list of hotels. Remove the `DoWork` method and replace it with the following code:

```
[ServiceContract(Namespace = "")]
[AspNetCompatibilityRequirements(RequirementsMode =
AspNetCompatibilityRequirementsMode.Allowed)]
public class HotelService
{
  [OperationContract]
  public List<Hotel> GetHotels()
  {
    return new List<Hotel>
    {
      new Hotel
      {
        Name = "Brussels Hotel",
        Price = 100,
        Location = "Brussels",
        Country = "Belgium"
      },
      new Hotel
      {
        Name = "London Hotel",
        Price = 200,
        Location = "London",
        Country = "United Kingdom"
      },
      new Hotel
      {
        Name = "Paris Hotel",
        Price = 150,
        Location = "Paris",
        Country = "France"
      },
      new Hotel
      {
```

```
            Name = "New York Hotel",
            Price = 230,
            Location = "New York",
            Country = "USA"
        }
    };
  }
}
```

Note the attributes that have been used in this class. The `ServiceContract` attribute specifies that the class contains a service contract that defines what functionality the service exposes. The `OperationContract` attribute is added to operations which can be invoked by clients on the service. This effectively means that if you add methods to the service without this attribute, it can't be invoked from a client

6. Now we'll build the solution and if no errors are encountered, we're ready for takeoff—takeoff for writing Silverlight code.

    Let's first make the service known to the Silverlight application. Right-click on the Silverlight application and select **Add Service Reference...**. In the dialog box that appears, as shown in the following screenshot, click on **Discover** and select your service. As it is in the same solution, the service will appear. Enter **HotelService** in the **Namespace** field.

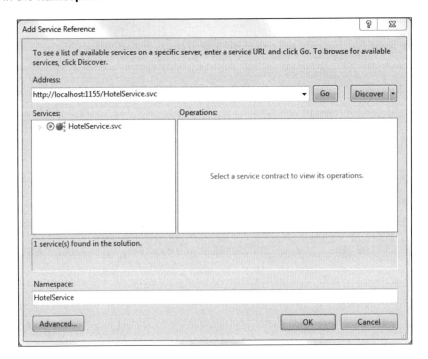

Click on the OK button to confirm. The service is now usable from the Silverlight application.

7. The UI was shown earlier and is quite easy. The XAML code for the `Grid` named `LayoutRoot` inside the `MainPage.xaml` file is as follows:

```xaml
<Grid x:Name="LayoutRoot" Width="400" Height="300"
      Background="LightGray">
  <Grid.RowDefinitions>
    <RowDefinition Height="50"></RowDefinition>
    <RowDefinition></RowDefinition>
  </Grid.RowDefinitions>
  <ComboBox x:Name="HotelComboBox" Width="250"
            SelectionChanged="HotelComboBox_SelectionChanged"
            DisplayMemberPath="Name"
            VerticalAlignment="Center">
  </ComboBox>
  <Grid x:Name="HotelDetailGrid" Grid.Row="1"
        VerticalAlignment="Top">
    <Grid.RowDefinitions>
      <RowDefinition></RowDefinition>
      <RowDefinition></RowDefinition>
      <RowDefinition></RowDefinition>
      <RowDefinition></RowDefinition>
    </Grid.RowDefinitions>
    <Grid.ColumnDefinitions>
      <ColumnDefinition></ColumnDefinition>
      <ColumnDefinition></ColumnDefinition>
    </Grid.ColumnDefinitions>
    <TextBlock x:Name="NameTextBlock"
               Grid.Row="0"
               Grid.Column="0"
               FontWeight="Bold"
               Text="Name: "
               HorizontalAlignment="Right">
    </TextBlock>
    <TextBlock x:Name="NameValueTextBlock"
               Grid.Row="0"
               Grid.Column="1"
               Text="{Binding Name}">
    </TextBlock>
    <TextBlock x:Name="LocationTextBlock"
               Grid.Row="1"
               Grid.Column="0"
               FontWeight="Bold"
               Text="Location: "
               HorizontalAlignment="Right">
```

```
        </TextBlock>
        <TextBlock x:Name="LocationValueTextBlock"
                   Grid.Row="1"
                   Grid.Column="1"
                   Text="{Binding Location}">
        </TextBlock>
        <TextBlock x:Name="CountryTextBlock"
                   Grid.Row="2"
                   Grid.Column="0"
                   FontWeight="Bold"
                   Text="Country: "
                   HorizontalAlignment="Right">
        </TextBlock>
        <TextBlock x:Name="CountryValueTextBlock"
                   Grid.Row="2"
                   Grid.Column="1"
                   Text="{Binding Country}">
        </TextBlock>
        <TextBlock x:Name="PriceTextBlock"
                   Grid.Row="3"
                   Grid.Column="0"
                   FontWeight="Bold"
                   Text="Price: "
                   HorizontalAlignment="Right">
        </TextBlock>
        <TextBlock x:Name="PriceValueTextBlock"
                   Grid.Row="3"
                   Grid.Column="1"
                   Text="{Binding Price}">
        </TextBlock>
      </Grid>
    </Grid>
```

8. In the code-behind class, MainPage.xaml.cs, we connect to the service and the results are used in a data binding scenario. We won't focus here on what's actually happening with the service call and the data binding; all this is covered in detail later in this book.

```
public MainPage()
{
  InitializeComponent();
  HotelService.HotelServiceClient proxy = new
    SilverlightHotelBrowser.HotelService.HotelServiceClient();
  proxy.GetHotelsCompleted += new EventHandler
    <SilverlightHotelBrowser.HotelService.
    GetHotelsCompletedEventArgs>
    (proxy_GetHotelsCompleted);
```

```
      proxy.GetHotelsAsync();
   }
   void proxy_GetHotelsCompleted(object sender,
      SilverlightHotelBrowser.HotelService.
      GetHotelsCompletedEventArgs e)
   {
      HotelComboBox.ItemsSource = e.Result;
   }


   private void HotelComboBox_SelectionChanged(object sender,
      SelectionChangedEventArgs e)
   {
      HotelDetailGrid.DataContext = (sender as ComboBox)
        .SelectedItem as HotelService.Hotel;
   }
```

8. We will compile the solution again and then press the *F5* button. The application should now run, allowing us to select a hotel in the ComboBox. Each selection change will trigger an event that shows the details of the selected item using data binding.

How it works...

Silverlight applications always have to run in the context of the browser. That's the reason why Visual Studio prompts us initially by asking how we want to host the Silverlight content.

Note that Silverlight 3 added out-of-browser capabilities to its previous version, thereby allowing Silverlight applications to run "standalone". However, they still run inside the browser sandbox. Silverlight 4 added the option to run a Silverlight application out of browser with elevated permissions, thereby giving it more permissions on the local system. We'll be looking at these later on in this book.

The default option is the **ASP.NET Web Application Project**. This option gives us the maximum number of possibilities for the configuration of the host project. It's the option that we will be using the most throughout this book because of the configuration options it offers towards working with services. The second option is **ASP.NET Web Site** and is a file-based website known from ASP.NET 2.0. Finally, we can also uncheck the **Host the Silverlight application in a new Web site** checkbox. This will result in Visual Studio generating an empty HTML page containing the Silverlight application whenever we build our solution. This option is not well suited for building Silverlight applications that work with services as we have no control over the generation process.

The solution and project structure

A new Silverlight solution thus contains normally two projects—a Silverlight project and a hosting application. Let's first take a look at the Silverlight project:

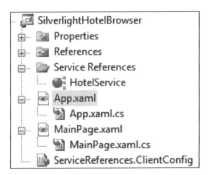

Silverlight applications contain XAML and C# (or VB.NET) files, among others. The XAML files contain the UI and are linked at runtime to the partial classes that make up the code-behind. By default, one page is added for free—called `MainPage`. It's not really a page, but a user control that is hosted. We can add UI code (such as controls, grids, and so on) to this file. We add UI logic in the code-behind.

One special case is the `App.xaml` file. It's the entry point of an application and is responsible for loading an instance of the `MainPage`, executing logic when an error occurs, and so on. Also, it can contain global resources such as styles that should be available over the entire application.

While building the solution, the Silverlight project is compiled into an assembly. In turn, this assembly—along with a manifest file that contains general information about the application and possible other resources—are wrapped into an XAP file. This XAP file is then copied into the hosting application. It shows up under the `ClientBin` directory in the web project as shown in the following screenshot:

The XAP file is basically a ZIP (archive) file. When renaming the `SilverlightHotelBrowser.xap` file to `SilverlightHotelBrowser.zip`, we can see the original files (`manifest` and `assembly`). The following screenshot shows the contents of the ZIP file:

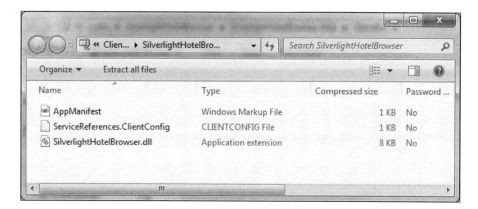

The generated ASPX page as well as the HTML page refer to the XAP file located in the `ClientBin` directory.

Services

Data is not readily available to a Silverlight application on the client side. So we need to retrieve it from the server. In Silverlight, this is done using services. Services need to be accessed asynchronously in Silverlight, hence the declaration of the callback method—`proxy_GetHotelsCompleted`. Silverlight has many options to communicate with services. These are covered in the recipes of this book.

Data binding

We use the rich data binding features available in Silverlight to connect the data with the UI in this application. Data binding allows us to bind properties of objects (the data) to properties of controls. In this particular example, we bind a list of `Hotel` instances to the `ComboBox` using the `ItemsSource` property. While changing the selection in the control, the `HotelComboBox_SelectionChanged` event handler fires and the selected item—a `Hotel` instance—is set as the `DataContext` for the `HotelDetailGrid`. This grid contains the controls in which we want to show the details. Each of these controls uses a `Binding` markup extension in XAML to specify which property needs to be bounded.

See also

Data binding was used in this application. It's also the topic of Chapter 3, where we delve deep into what data binding has to offer. We also connected with a WCF service. Connecting and communicating with services is covered in Chapter 6 and Chapter 7.

Using the workflow between Visual Studio 2010 and Blend 4

Expression Blend (currently at version 4) is part of Microsoft's Expression Suite. It's a designer tool that allows designers to create compelling user experiences for use with WPF and Silverlight. While aimed at designers, it's a tool that should be in a Silverlight developer's toolbox as well. In some areas, it offers a richer designer experience than Visual Studio does. One of the best examples of this is the timeline that makes it easy to create time-based animations.

In this recipe, we'll look at how Visual Studio and Blend integrate. When used together, they help us create our applications faster. In the next chapter, we'll take another look at Blend—namely at its features that support data binding.

Getting ready

After having read the *Getting our environment ready to start developing Silverlight applications* recipe, you should have Expression Blend 4 installed.

In this recipe, we are creating the sample from scratch. The completed solution can be found in the `Chapter01/Blend` folder in the code bundle that is available on the Packt website.

How to do it...

In this recipe, we'll recreate the Hotel Browser application. However, we'll do most of the work from Blend and switch back and forth to Visual Studio when it is recommended. We'll need to carry out the following steps:

1. Although we can start a new solution from Blend, we'll let Visual Studio create the solution for us. The main reason is that we'll be using services later on in this sample and working with services is easier if the hosting site is an ASP.NET web application. Adding an ASP.NET web application is possible from Visual Studio, but not from Blend. Therefore, open **Visual Studio 2010** and create a new Silverlight solution. Name it `SilverlightHotelBrowser` and make sure to select **ASP.NET Web Application Project** as the hosting website.

2. With the solution created in Visual Studio, right-click on one of the XAML files in the Silverlight project. In the context menu, select **Open in Expression Blend...** as shown in the following screenshot:

3. Expression Blend will open up and its workspace will be shown. The following is a screenshot of the interface containing some named references:

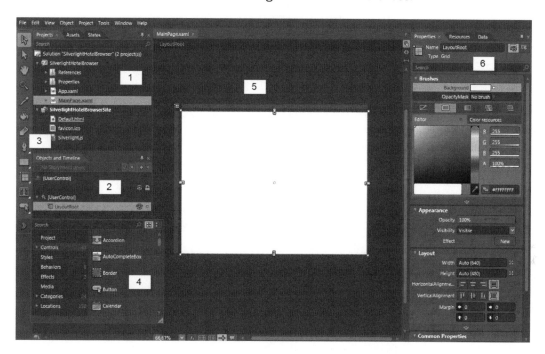

The following table describes some of the most important items on the Blend workspace:

Item	Name	Description
1	**Projects** window	Gives an overview of the loaded solution and its projects. It is comparable to the Solution Explorer in Visual Studio.
2	**Objects and Timeline**	By default, this window gives an overview of all the XAML objects in the currently loaded document. When we want to perform any action on an item (such as giving it a background color), we select it in the **Objects and Timeline** window. This opens the properties window for that item.
3	**Toolbox**	Comparable to what we know from Visual Studio, the toolbox contains all the tools available. Since Blend is a design tool, tools such as a Pen, Paint Bucket, and so on are available in the toolbox.
4	**Assets** window	The **Assets** window contains all controls (assets) that we can drag onto the design surface such as Buttons, ComboBoxes, and so on.

Item	Name	Description
5	**Design** workspace	This is where all the action takes place! We can drag items from the **Toolbox** or the **Assets** window, rearrange them and so on to create a compelling user experience.
6	**Properties** window	The **Properties** window allows us to change the properties of the selected item. We can change the color, layout properties, transform properties and so on.

4. Now that we know our way around the designer, we can get creative. We'll start with `MainPage.xaml` and split the main **Grid** (`LayoutRoot`) into two rows. Instead of writing the XAML code for this, we'll do this in the designer. Click on the icon on the top left of the user control in the designer so that the Grid will be in the Grid layout mode. This can be seen in the following screenshot:

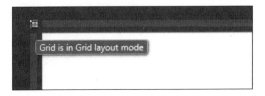

5. Now, click on the left bar next to the user control to add a row. It's possible to change the height of the created row by dragging the handle. The following screenshot shows a row added to the Grid::

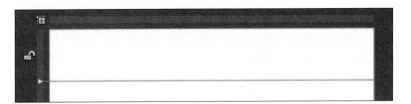

6. Select the **ComboBox** in the **Assets** window. Use the search function in this window to find it more quickly. On the designer, drag to create an instance of the `ComboBox` and place it on the top row that was just created. This can be seen in the next screenshot:

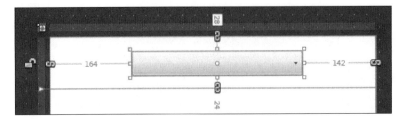

7. In the **Properties** window, give this `ComboBox` the name **HotelComboBox** and set the **DisplayMemberPath** property to **Name**. In the following screenshot, note that we are making use of the **Search** functionality within the **Properties** window. Simply enter part of the name of the property you are looking for (here **displ**) and Blend will filter the available properties.

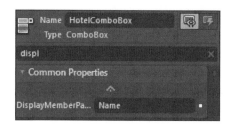

8. With the `ComboBox` still selected in the **Properties** window, change to the **Events** view (top arrow in the next screenshot). In the list of events, double-click on the **SelectionChanged** event, so Blend will create an event handler (bottom arrow in the next screenshot).

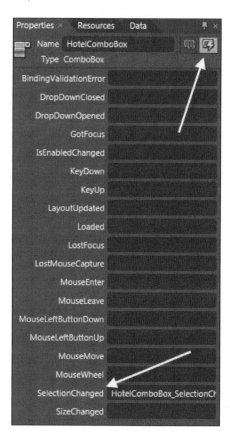

9. Let's now move back to the **Design** view of `MainPage.xaml`. Select the **Grid** item in the **Toolbox**. In the bottom cell of the `LayoutRoot` (the main grid control) drag to create a nested grid. Create four rows and two columns using the same technique as before. Columns are created quite logically by clicking on the top bar of the control. The result is shown in the following screenshot:

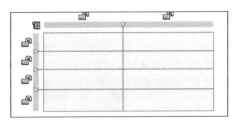

10. With this **Grid** still selected, change the name to **HotelDetailGrid** in the **Properties** window.

11. In each of the cells, drag a **TextBlock** from the **ToolBox**. For the **TextBlock** controls in the first column, change the `Text` property as shown in the following screenshot. Don't change the `Text` property of the controls in the second column; we'll look at these in the coming steps.

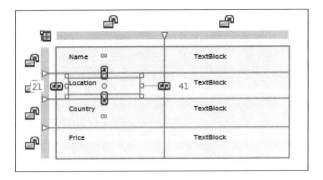

12. Let's now change the background color of the **LayoutRoot** grid. To do this, select the **LayoutRoot** node in the **Objects and Timeline** window and in the **Properties** window, change the background by selecting a different color in the editor.

13. In Chapter 2, we'll look at how we can make data binding in Blend easier. As of now, we'll just type the XAML code from Blend. In the top-right corner of the **Design Surface**, select either the **Split view** or the **XAML view**. Blend shows us the XAML code that it created in the background. Search for the `TextBlock` controls in the second column of the `HotelDetailGrid` and change it as shown in the following code. Note that the generated code might not always be exactly the same as values such as `Margin` could be different.

```xml
<TextBlock
  Margin="49,8,40,8"
  Grid.Column="1"
  Text="{Binding Name}"
  TextWrapping="Wrap"/>
<TextBlock
  Margin="49,8,40,8"
  Grid.Column="1"
  Grid.Row="1"
  Text="{Binding Location}"
  TextWrapping="Wrap"/>
<TextBlock
  Margin="49,8,40,8"
  Grid.Column="1"
  Grid.Row="2"
  Text="{Binding Country}"
  TextWrapping="Wrap"/>
<TextBlock
  Margin="49,8,40,8"
  Grid.Column="1"
  Grid.Row="3"
  Text="{Binding Price}"
  TextWrapping="Wrap"/>
```

14. The workflow between Blend and Visual Studio allows us to jump to Visual Studio for the tasks we can't achieve in Blend, for example, adding a WCF service and referencing it in the Silverlight project. In the **Projects** window, right-click on a file or a project and select **Edit in Visual Studio**. If Visual Studio is still open, it will reactivate. If not, a new instance will get launched with our solution.

15. In the website that was created with the project initialization (`SilverlightHotelBrowser.Web`), we need to have a service that will return the hotel information. A hotel is represented by an instance of the `Hotel` class as shown in the following code:

```csharp
[DataContract]
public class Hotel
{
  [DataMember]
    public string Name { get; set; }
  [DataMember]
    public string Location { get; set; }
  [DataMember]
    public string Country { get; set; }
  [DataMember]
    public double Price { get; set; }
}
```

16. Of course, we need to add the service as well. To do this, add a **Silverlight-enabled WCF service** called `HotelService`. Replace the `DoWork` sample method with the following code:

```
[OperationContract]
public List<Hotel> GetHotels()
{
   return new List<Hotel>
   {
     new Hotel
     {
       Name = "Brussels Hotel",
       Price = 100,
       Location = "Brussels",
       Country = "Belgium"
     },
     new Hotel
     {
       Name = "London Hotel",
       Price = 200,
       Location = "London",
       Country = "United Kingdom"
     },
     new Hotel
     {
       Name = "Paris Hotel",
       Price = 150,
       Location = "Paris",
       Country = "France"
     },
     new Hotel
     {
       Name = "New York Hotel",
       Price = 230,
       Location = "New York",
       Country = "USA"
     }
   };
}
```

17. Perform a build of the project so that the service is built and is ready to be referenced by the Silverlight application.

18. In the Silverlight project, add a service reference by right-clicking on the project and selecting **Add Service Reference...**. Click on the **Discover** button and the service should be found. Set the namespace to **HotelService**.

19. In the `MainPage.xaml.cs`, add the following code to load the hotels in the `ComboBox` control:

```
public MainPage()
{
  InitializeComponent();

  HotelService.HotelServiceClient proxy = new
    SilverlightHotelBrowser.HotelService.HotelServiceClient();
  proxy.GetHotelsCompleted += new
    EventHandler<SilverlightHotelBrowser.HotelService.
    GetHotelsCompletedEventArgs>(proxy_GetHotelsCompleted);
  proxy.GetHotelsAsync();
}
void proxy_GetHotelsCompleted(object sender,
  SilverlightHotelBrowser.HotelService.
  GetHotelsCompletedEventArgs e)
{
  HotelComboBox.ItemsSource = e.Result;
}
```

20. In the `SelectionChanged` event handler of the `ComboBox`, add the following code to load the details of a hotel once the user selects a different option:

```
private void HotelComboBox_SelectionChanged(object sender,
  System.Windows.Controls.SelectionChangedEventArgs e)
{
  HotelDetailGrid.DataContext = (sender as ComboBox).SelectedItem
    as HotelService.Hotel;
}
```

21. Build and run the application in Visual Studio.

With these steps completed, we have created the application using both Blend and Visual Studio. For an application as easy as this one, there is less profit in switching between the two environments. However, with larger applications requiring large teams containing both developers and designers, this strong integration can turn out to be very helpful.

How it works...

Visual Studio and Blend integrate nicely with each other. It's easy to jump from one application to the other. This allows a great workflow between designers and developers.

Designers can work in Blend and the changes made in this tool are automatically picked up by Visual Studio, and vice versa. This is achieved through the use of the same files (both code files and project files) by the two tools. A solution created in Blend will open in Visual Studio. The same holds true for a solution created in Visual Studio; Blend can work with it.

See also

In Chapter 2, we'll use some more features of Blend. We'll perform data binding directly from Blend.

Using source control in Visual Studio 2010 and Blend 4

When working on slightly larger projects in teams, source control is an absolute necessity. By far, the most popular source control system in the Microsoft world today is **Team Foundation Server** (**TFS**). This recipe explains all that we need to get TFS to work with Silverlight applications in Visual Studio and Blend. It doesn't explain how to work with TFS itself.

Getting ready

Before getting started, make sure that you have installed Blend 4 and the necessary developer tools as described in the *Getting our environment ready to start developing Silverlight applications* section.

How to do it...

To start using TFS as a versioning system with a Silverlight-enabled solution, we need to perform the following steps:

1. Using TFS source control with a Silverlight application in Visual Studio is exactly the same as using it with any other type of Visual Studio project. Team Explorer is used for this purpose and this is automatically installed out of the box with Visual Studio 2010. (For Visual Studio 2008, it has to be separately installed from `http://www.microsoft.com/downloads/details.aspx?FamilyID=0ed12659-3d41-4420-bbb0-a46e51bfca86&DisplayLang=en`.)

2. Blend 4 also supports source control out of the box. However, for Blend 3, TFS update KB967483 must be downloaded and installed from `http://code.msdn.microsoft.com/KB967483`. This update enables TFS source control for Expression Blend 3.

3. Once these are installed, we can use TFS source control from within Blend for any solution bound to the TFS source control. Right-click on any file in the Solution Explorer window to view the source control options just as we would do in Visual Studio's Solution Explorer window. We can now check out, check in, and merge files from Expression Blend.

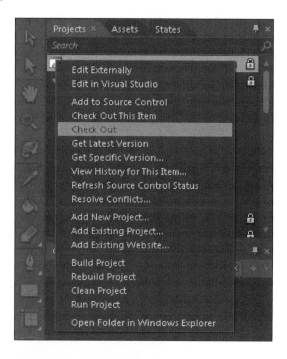

How it works...

Team Foundation Server source control is the preferred way of enabling version control on our projects. Explaining in detail how to work with TFS is beyond the scope of this book, but the following are a few basic steps and references:

1. We must make sure that we have the correct permissions on our Team Foundation Server to handle the tasks we need to do. We need different permissions to (for example) create projects than to check out files. Have a look at this MSDN article to learn how to set these permissions:
    `http://msdn.microsoft.com/en-us/library/ms252587.aspx`.

2. Next, we'll need to connect to TFS using Team Explorer. Have a look at this MSDN article to learn how to do that:
    `http://msdn.microsoft.com/en-us/library/ms181474.aspx`.

3. We'll now need to create a workspace on our machine. We can look at the workspace as a local folder containing copies of the source-controlled files on the TFS. For more information, have a look at this MSDN article: `http://msdn.microsoft.com/en-us/library/ms181384.aspx`.

4. After we've created a local workspace, we can download the files from the TFS to that local folder. More information about this can be found at `http://msdn.microsoft.com/en-us/library/ms181385.aspx`.

5. We're now able to open our source-controlled solution in Blend and/or Visual Studio and check out files, merge files, add projects, and so on depending on the permissions.

There's more...

While working a lot with TFS, an interesting feature to download is the Team Foundation Server Power Tools. This is a set of extra features that is added to TFS and is mainly aimed at power users. It can be downloaded at `http://msdn.microsoft.com/en-us/teamsystem/bb980963.aspx`.

Commonly used terms in TFS

A complete glossary of TFS terms can be found at `http://msdn.microsoft.com/en-us/library/ms242882.aspx`. As a reference, the following are a few of the more commonly used ones along with their brief explanation:

Term	Explanation
TFS workspace	A TFS workspace is a location on the **Team Foundation Server** (**TFS**) where a record of changes between local files and corresponding repository files is stored. It can also be thought of as a copy of the client-side directory, a staging ground where local changes are persisted until they are checked into the server, or a collection of working folder mappings that can be viewed and edited.
Working folder	A working folder should be seen as a client-side representation of the TFS workspace. Binding the TFS workspace to the client-side working folder is done through a TFS workspace mapping.
Check in	Check in refers to the task of committing a pending change/pending changes to a TFS repository. When you check in pending changes, a new changeset is created on the server.
Check out	Check out refers to the task of notifying the TFS server that you are changing the status of a resource from locked to writeable. When you check out for edit, TFS appends an edit to that resource.
Get latest	Get latest refers to the task of retrieving the most recent version of a file from the TFS source control to your local working folder.

Deploying a Silverlight application on the server

Once we have a Silverlight application ready, we will want to show it to the rest of the world. This means deploying it!

While Silverlight is a .NET technology, it doesn't require .NET to be installed on the server. Remember that it's a client-side technology. The Silverlight plugin on the client will download and run the application using the version of the **Common Language Runtime** (**CLR**) embedded in the Silverlight plugin. In this recipe, we'll look at how we can deploy a Silverlight application.

How to do it...

Deploying a Silverlight application is easy; the Silverlight code is compiled and wrapped into a *.xap file. Getting this file on the client side and running it from there is our only concern. The following steps are to be carried out for deploying a Silverlight application:

1. We'll use the DeployHelloWorld application to demonstrate deployment, which is available with the code downloads in the Chapter01/DeployHelloWorld folder. Build the application and notice that Visual Studio has created a *.xap file in the ClientBin directory. This file, which is nothing more than a *.zip file but with another extension, contains the assembly (one or more) to which our Silverlight application was compiled, optional resources, and the AppManifest.xaml file.

2. While looking at the files created by default by Visual Studio in the web project, a sample HTML (DeployHelloWorldTestPage.html) and ASPX (DeployHelloWorldTestPage.aspx) page are created for us as shown in the following screenshot:

3. Both pages have an `OBJECT` tag included. One of the parameters is named as `Source` and it has a reference to the `*.xap` file in the `ClientBin` as shown in the following code. If we want to deploy the `*.xap` file to another location, we need to update this reference. We'll use the default as of now.

```
<object data="data:application/x-silverlight-2,"
        type="application/x-silverlight-2"
        width="100%"
        height="100%">
  <param name="source" value="ClientBin/DeployHelloWorld.xap"/>
  <param name="onError" value="onSilverlightError" />
  <param name="background" value="white" />
  <param name="minRuntimeVersion" value="4.0.41108.0" />
  <param name="autoUpgrade" value="true" />
  <a href="http://go.microsoft.com/fwlink/?LinkID=149156&v=4.0.4
          1108.0"
     style="text-decoration:none">
    <img src="http://go.microsoft.com/fwlink/?LinkId=161376"
         alt="Get Microsoft Silverlight"
         style="border-style:none"/>
  </a>
</object>
```

Note that the value of `minRuntimeVersion` may differ slightly because of different Silverlight version releases.

4. If using the HTML page, the following files need to be copied:
   - `DeployHelloWorldTestPage.html`
   - `Silverlight.js`
   - `ClientBin/DeployHelloWorld.xap`

5. If using the ASPX page, we need to copy the following files:
   - `DeployHelloWorldTestPage.aspx`
   - `Silverlight.js`
   - `ClientBin/DeployHelloWorld.xap`
   - `bin` directory, if using code-behind for the ASPX page
   - `web.config`

6. We'll need to test the page in a browser. If it fails to load, check the MIME types served by the web server software. There should be `*.xap` and `*.xaml` in there. (They are specified as the data type in the `OBJECT` tag.)

How it works...

One of the best things about Silverlight is that it can run from any type of server. If we're using ASP.NET, PHP, JSP, or plain-old HTML, Silverlight can still be embedded. Silverlight runs on the client side. The plugin has a CLR embedded so that it hosts our application. On the server side, the only thing we need to do is to serve the files (most importantly, the *.xap file) that will be downloaded to the client side when requested.

Configuration changes on the server

If the Silverlight application isn't being shown, it might be that the server software (IIS or Apache) is not configured to serve the file types used by Silverlight (*.xap and *.xaml). Windows Vista SP1 and Windows Server ship with **Internet Information Services** (**IIS 7**) while Windows 7 and Windows Server 2008 R2 include IIS 7.5. On these OS versions, both IIS 7 and IIS 7.5 are configured out of the box to serve *.xap and *xaml files. On Windows Vista without SP1, we need to add these to the known MIME types. We can do this by opening **Internet Information Services (IIS) Manager** and selecting **MIME Types**. Then, we simply click on **Add** and add the following two items:

- ▶ .xap in the **File name extension:** field and application/x-silverlight-app in the **MIME type:** field

- ▶ .xaml in the **File name extension:** field and application/xaml+xml in the **MIME type:** field

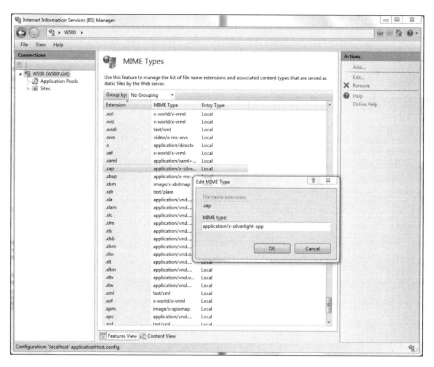

What if the server doesn't allow using XAP?

If the server environment doesn't allow adding MIME types (a shared hosting plan), there's no reason to panic. As a * . xap file is nothing more than a * . zip file but with another extension, Silverlight supports the * . xap file being deployed as a * . zip file.

To get things working, start by renaming the * . xap file in the ClientBin to * . zip. Also, replace the reference to the * . xap file to the new name as shown in the following code:

```
<object data="data:application/x-silverlight-2,"
        type="application/x-silverlight-2"
        width="100%"
        height="100%">
  <param name="source" value="ClientBin/DeployHelloWorld.zip"/>
    . . .
</object>
```

2
An Introduction to Data Binding

In this chapter, we will cover:

- ▶ Displaying data in Silverlight applications
- ▶ Creating dynamic bindings
- ▶ Binding data to another UI element
- ▶ Binding collections to UI elements
- ▶ Enabling a Silverlight application to automatically update its UI
- ▶ Obtaining data from any UI element it is bound to
- ▶ Using the different modes of data binding to allow persisting data
- ▶ Data binding from Expression Blend 4
- ▶ Using Expression Blend 4 for sample data generation

Introduction

Data binding allows us to build data-driven applications in Silverlight in a much easier and much faster way compared to old-school methods of displaying and editing data. This chapter and the following one take a look at how data binding works. We'll start by looking at the general concepts of data binding in Silverlight 4 in this chapter.

Analyzing the term **data binding** immediately reveals its intentions. It is a technique that allows us to bind properties of controls to objects or collections thereof.

The concept is, in fact, not new. Technologies such as ASP.NET, Windows Forms, and even older technologies such as MFC (Microsoft Foundation Classes) include data binding features. However, WPF's data binding platform has changed the way we perform data binding; it allows loosely coupled bindings. The `BindingsSource` control in Windows Forms has to know of the type we are binding to, at design time. WPF's built-in data binding mechanism does not. We simply define to which property of the source the target should bind. And at runtime, the actual data—the object to which we are binding—is linked. Luckily for us, Silverlight inherits almost all data binding features from WPF and thus has a rich way of displaying data.

A binding is defined by four items:

> ▸ **The source or source object**: This is the data we are binding to. The data that is used in data binding scenarios is in-memory data, that is, objects. Data binding itself has nothing to do with the actual data access. It works with the objects that are a result of reading from a database or communicating with a service. A typical example is a Customer object.

> ▸ **A property on the source object**: This can, for example, be the Name property of the Customer object.

> ▸ **The target control**: This is normally a visual control such as a `TextBox` or a `ListBox` control. In general, the target can be a `DependencyObject`. In Silverlight 2 and Silverlight 3, the target had to derive from `FrameworkElement`; this left out some important types such as transformations.

> ▸ **A property on the target control:** This will, in some way—directly or after a conversion—display the data from the property on the source.

The data binding process can be summarized in the following image:

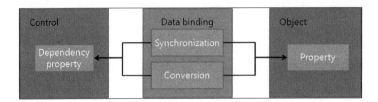

In the previous image, we can see that the data binding engine is also capable of synchronization. This means that data binding is capable of updating the display of data automatically. If the value of the source changes, Silverlight will change the value of the target as well without us having to write a single line of code. Data binding isn't a complete black box either. There are hooks in the process, so we can perform custom actions on the data flowing from source to target, and vice versa. These hooks are the **converters** and we'll look at converters in the next chapter.

Our applications can still be created without data binding. However, the manual process—that is getting data and setting all values manually on controls from code-behind—is error prone and tedious to write. Using the data-binding features in Silverlight, we will be able to write more maintainable code faster.

In this chapter, we'll explore how data binding works. We'll start by building a small data-driven application, which contains the most important data binding features, to get a grasp of the general concepts. We'll also see that data binding isn't tied to just binding single objects to an interface; binding an entire collection of objects is supported as well. We'll also be looking at the **binding modes**. They allow us to specify how the data will flow (from source to target, target to source, or both). We'll finish this chapter by looking at the support that Blend 4 provides to build applications that use data binding features. In the next chapter, we'll be looking at the more advanced concepts of data binding.

In the recipes of this chapter and the following one, we'll assume that we are building a simple banking application using Silverlight. Each of the recipes in this chapter will highlight a part of this application where the specific feature comes into play. The following screenshot shows the resulting Silverlight banking application:

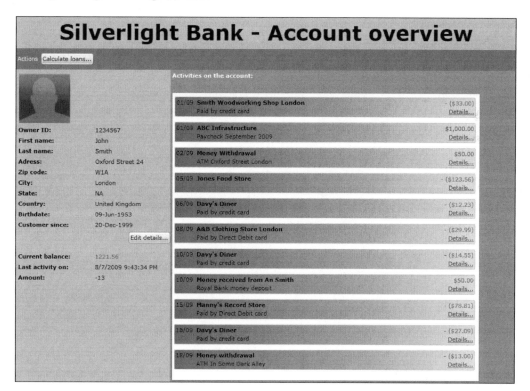

If you want to take a look at the complete application, run the solution found in the `Chapter02/SilverlightBanking` folder in the code bundle that is available on the Packt website.

Displaying data in Silverlight applications

When building Silverlight applications, we often need to display data to the end user. Applications such as an online store with a catalogue and a shopping cart, an online banking application and so on, need to display data of some sort.

Silverlight contains a rich data binding platform that will help us to write data-driven applications faster and using less code. In this recipe, we'll build a form that displays the data of the owner of a bank account using data binding.

Getting ready

To follow along with this recipe, you can use the starter solution located in the `Chapter02/SilverlightBanking_Displaying_Data_Starter` folder in the code bundle available on the Packt website. The finished application for this recipe can be found in the `Chapter02/SilverlightBanking_Displaying_Data_Completed` folder.

How to do it...

Let's assume that we are building a form, part of an online banking application, in which we can view the details of the owner of the account. Instead of wiring up the fields of the owner manually, we'll use data binding. To get data binding up and running, carry out the following steps:

1. Open the starter solution, as outlined in the *Getting Ready* section.

2. The form we are building will bind to data. Data in data binding is in-memory data, not the data that lives in a database (it can originate from a database though). The data to which we are binding is an instance of the `Owner` class. The following is the code for the class. Add this code in a new class file called `Owner` in the Silverlight project.

```
public class Owner
{
    public int OwnerId { get; set; }
    public string FirstName { get; set; }
    public string LastName { get; set; }
    public string Address { get; set; }
    public string ZipCode { get; set; }
    public string City { get; set; }
```

```
    public string State { get; set; }
    public string Country { get; set; }
    public DateTime BirthDate { get; set; }
    public DateTime CustomerSince { get; set; }
    public string ImageName { get; set; }
    public DateTime LastActivityDate { get; set; }
    public double CurrentBalance { get; set; }
    public double LastActivityAmount { get; set; }
}
```

3. Now that we've created the class, we are able to create an instance of it in the `MainPage.xaml.cs` file, the code-behind class of `MainPage.xaml`. In the constructor, we call the `InitializeOwner` method, which creates an instance of the `Owner` class and populates its properties.

```
private Owner owner;
public MainPage()
{
    InitializeComponent();
    //initialize owner data
    InitializeOwner();
}
private void InitializeOwner()
{
    owner = new Owner();
    owner.OwnerId = 1234567;
    owner.FirstName = "John";
    owner.LastName = "Smith";
    owner.Address = "Oxford Street 24";
    owner.ZipCode = "W1A";
    owner.City = "London";
    owner.Country = "United Kingdom";
    owner.State = "NA";
    owner.ImageName = "man.jpg";
    owner.LastActivityAmount = 100;
    owner.LastActivityDate = DateTime.Today;
    owner.CurrentBalance = 1234.56;
    owner.BirthDate = new DateTime(1953, 6, 9);
    owner.CustomerSince = new DateTime(1999, 12, 20);
}
```

4. Let's now focus on the form itself and build its UI. For this sample, we're not making the data editable. So for every field of the `Owner` class, we'll use a `TextBlock`. To arrange the controls on the screen, we'll use a `Grid` called `OwnerDetailsGrid`. This `Grid` can be placed inside the `LayoutRoot Grid`.

We will want the `Text` property of each `TextBlock` to be bound to a specific property of the `Owner` instance. This can be done by specifying this binding using the `Binding` "markup extension" on this property.

```xml
<Grid x:Name="OwnerDetailsGrid"
      VerticalAlignment="Stretch"
      HorizontalAlignment="Left"
      Background="LightGray"
      Margin="3 5 0 0"
      Width="300" >
  <Grid.RowDefinitions>
    <RowDefinition Height="100"></RowDefinition>
    <RowDefinition Height="30"></RowDefinition>
    <RowDefinition Height="30"></RowDefinition>
    <RowDefinition Height="30"></RowDefinition>
    <RowDefinition Height="30"></RowDefinition>
    <RowDefinition Height="30"></RowDefinition>
    <RowDefinition Height="30"></RowDefinition>
    <RowDefinition Height="30"></RowDefinition>
    <RowDefinition Height="30"></RowDefinition>
    <RowDefinition Height="30"></RowDefinition>
    <RowDefinition Height="30"></RowDefinition>
    <RowDefinition Height="30"></RowDefinition>
    <RowDefinition Height="*"></RowDefinition>
  </Grid.RowDefinitions>
  <Grid.ColumnDefinitions>
    <ColumnDefinition></ColumnDefinition>
    <ColumnDefinition></ColumnDefinition>
  </Grid.ColumnDefinitions>
  <Image x:Name="OwnerImage"
         Grid.Row="0"
         Width="100"
         Height="100"
         Stretch="Uniform"
         HorizontalAlignment="Left"
         Margin="3"
         Source="/CustomerImages/man.jpg"
         Grid.ColumnSpan="2">
  </Image>
  <TextBlock x:Name="OwnerIdTextBlock"
```

```
                        Grid.Row="1"
                        FontWeight="Bold"
                        Margin="2"
                        Text="Owner ID:">
</TextBlock>

<TextBlock x:Name="FirstNameTextBlock"
           Grid.Row="2"
           FontWeight="Bold"
           Margin="2"
           Text="First name:">
</TextBlock>

<TextBlock x:Name="LastNameTextBlock"
           Grid.Row="3"
           FontWeight="Bold"
           Margin="2"
           Text="Last name:">
</TextBlock>

<TextBlock x:Name="AddressTextBlock"
           Grid.Row="4"
           FontWeight="Bold"
           Margin="2"
           Text="Adress:">
</TextBlock>

<TextBlock x:Name="ZipCodeTextBlock"
           Grid.Row="5"
           FontWeight="Bold"
           Margin="2"
           Text="Zip code:">
</TextBlock>

<TextBlock x:Name="CityTextBlock"
           Grid.Row="6"
           FontWeight="Bold"
           Margin="2"
           Text="City:">
</TextBlock>

<TextBlock x:Name="StateTextBlock"
           Grid.Row="7"
           FontWeight="Bold"
           Margin="2"
           Text="State:">
</TextBlock>

<TextBlock x:Name="CountryTextBlock"
           Grid.Row="8"
           FontWeight="Bold"
           Margin="2"
           Text="Country:">
```

```xml
    </TextBlock>
    <TextBlock x:Name="BirthDateTextBlock"
            Grid.Row="9"
            FontWeight="Bold"
            Margin="2"
            Text="Birthdate:">
    </TextBlock>
    <TextBlock x:Name="CustomerSinceTextBlock"
            Grid.Row="10"
            FontWeight="Bold"
            Margin="2"
            Text="Customer since:">
    </TextBlock>
    <TextBlock x:Name="OwnerIdValueTextBlock"
            Grid.Row="1"
            Grid.Column="1"
            Margin="2"
            Text="{Binding OwnerId}">
    </TextBlock>
    <TextBlock x:Name="FirstNameValueTextBlock"
            Grid.Row="2"
            Grid.Column="1"
            Margin="2"
            Text="{Binding FirstName}">
    </TextBlock>
    <TextBlock x:Name="LastNameValueTextBlock"
            Grid.Row="3"
            Grid.Column="1"
            Margin="2"
            Text="{Binding LastName}">
    </TextBlock>
    <TextBlock x:Name="AddressValueTextBlock"
            Grid.Row="4"
            Grid.Column="1"
            Margin="2"
            Text="{Binding Address}">
    </TextBlock>
    <TextBlock x:Name="ZipCodeValueTextBlock"
            Grid.Row="5"
            Grid.Column="1"
            Margin="2"
            Text="{Binding ZipCode}">
    </TextBlock>
    <TextBlock x:Name="CityValueTextBlock"
            Grid.Row="6"
            Grid.Column="1"
```

```
                    Margin="2"
                    Text="{Binding City}">
</TextBlock>
<TextBlock x:Name="StateValueTextBlock"
           Grid.Row="7"
           Grid.Column="1"
           Margin="2"
           Text="{Binding State}">
</TextBlock>
<TextBlock x:Name="CountryValueTextBlock"
           Grid.Row="8"
           Grid.Column="1"
           Margin="2"
           Text="{Binding Country}">
</TextBlock>
<TextBlock x:Name="BirthDateValueTextBlock"
           Grid.Row="9"
           Grid.Column="1"
           Margin="2"
           Text="{Binding BirthDate}">
</TextBlock>
<TextBlock x:Name="CustomerSinceValueTextBlock"
           Grid.Row="10"
           Grid.Column="1"
           Margin="2"
           Text="{Binding CustomerSince}">
</TextBlock>
<Button x:Name="OwnerDetailsEditButton"
        Grid.Row="11"
        Grid.ColumnSpan="2"
        Margin="3"
        Content="Edit details..."
        HorizontalAlignment="Right"
        VerticalAlignment="Top">
</Button>
<TextBlock x:Name="CurrentBalanceValueTextBlock"
           Grid.Row="12"
           Grid.Column="1"
           Margin="2"
           Text="{Binding CurrentBalance}" >
</TextBlock>
<TextBlock x:Name="LastActivityDateValueTextBlock"
           Grid.Row="13"
           Grid.Column="1"
           Margin="2"
           Text="{Binding LastActivityDate}" >
```

```
    </TextBlock>
    <TextBlock x:Name="LastActivityAmountValueTextBlock"
               Grid.Row="14"
               Grid.Column="1"
               Margin="2"
               Text="{Binding LastActivityAmount}" >
    </TextBlock>
</Grid>
```

5. At this point, all the controls know what property they need to bind to. However, we haven't specified the actual link. The controls don't know about the Owner instance we want them to bind to. Therefore, we can use DataContext. We specify the DataContext of the OwnerDetailsGrid to be the Owner instance. Each control within that container can then access the object and bind to its properties . Setting the DataContext in done using the following code:

```
public MainPage()
{
    InitializeComponent();
    //initialize owner data
    InitializeOwner();
    OwnerDetailsGrid.DataContext = owner;
}
```

The result can be seen in the following screenshot:

Owner ID:	1234567
First name:	John
Last name:	Smith
Adress:	Oxford Street 24
Zip code:	W1A
City:	London
State:	NA
Country:	United Kingdom
Birthdate:	6/9/1953 12:00:00 AM
Customer since:	12/20/1999 12:00:00 AM

Edit details...

Current balance:	1234.56
Last activity on:	1/3/2010 12:00:00 AM
Amount:	100

How it works...

Before we take a look at the specifics of data binding, let's see what code we would need to write if Silverlight did not support data binding. The following is the `ManualOwner` class and we will be binding an instance of this class manually:

```
public class ManualOwner
{
  public int OwnerId { get; set; }
  public string FirstName { get; set; }
  public string LastName { get; set; }
  public string Address { get; set; }
  public string ZipCode { get; set; }
  public string City { get; set; }
  public string State { get; set; }
  public string Country { get; set; }
  public DateTime BirthDate { get; set; }
  public DateTime CustomerSince { get; set; }
  public string ImageName { get; set; }
  public DateTime LastActivityDate { get; set; }
  public double CurrentBalance { get; set; }
  public double LastActivityAmount { get; set; }
}
```

The XAML code would look the same, apart from the binding markup extensions that are absent as we aren't using the data binding functionality. The following is a part of the code that has no data binding markup extensions:

```
<TextBlock x:Name="OwnerIdValueTextBlock"
           Grid.Row="1"
           Grid.Column="1"
           Margin="2" >
</TextBlock>
<TextBlock x:Name="FirstNameValueTextBlock"
           Grid.Row="2"
           Grid.Column="1"
           Margin="2" >
</TextBlock>
<TextBlock x:Name="LastNameValueTextBlock"
           Grid.Row="3"
           Grid.Column="1"
           Margin="2" >
</TextBlock>
<TextBlock x:Name="AddressValueTextBlock"
           Grid.Row="4"
           Grid.Column="1"
           Margin="2" >
</TextBlock>
```

Of course, the `DataContext` would also not be needed. Instead, we would manually have to link all the `TextBlock` controls with a property of the `ManualOwner` from code-behind as shown in the following code. As can be seen, this is not the most exciting code one can write!

```
public MainPage()
{
  InitializeComponent();
  //initialize owner data
  InitializeOwner();
  SetOwnerValues();
}
private void SetOwnerValues()
{
  OwnerIdValueTextBlock.Text = owner.OwnerId.ToString();
  FirstNameValueTextBlock.Text = owner.FirstName;
  LastNameValueTextBlock.Text = owner.LastName;
  AddressValueTextBlock.Text = owner.Address;
  //other values go here
}
```

It's also easy to make errors this way. When a field gets added to the `ManualOwner`, we need to remember the places in which we have to update our code manually.

However, we can do better using data binding. Data binding enables us to write less code and have fewer opportunities to make errors.

Silverlight's data binding features allow us to bind the properties of the `Owner` instance to the `Text` property of the `TextBlock` controls using the `Binding` "markup extension". A markup extension can be recognized by a pair of curly braces ({ }). It's basically a signal for the XAML parser that more needs to be done than simple attribute parsing. In this case, an instance of the `System.Windows.Data.Binding` is to be created for data binding to happen. The created `Binding` instance will bind the source object with the target control.

Looking back at the XAML code, we find that this binding is achieved for each `TextBlock` using the following code:

```
<TextBlock Text="{Binding CustomerSince}" />
```

This is, in fact, the shortened format. We could have written it as the following code:

```
<TextBlock Text="{Binding Path=CustomerSince}" />
```

The format for the binding is generally the following:

```
<TargetControl TargetProperty="{Binding SourceProperty,
  SomeBindingProperties}" />
```

Note that using `SomeBindingProperties`, more options can be specified when creating t he binding. For example, we can specify that data should not only flow from source object to target control, but also vice versa. We'll explore a whole list of extra binding properties in the next recipes.

Are we missing something? Each control knows what it should bind to, but we haven't specified the actual source of the data. This is done using the `DataContext`. We set the `Owner` instance to be the `DataContext` of the `Grid` containing the controls. All controls within the `Grid` can access the data. We'll look at the `DataContext` in a later recipe.

Finally, there is one important point to note; we can't just bind everything. Basically, there are two rules we must follow:

1. The target object must be a `DependencyObject` (`System.Windows.DependencyObject`). In Silverlight 2 and Silverlight 3, the target could be a `FrameworkElement` instance only. `FrameworkElement` is lower in the class hierarchy than `DependencyObject`. Because of this, some important objects could not be used in data binding scenarios such as `Transformations`. Silverlight 4 has solved this problem.

2. The target property must be a dependency property. Again, don't panic, as almost all properties on UI controls (such as text, foreground and so on) are dependency properties.

> Dependency properties were introduced with WPF and can be considered as properties on steroids. They include a mechanism that at any point in time determines what the value of the property should be, based on several influences working on the property such as data binding, styling, and so on. They can be considered as the enabler for animations, data binding, styling, and so on.
>
> More on dependency properties can be found at `http://msdn.microsoft.com/en-us/library/system.windows.dependencyproperty.aspx`.

There's more...

Instead of creating the `Owner` instance in code, we can create it from XAML as well. First, we need to map the CLR namespace to an XML namespace as follows:

```
xmlns:local="clr-namespace:SilverlightBanking"
```

In the `Resources` collection of the container (the `UserControl`), we instantiate the type like this:

```
<UserControl.Resources>
  <local:Owner x:Key="localOwner"
               City="London"
               Country="United Kingdom"
               FirstName="John"
               LastName="Smith"
               OwnerId="1234567 ...>
  </local:Owner>
</UserControl.Resources>
```

The actual binding is almost the same, apart from specifying the source. We are not using the `DataContext` now, but we need to use the `Source` in each binding, referring to the item in the `Resources`:

```
<TextBlock x:Name="OwnerIdValueTextBlock"
           Grid.Row="1"
           Grid.Column="1"
           Margin="2"
           Text="{Binding OwnerId,
             Source={StaticResource localOwner}}" >
</TextBlock>
<TextBlock x:Name="FirstNameValueTextBlock"
           Grid.Row="2"
           Grid.Column="1"
           Margin="2"
           Text="{Binding FirstName,
             Source={StaticResource localOwner}}" >
</TextBlock>
<TextBlock x:Name="LastNameValueTextBlock"
           Grid.Row="3"
           Grid.Column="1"
           Margin="2"
           Text="{Binding LastName,
             Source={StaticResource localOwner}}" >
</TextBlock>
```

Whether binding from XAML is useful or not depends on the scenario. In most scenarios, we bind to objects that are created at runtime from code-behind. In this case, binding from XAML isn't possible.

See also

The `DataContext` makes its first appearance in this recipe, but we'll look at it in more detail in the *Obtaining data from any UI element it is bound to* recipe in this chapter.

■How to use the Ferrite core

Caution

● Please use the supplied two Ferrite cores to comply with the EMC standard - EN55022.

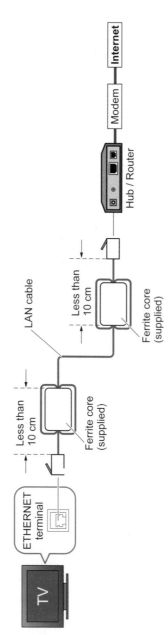

ETHERNET terminal

TV

Less than 10 cm

LAN cable

Ferrite core (supplied)

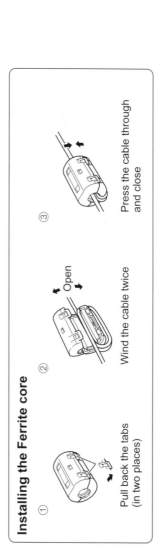

Less than 10 cm

Ferrite core (supplied)

Hub / Router

Modem

Internet

Installing the Ferrite core

① Pull back the tabs (in two places)

② Open — Wind the cable twice

③ Press the cable through and close

TQD0E19015

Creating dynamic bindings

In the previous recipe, you've learned how to use **data binding** in XAML. This is often useful because it allows you to show data easily to your user, for example, showing user information or a list of products. In this recipe, you'll learn how to do exactly the same in C# code, instead of XAML. This can be useful in situations where you want to bind a dependency property to the property of an object that you'll know only at runtime.

Getting ready

For this recipe, we can continue from the solution that was completed in the previous recipe. Alternatively, you can find the starter solution in the `Chapter02/SilverlightBanking_ Dynamic_Bindings_Starter` folder in the code bundle that is available on the Packt website. Also, the completed solution can be found in the `Chapter02/SilverlightBanking_ Dynamic_Bindings_Completed` folder.

How to do it...

We're going to change the code from the previous recipe, so we can create the bindings in C#, instead of XAML. To do this, we'll carry out the following steps:

1. Open the solution created in the previous recipe, *Displaying data in Silverlight applications*, locate the grid named `OwnersDetailsGrid` in `MainPage.xaml`, and remove the `Binding` syntax from the XAML code for each `TextBlock` as shown in the following code:

```
<TextBlock x:Name="OwnerIdValueTextBlock"
           Grid.Row="1"
           Grid.Column="1"
           Margin="2">
</TextBlock>
<TextBlock x:Name="FirstNameValueTextBlock"
           Grid.Row="2"
           Grid.Column="1"
           Margin="2">
</TextBlock>
<TextBlock x:Name="LastNameValueTextBlock"
           Grid.Row="3"
           Grid.Column="1"
           Margin="2">
</TextBlock>
<TextBlock x:Name="AddressValueTextBlock"
           Grid.Row="4"
           Grid.Column="1"
           Margin="2">
```

```xml
        </TextBlock>
        <TextBlock x:Name="ZipCodeValueTextBlock"
                   Grid.Row="5"
                   Grid.Column="1"
                   Margin="2">
        </TextBlock>
        <TextBlock x:Name="CityValueTextBlock"
                   Grid.Row="6"
                   Grid.Column="1"
                   Margin="2">
        </TextBlock>
        <TextBlock x:Name="StateValueTextBlock"
                   Grid.Row="7"
                   Grid.Column="1"
                   Margin="2">
        </TextBlock>
        <TextBlock x:Name="CountryValueTextBlock"
                   Grid.Row="8"
                   Grid.Column="1"
                   Margin="2">
        </TextBlock>
        <TextBlock x:Name="BirthDateValueTextBlock"
                   Grid.Row="9"
                   Grid.Column="1"
                   Margin="2">
        </TextBlock>
        <TextBlock x:Name="CustomerSinceValueTextBlock"
                   Grid.Row="10"
                   Grid.Column="1"
                   Margin="2">
        </TextBlock>
```

2. Open the code-behind `MainPage.xaml.cs` file. Here, we're going to create the same bindings in the C# code. In the constructor, after the call to `InitializeComponent()`, add the following code:

```csharp
OwnerIdValueTextBlock.SetBinding(TextBlock.TextProperty,
  new Binding("OwnerId"));
FirstNameValueTextBlock.SetBinding(TextBlock.TextProperty,
  new Binding("FirstName"));
LastNameValueTextBlock.SetBinding(TextBlock.TextProperty,
  new Binding("LastName"));
AddressValueTextBlock.SetBinding(TextBlock.TextProperty,
  new Binding("Address"));
ZipCodeValueTextBlock.SetBinding(TextBlock.TextProperty,
  new Binding("ZipCode"));
CityValueTextBlock.SetBinding(TextBlock.TextProperty,
```

```
      new Binding("City"));
StateValueTextBlock.SetBinding(TextBlock.TextProperty,
      new Binding("State"));
CountryValueTextBlock.SetBinding(TextBlock.TextProperty,
      new Binding("Country"));
BirthDateValueTextBlock.SetBinding(TextBlock.TextProperty,
      new Binding("BirthDate"));
CustomerSinceValueTextBlock.SetBinding(TextBlock.TextProperty,
      new Binding("CustomerSince"));
```

3. We can now build and run the application, and you'll notice that the correct data is still displayed in the details form. The result can be seen in the following screenshot:

How it works...

This recipe shows you how to set the binding using C# syntax. `Element.SetBinding` expects two parameters, a dependency property and a binding object. The first parameter defines the DependencyProperty of the element you want to bind. The second parameter defines the binding by passing a string that refers to the property path of the object to which you are binding.

There's more...

In our example, we've used `new Binding("path")` as the syntax. The binding object, however, has different properties that you can set and which can be of interest. A few of these properties are `Converter`, `ConverterParameter`, `ElementName`, `Path`, `Mode`, and `ValidatesOnExceptions`.

To know when and how to use these properties, have a look at the other recipes in this chapter and the next which explain all the possibilities in detail. They are, however, already mentioned in this recipe to make it clear you can do everything that is required as far as bindings are concerned in both C# and XAML.

Binding data to another UI element

Sometimes, the value of the property of an element is directly dependent on the value of the property of another element. In this case, you can create a binding in XAML called an **element binding** or **element-to-element binding**. This binding links both values. If needed, the data can flow bidirectionally.

In the banking application, we can add a loan calculator that allows the user to select an amount and the number of years in which they intend to pay the loan back to the bank, including (of course) a lot of interest.

Getting ready

To follow this recipe, you can either continue with your solution from the previous recipe or use the provided solution that can be found in the `Chapter02/SilverlightBanking_Element_Binding_Starter` folder in the code bundle that is available on the Packt website. The finished application for this recipe can be found in the `Chapter02/SilverlightBanking_Element_Binding_Completed` folder.

How to do it...

To build the loan calculator, we'll use `Slider` controls. Each `Slider` is bound to a `TextBlock` using an element-to-element binding to display the actual value. Let's take a look at the steps we need to follow to create this binding:

1. We will build the loan calculator as a separate screen in the application. Add a new child window called `LoanCalculation.xaml`. To do so, right-click on the Silverlight project in the Solution Explorer, select **Add | New Item...**, and choose **Silverlight Child Window** under Visual C#.

2. Within `MainPage.xaml`, add a `Click` event on the `LoanCalculationButton` as shown in the following code:

```
<Button x:Name="LoanCalculationButton"
        Click="LoanCalculationButton_Click" />
```

3. In the code-behind's event handler for this `Click` event, we can trigger the display of this new screen with the following code:

```
private void LoanCalculationButton_Click(object sender,
  RoutedEventArgs e)
{
  LoanCalculation loanCalculation = new LoanCalculation();
  loanCalculation.Show();
}
```

4. The UI of the `LoanCalculation.xaml` is quite simple—it contains two `Slider` controls. Each `Slider` control has set values for its `Minimum` and `Maximum` values (not all UI code is included here; the complete listing can be found in the finished sample code) as shown in the following code:

```
<Slider x:Name="AmountSlider"
        Minimum="10000"
        Maximum="1000000"
        SmallChange="10000"
        LargeChange="10000"
        Width="300" >
</Slider>
<Slider x:Name="YearSlider"
        Minimum="5"
        Maximum="30"
        SmallChange="1"
        LargeChange="1"
        Width="300"
        UseLayoutRounding="True">
</Slider>
```

5. As dragging a `Slider` does not give us proper knowledge of where we are exactly between the two values, we add two `TextBlock` controls. We want the `TextBlock` controls to show the current value of the `Slider` control, even while dragging. This can be done by specifying an element-to-element binding as shown in the following code:

```
<TextBlock x:Name="AmountTextBlock"
           Text="{Binding ElementName=AmountSlider, Path=Value}">
</TextBlock>
<TextBlock x:Name="MonthTextBlock"
           Text="{Binding ElementName=YearSlider, Path=Value}">
</TextBlock>
```

6. Add a `Button` that will perform the actual calculation called `CalculateButton` and a `TextBlock` called `PaybackTextBlock` to show the results. This can be done using the following code:

```
<Button x:Name="CalculateButton"
        Content="Calculate"
        Click="CalculateButton_Click">
</Button>
<TextBlock x:Name="PaybackTextBlock"></TextBlock>
```

7. The code for the actual calculation that is executed when the **Calculate** button is clicked uses the actual value for either the `Slider` or the `TextBlock`. This is shown in the following code:

```
private double percentage = 0.0345;
private void CalculateButton_Click(object sender,
  RoutedEventArgs e)
{
   double requestedAmount = AmountSlider.Value;
   int requestedYears = (int)YearSlider.Value;
   for (int i = 0; i < requestedYears; i++)
   {
      requestedAmount += requestedAmount * percentage;
   }
   double monthlyPayback =
      requestedAmount / (requestedYears * 12);
   PaybackTextBlock.Text =
      "€" + Math.Round(monthlyPayback, 2);
}
```

Having carried out the previous steps, we now have successfully linked the value of the `Slider` controls and the text of the `TextBlock` controls. The following screenshot shows the `LoanCalculation.xaml` screen as it is included in the finished sample code containing some extra markup:

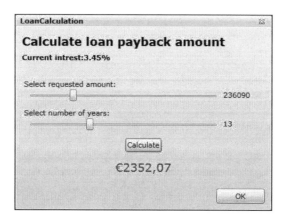

How it works...

An **element binding** links two properties of two controls directly from XAML. It allows creating a `Binding` where the source object is another control. For this to work, we need to create a `Binding` and specify the source control using the `ElementName` property. This is shown in the following code:

```
<TextBlock Text="{Binding ElementName=YearSlider, Path=Value}" >
</TextBlock>
```

Element bindings were added in Silverlight 3. Silverlight 2 did not support this type of binding.

There's more...

An element binding can also work in both directions, that is, from source to target and vice versa. This can be achieved by specifying the `Mode` property on the `Binding` and setting it to `TwoWay`.

The following is the code for this. In this code, we replaced the `TextBlock` by a `TextBox`. When entering a value in the latter, the `Slider` will adjust its position:

```
<TextBox x:Name="AmountTextBlock"
         Text="{Binding ElementName=AmountSlider, Path=Value,
           Mode=TwoWay}" >
</TextBox>
```

Element bindings without bindings

Achieving the same effect in Silverlight 2—which does not support this feature—is also possible, but only through the use of an event handler as shown in the following code. Element bindings eliminate this need:

```
private void AmountSlider_ValueChanged(object sender,
   RoutedPropertyChangedEventArgs<double> e)
{
   AmountSlider.Value = Math.Round(e.NewValue);
   AmountTextBlock.Text = AmountSlider.Value.ToString();
}
```

See also

Element-to-element bindings can be easily extended to use converters. For more information on TwoWay bindings, take a look at the *Using the different modes of data binding to allow persisting data* recipe in this chapter.

Binding collections to UI elements

Often, you'll want to display lists of data in your application such as a list of shopping items, a list of users, a list of bank accounts, and so on. Such a list typically contains a bunch of items of a certain type that have the same properties and need to be displayed in the same fashion.

We can use data binding to easily bind a collection to a Silverlight control (such as a `ListBox` or `DataGrid`) and use the same data binding possibilities to define how every item in the collection should be bound. This recipe will show you how to achieve this.

Getting ready

For this recipe, you can find the starter solution in the `Chapter02/SilverlightBanking_Binding_Collections_Starter` folder and the completed solution in the `Chapter02/SilverlightBanking_Binding_Collections_Completed` folder in the code bundle that is available on the Packt website.

How to do it...

In this recipe, we'll create a `ListBox` bound to a collection of activities. To complete this task, carry out the following steps:

1. We'll need a collection of some kind. We'll create a new type, that is, `AccountActivity`. Add the `AccountActivity` class to your Silverlight project as shown in the following code:

```
public class AccountActivity
{
  public int ActivityId {get; set;}
  public double Amount { get; set; }
  public string Beneficiary { get; set; }
  public DateTime ActivityDate { get; set; }
  public string ActivityDescription { get; set; }
}
```

Add an `ObservableCollection` of `AccountActivity` to `MainPage.xaml.cs` using the following code:

```
private ObservableCollection<AccountActivity>
  accountActivitiesCollection;
```

2. Now, we'll instantiate `accountActivitiesCollection` and fill it with data. To do this, add the following code to `MainPage.xaml.cs`:

```
private void InitializeActivitiesCollection()
{
  accountActivitiesCollection = new
    ObservableCollection<AccountActivity>();
  AccountActivity accountActivity1 = new AccountActivity();
  accountActivity1.ActivityId = 1;
  accountActivity1.Amount = -33;
  accountActivity1.Beneficiary = "Smith Woodworking Shop London";
  accountActivity1.ActivityDescription = "Paid by credit card";
  accountActivity1.ActivityDate = new DateTime(2009, 9, 1);
  accountActivitiesCollection.Add(accountActivity1);
  AccountActivity accountActivity2 = new AccountActivity();
  accountActivity2.ActivityId = 2;
  accountActivity2.Amount = 1000;
  accountActivity2.Beneficiary = "ABC Infrastructure";
  accountActivity2.ActivityDescription = "Paycheck September
    2009";
  accountActivity2.ActivityDate = new DateTime(2009, 9, 1);
  accountActivitiesCollection.Add(accountActivity2);
}
```

This creates a collection with two items. You can add more if you want to.

3. Add the following code to the `MainPage` constructor to call the method you created in the previous step:

```
InitializeActivitiesCollection();
```

4. We're going to need a control to display these `AccountActivity` items. To do this, add a `ListBox` called `AccountActivityListBox`. This `ListBox` defines a `DataTemplate` that defines how each `AccountActivity` is displayed.

```xml
<ListBox x:Name="AccountActivityListBox"
         Width="600"
         Grid.Row="1">
  <ListBox.ItemTemplate>
    <DataTemplate>
      <Grid>
        <Grid.RowDefinitions>
          <RowDefinition></RowDefinition>
          <RowDefinition></RowDefinition>
        </Grid.RowDefinitions>
        <Grid.ColumnDefinitions>
          <ColumnDefinition Width="150">
          </ColumnDefinition>
          <ColumnDefinition Width="330">
          </ColumnDefinition>
          <ColumnDefinitionWidth="100">
          </ColumnDefinition>
        </Grid.ColumnDefinitions>
        <TextBlock
          Grid.Row="0"
          Grid.Column="0"
          Grid.RowSpan="2"
          Text="{Binding ActivityDate}">
        </TextBlock>
        <TextBlock
          Grid.Row="0"
          Grid.Column="1"
          Text="{Binding Beneficiary}"
          FontWeight="Bold">
        </TextBlock>
        <TextBlock
          Grid.Row="0"
          Grid.Column="2"
          HorizontalAlignment="Right"
          Text="{Binding Amount}">
        </TextBlock>
        <TextBlock
          Grid.Row="1"
          Grid.Column="1"
          Text="{Binding ActivityDescription}">
```

```
            </TextBlock>
          </Grid>
        </DataTemplate>
      </ListBox.ItemTemplate>
    </ListBox>
```

5. In the `MainPage` constructor, set the `ObservableCollection` of
    `AccountActivity` you created in step 2 as the `ItemsSource`
    of the `ListBox` as shown in the following code:

    ```
    AccountActivityListBox.ItemsSource = accountActivitiesCollection;
    ```

6. If we build and run the application now, we'll see that a list of `AccountActivity`
    items is displayed as shown in the following screenshot:

9/1/2009 12:00:00 AM	**Smith Woodworking Shop London** Paid by credit card	-33
9/1/2009 12:00:00 AM	**ABC Infrastructure** Paycheck September 2009	1000
9/2/2009 12:00:00 AM	**Money Withdrawal** ATM Oxford Street London	50
9/5/2009 12:00:00 AM	**Jones Food Store**	-123.56
9/6/2009 12:00:00 AM	**Davy's Diner** Paid by credit card	-12.23
9/8/2009 12:00:00 AM	**A&B Clothing Store London** Paid by Direct Debit card	-29.99
9/10/2009 12:00:00 AM	**Davy's Diner** Paid by credit card	-14.55

How it works...

The first three steps aren't important for people who have worked with collections
before. A class is created to define the type of items that are held by the collection, which
is initialized and then items are added to it. The default collection type to use in Silverlight
is **ObservableCollection**. We're using this collection type here. (For more information about
this, have a look at the *There's more...* section in this recipe.)

The real magic happens in steps 4 and 5. In step 4, we are creating a `ListBox`,
which has an `ItemTemplate` property. This `ItemTemplate` property should contain
a `DataTemplate`, and it's this `DataTemplate` that defines how each item of the collection
should be visualized. So, the `DataTemplate` corresponds to one item of your collection:
one `AccountActivity`. This means we can use the **data binding** syntax that binds
to properties of an `AccountActivity` in this `DataTemplate`.

When the `ItemsSource` property of the `ListBox` gets set to the `ObservableCollection`
of `AccountActivity`, each `AccountActivity` in the collection is evaluated and visualized
as defined in the `DataTemplate`.

There's more...

An `ObservableCollection` is the default collection type you'll want to use in a Silverlight application because it's a collection type that implements the `INotifyCollectionChanged` interface. This makes sure that the UI can automatically be updated when the collection is changed (by adding or deleting an item). More on this can be found in the *Enabling a Silverlight application to automatically update its UI* recipe.

The same principle applies for the properties of classes that implement the `INotifyPropertyChanged` interface. More on this can be found in the same recipe, that is, *Enabling a Silverlight application to automatically update its UI*.

In this recipe, we're using a `ListBox` to visualize our `ObservableCollection`. However, every control that inherits the `ItemsControl` class (directly or indirectly) can be used in this way, such as a `ComboBox`, `TreeView`, `DataGrid`, `WrapPanel`, and so on. For more information on what operations can be performed using `DataGrid`, have a look at Chapter 4, *The Data Grid*.

See also

To learn how an `ObservableCollection` enables a UI to be automatically updated, have a look at the *Enabling a Silverlight application to automatically update its UI* recipe.

Enabling a Silverlight application to automatically update its UI

In the previous recipes, we looked at how we can display data more easily using data binding for both single objects as well as collections. However, there is another feature that data binding offers us for free, that is, **automatic synchronization** between the target and the source. This synchronization will make sure that when the value of the source property changes, this change will be reflected in the target object as well (being a control on the user interface). This also works in the opposite direction—when we change the value of a bound control, this change will be pushed to the data object as well. Silverlight's data binding engine allows us to opt-in to this synchronization process. We can specify if we want it to work—and if so, in which direction(s)—using the mode of data binding.

The synchronization works for both single objects bound to the UI as well as entire collections. But for it to work, an interface needs to be implemented in either case.

This synchronization process is what we'll be looking at in this recipe.

Getting ready

If you want to follow along with this recipe, you can either use the code from the previous recipes or use the provided solution in the `Chapter02/SilverlightBanking_Update_UI_Starter` folder in the code bundle that is available on the Packt website. The finished solution for this recipe can be found in the `Chapter02/SilverlightBanking_Update_UI_Completed` folder.

How to do it...

In this recipe, we'll look at how Silverlight does automatic synchronization, both for a single object and for a collection of objects. To demonstrate both types of synchronization, we'll use a timer that adds another activity on the account every 10 seconds. A single instance of the `Owner` class is bound to the UI. However, the newly added activities will cause the `CurrentBalance`, `LastActivity`, and `LastActivityAmount` properties of the `Owner` class to get updated. Also, these activities on the account will be reflected in the list of activities. The following are the steps to achieve automatic synchronization:

1. For the data binding engine to notice changes on the source object, the source needs to send a notification that the value of one of its properties has changed. By default, the `Owner` class does not do so. The original `Owner` class is shown by the following code:

```
public class Owner
{
    public int OwnerId { get; set; }
    public string FirstName { get; set; }
    public string LastName { get; set; }
    public string Address { get; set; }
    public string ZipCode { get; set; }
    public string City { get; set; }
    public string State { get; set; }
    public string Country { get; set; }
    public DateTime BirthDate { get; set; }
    public DateTime CustomerSince { get; set; }
    public string ImageName { get; set; }
    public DateTime LastActivityDate { get; set; }
    public double CurrentBalance { get; set; }
    public double LastActivityAmount { get; set; }
}
```

2. To make this class support notifications, an interface has to be implemented, namely the INotifyPropertyChanged interface. This interface defines one event, that is, the PropertyChanged event. Whenever one of the properties changes, this event should be raised. The changed Owner class is shown in the following code. (Only two properties are shown as they are all similar; the rest can be found in the finished solution in the book sample code.)

```
public class Owner : INotifyPropertyChanged
{
  private double currentBalance;
  private string firstName;
  public event PropertyChangedEventHandler PropertyChanged;
  public string FirstName
  {
    get
    {
      return firstName;
    }
    set
    {
      firstName = value;
      if(PropertyChanged != null)
        PropertyChanged(this, new
          PropertyChangedEventArgs("FirstName"));
    }
  }
  public double CurrentBalance
  {
    get
    {
      return currentBalance;
    }
    set
    {
      currentBalance = value;
      if(PropertyChanged != null)
        PropertyChanged(this, new
          PropertyChangedEventArgs("CurrentBalance"));
    }
  }
}
```

3. To simulate updates, we'll use a `DispatcherTimer` in the `MainPage`. With every tick of this timer, a new activity on the account is created. We'll count the new value of the `CurrentBalance` with every tick and update the value of the `LastActivityDate` and `LastActivityAmount` as shown in the following code:

```
private DispatcherTimer timer;
private int currentActivityId = 11;
public MainPage()
{
   InitializeComponent();
   //initialize owner data
   InitializeOwner();
   OwnerDetailsGrid.DataContext = owner;
   timer = new DispatcherTimer();
   timer.Interval = new TimeSpan(0, 0, 10);
   timer.Tick += new EventHandler(timer_Tick);
   timer.Start();
}
void timer_Tick(object sender, EventArgs e)
{
   currentActivityId++;
   double amount = 0 - new Random().Next(100);
   AccountActivity newActivity = new AccountActivity();
   newActivity.ActivityId = currentActivityId;
   newActivity.Amount = amount;
   newActivity.Beneficiary = "Money withdrawal";
   newActivity.ActivityDescription = "ATM In Some Dark Alley";
   newActivity.ActivityDate = new DateTime(2009, 9, 18);
   owner.CurrentBalance += amount;
   owner.LastActivityDate = DateTime.Now;
   owner.LastActivityAmount = amount;
}
```

4. In XAML, the `TextBlock` controls are bound as mentioned before. If no `Mode` is specified, `OneWay` is assumed. This causes updates of the source to be reflected in the target as shown in the following code:

```
<TextBlock x:Name="CountryValueTextBlock"
           Grid.Row="8"
           Grid.Column="1"
           Margin="2"
           Text="{Binding Country}" >
</TextBlock>
<TextBlock x:Name="BirthDateValueTextBlock"
```

```
                Grid.Row="9"
                Grid.Column="1"
                Margin="2"
                Text="{Binding BirthDate}" >
  </TextBlock>
  <TextBlock x:Name="CustomerSinceValueTextBlock"
                Grid.Row="10"
                Grid.Column="1"
                Margin="2"
                Text="{Binding CustomerSince}"   >
  </TextBlock>
```

5. If we run the application now, after 10 seconds, we'll see the values changing. The values can be seen in the following screenshot:

Current balance:	1183.56
Last activity on:	8/2/2009 5:48:55 PM
Amount:	-30

6. In the *Binding collections to UI elements* recipe, we saw how to bind a list of AccountActivity items to a ListBox. If we want the UI to update automatically when changes occur in the list (when a new item is added or an existing item is removed), then the list to which we bind should implement the INotifyCollectionChanged interface. Silverlight has a built-in list that implements this interface, namely the ObservableCollection<T>. If we were binding to a List<T>, then these automatic updates wouldn't work. Working with an ObservableCollection<T> is no different than working with a List<T>. In the following code, we're creating the ObservableCollection<AccountActivity> and adding items to it:

```
private ObservableCollection<AccountActivity>
  accountActivitiesCollection;
private void InitializeActivitiesCollection()
{
  accountActivitiesCollection = new
    ObservableCollection<AccountActivity>();
  AccountActivity accountActivity1 = new AccountActivity();
  accountActivity1.ActivityId = 1;
  accountActivity1.Amount = -33;
  accountActivity1.Beneficiary = "Smith Woodworking Shop London";
  accountActivity1.ActivityDescription = "Paid by credit card";
  accountActivity1.ActivityDate = new DateTime(2009, 9, 1);
  accountActivitiesCollection.Add(accountActivity1);
}
```

7. Update the `Tick` event, so that each new `Activity` is added to the collection:

```
void timer_Tick(object sender, EventArgs e)
{
  . . .
  AccountActivity newActivity = new AccountActivity();
  . . .
  accountActivitiesCollection.Add(newActivity);
  . . .
}
```

8. To bind this collection to the `ListBox`, we use the `ItemsSource` property. The following code can be added to the constructor to create the collection and perform the binding:

```
InitializeActivitiesCollection();
AccountActivityListBox.ItemsSource = accountActivitiesCollection;
```

When we run the application now, we see that all added activities appear in the `ListBox` control. With every tick of the `Timer`, a new activity is added and the UI refreshes automatically.

How it works...

In some scenarios, we might want to view changes to the source object in the user interface immediately. Silverlight's data binding engine can automatically synchronize the source and target for us, both for single objects and for collections.

Single objects

If we want the target controls on the UI to update automatically if a property value of an instance changes, then the class to which we are binding should implement the `INotifyPropertyChanged` interface. This interface defines just one event—`PropertyChanged`. It is defined in the `System.ComponentModel` namespace using the following code:

```
public interface INotifyPropertyChanged
{
  event PropertyChangedEventHandler PropertyChanged;
}
```

This event should be raised whenever the value of a property changes. The name of the property that has changed is passed as the parameter for the instance of `PropertyChangedEventArgs`.

A binding in XAML is set to `OneWay` by default. `OneWay` allows updates to be passed on to the target. (For more information on binding modes, refer to the *Using the different modes of data binding to allow persisting data* recipe.) If we had set the binding to `Mode=OneTime`, then only the initial values would have been loaded.

Now, what exactly happens when we bind to a class that implements this interface? Whenever we do so, Silverlight's data binding engine will notice this and will automatically start to check if the `PropertyChanged` event is raised by an instance of the class. It will react to this event, thereby resulting in an update of the target.

Collections

Whenever a **collection** changes, we might want to get updates of this collection as well. In this example, we want to view the direct information of all the activities on the account. Normally, we would have placed these in a `List<T>`. However, `List<T>` does not raise an event when items are being added or deleted. Similar to `INotifyPropertyChanged`, an interface exists so that a list/collection should implement for data binding to pick up those changes. This interface is known as `INotifyCollectionChanged`.

We didn't directly create a class that implements this interface. However, we used an `ObservableCollection<T>`. This collection already implemented this interface for us.

Whenever items are being added, deleted, or the collection gets refreshed, an event will be raised on which the data binding engine will bind itself. As for single objects, changes will be reflected in the UI immediately.

Cleaning up the code

In the code for the `Owner` class, we have inputted all the properties as shown in the following code:

```
public double CurrentBalance
{
  get
  {
    return currentBalance;
  }
  set
  {
    currentBalance = value;
    if(currentBalance != null)
      PropertyChanged(this, new
        PropertyChangedEventArgs("CurrentBalance"));
  }
}
```

It's a good idea to move the check whether the event is null (which means that there is no one actually subscribed to the event) and the raising of the event to a separate method as shown in the following code:

```
public void OnPropertyChanged(string propertyName)
{
  if (PropertyChanged != null)
  {
```

```
        PropertyChanged(this, new
           PropertyChangedEventArgs(propertyName));
      }
   }
   public double CurrentBalance
   {
     get
     {
       return currentBalance;
     }
     set
     {
       if (currentBalance != value)
       {
         currentBalance = value;
         OnPropertyChanged("CurrentBalance");
       }
     }
   }
}
```

It may also be a good idea to move this method to a base class and have the entities inherit
from this class as shown in the following code:

```
   public class BaseEntity : INotifyPropertyChanged
   {
     public event PropertyChangedEventHandler PropertyChanged;
     public void OnPropertyChanged(string propertyName)
     {
       if (PropertyChanged != null)
       {
         PropertyChanged(this, new
           PropertyChangedEventArgs(propertyName));
       }
     }
   }
   public class Owner : BaseEntity
   {
     ...
   }
```

While automatic synchronization is a nice feature that comes along with data binding for
free, it's not always needed. Sometimes it's not even wanted. Therefore, implement the
interfaces that are described here only when the application needs them. It's an
opt-in model.

Obtaining data from any UI element it is bound to

When a user who is working with your application performs a certain action, it's often essential to know on what object this action will be executed. For example, if a user clicks on a *Delete* button on an item, it's essential that you know which item is clicked so that you can write the correct code to delete that item. Also, when a user wants to edit an item in a list, it's necessary that you—the programmer—know which item in the list the user wants to edit.

In Silverlight, there is a very easy mechanism called `DataContext` that helps us in this task. In this recipe, we're going to use the `DataContext` to get the data when we need it.

Getting ready

If you want to follow along with this recipe, you can either use the code from the previous recipes or use the provided solution in the `Chapter02/SilverlightBanking_ Obtaining_Data_Starter` folder in the code bundle that is available on the Packt website. The completed solution for this recipe can be found in the `Chapter02/ SilverlightBanking_Obtaining_Data_Completed` folder.

How to do it...

We're going to create a **Details...** button for each item in the `ListBox` containing `AccountActivities`. This **Details...** button will open a new `ChildWindow` that will display details about the selected `AccountActivity`. To achieve this, carry out the following steps:

1. We'll start by opening the solution we've created by following all the steps of the *Binding data to collections* recipe. We add a new item to the Silverlight project—a `ChildWindow` named `ActivityDetailView`—and add the following code to the XAML defining this new control:

    ```
    <Grid x:Name="LayoutRoot" Margin="2">
      <Grid.RowDefinitions>
        <RowDefinition />
        <RowDefinition Height="Auto" />
      </Grid.RowDefinitions>
    <Grid x:Name="OwnerDetailsGrid">
      <Grid.RowDefinitions>
        <RowDefinition Height="30"></RowDefinition>
        <RowDefinition Height="30"></RowDefinition>
        <RowDefinition Height="30"></RowDefinition>
        <RowDefinition Height="30"></RowDefinition>
        <RowDefinition Height="30"></RowDefinition>
        <RowDefinition Height="30"></RowDefinition>
        <RowDefinition Height="30"></RowDefinition>
    ```

```xml
      <RowDefinition Height="30"></RowDefinition>
      <RowDefinition Height="30"></RowDefinition>
      <RowDefinition Height="30"></RowDefinition>
      <RowDefinition Height="30"></RowDefinition>
      <RowDefinition Height="*"></RowDefinition>
    </Grid.RowDefinitions>
    <Grid.ColumnDefinitions>
      <ColumnDefinition></ColumnDefinition>
      <ColumnDefinition></ColumnDefinition>
    </Grid.ColumnDefinitions>
      <TextBlock x:Name="ActivityIdTextBlock"
                 Grid.Row="0"
                 FontWeight="Bold"
                 Margin="2"
                 Text="Activity ID:">
      </TextBlock>
      <TextBlock x:Name="BeneficiaryTextBlock"
                 Grid.Row="1"
                 FontWeight="Bold"
                 Margin="2"
                 Text="Beneficiary:">
      </TextBlock>
      <TextBlock x:Name="AmountTextBlock"
                 Grid.Row="2"
                 FontWeight="Bold"
                 Margin="2"
                 Text="Amount:">
      </TextBlock>
      <TextBlock x:Name="ActivityDateTextBlock"
                 Grid.Row="3"
                 FontWeight="Bold"
                 Margin="2"
                 Text="Date:">
      </TextBlock>
      <TextBlock x:Name="DescriptionTextBlock"
                 Grid.Row="4"
                 FontWeight="Bold"
                 Margin="2"
                 Text="Description:">
      </TextBlock>
      <TextBlock x:Name="ActivityIdTextBlockValue"
                 Grid.Row="0"
                 Grid.Column="1"
                 Margin="2"
                 Text="{Binding ActivityId}" >
      </TextBlock>
      <TextBlock x:Name="BeneficiaryTextBlockValue"
                 Grid.Row="1"
```

```
                    Grid.Column="1"
                    Margin="2"
                    Text="{Binding Beneficiary}" >
        </TextBlock>
        <TextBlock x:Name="AmountTextBlockValue"
                    Grid.Row="2"
                    Grid.Column="1"
                    Margin="2"
                    Text="{Binding Amount}" >
        </TextBlock>
        <TextBlock x:Name="ActivityDateTextBlockValue"
                    Grid.Row="3"
                    Grid.Column="1"
                    Margin="2"
                    Text="{Binding ActivityDate}" >
        </TextBlock>
        <TextBlock x:Name="DescriptionTextBlockValue"
                    Grid.Row="4"
                    Grid.Column="1"
                    Margin="2"
                    Text="{Binding ActivityDescription}"
                        TextWrapping="Wrap">
        </TextBlock>
    </Grid>
      <Button x:Name="btnOK"
              Content="OK"
              Click="btnOK_Click"
              Width="75"
              Height="23"
              HorizontalAlignment="Right"
              Margin="0,12,0,0"
              Grid.Row="1" />
    </Grid>
```

2. Next, we open `ActivityDetailView.xaml.cs` and add the following code:

```
public ActivityDetailView(AccountActivity activity)
{
    InitializeComponent();
    this.DataContext = activity;
}
private void btnOK_Click(object sender, RoutedEventArgs e)
{
    this.DialogResult = true;
}
```

3. Now, we open `MainPage.xaml`, locate the `ListBox` named `AccountActivityListBox`, and add a button named `btnDetails` to the `DataTemplate` of that `ListBox`. This is shown in the following code:

```
<Button x:Name="btnDetails"
        Grid.Row="1"
        Grid.Column="2"
        HorizontalAlignment="Right"
        Content="Details..."
        Click="btnDetails_Click">
</Button>
```

4. Add the following C# code to `MainPage.xaml.cs` to handle the `Click` event of the button we've added in the previous step:

```
private void btnDetails_Click(object sender, RoutedEventArgs e)
{
    ActivityDetailView activityDetailView = new ActivityDetailView
    ((AccountActivity)((Button)sender).DataContext);
    activityDetailView.Show();
}
```

5. We can now build and run the solution. When you click on the **Details...** button, you'll see the details of the selected `AccountActivity` in a `ChildWindow`. You can see the result in the following screenshot:

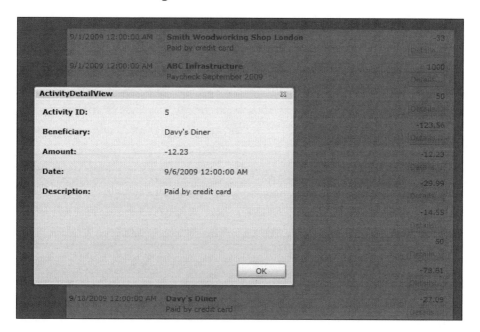

How it works...

Once the `DataContext` of a general control has been set (any CLR object can be used as `DataContext`), each child item of that control refers to the same `DataContext`.

For example, if we have a `UserControl` containing a `Grid` that has three columns, with a `TextBox` in the first two and a `Button` in the last column, and if the `DataContext` of the `UserControl` gets set to an object of the `Person` type, then the `Grid`, `TextBox`, and `Button` would have that same `Person` object as their `DataContext`. To be more precise, if the `DataContext` of an item hasn't been set, then Silverlight will find out if the parent of that item in the visual tree has its `DataContext` set to an object and use that `DataContext` as the `DataContext` of the child item. Silverlight keeps on trickling right up to the uppermost level of the application.

If you use an `ItemsControl` such as a `ListBox` and give it a collection as an `ItemsSource`, then the `DataContext` of that `ListBox` is the collection you bound it to.

Following the same logic, the `DataContext` of one `ListBoxItem` is one item from the collection. In our example, one item is defined by a `DataTemplate` containing a `Grid`, various `TextBlocks`, and a `Button`. Due to the fact that Silverlight keeps on trickling up to look for a valid `DataContext`, the `DataContext` of the `Grid`, all the `TextBlocks`, and the `Button` are the same; they're one item from the `ItemsSource` collection of the `ListBox`.

With this in mind, we can now access the data that is bound to any UI element of our `ListBoxItem`. The data we need is the `DataContext` of the button we're clicking.

The click event of this button has a sender parameter—the `Button` itself. To access the `DataContext`, we cast the sender parameter to a `Button` object. As we know that the `ListBox` is bound to an `ObservableCollection` of `AccountActivity`, we can cast the `DataContext` to type `AccountActivity`. To show the details window, all we need to do now is pass this object to the constructor of the details `ChildWindow`.

See also

The `DataContext` is important when you're working with **data binding** as it's the `DataContext` of an element that's looked at as the source of the binding properties. You can learn more about data binding and the various possibilities it offers by looking at almost any recipe in this chapter.

Using the different modes of data binding to allow persisting data

Until now, the data has flowed from the source to the target (the UI controls). However, it can also flow in the opposite direction, that is, from the target towards the source. This way, not only can data binding help us in displaying data, but also in **persisting data**.

The direction of the flow of data in a data binding scenario is controlled by the `Mode` property of the `Binding`. In this recipe, we'll look at an example that uses all the `Mode` options and in one go, we'll push the data that we enter ourselves to the source.

Getting ready

This recipe builds on the code that was created in the previous recipes, so if you're following along, you can keep using that codebase. You can also follow this recipe from the provided start solution. It can be found in the `Chapter02/SilverlightBanking_Binding_Modes_Starter` folder in the code bundle that is available on the Packt website. The `Chapter02/SilverlightBanking_Binding_Modes_Completed` folder contains the finished application of this recipe.

How to do it...

In this recipe, we'll build the "edit details" window of the Owner class. On this window, part of the data is editable, while some isn't. The editable data will be bound using a TwoWay binding, whereas the non-editable data is bound using a OneTime binding. The **Current balance** of the account is also shown—which uses the automatic synchronization—based on the INotifyPropertyChanged interface implementation. This is achieved using OneWay binding. The following is a screenshot of the details screen:

Let's go through the required steps to work with the different binding modes:

1. Add a new Silverlight child window called OwnerDetailsEdit.xaml to the Silverlight project.

2. In the code-behind of this window, change the default constructor—so that it accepts an instance of the Owner class—as shown in the following code:

```
private Owner owner;
public OwnerDetailsEdit(Owner owner)
{
    InitializeComponent();
    this.owner = owner;
}
```

3. In `MainPage.xaml`, add a `Click` event on the `OwnerDetailsEditButton`:

```
<Button x:Name="OwnerDetailsEditButton"
        Click="OwnerDetailsEditButton_Click" >
```

4. In the event handler, add the following code, which will create a new instance of the `OwnerDetailsEdit` window, passing in the created `Owner` instance:

```
private void OwnerDetailsEditButton_Click(object sender,
    RoutedEventArgs e)
{
    OwnerDetailsEdit ownerDetailsEdit = new OwnerDetailsEdit(owner);
    ownerDetailsEdit.Show();
}
```

5. The XAML of the `OwnerDetailsEdit` is pretty simple. Take a look at the completed solution (Chapter02/ SilverlightBanking_Binding_Modes_Completed)for a complete listing. Don't forget to set the passed `Owner` instance as the `DataContext` for the `OwnerDetailsGrid`. This is shown in the following code:

```
OwnerDetailsGrid.DataContext = owner;
```

6. For the `OneWay` and `TwoWay` bindings to work, the object to which we are binding should be an instance of a class that implements the `INotifyPropertyChanged` interface. In our case, we are binding an `Owner` instance. This instance implements the interface correctly. The following code illustrates this:

```
public class Owner : INotifyPropertyChanged
{
    public event PropertyChangedEventHandler PropertyChanged;
    ...
}
```

7. Some of the data may not be updated on this screen and it will never change. For this type of binding, the `Mode` can be set to `OneTime`. This is the case for the `OwnerId` field. The users should neither be able to change their ID nor should the value of this field change in the background, thereby requiring an update in the UI. The following is the XAML code for this binding:

```
<TextBlock x:Name="OwnerIdValueTextBlock"
           Text="{Binding OwnerId, Mode=OneTime}" >
</TextBlock>
```

8. The `CurrentBalance TextBlock` at the bottom does not need to be editable by the user (allowing a user to change his or her account balance might not be beneficial for the bank), but it does need to change when the source changes. This is the automatic synchronization working for us and it is achieved by setting the `Binding` to `Mode=OneWay`. This is shown in the following code:

```
<TextBlock x:Name="CurrentBalanceValueTextBlock"
           Text="{Binding CurrentBalance, Mode=OneWay}" >
</TextBlock>
```

9. The final option for the `Mode` property is `TwoWay`. `TwoWay` bindings allow us to persist data by pushing data from the UI control to the source object. In this case, all other fields can be updated by the user. When we enter a new value, the bound `Owner` instance is changed. `TwoWay` bindings are illustrated using the following code:

```
<TextBox x:Name="FirstNameValueTextBlock"
         Text="{Binding FirstName, Mode=TwoWay}" >
</TextBox>
```

We've applied all the different binding modes at this point. Notice that when you change the values in the pop-up window, the details on the left of the screen are also updated. This is because all controls are in the background bound to the same source object as shown in the following screenshot:

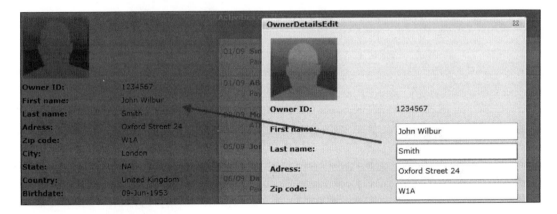

How it works...

When we looked at the basics of data binding, we saw that a binding always occurs between a source and a target. The first one is normally an in-memory object, but it can also be a UI control. The second one will always be a UI control.

Normally, data flows from source to target. However, using the `Mode` property, we have the option to control this.

A `OneTime` binding should be the default for data that does not change when displayed to the user. When using this mode, the data flows from source to target. The target receives the value initially during loading and the data displayed in the target will never change. Quite logically, even if a `OneTime` binding is used for a `TextBox`, changes done to the data by the user will not flow back to the source. IDs are a good example of using `OneTime` bindings. Also, when building a catalogue application, `OneTime` bindings can be used, as we won't change the price of the items that are displayed to the user (or should we...?).

We should use a OneWay binding for binding scenarios in which we want an up-to-date display of data. Data will flow from source to target here also, but every change in the values of the source properties will propagate to a change of the displayed values. Think of a stock market application where updates are happening every second. We need to push the updates to the UI of the application.

The TwoWay bindings can help in **persisting data**. The data can now flow from source to target, and vice versa. Initially, the values of the source properties will be loaded in the properties of the controls. When we interact with these values (type in a textbox, drag a slider, and so on), these updates are pushed back to the source object. If needed, conversions can be done in both directions.

There is one important requirement for the OneWay and TwoWay bindings. If we want to display up-to-date values, then the INotifyPropertyChanged interface should be implemented. The OneTime and OneWay bindings would have the same effect, even if this interface is not implemented on the source. The TwoWay bindings would still send the updated values if the interface was not implemented; however, they wouldn't notify about the changed values. It can be considered as a good practice to implement the interface, unless there is no chance that the updates of the data would be displayed somewhere in the application. The overhead created by the implementation is minimal.

There's more...

Another option in the binding is the UpdateSourceTrigger. It allows us to specify when a TwoWay binding will push the data to the source. By default, this is determined by the control. For a TextBox, this is done on the LostFocus event; and for most other controls, it's done on the PropertyChanged event.

The value can also be set to Explicit. This means that we can manually trigger the update of the source.

```
BindingExpression expression = this.FirstNameValueTextBlock.
   GetBindingExpression(TextBox.TextProperty);
expression.UpdateSource();
```

See also

Changing the values that flow between source and target can be done using converters. We'll look at these in the next chapter.

Data binding from Expression Blend 4

While creating data bindings is probably a task mainly reserved for the developer(s) in the team, Blend 4—the design tool for Silverlight applications—also has strong support for creating and using bindings.

In this recipe, we'll build a small data-driven application that uses data binding. We won't manually create the data binding expressions; we'll use Blend 4 for this task.

How to do it...

For this recipe, we'll create a small application from scratch that allows us to edit the details of a bank account owner. In order to achieve this, carry out the following steps:

1. We'll need to open Blend 4 and go to **File | New Project...**. In the **New Project** dialog box, select **Silverlight 4 Application + Website**. Name the project `SilverlightOwnerEdit` and click on the **OK** button. Blend will now create a Silverlight application and a hosting website.

2. We'll start by adding a new class called `Owner`. Right-click on the Silverlight project and select **Add New Item...**. In the dialog box that appears, select the **Class** template and click on the **OK** button. The following is the code for the `Owner` class and it can be edited inside Blend 4:

   ```
   public class Owner
   {
     public string Name {get; set;}
     public int CurrentBalance {get;set;}
     public DateTime LastActivityDate {get;set;}
   }
   ```

3. In the code-behind of `MainPage.xaml`, create an instance of the `Owner` class and set it as the `DataContext` for the `LayoutRoot` of the page.

   ```
   public partial class MainPage : UserControl
   {
     public Owner owner;
     public MainPage()
     {
       // Required to initialize variables
       InitializeComponent();
       owner = new Owner()
       {
         Name="Gill Cleeren",
         CurrentBalance=300,
   ```

```
        LastActivityDate=DateTime.Now.Date
    };
    LayoutRoot.DataContext = owner;
  }
}
```

4. Build the solution, so that the `Owner` class is known to Blend and it can use the class in its dialog boxes.

5. Now, in the designer, add a `Grid` containing three `TextBlock` and three `TextBox` controls as shown in the following screenshot:

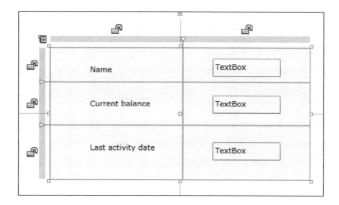

6. We're now ready to add the data binding functionality. Select the first `TextBox` and in the **Properties** window, search for the `Text` property. Instead of typing a value, click on the small square for the **Advanced property options** next to the text field. Select **Data Binding...** in the menu. The following screenshot shows how to access this option:

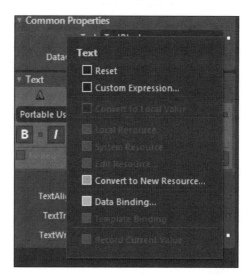

7. In the dialog box that appears, we can now couple the `Name` property of the `Owner` type to the `Text` property of the `TextBox`. Under the **Explicit Data Context** tab, mark the **Use a custom path expression** checkbox and enter **Name** as the value. Click on the down arrow so that the advanced properties are expanded and mark **TwoWay** as the **Binding direction**. The other properties are similar as shown in the following screenshot:

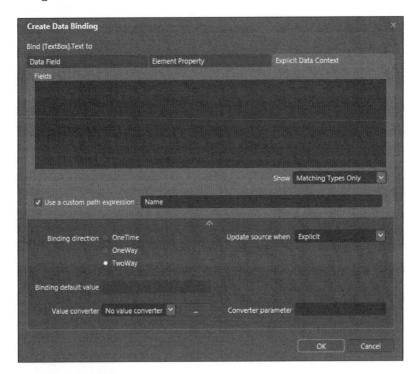

How it works...

Let's look at the resulting XAML code for a moment. Blend created the bindings for us automatically taking into account the required options such as `Mode=TwoWay`. This is shown in the following code:

```
<TextBox Grid.Column="1"
         Text="{Binding Name, Mode=TwoWay,
           UpdateSourceTrigger=Default}"
         TextWrapping="Wrap"/>
<TextBox Grid.Column="1"
         Grid.Row="2"
         Text="{Binding LastActivityDate, Mode=TwoWay,
           UpdateSourceTrigger=Default}"
         TextWrapping="Wrap"/>
<TextBox Grid.Column="1"
```

```
Grid.Row="1"
Text="{Binding CurrentBalance, Mode=TwoWay,
   UpdateSourceTrigger=Default}"
TextWrapping="Wrap"/>
```

When we have to create many bindings, it's often easier to do so through these dialog boxes than typing them manually in Visual Studio.

Using Expression Blend 4 for sample data generation

Expression Blend 4 contains a feature that is capable of generating the sample data while developing an application. It visualizes the data on which we are working and provides us with an easier way to create an interface for a data-driven application. This feature was added to Blend in version 3.

How to do it...

In this recipe, we'll build a small management screen for the usage of the bank employees. It will show an overview of the bank account owners. We wouldn't want to waste time with the creation of (sample) data, so we'll hand over this task to Blend. The following are the steps we need to follow for the creation of this data:

1. Open Blend 4 and go to **File | New Project...**. In the dialog box that appears, select **Silverlight 4 Application + Website**. Name the project as **SilverlightBankingManagement** and click on the **OK** button. Blend will now create a Silverlight application and a hosting website.

2. With `MainPage.xaml` open in either the **Design View** or the **Split View**, go to the **Data** window. In this window, click on the **Add sample data source** icon and select **Define New Sample Data...** as shown in the following screenshot:

3. In the **Define New Sample Data** dialog box that appears, specify the **Data source name** as **OwnerDataSource**. We have the option to either embed this data source in the usercontrol (**This document**) or make it available for the entire project (**Project**). Select the latter option by selecting the **Project** radio button and clicking on the **OK** button.

The last option in this window—**Enable sample data when application is running**—allows us to switch off the sample data while running the compiled application. If we leave the checkbox checked, then the sample data will be used for the design time as well as the runtime. We'll keep this option enabled.

Blend will now generate the data source for us. The result is shown in the following screenshot:

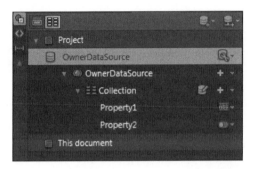

4. By default, a **Collection** is created and it contains items with two properties. Each property has a type. Start by adding two more properties by clicking on the **+** sign next to the **Collection and select the Add simple property option**.

    Rename **Property1** to **Name**. Now, change the type options by clicking on the **Change property type** icon and selecting **Name** as the format. The other properties are similar and are shown in the following screenshot:

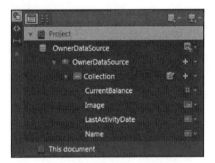

5. For the **Image** type, we can select a folder that contains images. Blend will then copy these images to the `SampleData` subfolder inside the project.

6. We're now ready to use the sample data—for example—in a master-detail scenario. A `ListBox` will contain all the `Owner` data from which we can select an instance. The details are shown in a `Grid` using some `TextBlock` controls. Make sure that the **Data** window is set to **List Mode** and drag the collection on to the design surface. This will trigger the creation of a listbox in which the items are formatted, so we can see the details.

7. Now, to view the details, we have to set the **Data** window to the **Details Mode**. Then, instead of dragging the collection, we select the properties that we want to see in the detail view and drag those onto the design surface. The result should be similar to the following screenshot:

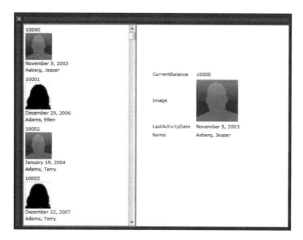

Thus, Blend created all the data binding code in XAML as well as the sample data. For each different type, it generated different values.

3
Advanced Data Binding

In this chapter, we will cover:

- ▶ Hooking into the data binding process
- ▶ Replacing converters with Silverlight 4 BindingBase properties
- ▶ Validating data bound input
- ▶ Validating data input using attributes
- ▶ Validating using IDataErrorInfo and INotifyDataErrorInfo
- ▶ Using templates to customize the way data is shown by controls
- ▶ Building a change-aware collection type
- ▶ Combining converters, data binding, and DataContext into a custom DataTemplate

Introduction

In the previous chapter, we explained in detail the concepts behind data binding and their implementation in Silverlight 4. Reflecting on what we learned in the previous chapter, we may start to think that data binding works as some kind of black box into which we insert the data and it just displays it. However, this is not the case. The data binding engine gives us many points where we can extend or change this process.

The most obvious hooks we have in data binding are **converters**. Converters allow us to grab a value when it's coming in from a source object, perform some action on it, and then pass it to the target control. The most obvious action that we can take is formatting, though many more are possible. We'll look at converters and their possibilities in this chapter.

Data binding also allows us to perform **validations**. When entering data in data-bound controls such as a TextBox, it's important that we validate the data before it's sent back to the source. Silverlight 4 has quite a few options to perform this validation. We'll look at these in this chapter as well.

We can also change the way our data is being displayed using **data templates**. Data templates allow us to override the default behavior of controls such as a ListBox. We will build some templates in this chapter to complete the look of the Silverlight Banking application.

This chapter continues to use the same sample application, Silverlight Banking, which we have already used in the previous chapter. If you want to run the completed application, take a look at the code within the Chapter02/SilverlightBanking folder in the code bundle that is available on the Packt website.

Hooking into the data binding process

We may want to perform some additional formatting for some types of data that we want to display using data binding. Think of a date. Normally, a date is stored in the database as a combination of a date and time. However, we may only want to display the date part—perhaps formatted according to a particular culture. Another example is a currency; the value is normally stored in the database as a double. In an application, we may want to format it by putting a dollar or a euro sign in front of it.

Silverlight's data binding engine offers us a hook in the data binding process, thereby allowing us to format, change, or do whatever we want to do with the data in both directions. This is achieved through the use of a converter.

Getting ready

This recipe builds on the code that was created in the recipes of the previous chapter. If you want to follow along, you can keep using your own code or use the provided starter solution that is located in the Chapter03/SilverlightBanking_Converters_Starter folder. The Chapter03/SilverlightBanking_Converters_Completed folder contains the completed solution for this recipe.

How to do it...

In this recipe, we'll build two converters. We'll start with a currency converter. This is quite basic. It will take a value and format it as a currency using the currency symbol based on the current culture. The second converter will be more advanced; it will convert from a numeric value to a color.

In the sample code of the book, some more converters have been added.

Carry out the following steps in order to get converters to work in a Silverlight application:

1. We'll start by creating the currency converter. A converter is nothing more than a class, in this sample called CurrencyConverter, which implements the IValueConverter interface. This interface defines two methods, that is, `Convert` and `ConvertBack`. Place the `CurrencyConverter` class in a folder called `Converters` within the Silverlight project. The following is the code for this class:

```
public class CurrencyConverter : IValueConverter
{
    public object Convert(object value, Type targetType, object
      parameter, System.Globalization.CultureInfo culture)
    {
      throw new NotImplementedException();
    }
    public object ConvertBack(object value, Type targetType, object
      parameter, System.Globalization.CultureInfo culture)
    {
      throw new NotImplementedException();
    }
}
```

2. The code in the `Convert` method will be applied to the data when it flows from the source to the target. Similarly, the `ConvertBack` method is called when the data flows from the target to the source, so when a `TwoWay` binding is active. The original value is passed in the `value` parameter. We have access to the current culture via the `culture` parameter. Also, we add a "minus" sign to the string value that is returned if the value is less than zero. This is shown in the following code:

```
public object Convert(object value, Type targetType, object
  parameter, System.Globalization.CultureInfo culture)
{
    double amount = double.Parse(value.ToString());
    if (amount < 0)
      return "- " + amount.ToString("c", culture);
    else
      return amount.ToString("c", culture);
}
```

3. Simply creating the converter doesn't do anything. An instance of the converter has to be created and passed along with the binding using the `Converter` property. This is to be done in the resources collection of the XAML file in which we will be using the converter or in `App.xaml`. The following code shows this instantiation in `App.xaml`. Note that we also need to add the namespace mapping.

```xml
<Application
  xmlns="http://schemas.microsoft.com/winfx/2006/xaml/
    presentation"
  xmlns:x="http://schemas.microsoft.com/winfx/2006/xaml"
  x:Class="SilverlightBanking.App"
  xmlns:converters="clr-namespace:SilverlightBanking.Converters">

  <Application.Resources>

    <converters:CurrencyConverter x:Key="localCurrencyConverter">

    </converters:CurrencyConverter>

  </Application.Resources>

</Application>
```

4. After that, we specify this converter as the value for the `Converter` property in the `Binding` declaration. This is shown in the following code:

```xml
<TextBlock Text="{Binding Amount,
              Converter={StaticResource localCurrencyConverter}}"
           FontSize="12"
           FontWeight="Bold">

</TextBlock>
```

5. While this simple converter converts a double into a string, more advanced conversions can be performed. What if, for example, we want to color negative amounts red and positive amounts green? The `Convert` method looks quite similar, except that it now returns a `SolidColorBrush`. This is shown in the following code:

```csharp
public object Convert(object value, Type targetType, object
    parameter, System.Globalization.CultureInfo culture)
{
  double amount = (double)value;
  if (amount >= 0)
    return new SolidColorBrush(Colors.Green);
  else
    return new SolidColorBrush(Colors.Red);
}
```

6. This type of converter can be applied in a `Binding` expression on a property that expects a `SolidColorBrush`, for example, the `Foreground`. This is shown in the following code:

```
<TextBlock Text="{Binding Amount,
         Converter={StaticResource localCurrencyConverter}}"
         Foreground="{Binding Amount,
         Converter={StaticResource
             localAmountToColorConverter}}">
</TextBlock>
```

The result of the the conversion can be seen in the following screenshot. The balance is positive, so the value is colored green.

Current balance:	$1,234.56
Last activity on:	04-11-2010
Amount:	$100.00

How it works...

A **converter** is a handy way of allowing us to get a hook in the data binding process. It allows us to change a value to another format or even another type (for example, a double value into a `SolidColorBrush`).

A converter is nothing more than a class that implements an interface called `IValueConverter`. This interface defines two methods: `Convert` and `ConvertBack`. When a binding specifies a converter, the `Convert` method is called automatically when the data flows from the source to the target. The same holds true for the `ConvertBack` method: this method is applied when the binding is happening, with data flowing from the target to the source. Thus the latter happens when the `Mode` of the binding is set to `TwoWay` and can be used to convert a value back into a format that is understood by the data store.

The ConvertParameter

The `Convert` as well as the `ConvertBack` methods of the `IValueConverter` interface also define an extra parameter that can be used to pass extra information into the converter to influence the conversion process. Take for example a `DateConverter`, which would require an extra parameter that defines the formatting of the date to be passed in. The following code shows the `Convert` method of such a converter:

```
public object Convert(object value, Type targetType, object
  parameter, System.Globalization.CultureInfo culture)
{
  DateTime dt = (DateTime)value;
  return dt.ToString(parameter.ToString(), culture);
}
```

The `ConvertParameter` is used in the `Binding` expression to pass the value to the parameter. This is shown in the following code:

```
<TextBlock x:Name="CustomerSinceValueTextBlock"
           Text="{Binding CustomerSince,
              Converter={StaticResource localDateConverter},
              ConverterParameter='dd-MMM-yyyy'}" >
</TextBlock>
```

Here, we are specifying to the converter that a date should be formatted as dd-MMM-yyyy.

Displaying images based on a URL with converters

Another nice way of using a converter is shown in the following code. Let's assume that in the database, we store the name of an image of the user. Of course, we want to display the image, and not the name of the image. The `Source` property of an `Image` control is of type `ImageSource`. The class best suited for this is the `BitmapImage`. The converter that we need for this type of conversion is shown in the following code:

```
public class ImageConverter:IValueConverter
{
  private string baseUri = "http://localhost:1234/CustomerImages/";
  public object Convert(object value, Type targetType, object
    parameter, System.Globalization.CultureInfo culture)
  {
    if (value != null)
    {
      Uri imageUri = new Uri(baseUri + value);
      return new BitmapImage(imageUri);
    }
    else
      return "";
  }
  . . .
}
```

Using the converter in the XAML binding code is similar.

Replacing converters with Silverlight 4 BindingBase properties

In the previous recipe, we saw that using converters in data binding expressions can help us with a variety of things we want to do with the value that's being bound. It helps us in formatting the value as well as switching between colors. However, creating the converter can be a bit cumbersome for some tasks. To use it, we have to create the class that implements the IValueConverter interface, instantiate it, and change the binding expression. Silverlight 4 has added some properties on the `BindingBase` class that can relieve us from writing a converter in some occasions.

In this recipe, we'll look at how these three new properties, namely `TargetNullValue`, `StringFormat`, and `FallbackValue`, can be used instead of writing a converter.

Getting ready

This recipe builds on the code that was created in the previous recipe. If you want to follow along with this recipe, you can continue using your own code. Alternatively, you can use the start solution that can be found in the `Chapter03/SilverlightBanking_BindingBase_Properties_Starter` folder. The completed solution for this recipe can be found in the `Chapter03/SilverlightBanking_BindingBase_Properties_Completed` folder.

How to do it...

The newly added options that are at our disposal in Silverlight 4 allow us to skip writing a converter during specific scenarios. We wrote quite a few in the previous example, some of which can be replaced by applying one or more of the new properties on the data binding expression. Let's take a look at how we can use these properties.

1. Let's first take a look at the `TargetNullValue` property. The value that we specify for `TargetNullValue` will be applied in the data binding expression if the value of the property is null. For the purpose of this example, let's say that a customer can also leave the bank. This `DateTime` value can be stored in the `NoMoreCustomerSince` property, which is a part of the `Owner` class. Add the following field and accompanying property to the `Owner` class:

```
private DateTime? noMoreCustomerSince;
public DateTime? NoMoreCustomerSince
{
  get
  {
    return noMoreCustomerSince;
  }
  set
  {
    if (noMoreCustomerSince != value)
    {
      noMoreCustomerSince = value;
      OnPropertyChanged("NoMoreCustomerSince");
    }
  }
}
```

3. For active customers, this value will be null. If we do not change anything in the initialization of the `Owner` instance in the `MainPage.xaml.cs`, then the value will be equal to null—that is, its default value. To display a value in the UI in any manner, we can use `TargetNullValue` and set it to "NA" (Not Available) using the following data binding expression:

```
<TextBlock x:Name="NoMoreCustomerSinceValueTextBlock"
           Text="{Binding NoMoreCustomerSince,
             TargetNullValue='NA'}" >
</TextBlock>
```

4. Very often, converters need to be written to format a value (as we did in the previous recipe). Formatting a currency or formatting a date is a task that we often encounter in business applications. Some of these can be replaced with another property of the `BindingBase`, that is, the `StringFormat` property. Instead of writing a converter to format all the dates, we use this property as shown in the following code. (We're showing `CustomerSince` here, but all others are similar.)

```
<TextBlock x:Name="CustomerSinceValueTextBlock"
        Text="{Binding CustomerSince, StringFormat='MM-dd-yyyy'}" >
</TextBlock>
```

5. `StringFormat` can also be used for currency formatting. The `LastActivityAmount` is formatted using this property as shown in the following code:

```
<TextBlock x:Name="LastActivityAmountValueTextBlock"
           Text="{Binding LastActivityAmount, StringFormat=C}" >
</TextBlock>
```

6. If we're binding to a property that does not exist, then the data binding engine will swallow the error and not display anything. This can be annoying in some situations. In such situations, the `FallbackValue` property can help. For example, assume that we have a class called `PreferredOwner` that inherits from `Owner` as shown in the following code:

```
public class PreferredOwner: Owner
{
  private DateTime preferredSince { get; set; }
  public DateTime PreferredSince
  {
    get
    {
      return preferredSince;
    }
    set
    {
      if (preferredSince != value)
      {
```

```
            preferredSince = value;
            OnPropertyChanged("PreferredSince");
        }
    }
  }
}
```

7. A situation may arise when an interface would bind to either an instance of
   Owner or PreferredOwner. The PreferredSince property is available only
   on PreferredOwner. If we are binding an Owner instance, no value would be
   displayed for this property. The FallbackValue can be used in this case to
   indicate that if the property is not found, a fallback value should be used. This
   can be seen in the following code:

```
<TextBlock x:Name="PreferredSinceValueTextBlock"
           Text="{Binding PreferredSince,
             StringFormat='MM-dd-yyyy', FallbackValue='NA'}" >
</TextBlock>
```

With these three new properties in action, the UI looks like the following screenshot when an
Owner instance is bound.

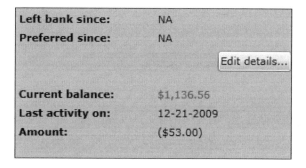

How it works...

Converters are a way of hooking into the data binding process. They allow operations to
be executed on the data before it is displayed. While converters can be used for all kinds
of operations, they require quite some code to be written.

In Silverlight 4, the BindingBase class—the abstract base class for the Binding class—has
been extended with some properties that can do some particular tasks for which we would
have needed to write a converter.

The TargetNullValue property allows us to react to the value of the source property being
null. If the value for the property is null, then the value specified for the TargetNullValue
will be displayed.

`StringFormat` makes it possible to perform the formatting of the value of the source property. Formatting parameters such as percentage, currency and dates can be formatted without the need of writing a converter.

Finally, the `FallbackValue` allows us to display a value when the data binding fails. Assume that we are binding to a property that is not defined on the type. Data binding will fail, but it will not cause an exception. No value will be displayed, but the application will keep running. If we specify the `FallbackValue`, this value will be displayed.

See also

In the previous recipe, we looked at writing converters.

Validating databound input

Validation of your data is a requirement for almost every application. By using validation, you make sure that no invalid data is (eventually) persisted in your datastore. When you don't implement validation, there is a risk that a user will input wrongly formatted or plain incorrect data on the screen and even persist this data in your datastore. This is something you should definitely avoid.

In this recipe, we'll learn about implementing client-side validation on the bound fields in the UI.

Getting ready

To get ready for this recipe, you can either use the code from one of the previous recipes or use the provided starter solution in the `Chapter03/SilverlightBanking_Validation_Starter` folder in the code bundle available on the Packt website. The completed solution for this recipe can be found in the `Chapter03/SilverlightBanking_Validation_Completed` folder.

How to do it...

We're going to add validation logic to the **OwnerDetailsEdit** screen you created by following all the steps of the *Using the different modes of data binding to allow persisting data* recipe in the previous chapter. (Alternatively, you can use the starter solution.) To achieve this, we'll carry out the following steps:

1. Open the solution that you created in the *Using the different modes of data binding to allow persisting data* recipe (or the starter solution) and locate the `OwnerDetailsEdit.xaml` file. In this XAML file, locate and change the `LastNameValueTextBlock` and the `BirthDateValueTextBlock` by adding `NotifyOnValidationError=true` and `ValidatesOnExceptions=true` to the `Binding` syntax. This is shown in the following code:

```
<TextBox x:Name="LastNameValueTextBlock"
         Grid.Row="3"
         Grid.Column="1"
         Margin="2"
         Text="{Binding LastName, Mode=TwoWay,
           NotifyOnValidationError=true,
           ValidatesOnExceptions=true}" >
</TextBox>
<TextBox x:Name="BirthDateValueTextBlock"
         Grid.Row="9"
         Grid.Column="1"
         Margin="2"
         Text="{Binding BirthDate, Mode=TwoWay,
           NotifyOnValidationError=true,
           ValidatesOnExceptions=true}" >
</TextBox>
```

2. Add a handler to the surrounding `Grid`, that is, `OwnerDetailsGrid`. This is shown in the following code:

```
<Grid x:Name="OwnerDetailsGrid"
      BindingValidationError="OwnerDetailsGrid_
        BindingValidationError">
```

3. Add the following C# code to `OwnerDetailsEdit.xaml.cs`. This implements the handler we defined in the previous step.

```
private void OwnerDetailsGrid_BindingValidationError(object
  sender, ValidationErrorEventArgs e)
{
  if (e.Action == ValidationErrorEventAction.Added)
    OwnerDetailsGrid.Background = new
      SolidColorBrush(Color.FromArgb(25, 255, 0, 0));
    if (e.Action == ValidationErrorEventAction.Removed)
      OwnerDetailsGrid.Background = new
        SolidColorBrush(Color.FromArgb(0, 0, 0, 0));
}
```

4. Locate the `Owner.cs` file, which represents the type of `DataContext` of the **OwnerDetailsEdit** control. Add the following code to the `set` accessor of `LastName` to make sure that a validation error is thrown when needed.

```
set
{
  if (lastName != value)
  {
    if (value.Length > 20)
    {
      throw new Exception("Length must be <= 20");

    else
    {
      lastName = value;
      OnPropertyChanged("LastName");
    }
  }
}
```

5. We can now build and run the solution. When invalid data is inputted (a string that's too long for the **Last name** field or a value that isn't in a correct format for the **Birthdate** field), a validation error will occur.

   The result can be observed in the following screenshot:

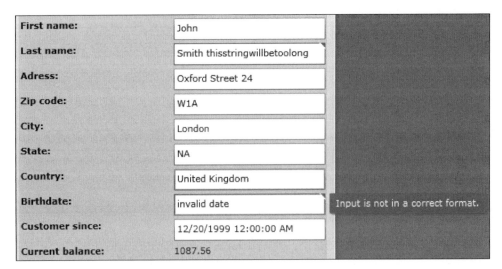

How it works...

Silverlight automatically reports a validation error in a few cases. These include when type conversion fails on binding, when an exception is thrown in a property's `set` accessor, or when a value doesn't correspond to the applied validation attribute (more on this can be found in the next recipe, *Validating data input using attributes*).

In our example, we're throwing an exception in the property's `set` accessor. This means Silverlight will report the error. Next to that, Silverlight will also report an error when you try to input a value that doesn't correspond with the underlying type (you can try to input an invalid date value in the **Birthdate:** field)

If you look at the `Binding` syntax in XAML, you'll see that we've added a few things, that is, `ValidatesOnExceptions` and `NotifyOnValidationError` are set to true.

Setting `ValidatesOnExceptions` to true makes sure that Silverlight will provide visual feedback for the validation errors it reports. Setting `NotifyOnValidationError` to true makes sure that the binding engine raises the `BindingValidationError` event when a validation error occurs.

In the parent grid, this `BindingValidationError` event gets handled. We've written code that will change the background color of the complete box if an error occurs (this is optional).

Client-side validation is easily implemented by bringing these three principles together in the example you've just created.

There's more...

Along with reporting a validation error when type conversion fails on binding or when an exception is thrown in a property's `set` accessor, Silverlight also reports an error when a value doesn't correspond to the applied validation attribute. More on this can be found in the next recipe, *Validating data input using attributes*.

As you've noticed while running the solution we've created, Silverlight has a default style for showing the validation error. This can, of course, be customized by changing the control's default ControlTemplate. More information on customizing templates can be found in the *Using templates to customize the way data is shown by controls* recipe.

And last but not least, we can provide more detailed validation reporting by using the `ValidationSummary` control. This `ValidationSummary` control will automatically receive the `BindingValidationError` events of its parent container. On each `BindingValidationError`, the `ValidationSummary` receives a newly created `ValidationSummaryItem` (added to `ValidationSummary.Errors`) with corresponding `Message`, `MessageHeader`, `ItemType`, and `Context` properties. Next to that, a new `ValidationSummaryItemSource` is created (and added to `ValidationSummaryItem.Sources`) with corresponding `Control` and `PropertyName` properties.

To use a `ValidationSummary` in the example created in this recipe, we have to add a reference to `System.Windows.Controls.Data.Input` in the Silverlight project and add the following code to the `OwnerDetailsEdit` control:

```
xmlns:datainput="clr-namespace:System.Windows.Controls;
assembly=System.Windows.Controls.Data.Input"
```

This will make sure that we can use the `ValidationSummary`. Next, we'll have to locate the **OK** button and add a `ValidationSummary` control. This is shown in the following code:

```
<datainput:ValidationSummary Grid.Row="1"
                                    Margin="2,5,2,5">
</datainput:ValidationSummary>
<Button x:Name="OKButton"
        Content="OK"
        Click="OKButton_Click"
        Width="75"
        Height="23"
        HorizontalAlignment="Right"
        Margin="0,12,0,0"
        Grid.Row="2" />
```

When we run our solution and input invalid data, a validation summary will be shown. This can be seen in the following screenshot:

See also

If you want to learn more about validation, you might want to take a look at the next two recipes, *Validating data input using attributes* and *Validating using IDataErrorInfo and INotifyDataErrorInfo*. To learn more about two-way data binding, have a look at the *Using the different modes of data binding to allow persisting data* recipe in Chapter 2.

Validating data input using attributes

Validation of your data is a requirement for almost every application. By using validation, you make sure that no invalid data is (eventually) persisted in your datastore. When you don't implement validation, there's a risk that a user will input wrongly formatted or plain incorrect data on the screen and even persist this data in your datastore. This is something you should definitely avoid.

In this recipe, we'll learn about implementing client-side validation on the bound fields in the UI using attributes (**Data Annotations**).

Getting ready

To get ready for this recipe, you can either use the code from the previous recipe or use the provided starter solution in the `Chapter03/SilverlightBanking_Validation_Attributes_Starter` folder in the code bundle available on the Packt website. The completed solution for this recipe can be found in the `Chapter03/SilverlightBanking_Validation_Attributes_Completed` folder.

How to do it...

In this recipe, we're going to replace the validation on `LastName` by using attributes or, to be more specific, by using data annotations. To achieve this, we'll carry out the following steps:

1. We have to add a reference to `System.ComponentModel.DataAnnotations` in our Silverlight project.

2. Locate `Owner.cs` and add the following `using` statement:

   ```
   using System.ComponentModel.DataAnnotations;
   ```

3. Next, we should locate the `LastName` property and change it by adding a data annotation attribute to limit the maximum length. Add the following code to actually validate this property:

   ```
   [StringLength(20, ErrorMessage="Length must be <= 20")]
   public string LastName
   {
     get
   ```

```
      {
        return lastName;
      }
      set
      {
        if (lastName != value)
        {
          Validator.ValidateProperty(value,
            new ValidationContext(this, null, null)
            { MemberName ="LastName" });
          lastName = value;
          OnPropertyChanged("LastName");
        }
      }
    }
  }
```

4. We can now build and run the solution. When a string having more than 20 characters in length is inputted in the **Last name** field, the correct error message will be shown. This can be seen in the following screenshot:

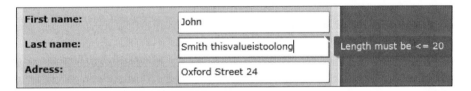

How it works...

Silverlight automatically reports a validation error in a few cases such as when type conversion fails on binding, when an exception is thrown in a property's `set` accessor, or when a value doesn't correspond to the applied validation attribute. To learn about the first two cases, have a look at the previous recipe, *Validating data bound input*.

In our example, we've added a `StringLength` attribute to the `LastName` property, hereby passing in the length and the error message that should be shown. Next to that, we've added a `ValidateProperty` call. This will make sure that the property is validated. When you don't add this, no data validation using attributes occurs.

If you look at the `Binding` syntax in XAML, you'll see that we've added a few things, that is, `ValidatesOnExceptions` and `NotifyOnValidationError` are set to true.

Setting `ValidatesOnExceptions` to true makes sure that Silverlight will provide visual feedback for the validation errors it reports. Setting `NotifyOnValidationError` to true makes sure that the binding engine raises the `BindingValidationError` event when a validation error occurs.

Client-side validation is easily implemented by bringing these principles together in the example we've just created.

There's more...

In this example, we've only used one data annotation attribute for validation—`StringLength`—to explain the principle. However, there are some more attributes you can use such as `CustomValidation`, `DataType`, `EnumDataType`, `Range`, `RegularExpression`, and `Required`.

Next to that, you'll notice we've inputted only one NamedParameter value, that is, `ErrorMessage`. Most validation attributes accept more NamedParameter values that can be used to customize the way validation is handled such as `ErrorMessageResourceName`, `ErrorMessageResourceType`, and so on depending on the validation attribute you're using.

Other uses of data annotations

There are various other data annotations that can be used for validation, such as displaying attributes and modeling attributes. These are used to control how certain information should be displayed or how certain properties should relate to each other. Data annotations are heavily used by RIA Services and the DataForm control. You can learn more about this by looking at the corresponding chapters in this book.

See also

If you want to know more about validation, you might want to take a look at the previous recipe, *Validating data bound input* or the next recipe, *Validating using IDataErrorInfo and INotifyDataErrorInfo*. To learn more about two-way data binding, have a look at the *Using the different modes of data binding to allow persisting data* recipe in Chapter 2.

Validating using IDataErrorInfo and INotifyDataErrorInfo

Validation of your data is a requirement for almost every application. By using validation, you make sure that no invalid data is (eventually) persisted in your datastore. When you don't implement validation, there's a risk that a user will input wrongly formatted or plain incorrect data on the screen and even persist this data in your datastore. This is something you should definitely avoid.

In Silverlight 4, a new way of validating your data is possible by using `IDataErrorInfo` or `INotifyDataErrorInfo`. This allows us to invalidate the properties without throwing exceptions and the validation code doesn't have to reside in the set accessor of the property. It can be called whenever it's needed.

In this recipe, we'll learn about implementing validation on the bound fields in the UI using `IDataErrorInfo` and `INotifyDataErrorInfo`.

Getting ready

To get ready for this recipe, you can either use the code from one of the previous recipes such as the *Using the different modes of data binding to allow persisting data* recipe in Chapter 2 or use the provided starter solution in the `Chapter03/SilverlightBanking_ Validation_DataError_Starter` folder in the code bundle available on the Packt website. The completed solution for this recipe can be found in the `Chapter03/ SilverlightBanking_Validation_DataError_Completed` folder.

How to do it...

We're going to add validation logic to the **OwnerDetailsEdit** screen, just as we did in the previous validation recipes. However, this time we're going to notify the UI through `INotifyDataErrorInfo`, rather than throwing exceptions. To achieve this, carry out the following steps:

1. Open the solution you created in the *Using the different modes of data binding to allow persisting data* recipe in Chapter 2 (or the starter solution) and locate the `OwnerDetailsEdit.xaml` file. In this XAML file, locate and change the `LastNameValueTextBlock` by adding `NotifyOnValidationError=true` to the `Binding` syntax. This can be seen in the following code:

```
<TextBox x:Name="LastNameValueTextBlock"
         Grid.Row="3"
         Grid.Column="1"
         Margin="2"
         Text="{Binding LastName, Mode=TwoWay,
           NotifyOnValidationError=true }" >

</TextBox>
```

2. Add a button named `ValidateButton` next to the `OKButton` as shown in the following code:

```
<StackPanel Orientation="Horizontal"
            Grid.Row="1">
  <Button x:Name="ValidateButton"
          Content="Validate"
          Click="ValidateButton_Click"
          Width="75"
          Height="23"
          HorizontalAlignment="Right"
          Margin="0,12,0,0" />
  <Button x:Name="OKButton"
          Content="OK"
```

```
                    Click="OKButton_Click"
                    Width="75"
                    Height="23"
                    HorizontalAlignment="Right"
                    Margin="0,12,0,0"
                    Grid.Row="1" />
    </StackPanel>
```

3. Add the following C# code to `OwnerDetailsEdit.xaml.cs`. This implements the `ValidateButton` handler we defined in the previous step.

```csharp
private void ValidateButton_Click(object sender,
    RoutedEventArgs e)
{
    owner.FireValidation();
}
```

4. Locate the `Owner.cs` file, which represents the type of `DataContext` of the `OwnerDetailsEdit` control, and let it implement the `INotifyDataErrorInfo` interface as shown in the following code:

```csharp
public class Owner : INotifyPropertyChanged, INotifyDataErrorInfo
{
    private Dictionary<string, string> FailedRules
    { get; set; }
    public event EventHandler<DataErrorsChangedEventArgs>
        ErrorsChanged;
    public IEnumerable GetErrors(string propertyName)
    {
        if (FailedRules.ContainsKey(propertyName))
            return FailedRules[propertyName];
        else
            return FailedRules.Values;
    }
    public bool HasErrors
    {
        get { return FailedRules.Count > 0; }
    }
    private void NotifyErrorsChanged(string propertyName)
    {
        if (ErrorsChanged != null)
            ErrorsChanged(this, new
                DataErrorsChangedEventArgs(propertyName));
    }
}
```

5. Add a constructor to `Owner.cs` to initialize the `FailedRules` dictionary as shown in the following code:

```
public Owner()
{
   FailedRules = new Dictionary<string, string>();
}
```

6. Implement the `FireValidation` method, which is called in `OwnerDetailsEdit.xaml.cs`, as shown in the following code:

```
internal void FireValidation()
{
   if (lastName.Length > 20)
   {
     if (!FailedRules.ContainsKey("LastName"))
       FailedRules.Add("LastName",
         "Last name cannot have more than 20 characters");
   }
   else
   {
     if (FailedRules.ContainsKey("LastName"))
       FailedRules.Remove("LastName");
   }
   NotifyErrorsChanged("LastName");
}
```

7. We can now build and run the solution. When the **Validate** button is clicked and there are more than 20 characters entered in the **Last name** field, a validation error will be shown.

The result can be observed in the following screenshot:

How it works...

The Silverlight controls observe the `INotifyDataErrorInfo` interface automatically. This means the control will display the correct error (invalid state) when a validation rule is violated by an entity.

In this example, we're firing validation on the `LastName` property when the **Validate** button is clicked. If the **Last name** field contains too many characters, then the validation rule will be violated and the UI will show the typical "invalid value" tooltip automatically.

We could have achieved the same result by throwing an exception in the `LastName` property's `set` accessor. However, the main difference is that we can now validate and have the UI react to it without having to write the validation code in the `LastName` property's `set` accessor. We can call it from anywhere and the UI will still react to it. This is how we can use the `INotifyDataErrorInfo` to perform server-side validation and make our UI react to it. You could call a server-side method in your property's `set` accessor and notify the UI through the `INotifyDataErrorInfo` in the callback of that method.

Nevertheless, in this case, the property's set accessor is probably a better place to do the validation (through INotifyDataErrorInfo). But for demonstration purposes, it's done in the click handler of the button.

When we implement the INotifyDataErrorInfo interface, we get an ErrorsChanged event handler, a GetErrors method that must return the correct error message as IEnumerable, and a HasErrors method. We need to implement these methods. To do this, we create a Dictionary called FailedRules, which we initialize in the class constructor and which will contain a list of errors. The GetErrors method, which accepts a propertyName parameter, fetches the correct error (or errors, if you keep a list of errors) from the FailedRules dictionary, while the HasErrors method is implemented by returning whether or not there are errors in the dictionary.

On clicking the button, the FireValidation method is called. This method will check if the LastName has more than 20 characters and will add an error to the FailedRules dictionary if the validation fails (or remove the error if the validation succeeds). After this, the NotifyErrorsChanged method is called, which fires the ErrorsChanged event. This event will make sure that the UI is notified (if the Binding syntax states that NotifyOnValidationError should be true) and will let Silverlight display errors where applicable.

There's more...

In this recipe, we've implemented validation using the INotifyDataErrorInfo interface. However, another interface of the same family exists, that is, the IDataErrorInfo interface. The INotifyDataErrorInfo interface is typically used for more complex scenarios such as the need for async server-side validation to which the UI has to react, or when multiple errors have to be represented with different messages. The IDataErrorInfo interface is used for simpler, client-side validation.

When you implement the IDataErrorInfo interface, you get an Item property (accessible through an indexer in C#) and an Error property. The first one is used to get a specific error message on a certain property of your entity, while the second one is typically used to get an error message related to the complete entity.

See also

If you want to learn more about validation, you might want to take a look at the previous two recipes, *Validating data bound input* and *Validating data input using attributes*. To learn more about two-way data binding, have a look at the *Using the different modes of data binding to allow persisting data* recipe in Chapter 2.

Using templates to customize the way data is shown by controls

Normally when we ask Silverlight to visualize an object, for example a person or a customer, it will simply display the result of the ToString() method—which is, of course, a string. This can be seen when we're binding a collection of items to a ListBox. If we don't specify a value for the DisplayMemberPath property, we simply see the name of the type (unless we overloaded the ToString() method). However, it's possible to specify a **template** called a DataTemplate, which will be used to visualize an object. It's in fact nothing more than a block of XAML code that gets rendered when an item of a particular type is visualized.

In this recipe, we'll build a DataTemplate to render the activities in a ListBox occurring on an account.

Getting ready

To follow along with this recipe, you can either use your own code that has been created from the previous recipes or use the starter solution that is located in the Chapter03/ SilverlightBanking_DataTemplates_Starter folder in the code bundle available on the Packt website. The completed solution for this recipe can be found in the Chapter03/ SilverlightBanking_DataTemplates_Completed folder.

How to do it...

Instead of immediately building the template, we'll go through a few steps. We'll start from the simple text representation and finish with a complete DataTemplate. Let's get started!

1. The collection of AccountActivity items is displayed in a ListBox. The following is the XAML code for this control:

    ```
    <ListBox x:Name="AccountActivityListBox"
             Width="600"
             Grid.Row="1">
    </ListBox>
    ```

2. Getting the items in the ListBox is achieved through setting the ItemsSource property to the ObservableCollection<AccountActivity> called accountActivitiesCollection. This is shown in the following code:

    ```
    AccountActivityListBox.ItemsSource = accountActivitiesCollection;
    ```

3. When populating this `ListBox` with `AccountActivity` objects and omitting any information that tells the `ListBox` what to display (as we did here), it will simply call the `ToString()` implementation of the object. This mostly results in displaying the string representation of the type of the object, as shown in the following screenshot:

4. We can tell the `ListBox` which property it should display through the `DisplayMemberPath`. For example, we can ask it to display the `Amount` property. This is shown in the following code:

```
<ListBox x:Name="AccountActivityListBox"
         DisplayMemberPath="Amount">

</ListBox>
```

The `ListBox` now displays the value of the `Amount` property, as can be seen in the following screenshot:

Activities on the account:

-33
1000
50
-123.56
-12.23
-29.99
-14.55

5. We can all agree that this is not the best way of displaying data! Now, let's start by creating an easy `DataTemplate`. Such a template is in fact nothing more than some XAML that contains some data binding statements. (Although it's not mandatory, it won't make sense to create a template without data binding.) Our first simple template contains a `StackPanel` with three `TextBlock` controls and a `Button`. We specify this template as a value for the `ItemTemplate`. This is shown in the following code:

```
<ListBox x:Name="AccountActivityListBox">
  <ListBox.ItemTemplate>
    <DataTemplate>
      <StackPanel Orientation="Horizontal">
        <TextBlock Text="{Binding Beneficiary}"
                   FontSize="12" >
        </TextBlock>
        <TextBlock Text=" - "
                   FontSize="12">
        </TextBlock>
        <TextBlock Text="{Binding Amount,
                   Converter={StaticResource
                   localCurrencyConverter}}"
                   FontSize="12"
                   FontWeight="Bold">
        </TextBlock>
        <Button x:Name="DetailButton"
                Click="DetailButton_Click"
                Content="More..."
                Margin="3 0 0 0">
        </Button>
      </StackPanel>
    </DataTemplate>
  </ListBox.ItemTemplate>
</ListBox>
```

The following screenshot shows the template in action:

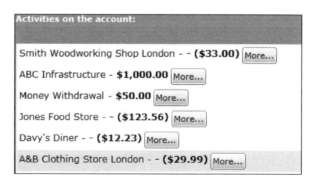

6. If we want to reuse the template several times throughout the application, then it should be moved to the Resources collection of the App.xaml file. If we want to limit the scope, we can also place it in the Resources of a container such as a Grid or the UserControl. However, when placing the template in the Resources, we need to give it a name using the x:Key property. This key is then used for specifying which template is to be used. This can be seen in the following code:

```
<UserControl.Resources>
  <DataTemplate x:Key="SimpleTemplate">
    . . .
  </DataTemplate>
</UserControl.Resources>
```

The following code shows how we should apply the template in a ListBox:

```
<ListBox x:Name="AccountActivityListBox"
         ItemTemplate="{StaticResource ComplexTemplate}">
</ListBox>
```

7. A template can also contain complex controls along with the simple controls placed in a StackPanel. The following code shows a more complex template. It contains a Border with a LinearGradientBrush. Nested inside this border is a Grid, which contains some TextBlock controls, bound to a specific property. Note that we can also specify events such as the MouseLeftButtonDown inside the template.

```
<DataTemplate x:Key="ComplexTemplate">
  <Border BorderBrush="LightGray"
          BorderThickness="1"
          CornerRadius="2"
          Margin="0 3 0 1"
          Padding="2" >
    <Border.Background>
      <LinearGradientBrush EndPoint="1.207,0.457"
                           StartPoint="-0.017,0.467">
        <GradientStop Color="#FF807777"/>
        <GradientStop Color="White" Offset="0.949"/>
      </LinearGradientBrush>
    </Border.Background>
    <Grid Width="580" >
      <Grid.RowDefinitions>
        <RowDefinition></RowDefinition>
        <RowDefinition></RowDefinition>
      </Grid.RowDefinitions>
      <Grid.ColumnDefinitions>
        <ColumnDefinition Width="40"></ColumnDefinition>
        <ColumnDefinition></ColumnDefinition>
```

```xml
            <ColumnDefinition></ColumnDefinition>
        </Grid.ColumnDefinitions>
        <TextBlock Grid.Row="0"
                Grid.Column="0"
                Grid.RowSpan="2"
                Text="{Binding ActivityDate,
                    Converter={StaticResource
                    localShortDateConverter}}">
        </TextBlock>
        <TextBlock Grid.Row="0"
                Grid.Column="1"
                Text="{Binding Beneficiary}"
                FontWeight="Bold">
        </TextBlock>
        <TextBlock Grid.Row="0"
                Grid.Column="2"
                HorizontalAlignment="Right"
                Text="{Binding Amount,
                    Converter={StaticResource
                    localCurrencyConverter}}"
                Foreground="{Binding Amount,
                    Converter={StaticResource
                    localAmountToColorConverter}}">
        </TextBlock>
        <TextBlock Grid.Row="1"
                Grid.Column="1"
                Text="{Binding ActivityDescription}">
        </TextBlock>
        <TextBlock x:Name="DetailsTextBlock"
                Grid.Row="1"
                Grid.Column="2"
                HorizontalAlignment="Right"
                Text="Details..."
                Tag="{Binding ActivityId}"
                MouseLeftButtonDown=
                    "DetailsTextBlock_MouseLeftButtonDown"
                TextDecorations="Underline"
                Foreground="Blue" >
        </TextBlock>
    </Grid>
  </Border>
</DataTemplate>
```

The result of this template is shown in the following screenshot:

01/09	**Smith Woodworking Shop London**	- ($33.00)
	Paid by credit card	Details...
01/09	**ABC Infrastructure**	$1,000.00
	Paycheck September 2009	Details...
02/09	**Money Withdrawal**	$50.00
	ATM Oxford Street London	Details...
05/09	**Jones Food Store**	- ($123.56)
		Details...

How it works...

A `DataTemplate` allows us to define how a data object should be visualized. They work really well when binding data to an `ItemsControl`, such as a `ListBox`. By default, while binding the items to this control, it will render the items as a string, coming from the `ToString()` method. When specifying a `DataTemplate`, for each item bound to the `ListBox`, Silverlight will render the XAML code specified in the template by taking into account the data binding expressions contained in the template.

A `DataTemplate` can contain all types of controls, varying from grids to buttons. Events such as a click on a `Button` or a `MouseLeftButtonDown` on a `TextBlock` from within a template are supported as well. To find out which item was clicked, we can use the `DataContext`. The `DataContext` for each item in the list is an `AccountActivity`. The following line of code displays a detail window based on the selected item:

```
ActivityDetailView activityDetailView = new
    ActivityDetailView(accountActivitiesCollection.
    Where<AccountActivity>(a => a.ActivityId ==
    ((AccountActivity)((TextBlock)sender).DataContext).
    ActivityId).First<AccountActivity>());
```

A `DataTemplate` can be specified on the control itself. For a `ListBox`, this is done by specifying the template as a value for the `ItemTemplate`. However, it's more often useful to specify the template at a higher level in the XAML hierarchy, such as the `UserControl` or (even better) the `App.xaml` file. While using the latter, the template will be available throughout the entire application. One thing to note here is that the template should then be given a name that is specified through the `x:Key` property. This value is then used for retrieving the correct template in the resources collection.

Building a change-aware collection type

We may not always have the option of binding to a collection that implements the `INotifyCollectionChanged` interface. For example, what if we have a service that returns `IList<T>`? Can't we use the automatic synchronization features that Silverlight's data binding engine offers us?

The good news is that we can. For that, we need to build a wrapper class around the `IList<T>`. This class will implement the necessary interface and will allow data binding to work in the manner we are used to.

Getting ready

The finished solution for this recipe can be found in the `Chapter03/CustomCollections` folder in the code bundle available on the Packt website.

How to do it...

For this recipe, we'll assume that we need to work with an external assembly called `UnchangeableCode` in the sample code, which we simply can't change it. Inside the assembly, a class returns a list of `Owner` instances as `IList<Owner>`. However, in our Silverlight application, we would still like to use the synchronization that data binding offers us. We'll implement this by building a wrapper class. We need to perform the following steps in order to achieve this:

1. The `UnchangeableCode` project contains a class called `OwnerService`. This class contains a `List<Owner>` as shown in the following code:

```
public class OwnerService
{
    private List<Owner> owners;
    public List<Owner> Owners
    {
        get { return owners; }
        set { owners = value; }
    }
    public OwnerService()
    {
        owners = new List<Owner>();
        Owner o1 = new Owner()
            {
                Name = "Gill Cleeren",
                CurrentBalance = 100
            };
```

```
Owner o2 = new Owner()
  {
    Name = "Kevin Dockx",
    CurrentBalance = 200
  };
Owner o3 = new Owner()
  {
    Name = "Marina Smith",
    CurrentBalance = 300
  };
Owner o4 = new Owner()
  {
    Name = "Lindsey Smith",
    CurrentBalance = 400
  };
owners.Add(o1);
owners.Add(o2);
owners.Add(o3);
owners.Add(o4);
    }
}
```

2. In our Silverlight application, we would like to bind to the list of `Owner` instances not only for displaying the data, but also for viewing any changes done to the list immediately. We'll create a class that wraps around the `List<Owner>`. This class will also implement the `INotifyCollectionChanged` interface as shown in the following code:

```
public class CustomOwnerList : IList<Owner>,
  INotifyCollectionChanged
{
  private IList<Owner> owners;
  public CustomOwnerList(IList<Owner> owner)
  {
    this.owners = owner;
  }
}
```

3. We can now start implementing all the methods that are defined by both interfaces. The `INotifyCollectionChanged` interface defines only one event, which is called the `CollectionChanged` event. This is shown in the following line of code:

```
public event NotifyCollectionChangedEventHandler
  CollectionChanged;
```

4. The `IList` interface contains quite a lot of methods that we need to implement. The following is the code for the `Insert` method. Notice that we're manually calling the `CollectionChanged` event when something changes in the list. We wrap the call

of the `CollectionChanged` event in the `OnCollectionChanged` method. This method includes checking that the event isn't null. The other methods are similar and the code for these methods can be found in the code bundle available on the Packt website.

```
public void Insert(int index, Owner item)
{
  owners.Insert(index, item);
  OnCollectionChanged(new NotifyCollectionChangedEventArgs
    (NotifyCollectionChangedAction.Add, item, index));
}
private void OnCollectionChanged(NotifyCollectionChangedEventArgs
  notifyCollectionChangedEventArgs)
{
  if (CollectionChanged != null)
    CollectionChanged(this,notifyCollectionChangedEventArgs);
}
```

5. Now that we have the wrapper, we can work with the list as if it's a regular `ObservableCollection`. Whenever we add, remove, or change items in the list, we'll see those changes directly in the UI. The following code shows the instantiation of the new collection and sets it as the `DataContext` for a `ListBox` control:

```
OwnerService someOldClass = new OwnerService();
CustomOwnerList list = new CustomOwnerList(someOldClass.Owners);
OwnerListBox.ItemsSource = list;
```

How it works...

If we want to make use of the automatic synchronization offered by Silverlight's data binding for a collection, then this collection should implement the `INotifyCollectionChanged` interface. If it doesn't do this, we can still bind and show the items in the collection. However, changes to the collection won't be propagated into the UI. Although using the `ObservableCollection` is advised, sometimes we need to work with a service or an assembly from a third party that returns, for example, a generic list.

If we want the data of the generic list to be bound to the UI and the changes to the list to be visualized, then we need to build a class that wraps around the list. This class needs to implement the `IList<T>` interface. As a result, while implementing the methods, we work with the original list itself. For example, while implementing the `Insert` method, we insert an item in a specific location in the underlying list.

Also, the class needs to implement the `INotifyCollectionChanged` interface. For every change that is done in the list (such as adding an item), our wrapper class will raise the `CollectionChanged` event.

Now, whenever we want to bind, we bind to an instance of our wrapper class. Silverlight notices that this class implements the INotifyCollectionChanged interface, so it will register for the events that are raised by an instance of the wrapper class.

See also

Binding to regular collections is explained in the *Binding collections to UI elements* recipe of the previous chapter.

Combining converters, data binding, and DataContext into a custom DataTemplate

A lot of things we've talked about in this chapter are great features on their own, but they really shine when you combine them and let them work together. This recipe will show you how to bring some of the most powerful, built-in features of the Silverlight SDK together or, to put it differently, how to program "The Silverlight Way". We're going to create an editable ComboBox of people using a custom DataTemplate, the DataContext, an ObservableCollection with two-way data binding, and Converters to make the UI fluid, interactive, and responsive.

Getting ready

We're starting off with a completely new, blank Silverlight solution for this recipe. So, to get started, make sure you have one of those. To create an empty Silverlight solution, start a new Silverlight project in Visual Studio by selecting **File | New | Project...** and let it create an accompanying web application automatically for hosting the Silverlight application.

You can find the completed solution for this recipe in the Chapter03/Combining_ Converters_Databinding_And_DataContext_Completed folder in the code bundle available on the Packt website.

How to do it...

We want to end up with a ComboBox that displays the names of a few people. Each person's name should be editable from inside the list of items in the ComboBox. To achieve this, we'll need to carry out the following steps:

1. We're going to start by adding a new class to our Silverlight project. This class is named Person and it has three properties: an ID, a Name, and a field that represents the current edit state of the person—InEditMode. This class implements the INotifyPropertyChanged interface as shown in the following code:

```csharp
public class Person : INotifyPropertyChanged
{
  public int PersonID { get; set; }
  private bool pInEditMode;
  public bool InEditMode
  {
    get
    {
      return pInEditMode;
    }
    set
    {
      pInEditMode = value;
      NotifyPropertyChanged("InEditMode");
    }
  }
  private string pName;
  public string Name
  {
    get
    {
      return pName;
    }
    set
    {
      pName = value;
      NotifyPropertyChanged("Name");
    }
  }
  #region INotifyPropertyChanged Members
  public event PropertyChangedEventHandler PropertyChanged;
  public void NotifyPropertyChanged(string propertyName)
  {
    if (PropertyChanged != null)
    {
      PropertyChanged(this, new
        PropertyChangedEventArgs(propertyName));
    }
  }
  #endregion
}
```

2. Next, we're going to add another class to our Silverlight project. This class is named `BoolToVisibilityConverter`. It will implement the `IValueConverter` interface and convert a `Boolean` value to a `Visibility` value. This is shown in the following code:

```
public class BoolToVisibilityConverter : IValueConverter
{
  #region IValueConverter Members
  public object Convert(object value, Type targetType,
    object parameter, System.Globalization.CultureInfo culture)
  {
    bool normalDirection = true;
    if (parameter != null)
    {
      if (parameter.ToString().Trim().ToLower() ==
        "trueiscollapsed")
        normalDirection = false;
    }
    if (value is bool)
    {
      if ((bool)value)
      {
        return normalDirection ?
          Visibility.Visible : Visibility.Collapsed;
      }
      else
      {
        return normalDirection ?
          Visibility.Collapsed : Visibility.Visible;
      }
    }
    else
    {
      return Visibility.Visible;
    }
  }
  public object ConvertBack(object value, Type targetType,
    object parameter, System.Globalization.CultureInfo culture)
  {
    bool normalDirection = true;
    if (parameter.ToString().Trim().ToLower() ==
      "trueiscollapsed")
      normalDirection = false;
```

```
if (value is Visibility)
{
  if ((Visibility)value == Visibility.Visible)
  {
    return normalDirection ? true : false;
  }
  else
  {
    return normalDirection ? false : true;
  }
}
else
{
  return true;
}
}
#endregion
}
```

3. Open the `MainPage.xaml` file. We'll add the following code to represent our UI. It includes the `Binding` syntax for the person objects visible in our `ComboBox`, the necessary `Converter` syntax, and an event handler for the `Click` events of our **Edit** and **Save** buttons.

```
<UserControl x:Class="Editable_Combobox.MainPage"
  xmlns="http://schemas.microsoft.com/winfx/2006/
    xaml/presentation"
  xmlns:x="http://schemas.microsoft.com/winfx/2006/xaml"
  xmlns:d="http://schemas.microsoft.com/expression/blend/2008"
  xmlns:mc="http://schemas.openxmlformats.org/markup-
    compatibility/2006"
  mc:Ignorable="d" d:DesignWidth="640" d:DesignHeight="480"
  xmlns:local="clr-namespace:Editable_Combobox">
  <UserControl.Resources>
    <local:BoolToVisibilityConverter
      x:Name="BoolToVisibilityConverter" />
  </UserControl.Resources>
  <Grid x:Name="LayoutRoot" Margin="10" >
    <Grid.RowDefinitions>
      <RowDefinition Height="30"></RowDefinition>
      <RowDefinition></RowDefinition>
    </Grid.RowDefinitions>
    <TextBlock Text="An editable ComboBox"
```

```xml
                    HorizontalAlignment="Left"
                    VerticalAlignment="Top" >

</TextBlock>
<ComboBox x:Name="cmbPersons" Grid.Row="1"
            Width="220" Height="30"
            HorizontalAlignment="Left"
            VerticalAlignment="Top">
  <ComboBox.ItemTemplate>
    <DataTemplate>
      <Grid Width="280" Height="30">
        <Grid.ColumnDefinitions>
          <ColumnDefinition Width="200"></ColumnDefinition>
          <ColumnDefinition></ColumnDefinition>
        </Grid.ColumnDefinitions>
        <TextBlock Text="{Binding Name, Mode=TwoWay}"
                   HorizontalAlignment="Left"
                   VerticalAlignment="Center"
                   IsHitTestVisible="False"
                   Width="180"
                   Visibility="{Binding InEditMode,
                     Converter={StaticResource
                     BoolToVisibilityConverter},
                     ConverterParameter=trueiscollapsed}"/>
        <TextBox Text="{Binding Name, Mode=TwoWay}"
                   Width="180" HorizontalAlignment="Left"
                   VerticalAlignment="Center"
                   Visibility="{Binding InEditMode,
                     Converter={StaticResource
                     BoolToVisibilityConverter},
                     ConverterParameter=trueisvisible}"/>
        <Button x:Name="btnEdit" Width="70" Height="20"
                   Click="btnEditSave_Click"
                   Content="Edit" Grid.Column="1"
                   Visibility="{Binding InEditMode,
                     Converter={StaticResource
                     BoolToVisibilityConverter},
                     ConverterParameter=trueiscollapsed}" />
        <Button x:Name="btnSave" Width="70" Height="20"
                   Click="btnEditSave_Click"
                   Content="Save" Grid.Column="1"
                   Visibility="{Binding InEditMode,
                     Converter={StaticResource
                     BoolToVisibilityConverter}}"/>
      </Grid>
    </DataTemplate>
  </ComboBox.ItemTemplate>
```

```
    </ComboBox>
  </Grid>
</UserControl>
```

4. Open the `MainPage.xaml.cs` file. This is our code-behind file in which we'll write the following code to handle the `Click` events of our buttons as well as to initialize an `ObservableCollection` of the `Person` type:

```
public partial class MainPage : UserControl
{
  public ObservableCollection<Person> Persons
  { get; set; }
  public MainPage()
  {
    InitializeComponent();
    InitializeCollection();
  }
  private void InitializeCollection()
  {
    Persons = new ObservableCollection<Person>()
    {
      new Person()
      {
        PersonID=1, Name="Gill Cleeren", InEditMode = false
      },
      new Person()
      {
        PersonID=2, Name="Kevin Dockx", InEditMode = false
      }
    };
    cmbPersons.ItemsSource = Persons;
  }
private void btnEditSave_Click(object sender, RoutedEventArgs e)
{
  Person p = (Person)(((Button)sender).DataContext);
  p.InEditMode = !p.InEditMode;
}
```

5. We can now build and run this project. The result can be observed in the following screenshot:

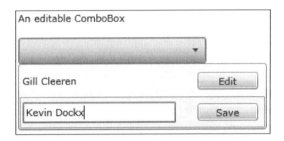

How it works...

This recipe brings together quite a few Silverlight principles into one project. Let's start off with the `Person` class. This class represents the people shown in our editable `ComboBox`. It implements the `INotifyPropertyChanged` interface, which makes sure that the UI is notified when one of the properties changes.

Our converter converts a `Boolean` value to a `Visibility` value. We bind the visibility property of our `TextBlock`, `TextBox`, and `Buttons` to the `InEditMode` property of the `Person` class. This is done by using the converter to convert the `Boolean` value to a `Visibility` value and by using the `ConverterParameter` to decide how the value should be converted. As a result of this, the `TextBlock` and the **Edit** button will be `Visible` when the `InEditMode` property is false, and `Collapsed` when it's true. On the other hand, the `TextBox` and the **Save** button will be `Collapsed` when the `InEditMode` property is false and `Visible` when it's true.

Next, we've got the `Click` event handler on our buttons. In this handler, we can get the `DataContext` of the sender. Due to the fact that the `ItemsSource` in a `ComboBox` is a collection of persons, the `DataContext` of this `Button` is always exactly one person. We can then cast this `DataContext` in the `Person` and change its `InEditMode` property.

Bringing it all together, the `ObservableCollection` of the `Person` represents the data shown in the `ComboBox`. The `Converter` makes sure that the correct pieces of the UI are shown. Due to the `DataContext`, we can easily access our `Person` object on the click of a button. Also, as the `INotifyPropertyChanged` interface is implemented on the `InEditMode` property, the UI is updated when we change this property. Finally, the two-way data binding makes sure that the changes we make to a person's name are automatically persisted in the underlying object.

See also

This recipe brought together most of the principles that are covered in this book. To learn more about **data binding**, have a look at the following recipes in Chapter 2:

- ▶ *Displaying data in Silverlight applications*
- ▶ *Creating dynamic bindings*
- ▶ *Binding data to another UI element*
- ▶ *Binding collections to UI elements*
- ▶ *Enabling a Silverlight application to automatically update its UI*

To learn more about the `DataContext`, you can refer to the *Obtaining data from any UI element it is bound to* recipe in Chapter 2. Additionally, **Converters** are covered in the *Hooking into the data binding process* recipe in this chapter, and for more information on the `ObservableCollection`, have a look at the *Binding collections to UI elements* recipe in Chapter 2.

4
The Data Grid

This chapter takes an in-depth look at working with the `DataGrid` using the following recipes:

- ▶ Displaying data in a customized DataGrid
- ▶ Inserting, updating, and deleting data in a DataGrid
- ▶ Sorting and grouping data in a DataGrid
- ▶ Filtering and paging data in a DataGrid
- ▶ Using custom columns in the DataGrid
- ▶ Implementing master-detail in the DataGrid
- ▶ Validating the DataGrid

Introduction

If we want to build applications that deal with large amounts of data, then a control such as a data grid is vital. This control shows the data in a tabular format and allows for adding, editing, and deleting the data inline. It allows the sorting of data into columns by clicking on a column header. Finally, a data grid should support grouping, so that we can create levels in the data.

Silverlight included a data grid from version 2 onwards, even before WPF had one. It's very powerful, supports all the features outlined previously, and is thus a good solution to work with large amounts of data in the browser. It lives in the `System.Windows.Controls` namespace. However, it's not included in the default assemblies that are installed with the Silverlight core. When using it in our application, Visual Studio will embed several assemblies into the XAP file.

In order to maintain its performance, Silverlight's DataGrid control features UI virtualization. This feature means that Silverlight will only create the items that are currently visible. As a result of this, even if we are displaying thousands, or even millions of rows, the DataGrid will still keep running fluently.

In the recipes of this chapter, we'll look at how to work with the DataGrid. This is an essential control for applications that rely on (collections of) data.

Displaying data in a customized DataGrid

Displaying data is probably the most straightforward task we can ask the DataGrid to do for us. In this recipe, we'll create a collection of data and hand it over to the DataGrid for display. While the DataGrid may seem to have a rather fixed layout, there are many options available on this control that we can use to customize it.

In this recipe, we'll focus on getting the data to show up in the DataGrid and customize it to our likings.

Getting ready

In this recipe, we'll start from an empty Silverlight application. The finished solution for this recipe can be found in the Chapter04/Datagrid_Displaying_Data_Completed folder in the code bundle that is available on the Packt website.

How to do it...

We'll create a collection of Book objects and display this collection in a DataGrid. However, we want to customize the DataGrid. More specifically, we want to make the DataGrid fixed. In other words, we don't want the user to make any changes to the bound data or move the columns around. Also, we want to change the visual representation of the DataGrid by changing the background color of the rows. We also want the vertical column separators to be hidden and the horizontal ones to get a different color. Finally, we'll hook into the LoadingRow event, which will give us access to the values that are bound to a row and based on that value, the LoadingRow event will allow us to make changes to the visual appearance of the row.

To create this DataGrid, you'll need to carry out the following steps:

1. Start a new Silverlight solution called **DatagridDisplayingData** in Visual Studio.

    We'll start by creating the Book class. Add a new class to the Silverlight project in the solution and name this class as Book. Note that this class uses two enumerations—one for the Category and the other for the Language. These can be found in the sample code. The following is the code for the Book class:

```
public class Book
{
    public string Title { get; set; }
    public string Author { get; set; }
    public int PageCount { get; set; }
    public DateTime PurchaseDate { get; set; }
    public Category Category { get; set; }
    public string Publisher { get; set; }
    public Languages Language { get; set; }
    public string ImageName { get; set; }
    public bool AlreadyRead { get; set; }
}
```

2. In the code-behind of the generated `MainPage.xaml` file, we need to create a generic list of `Book` instances (`List<Book>`) and load data into this collection. This is shown in the following code:

```
private List<Book> bookCollection;
public MainPage()
{
    InitializeComponent();
    LoadBooks();
}
private void LoadBooks()
{
    bookCollection = new List<Book>();
    Book b1 = new Book();
    b1.Title = "Book AAA";
    b1.Author = "Author AAA";
    b1.Language = Languages.English;
    b1.PageCount = 350;
    b1.Publisher = "Publisher BBB";
    b1.PurchaseDate = new DateTime(2009, 3, 10);
    b1.ImageName = "AAA.png";
    b1.AlreadyRead = true;
    b1.Category = Category.Computing;
    bookCollection.Add(b1);
    ...
}
```

3. Next, we'll add a `DataGrid` to the `MainPage.xaml` file. For now, we won't add any extra properties on the `DataGrid`. It's advisable to add it to the page by dragging it from the toolbox, so that Visual Studio adds the correct references to the required assemblies in the project, as well as adds the namespace mapping in the XAML code. Remove the `AutoGenerateColumns="False"` for now so that we'll see all the properties of the Book class appear in the `DataGrid`. The following line of code shows a default `DataGrid` with its name set to `BookDataGrid`:

```
<sdk:DataGrid x:Name="BookDataGrid"></sdk:DataGrid>
```

4. Currently, no data is bound to the `DataGrid`. To make the `DataGrid` show the book collection, we set the `ItemsSource` property from the code-behind in the constructor. This is shown in the following code:

```
public MainPage()
{
   InitializeComponent();
   LoadBooks();
   BookDataGrid.ItemsSource = bookCollection;
}
```

5. Running the code now shows a default `DataGrid` that generates a column for each public property of the `Book` type. This happens because the `AutoGenerateColumns` property is `True` by default.

6. Let's continue by making the `DataGrid` look the way we want it to look. By default, the `DataGrid` is user-editable, so we may want to change this feature. Setting the `IsReadOnly` property to `True` will make it impossible for a user to edit the data in the control. We can lock the display even further by setting both the `CanUserResizeColumns` and the `CanUserReorderColumns` properties to `False`. This will prohibit the user from resizing and reordering the columns inside the `DataGrid`, which are enabled by default. This is shown in the following code:

```
<sdk:DataGrid x:Name="BookDataGrid"
              AutoGenerateColumns="True"
              CanUserReorderColumns="False"
              CanUserResizeColumns="False"
              IsReadOnly="True">
</sdk:DataGrid>
```

7. The `DataGrid` also offers quite an impressive list of properties that we can use to change its appearance. By adding the following code, we specify alternating the background colors (the `RowBackground` and `AlternatingRowBackground` properties), column widths (the `ColumnWidth` property), and row heights (the `RowHeight` property). We also specify how the gridlines should be displayed (the `GridLinesVisibility` and `HorizontalGridLinesBrush` properties). Finally, we specify that we also want a row header to be added (the `HeadersVisibility` property).

```
<sdk:DataGrid x:Name="BookDataGrid"
               AutoGenerateColumns="True"
               CanUserReorderColumns="False"
               CanUserResizeColumns="False"
               RowBackground="#999999"
               AlternatingRowBackground="#CCCCCC"
               ColumnWidth="90"
               RowHeight="30"
               GridLinesVisibility="Horizontal"
               HeadersVisibility="All"
               HorizontalGridLinesBrush="Blue">
</sdk:DataGrid>
```

8. We can also get a hook into the loading of the rows. For this, the `LoadingRow` event has to be used. This event is triggered when each row gets loaded. Using this event, we can get access to a row and change its properties based on custom code. In the following code, we are specifying that if the book is a thriller, we want the row to have a red background:

```
private void BookDataGrid_LoadingRow(object sender,
  DataGridRowEventArgs e)
{
  Book loadedBook = e.Row.DataContext as Book;
  if (loadedBook.Category == Category.Thriller)
  {
    e.Row.Background = new SolidColorBrush(Colors.Red);
    //It's a thriller!
    e.Row.Height = 40;
  }
  else
  {
    e.Row.Background = null;
  }
}
```

After completing these steps, we have the `DataGrid` that we wanted. It displays the data (including headers), fixes the columns and makes it impossible for the user to edit the data. Also, the color of the rows and alternating rows is changed, the vertical grid lines are hidden, and a different color is applied to the horizontal grid lines. Using the `LoadingRow` event, we have checked whether the book being added is of the "Thriller" category, and if so, a red color is applied as the background color for the row. The result can be seen in the following screenshot:

How it works...

The `DataGrid` allows us to display the data easily, while still offering us many customization options to format the control as needed.

The `DataGrid` is defined in the `System.Windows.Controls` namespace, which is located in the `System.Windows.Controls.Data` assembly. By default, this assembly is not referenced while creating a new Silverlight application. Therefore, the following extra references are added while dragging the control from the toolbox for the first time:

- System.ComponentModel.DataAnnotations
- System.Windows.Controls.Data
- System.Windows.Controls.Data.Input
- System.Windows.Data

While compiling the application, the corresponding assemblies are added to the XAP file (as can be seen in the following screenshot, which shows the contents of the XAP file). These assemblies need to be added because while installing the Silverlight plugin, they aren't installed as a part of the CLR. This is done in order to keep the plugin size small. However, when we use them in our application, they are embedded as part of the application. This results in an increase of the download size of the XAP file. In most circumstances, this is not a problem. However, if the file size is an important requirement, then it is essential to keep an eye on this.

Also, Visual Studio will include the following namespace mapping into the XAML file:

```
xmlns:sdk="clr-namespace:System.Windows.Controls;
    assembly=System.Windows.Controls.Data"
```

From then on, we can use the control as shown in the following line of code:

```
<sdk:DataGrid x:Name="BookDataGrid"> </sdk:DataGrid>
```

Once the control is added on the page, we can use it in a data binding scenario. To do so, we can point the ItemsSource property to any IEnumerable implementation. Each row in the DataGrid will correspond to an object in the collection.

When AutoGenerateColumns is set to True (the default), the DataGrid uses a reflection on the type of objects bound to it. For each public property it encounters, it generates a corresponding column. Out of the box, the DataGrid includes a text column, a checkbox column, and a template column. For all the types that can't be displayed, it uses the ToString method and a text column.

If we want the DataGrid to feature automatic synchronization, the collection should implement the INotifyCollectionChanged interface. If changes to the objects are to be reflected in the DataGrid, then the objects in the collection should themselves implement the INotifyPropertyChanged interface.

There's more

While loading large amounts of data into the DataGrid, the performance will still be very good. This is the result of the DataGrid implementing UI virtualization, which is enabled by default.

Let's assume that the DataGrid is bound to a collection of 1,000,000 items (whether or not this is useful is another question). Loading all of these items into memory would be a time-consuming task as well as a big performance hit. Due to UI virtualization, the control loads only the rows it's currently displaying. (It will actually load a few more to improve the scrolling experience.) While scrolling, a small lag appears when the control is loading the new items. Since Silverlight 3, the ListBox also features UI virtualization.

See also

In the *Using custom columns in the DataGrid* recipe of this chapter, we'll look at how we can specify which columns should be included in the DataGrid.

Inserting, updating, and deleting data in a DataGrid

The DataGrid is an outstanding control to use while working with large amounts of data at the same time. Through its Excel-like interface, not only can we easily view the data, but also add new records or update and delete existing ones.

In this recipe, we'll take a look at how to build a DataGrid that supports all of the above actions on a collection of items.

Getting ready

This recipe builds on the code that was created in the previous recipe. To follow along with this recipe, you can keep using your code or use the starter solution located in the Chapter04/Datagrid_Editing_Data_Starter folder in the code bundle available on the Packt website. The finished solution for this recipe can be found in the Chapter04/Datagrid_Editing_Data_Completed folder.

How to do it...

In this recipe, we'll work with the same Book class as in the previous recipe. Through the use of a DataGrid, we'll manage an ObservableCollection<Book>. We'll make it possible to add, update, and delete the items in the collection through the DataGrid. An ObservableCollection raises an event when items are added, removed, and so on, and Silverlight will listen for this event. The existing data will be edited by doing inline edits to the rows, which will be pushed back to the underlying collection. We'll allow the user to add or delete an item in the DataGrid by clicking on a button. Behind the scene, an item is added to or removed from the underlying collection. We'll also include a detail panel where the user can view more properties on the selected item in the DataGrid.

The following are the steps we need to perform:

1. In the `MainPage.xaml.cs` file, we bind to a generic list of `Book` instances (`List<Book>`). For the `DataGrid` to react to the changes in the bound collection, the collection itself should implement the `INotifyCollectionChanged` interface. Thus, instead of a `List<Book>`, we'll use an `ObservableCollection<Book>` as shown in the following line of code:

   ```
   ObservableCollection<Book> bookCollection =
       new ObservableCollection<Book>();
   ```

2. Let's first look at deleting the items. We may want to link the hitting of the *Delete* key on the keyboard with the removal of a row in the `DataGrid`. In fact, we're asking to remove the currently selected item from the bound collection. For this, we register for the `KeyDown` event on the `DataGrid` as shown in the following code:

   ```
   <sdk:DataGrid x:Name="BookDataGrid"
                   KeyDown="BookDataGrid_KeyDown" ...>
   ```

3. In the event handler, we'll need to check whether the key was the *Delete* key. Also, the required code for inserting the data—triggered by hitting the *Insert* key—is included. This is shown in the following code:

   ```
   private bool cellEditing = false;
   private void BookDataGrid_KeyDown(object sender, KeyEventArgs e)
   {
       if (e.Key == Key.Delete && !cellEditing)
       {
           RemoveBook();
       }
       else if (e.Key == Key.Insert && !cellEditing)
       {
           AddEmptyBook();
       }
   }
   ```

4. Note the `!cellEditing` in the previous code. It's a Boolean field that we are using to check whether we are currently editing a value that is in a cell or we simply have a row selected. In order to carry out this check, we should add both the `BeginningEdit` and the `CellEditEnded` events in the `DataGrid` as shown in the following code. These will be triggered when the cell enters or leaves the edit mode respectively.

   ```
   <sdk:DataGrid x:Name="BookDataGrid"
                   BeginningEdit="BookDataGrid_BeginningEdit"
                   CellEditEnded="BookDataGrid_CellEditEnded" ...>
   ```

5. In the event handlers, we change the value of the `cellEditing` variable as shown in the following code:

```
private void BookDataGrid_BeginningEdit(object sender,
  DataGridBeginningEditEventArgs e)
{
  cellEditing = true;
}
private void BookDataGrid_CellEditEnded(object sender,
  DataGridCellEditEndedEventArgs e)
{
  cellEditing = false;
}
```

6. Next, we need to write the code either to add an empty `Book` object or to remove an existing one. Here, we're actually working with the `ObservableCollection<Book>`. We're adding items to the collection or removing them from it. The application UI contains two buttons. We can add two `Click` event handlers that will trigger adding or removing an item using the following code. Note that while deleting, we are checking whether an item is selected.

```
private void AddButton_Click(object sender, RoutedEventArgs e)
{
  AddEmptyBook();
}
private void DeleteButton_Click(object sender, RoutedEventArgs e)
{
  RemoveBook();
}
private void AddEmptyBook()
{
  Book b = new Book();
  bookCollection.Add(b);
}
private void RemoveBook()
{
  if (BookDataGrid.SelectedItem != null)
  {
    Book deleteBook = BookDataGrid.SelectedItem as Book;
    bookCollection.Remove(deleteBook);
  }
}
```

7. Finally, let's take a look at updating the items. In fact, simply typing in new values for the existing items in the `DataGrid` will push the updates back to the bound collection. Add a `Grid` containing the `TextBlock` controls in order to see this. The entire `Grid` should be bound to selected row of the `DataGrid`. This is done by means of an element data binding. The following code is a part of this code. The remaining code can be found in the completed solution in the code bundle.

```
<Grid DataContext="{Binding ElementName=BookDataGrid,
        Path=SelectedItem}" >
    <TextBlock Text="Title:"
                FontWeight="Bold"
                Grid.Row="1"
                Grid.Column="0">
    </TextBlock>
    <TextBlock Text="{Binding Title}"
                Grid.Row="1"
                Grid.Column="1">
    </TextBlock>
</Grid>
```

We now have a fully working application to manage the data of the Book collection. We have a data-entry application that allows us to perform **CRUD** (**create**, **read**, **update**, and **delete**) operations on the data using the `DataGrid`. The final application is shown in the following screenshot:

Book Library

Actions | Add book | Delete book

Title	Author	PageCount	PurchaseDate	Category	Publisher	Language	ImageName	AlreadyRead
Book AAA	Author AAA	350	3/10/2009 12:00:00 AM	Computing	Publisher BBB	English	AAA.png	✓
Book BBB	Author AAA	667	4/11/2009 12:00:00 AM	Thriller	Publisher AAA	Dutch	BBB.png	☐
Book CCC	Author AAA	289	12/10/2009 12:00:00 AM	Fiction	Publisher AAA	French	CCC.png	✓
Book DDD	Author BBB	200	1/20/2009 12:00:00 AM	Thriller	Publisher DDD	German	DDD.png	☐
Book EEE	Author BBB	403	3/1/2007 12:00:00 AM	Biography	Publisher DDD	German	EEE.png	✓
Book FFF	Author AAA	296	9/4/2009 12:00:00 AM	Comics	Publisher AAA	English	FFF.png	✓
Book HHH	Author CCC	675	1/31/2007 12:00:00 AM	Fiction	Publisher CCC	Dutch	HHH.png	☐
Book HHH	Author CCC	675	1/31/2007 12:00:00 AM	Fiction	Publisher CCC	Dutch	HHH.png	☐
Book III	Author DDD	1300	7/1/2008 12:00:00 AM	Computing	Publisher DDD	French	III.png	✓

Book details

Title:	Book EEE
Author:	Author BBB
Pagecount:	403
Publisher:	Publisher DDD

How it works...

The `DataGrid` is bound to an `ObservableCollection<Book>`. This way, changes to the collection are reflected in the control immediately because of the automatic synchronization that data binding offers us on collections that implement the `INotifyCollectionChanged` interface. If the class (in our case, the `Book` class) itself implements the `INotifyPropertyChanged` interface, then the changes to the individual items are also reflected. Implicitly, a `DataGrid` implements a `TwoWay` binding. We don't have to specify this anywhere.

To remove an item by hitting the *Delete* key, we first need to check that we're not editing the value of the cell. If we are, then the row shouldn't be deleted. This is done using the `BeginningEdit` and `CellEditEnded` events. The former one is called before the user can edit the value. It can also be used to perform some action on the value in the cell such as formatting. The latter event is called when the focus moves away from the cell.

In the end, managing (inserting, deleting, and so on) the data in the `DataGrid` comes down to managing the items in the collection. We leverage this here. We aren't adding any items to the `DataGrid` itself, but we are either adding items to the bound collection or removing items from the bound collection.

See also

For more information on the data binding features, take a look at Chapter 2 and Chapter 3, where we look carefully at all the features offered by Silverlight.

Sorting and grouping data in a DataGrid

Sorting the values within a column in a control such as a `DataGrid` is something that we take for granted. Silverlight's implementation has some very strong sorting options working out of the box for us. It allows us to sort by clicking on the header of a column, amongst other things.

Along with sorting, the `DataGrid` enables the grouping of values. Items possessing a particular property (that is, in the same column) and having equal values can be visually grouped within the `DataGrid`.

All of this is possible by using a view on top of the bound collection. In this recipe, we'll look at how we can leverage this view to customize the sorting and grouping of data within the `DataGrid`.

Getting ready

This sample continues with the same code that was created in the previous recipes of this chapter. If you want to follow along with this recipe, you can continue using your code or use the provided start solution located in the `Chapter04/Datagrid_Sorting_And_Grouping_Starter` folder in the code bundle that is available on the Packt website. The finished code for this recipe can be found in the `Chapter04/Datagrid_Sorting_And_Grouping_Completed` folder.

How to do it...

We'll be using the familiar list of `Book` items again in this recipe. This list, which is implemented as an `ObservableCollection<Book>`, will not be directly bound to the `DataGrid` in this case. Instead, we'll use a `PagedCollectionView` that acts as a view on top of the collection. We'll change the way the `DataGrid` is sorted by default as well as introduce grouping within the control. The following are the steps to achieve all of this:

1. Instead of using the `AutoGenerateColumns` feature, we'll define the columns that we want to see manually. We'll make use of several `DataGridTextColumns`, a `DataGridCheckBoxColumn` and a `DataGridTemplateColumn`. The following is the code for the `DataGrid`:

```
<sdk:DataGrid x:Name="CopyBookDataGrid"
              AutoGenerateColumns="False" ... >
  <sdk:DataGrid.Columns>
    <sdk:DataGridTextColumn x:Name="CopyTitleColumn"
                            Binding="{Binding Title}"
                            Header="Title">
    </sdk:DataGridTextColumn>
    <sdk:DataGridTextColumn x:Name="CopyAuthorColumn"
                            Binding="{Binding Author}"
                            Header="Author">
    </sdk:DataGridTextColumn>
    <sdk:DataGridTextColumn x:Name="CopyPublisherColumn"
                            Binding="{Binding Publisher}"
                            Header="Publisher">
    </sdk:DataGridTextColumn>
    <sdk:DataGridTextColumn x:Name="CopyLanguageColumn"
                            Binding="{Binding Language}"
                            Header="Language">
    </data:DataGridTextColumn>
    <data:DataGridTextColumn x:Name="CopyCategoryColumn"
                            Binding="{Binding Category}"
                            Header="Category">
    </sdk:DataGridTextColumn>
```

```
<sdk:DataGridCheckBoxColumn x:Name="CopyAlreadyReadColumn"
                            Binding="{Binding AlreadyRead,
                              Mode=TwoWay}"
                            Header="Already read">
</sdk:DataGridCheckBoxColumn>
<sdk:DataGridTemplateColumn Header="Purchase date"
                            x:Name="CopyPurchaseDateColumn">
  <sdk:DataGridTemplateColumn.CellTemplate>
    <DataTemplate>
      <controls:DatePicker SelectedDate="{Binding
                            PurchaseDate}">
      </controls:DatePicker>
    </DataTemplate>
  </sdk:DataGridTemplateColumn.CellTemplate>
</sdk:DataGridTemplateColumn>
</sdk:DataGrid.Columns>
</sdk:DataGrid>
```

2. In order to implement both sorting and grouping, we'll use the `PagedCollectionView`. It offers us a view on top of our data and allows the data to be sorted, grouped, filtered and so on without changing the underlying collection. The `PagedCollectionView` is instantiated using the following code. We pass in the collection (in this case, the `bookCollection`) on which we want to put the view.

```
PagedCollectionView view = new
  PagedCollectionView(bookCollection);
```

3. In order to change the manner of sorting from the code, we need to add a new `SortDescription` to the `SortDescriptions` collection of the view. In the following code, we are specifying that we want the sorting to occur on the `Title` property of the books in a descending order:

```
view.SortDescriptions.Add(new SortDescription("Title",
  ListSortDirection.Descending));
```

4. If we want our data to appear in groups, we can make it so by adding a new `PropertyGroupDescription` to the `GroupDescriptions` collection of the view. In this case, we want the grouping to be based on the value of the `Language` property. This is shown in the following code:

```
view.GroupDescriptions.Add(new
  PropertyGroupDescription("Language"));
```

5. The `DataGrid` will not bind to the collection, but to the view. We specify this by setting the `ItemsSource` property to the instance of the `PagedCollectionView`. The following code should be placed in the constructor as well:

```
public MainPage()
{
  InitializeComponent();
  LoadBooks();
  view = new PagedCollectionView(bookCollection);
  view.SortDescriptions.Add(new SortDescription("Title",
    ListSortDirection.Descending));
  view.GroupDescriptions.Add(new
    PropertyGroupDescription("Language"));
  BookDataGrid.ItemsSource = view;
}
```

We have now created a `DataGrid` that allows the user to sort the values in a column as well as group the values based on a value in the column. The resulting `DataGrid` is shown in the following screenshot:

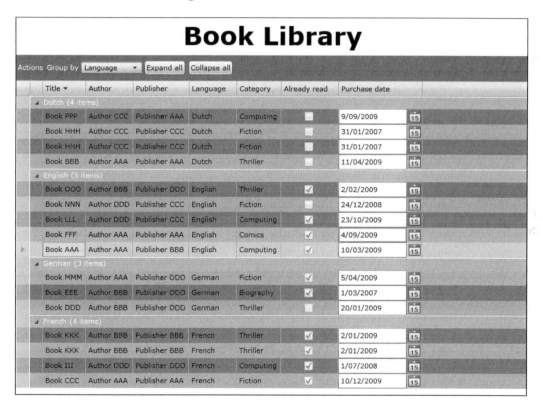

How it works...

The actions such as sorting, grouping, filtering and so on don't work on an actual collection of data. They are applied on a view that sits on top of the collection (either a `List<T>` or an `ObservableCollection<T>`). This way, the original data is not changed. Due to this, we can show the same collection more than once in a different format on the same screen. Different views are applied on the same source data (for example, sorted in one `DataGrid` by `Title` and in another one by `Author`). This view is implemented through the `PagedCollectionView` class.

To change the sorting, we can add a new `SortDescription` to the `SortDescriptions` collection that the view encapsulates. Note that `SortDescriptions` is a collection in which we can add more than one sort field. The second `SortDescription` value will be used only when equal values are encountered for the first `SortDescription` value.

Grouping (using the `PropertyGroupDescription`) allows us to split the grid into different levels. Each section will contain items that have the same value for a particular property. Similar to sorting, we can add more than one `PropertyGroupDescription`, which results in nested groups.

There's more...

From code, we can control all groups to expand or collapse. The following code shows us how to do so:

```
private void CollapseGroupsButton_Click(object sender,
  RoutedEventArgs e)
{
  foreach (CollectionViewGroup group in view.Groups)
  {
    BookDataGrid.CollapseRowGroup(group, true);
  }
}
private void ExpandGroupsButton_Click(object sender,
  RoutedEventArgs e)
{
  foreach (CollectionViewGroup group in view.Groups)
  {
    BookDataGrid.ExpandRowGroup(group, true);
  }
}
```

Sorting a template column

If we want to sort a template column, we have to specify which value needs to be taken into account for the sorting to be executed. Otherwise, Silverlight has no clue which field it should take.

This is done by setting the `SortMemberPath` property as shown in the following code:

```
<sdk:DataGridTemplateColumn x:Name="PurchaseDateColumn"
                             SortMemberPath="PurchaseDate">
```

We'll look at the `DataGridTemplateColumn` in more detail in the *Using custom columns in the DataGrid* recipe of this chapter.

See also

In the next recipe, we'll use the `PagedCollectionView` once more.

Filtering and paging data in a DataGrid

Along with offering us support for the sorting and filtering of data, the `PagedCollectionView` has more up its sleeve. It is also the enabler for filtering rows in a `DataGrid` and, in combination with the `DataPager` control (a control added with Silverlight 3), it allows us to spread the data over several pages within the `DataGrid`.

In this recipe, we'll look at how we can filter based on a value specified by the user and we'll page the results based on the number of returned results, if needed.

Getting ready

This recipe builds on the code that was created in the previous recipes. You can continue using your code to follow this recipe. Alternatively, you can use the start solution located in the `Chapter04/Datagrid_Filtering_And_Paging_Starter` folder in the code bundle that is available on the Packt website. The finished code for this recipe can be found in the `Chapter04/Datagrid_Filtering_And_Paging_Completed` folder.

How to do it...

For this recipe, we'll again work with the `Book` class for which an `ObservableCollection<Book>` is created. This collection is then used as input for the `PagedCollectionView`, which offers a view on the collection. We'll add a search functionality on the collection of books using a filter and a paging functionality using the `DataPager`. The following are the steps to follow:

1. We'll add some XAML controls to the filter. These include a `TextBlock` for indicating the purpose of a field, a `TextBox` in which the user can enter a value, and a `Button`. This is shown in the following code:

```
<TextBlock x:Name="FilterTextBlock"
           Text="Search book titles"
           Margin="3"
           VerticalAlignment="Center"
           Foreground="White">
</TextBlock>
<TextBox x:Name="FilterTextBox"
         Width="200"
         VerticalAlignment="Center"
         HorizontalAlignment="Center"
         Margin="3">
</TextBox>
<Button x:Name="FilterButton"
        Content="Search"
        Margin="3"
        HorizontalAlignment="Center"
        VerticalAlignment="Center"
        Click="FilterButton_Click">
</Button>
```

2. The `DataGrid` is bound to the `PagedCollectionView`, which is a view over the items of a used collection. This is shown in the following code:

```
PagedCollectionView view = new
  PagedCollectionView(bookCollection);
BookDataGrid.ItemsSource = view;
```

3. Upon clicking on the `Button`, we need to search the collection. Searching means looping over the collection and checking whether or not each item satisfies the query. This sounds like a perfect job for a predicate and that's exactly how it's implemented. In the predicate, we'll check whether a book title contains the value entered by the user. This is shown in the following code:

```
private void FilterButton_Click(object sender, RoutedEventArgs e)
{
  view.Filter = null;
  view.Filter = new Predicate<object>(Search);
}
private bool Search(object b)
{
  Book book = b as Book;
  bool foundSearchHit = false;
  if (book != null)
  {
    if (book.Title.Contains(FilterTextBox.Text))
      foundSearchHit = true;
```

```
    }
    return foundSearchHit;
}
```

4. Finally, let's add paging support to the `DataGrid`. Paging is the job of the `DataPager`. This control adds paging support to controls such as the `ListBox` and the `DataGrid`. We simply add a `DataPager` on the XAML page and specify the `PageSize` property as five as shown in the following code:

```
<sdk:DataPager x:Name="BookPager"
               PageSize="5"
               DisplayMode="PreviousNextNumeric">

</sdk:DataPager>
```

5. To make the `DataPager` control display the pages, we need to set its `Source` to the same `PagedCollectionView` as the `DataGrid`. The following code shows us how to do this:

```
public MainPage()
{
    InitializeComponent();

    LoadBooks();

    view = new PagedCollectionView(bookCollection);

    BookDataGrid.ItemsSource = view;

    BookPager.Source = view;
}
```

We have now implemented a filter on the `DataGrid` using the `PagedCollectionView`. A user can search for a value and filtering of the in-memory data will be done. The resulting `DataGrid` is paged using a `DataPager`. The following screenshot shows the result:

How it works...

Just like sorting and grouping, **filtering** is not done on the collection itself, but it's done using a view on top of the collection. This way, the original collection remains intact and can be used on the same screen with different filter values more than once.

Filtering is done using a predicate. Silverlight will loop over all the items of the view and execute the method (in this case the `Search` method) being passed in as the parameter for each item. This method contains the logic that will check whether or not the item should be included in the result set.

Paging is not directly done by the `DataGrid`. A second control, that is, the `DataPager` comes to the rescue. This control does not have a direct link to the `DataGrid`. Both the `DataGrid.ItemsSource` and the `DataPager.Source` properties point to the same instance of the `PagedCollectionView`. This way, the `DataPager` knows on which control it should add the paging functionality.

The `DataPager` control has a `DisplayMode` property that requires a value of the `PagerDisplayMode` enumeration. The following table shows the different options in action:

PagerDisplayMode value	Visualization
FirstLastNumeric	◄ | 1 2 3 4 | ►I
FirstLastPreviousNext	I◄ ◄ | Page 1 of 4 | ► ►I
FirstLastPreviousNextNumeric	I◄ ◄ | 1 2 3 4 | ► ►I
Numeric	1 2 3 4
PreviousNext	◄ | Page 1 of 4 | ►
PreviousNextNumeric	◄ | 1 2 3 4 | ►

There's more...

The `DataPager` is not exclusively tied to the `DataGrid`; it can also be used with the `ListBox`. The following screenshot shows a `DataPager` working together with a `ListBox`:

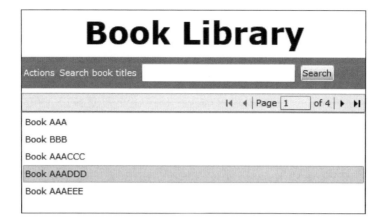

There is no difference code-wise. Both the `ListBox` and the `DataPager` refer to the same `PagedCollectionView` instance.

See also

In the previous recipe, *Sorting and grouping the data in a DataGrid*, we used the `PagedCollectionView` for sorting and grouping the data in a `DataGrid`. In the next recipe, we'll explain more about defining the columns that we want to appear in the `DataGrid`.

Using custom columns in the DataGrid

By default, the `DataGrid` will generate columns for us based on the type of objects that we pass to the control. We looked at this in the *Displaying the data in a customized DataGrid* recipe. However, we'll want more control over what is being displayed most of the time. We'll want to make decisions such as which columns should be shown, in what order and so on. On top of that, we may want to allow the user to select a value from a `ComboBox` for a particular column or entirely reformat a value.

In this recipe, we'll take full control over what will be displayed by the `DataGrid` by creating a number of columns ourselves.

Getting ready

To follow along with this recipe, you can continue using the code that was created in the previous recipes of this chapter. You can also use the start solution located in the `Chapter04/Datagrid_Custom_Columns_Starter` folder in the code bundle that is available on the Packt website. The completed solution for this recipe can be found in the `Chapter04/Datagrid_Custom_Columns_Completed` folder.

How to do it...

There are three types of columns from which we can choose—the `DataGridTextColumn`, the `DataGridCheckBoxColumn` and the `DataGridTemplateColumn`. We can either declare columns from XAML by adding them to the `Columns` collection of the `DataGrid` or add them from the code-behind. We'll again work with the `Book` class. We'll create an `ObservableCollection<Book>` in the code-behind and bind this to the `DataGrid`. We'll create a few custom columns in the following list of steps:

1. The `AutoGenerateColumns` property defaults to `True`. Therefore, in the declaration of the `DataGrid`, we set the property to `False`. The custom-created columns will be added to the `Columns` collection. This is shown in the following code:

```
<sdk:DataGrid x:Name="BookDataGrid"
                AutoGenerateColumns="False">
  <sdk:DataGrid.Columns>
  </sdk:DataGrid.Columns>
</sdk:DataGrid>
```

2. In order to display plain textual values such as the `Title`, the `Author`, and the `Publisher`, we can use the `DataGridTextColumn` as shown in the following code. We need to specify the `Binding` for each column. Note that we now need to set the `Mode` property to `TwoWay`. If we omit this, the value will not be pushed back to the underlying collection.

```
<sdk:DataGridTextColumn x:Name="TitleColumn"
                            Binding="{Binding Title}"
                            Header="Title">
</sdk:DataGridTextColumn>
<sdk:DataGridTextColumn x:Name="AuthorColumn"
                            Binding="{Binding Author}"
                            Header="Author">
</sdk:DataGridTextColumn>
<sdk:DataGridTextColumn x:Name="PublisherColumn"
                            Binding="{Binding Publisher,
                              Mode=TwoWay}"
                            Header="Publisher">
</sdk:DataGridTextColumn>
```

3. The `AlreadyRead` property of our `Book` class is of the `bool` type. We can bind such a value to a `DataGridCheckBoxColumn` as shown in the following code:

```
<sdk:DataGridCheckBoxColumn x:Name="AlreadyReadColumn"
                                Binding="{Binding AlreadyRead,
                                  Mode=TwoWay}"
                                Header="Already read">
</sdk:DataGridCheckBoxColumn>
```

4. The `DataGridTemplateColumn` is the most powerful column type. Using this type, we can specify the template for the column manually. The following is the code for the `ImageName` property. We specify a converter, which is used to convert the `ImageName` property of type string into a `BitmapImage`. This `BitmapImage` can then be used for setting the `Source` property of the `Image` control. The code for the converter can be found in the code bundle that is available on the Packt website.

```
<sdk:DataGridTemplateColumn x:Name="ImageColumn">
  <sdk:DataGridTemplateColumn.CellTemplate>
    <DataTemplate>
      <Image Source="{Binding ImageName,
              Converter={StaticResource localImageConverter}}"
          Margin="2">
      </Image>
    </DataTemplate>
  </sdk:DataGridTemplateColumn.CellTemplate>
</sdk:DataGridTemplateColumn>
```

5. A `CellTemplate` was defined in the previous template. However, we can also define a `CellEditingTemplate`. The cell will switch to the editing template when the user starts editing inside the cell. For the `Language` property in edit mode, we want to offer the user a `ComboBox` containing the available languages. First, we need to make it possible to retrieve the different languages. We can do so by creating a helper class called `LanguageHelper`, which defines a property. The return value of this property is a list of `Language` instances. This is shown in the following code:

```
public class LanguageHelper
    {
        public List<string> LanguageList
        {
            get
            {
                List<string> languages = new List<string>();
                Type lanugageType = typeof(Languages);
                var fields = from c in lanugageType.GetFields()
                             where c.IsLiteral
                             select c;

                foreach (var f in fields)
                {
                    var value = f.GetValue(lanugageType);
                    languages.Add(value.ToString());
                }
                return languages;
            }
        }
    }
```

6. We can instantiate this class in `MainPage.xaml` as shown in the following code:

```
<UserControl.Resources>
  <local:LanguageHelper x:Key="localLanguageHelper">
  </local:LanguageHelper>
</UserControl.Resources>
```

7. We can now use this instance to fill the `ComboBox`. The following is the code for the `Language` column. The normal, non-editing template shows a `TextBlock` and the editing template shows a `ComboBox`. The `ItemsSource` property defines the data binding between the `ComboBox` and the `LangnuageList` property on the instance of the `LanguageHelper` class:

```
<sdk:DataGridTemplateColumn x:Name="LanguageColumn"
                                 Header="Language">
  <sdk:DataGridTemplateColumn.CellTemplate>
    <DataTemplate>
      <TextBlock Text="{Binding Language}"
              VerticalAlignment="Center">
      </TextBlock>
    </DataTemplate>
  </sdk:DataGridTemplateColumn.CellTemplate>
  <sdk:DataGridTemplateColumn.CellEditingTemplate>
    <DataTemplate>
      <ComboBox VerticalAlignment="Center"
              SelectedItem="{Binding Language,
                Converter={StaticResource localEnumConverter},
                Mode=TwoWay}"
              ItemsSource="{Binding LanguageList,
                Source={StaticResource localLanguageHelper}}" >
      </ComboBox>
    </DataTemplate>
  </sdk:DataGridTemplateColumn.CellEditingTemplate>
</sdk:DataGridTemplateColumn>
```

Not all columns are shown here, but they are all similar to the previous samples. The completed sample code contains the remaining ones. All the columns have been added to the `DataGrid` as shown in the following screenshot:

Book Library

How it works...

In most cases, we will not use the auto-generate function of the DataGrid. We can specify the columns ourselves by adding them to the Columns collection. Three types are available, of which the DataGridTemplateColumn is the most powerful.

If we need to display plain text, then we can use the DataGridTextColumn. However, we only have limited control over the formatting of the text. For example, we can change the ForeGround, the FontSize, and the FontWeight properties. However, if we want the text to wrap, we need to use the ElementStyle property as shown in the following code:

```
<sdk:DataGridTextColumn x:Name="PublisherColumn"
                        Binding="{Binding Publisher, Mode=TwoWay}"
                        Header="Publisher">
  <sdk:DataGridTextColumn.ElementStyle>
    <Style TargetType="TextBlock">
      <Setter Property="TextWrapping"
              Value="Wrap">
      </Setter>
    </Style>
  </sdk:DataGridTextColumn.ElementStyle>
</sdk:DataGridTextColumn>
```

While displaying a `boolean` property, we can use a `DataGridCheckboxColumn`, which will render a checkbox per item.

As mentioned before, the real power lies in the `DataGridTemplateColumn` because we can specify how a column will render its contents. We specify a `DataTemplate` containing the data binding statements for the `CellTemplate` property. In this template, we can use whichever control we want (for example, a `DateTimePicker`, an `Image`, or a `ComboBox`).

Each column can have a `CellTemplate` as well as a `CellEditingTemplate`. When both are specified, the column renders the editing template when the user starts editing its content.

In this editing template, we can offer the user a way to make a selection from several options. We have allowed this using a `ComboBox`. However, we need some way to bind the list of possible options to this `ComboBox`. To do so, we can create a helper class that exposes a property that returns a `List<T>`. We can then instantiate this helper class in XAML and perform a data binding with this instance as the source.

There's more...

Silverlight 4 has added more sizing options for the columns of a `DataGrid`. Silverlight 2 and Silverlight 3 basically offered us two options. Under these options, we either needed to specify a width for a column, or else had to leave this task for Silverlight. In the latter case, Silverlight would basically do an auto-sizing (sizing a column according to its contents).

In Silverlight 4, three new options were added, bringing the total to five options to size the columns. The following table shows an overview of these size options:

Size option	Function
Auto	Sized to content and header
Pixel (Fixed)	Fixed width in pixels
SizeToCells	Sized to fit content of cells
SizeToHeader	Sized to fit header
Star	Size is a weighted proportion of the available space

The most interesting option is the star option, which works similarly to the star in a regular `Grid`. Using this option, we can now, for example, specify a cell to either take all of the remaining space or become twice as wide as another cell. The following screenshot shows how the `TitleColumn` is set to take all the remaining space, the `PurchaseDateColumn` and the `ImageColumn` are set to a size according to their cells, and the `AlreadyReadColumn` is set to a size according to its header.

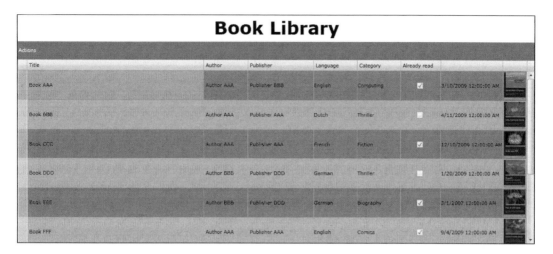

The following code shows how the cells are sized using these sizing options (only the relevant part of the code is posted here):

```
<sdk:DataGrid>
  <sdk:DataGrid.Columns>
    <sdk:DataGridTextColumn x:Name="TitleColumn"
                            Width="*">
    </sdk:DataGridTextColumn>
    <sdk:DataGridTextColumn x:Name="AuthorColumn"
                            Width="100">
    </sdk:DataGridTextColumn>
    <sdk:DataGridTextColumn x:Name="PublisherColumn"
                            Width="150">
    </sdk:DataGridTextColumn>
    <sdk:DataGridTemplateColumn x:Name="LanguageColumn"
                                Width="100">
    </sdk:DataGridTemplateColumn>
    <sdk:DataGridTemplateColumn x:Name="CategoryColumn"
                                Width="100">
    </sdk:DataGridTemplateColumn>
    <sdk:DataGridCheckBoxColumn x:Name="AlreadyReadColumn"
                                Width="SizeToHeader>
    </sdk:DataGridTemplateColumn>
    <sdk:DataGridCheckBoxColumn x:Name="PurchaseDateColumn"
                                Width="SizeToCells>
    </sdk:DataGridTemplateColumn>
    <sdk:DataGridTemplateColumn x:Name="ImageColumn"
                                Width="SizeToCells">
    </sdk:DataGridTemplateColumn>
  </sdk:DataGrid.Columns>
</sdk:DataGrid>
```

Implementing master-detail in the DataGrid

In order to save screen space, not creating too many columns in a DataGrid may be a good idea. A better solution in this case is to create a **master-detail implementation**. The master, being the original row in the DataGrid, would then contain a few columns only. When clicking on any row, the details of that row are shown. In the Silverlight DataGrid, this is possible due to the RowDetailsTemplate.

Getting ready

To follow along with this recipe, you can continue using the code that was created in the previous recipes. Alternatively, you can use the starter solution located in the Chapter04/Datagrid_Master_Detail_Starter folder in the code bundle that is available on the Packt website. The finished solution for this recipe can be found in the Chapter04/Datagrid_Master_Detail_Completed folder.

How to do it...

For this recipe, we'll again use an ObservableCollection<Book>, which is bound to a DataGrid. However, we'll display only the Title and the Author in the default view. When clicking on an item, the details would be shown using a RowDetailsTemplate. The following are the steps we need to follow in order to implement this:

1. We want the DataGrid to contain only two columns. One of the columns is needed for the Title property and the other one for the Author property. In the following code, both of these columns are declared as a DataGridTextColumn and they contain a Binding to the respective properties of the Book class:

```
<sdk:DataGrid x:Name="BookDataGrid"
              AutoGenerateColumns="False">
  <sdk:DataGrid.Columns>
    <sdk:DataGridTextColumn x:Name="TitleColumn"
                            Binding="{Binding Title}"
                            Header="Title">
    </sdk:DataGridTextColumn>
    <sdk:DataGridTextColumn x:Name="AuthorColumn"
                            Binding="{Binding Author}"
                            Header="Author">
    </sdk:DataGridTextColumn>
  </sdk:DataGrid.Columns>
</sdk:DataGrid>
```

2. A detail template is defined on the `DataGrid` itself as shown in the following code:

```
<sdk:DataGrid>
  <sdk:DataGrid.RowDetailsTemplate>
  </sdk:DataGrid.RowDetailsTemplate>
</sdk:DataGrid>
```

3. Similar to the `CellTemplate`, a `RowDetailsTemplate` is a `DataTemplate` that we can define ourselves. The following code defines a `DataTemplate` containing a `Border`. Inside this `Border`, a `Grid` is nested containing an `Image` control, several `TextBlock` controls, and a `DatePicker`. All of these are data bound to display the value of the selected `Book`.

```
<DataTemplate>
  <Border  Background="AntiqueWhite"
          BorderThickness="2"
          BorderBrush="Blue"
          CornerRadius="5">
    <Grid>
      <Grid.RowDefinitions>
        . . .
      </Grid.RowDefinitions>
      <Grid.ColumnDefinitions>
        . . .
      </Grid.ColumnDefinitions>
      <Image  Grid.Row="0"
             Grid.Column="0"
             Grid.RowSpan="2"
             Source="{Binding ImageName,
                Converter={StaticResource localImageConverter}}"
             Margin="2">
      </Image>
      <StackPanel  Grid.Row="0"
                  Grid.Column="1"
                  Orientation="Horizontal">
        <TextBlock  Text="Publisher:"
                   FontWeight="Bold"
                   HorizontalAlignment="Left">
        </TextBlock>
        <TextBlock  Text="{Binding Publisher}"
                   HorizontalAlignment="Left"
                   Margin="1">
        </TextBlock>
      </StackPanel>
      <StackPanel  Grid.Row="1"
                  Grid.Column="1"
```

```xml
                         Orientation="Horizontal">
          <TextBlock Text="Language:"
                     FontWeight="Bold"
                     HorizontalAlignment="Left">
          </TextBlock>
          <TextBlock Text="{Binding Language}"
                     HorizontalAlignment="Left"
                     Margin="1">
          </TextBlock>
     </StackPanel>
     <StackPanel Grid.Row="0"
                 Grid.Column="2"
                 Orientation="Horizontal">
          <TextBlock Text="Category:"
                     FontWeight="Bold"
                     HorizontalAlignment="Left">
          </TextBlock>
          <TextBlock Text="{Binding Category}"
                     HorizontalAlignment="Left"
                     Margin="1">
          </TextBlock>
     </StackPanel>
     <StackPanel Grid.Row="1"
                 Grid.Column="2"
                 Orientation="Horizontal">
          <TextBlock Text="Purchase date:"
                     FontWeight="Bold"
                     HorizontalAlignment="Left">
          </TextBlock>
          <controls:DatePicker SelectedDate="{Binding PurchaseDate}"
                               VerticalAlignment="Top"
                               Margin="1">
          </controls:DatePicker>
     </StackPanel>
     <StackPanel Grid.Row="0"
                 Grid.Column="3"
                 Orientation="Horizontal">
          <TextBlock Text="Already read:"
                     FontWeight="Bold"
                     HorizontalAlignment="Left">
```

```
            </TextBlock>
            <CheckBox IsChecked="{Binding AlreadyRead}">
            </CheckBox>
        </StackPanel>
    </Grid>
</Border>
</DataTemplate>
```

We have now created a master-detail scenario. This can be seen in the following screenshot:

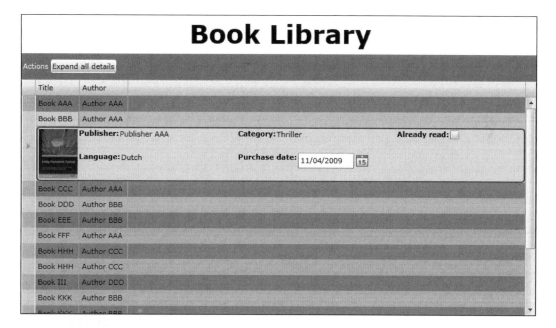

How it works...

For an easy way of implementing a master-detail scenario, the RowDetailsTemplate of the DataGrid is a perfect fit. It allows the user to view more details of a record when clicking on it.

The template is defined as a DataTemplate on the RowDetailsTemplate of the DataGrid control. Inside this template—just like other implementations of the DataTemplate—we can place whatever controls we want. We can use data binding to get the values inside the controls. Each detail template gets the object to which the selected row is bound as the input for this data binding. Inside the data template, the selected row serves as a data source for the data binding expressions within the template.

There's more...

What if we want to add a `Button` in the template and based on the selected item, want to perform a custom action such as navigating to an edit screen where we can edit the selected item?

This can be solved by binding the `Tag` property of the `Button` as shown in the following code:

```
<Button x:Name="SelectButton"
        Content="Select"
        Click="SelectButton_Click"
        Tag="{Binding Title}">
</Button>
```

In the `Click` event handler, we can cast the sender to a `Button` and get access to the value of a `Tag`. In the following code, we bound the `Title`:

```
private void SelectButton_Click(object sender, RoutedEventArgs e)
{
  Button templateButton = sender as Button;
  if (templateButton.Tag != null)
  {
    //do something
  }
}
```

Validating the DataGrid

Validation of your data is a requirement for almost every application in order to make sure that no invalid input is possible. If you're using a `DataGrid`, then you can easily implement validation by using **data annotations** on your classes or properties. This control picks up these validation rules automatically and even provides visual feedback. In this recipe, you'll learn how to get your `DataGrid` to implement this kind of validation.

Getting ready

You can find a starter solution for this recipe located in the `Chapter04\DataGrid_Validation_Starter` folder in the code bundle that is available on the Packt website. The finished solution for this recipe can be found in the `Chapter04\DataGrid_Validation_Completed` folder.

How to do it...

If you're starting from a blank solution, you'll need to create a `Person` class having `ID`, `FirstName`, `LastName`, and `DateOfBirth` properties. The `MainPage` should contain an `ObservableCollection` of `Person`.

We're going to add a `DataGrid` to this project and we'll make sure that it react to the validation attributes that we'll add to the `Person` class. To achieve this, carry out the following steps:

1. Open `MainPage.xaml` and add a `DataGrid` to this control. Your `LayoutRoot` grid looks as shown in the following code:

```
<Grid x:Name="LayoutRoot">
  <Grid.RowDefinitions>
    <RowDefinition Height="40" ></RowDefinition>
    <RowDefinition></RowDefinition>
  </Grid.RowDefinitions>
  <TextBlock Text="Working with the DataGrid"
             Margin="10"
             FontSize="14" >
  </TextBlock>
  <data:DataGrid x:Name="myDataGrid"
             Grid.Row="1"
             Width="400"
             Height="300"
             Margin="10"
             HorizontalAlignment="Left"
             VerticalAlignment="Top">
  </data:DataGrid>
</Grid>
```

2. Add the following namespace import to `MainPage.xaml` to make sure that the `DataGrid` can be used:

```
xmlns:data="clrnamespace:System.Windows.Controls;
  assembly=System.Windows.Controls.Data"
```

3. Add a reference to `System.ComponentModel.DataAnnotations` to your Silverlight project.

4. Open the `Person` class and add the following attributes to the `FirstName` property of this class:

```
[StringLength(30, MinimumLength=3,
  ErrorMessage="First name should have between 3 and 30
  characters")]
[Required(ErrorMessage="First name is required")]
public string FirstName { get; set; }
```

5. We can now build and run our solution. When you enter invalid data into the `FirstName` field, you notice that you get visual feedback for these validation errors and you aren't able to persist your changes unless they are valid. This can be seen in the following screenshot:

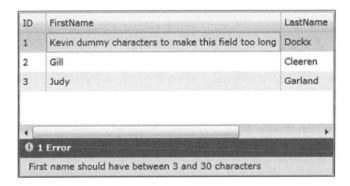

ID	FirstName	LastName
1	Kevin dummy characters to make this field too long	Dockx
2	Gill	Cleeren
3	Judy	Garland

❶ 1 Error

First name should have between 3 and 30 characters

How it works...

This recipe starts by adding a `DataGrid` and a corresponding namespace import to `MainPage.xaml`. As this is done, we can see how it reacts to data annotations.

In the `Person` class, we've added data annotations to the `FirstName` property—the `RequiredAttribute`, and the `StringLengthAttribute`. These data annotations tell that the `FirstName` is required and should have between 3 and 30 characters to any control that can interpret them. We've also added a custom error message by filling out the `ErrorMessage NamedParameter`.

As a `DataGrid` is automatically able to look for these validation rules, it will show the validation errors if validation fails. This feature comes out of the box with a `DataGrid` or a `DataForm` (have a look at the next chapter for more details on this), without us having to do any work. Therefore, you can easily enable validation by just using data annotations.

By using the named parameters in the constructors of your attributes, you can further customize how an attribute should behave. For example, an `ErrorMessage` enables you to customize the message that is shown when validation fails.

There's more...

In this recipe, we've used just a few of the possible data annotations. `DataTypeAttribute`, `RangeAttribute`, `RegularExpressionAttribute`, `RequiredAttribute`, `StringLengthAttribute`, and `CustomValidationAttribute` are the possible data annotations at your disposal.

For all of these attributes, named parameters are available to further customize the way validation should occur. `ErrorMessage`, `ErrorMessageResourceName`, and `ErrorMessageResourceType` are available on all the attributes, but many more are available depending on the attribute you use. You can check these parameters by looking at the IntelliSense tool tip that you get on the attribute constructor.

RIA Services and data annotations

Data annotations are heavily used by **RIA Services**. You can learn more about this by referring to Chapter 9, *Talking to WCF RIA Services*.

See also

If you want to learn more about the various uses of data annotations, have a look at Chapter 9, *Talking to WCF RIA Services*. If you want to learn more about how validation is done using data annotations and the `DataForm`—which is almost identical to the way it's shown in this recipe—have a look at the next chapter.

5

The DataForm

In this chapter, we'll take a look at working with the `DataForm` using the following recipes:

- ▸ Displaying and editing an object using the DataForm
- ▸ Displaying and editing a collection using the DataForm
- ▸ Customizing the DataForm using Data Annotations
- ▸ Customizing the DataForm using a custom DataTemplate
- ▸ Customizing the DataForm template
- ▸ Validating the DataForm

Introduction

If we want to build applications that deal with large amounts of data, it is necessary to have some sort of control that can handle these massive amounts of data. The `DataForm` is such a control; displaying and manipulating (collections of) data can be achieved by using it.

This is a control from the **Silverlight Toolkit** and it is essentially what the name suggests—a form. It is a really powerful form that provides built-in support for field generation, committing or cancelling changes (through `IEditableObject` support), validation on both the field level and the entity level, and built-in paging/navigation. Besides that, it's also highly customizable. This makes the `DataForm` a perfect companion for **Rapid Application Development (RAD)**.

In the recipes of this chapter, we'll look at how we can work with the `DataForm`, which is an essential control for the applications that rely on (collections of) data.

Displaying and editing an object using the DataForm

Letting a user work with groups of related data is a requirement of almost every application. It includes displaying a group of people, editing product details, and so on. These groups of data are generally contained in forms and the Silverlight `DataForm` (from the Silverlight Toolkit) is just that—a form.

In the next few recipes, you'll learn how to work with this `DataForm`. As of now, let's start off with the basics, that is, displaying and editing the data.

Getting ready

For this recipe, we're starting with a blank solution, but you do need to install the Silverlight Toolkit as the assemblies containing the `DataForm` are offered through this. You can download and install it from `http://www.codeplex.com/Silverlight/`. You can find the completed solution in the `Chapter05/Dataform_DisplayAndEdit_Completed` folder in the code bundle that is available on the Packt website.

How to do it...

We're going to create a `Person` object, which will be displayed through a `DataForm`. To achieve this, we'll carry out the following steps:

1. Start a new Silverlight solution, name it **DataFormExample**, and add a reference to `System.Windows.Controls.Data.DataForm.Toolkit` (from the Silverlight Toolkit). Alternatively, you can drag the `DataForm` from the **Toolbox** to the design surface.

2. Open `MainPage.xaml` and add a namespace import statement at the top of this file (in the `<UserControl>` tag) as shown in the following code. This will allow us to use the `DataForm`, which resides in the assembly that we've just referenced.

   ```
   xmlns:df="clr-namespace:System.Windows.Controls;
     assembly=System.Windows.Controls.Data.DataForm.Toolkit"
   ```

3. Add a `DataForm` to `MainPage.xaml` and name it as `myDataForm`. In the `DataForm`, set `AutoEdit` to `False` and `CommandButtonsVisibility` to `All` as shown in the following code:

   ```
   <Grid x:Name="LayoutRoot">
     <Grid.RowDefinitions>
       <RowDefinition Height="40" ></RowDefinition>
   ```

```
    <RowDefinition></RowDefinition>
</Grid.RowDefinitions>
<TextBlock Text="Working with the DataForm"
           Margin="10"
           FontSize="14" >
</TextBlock>
<df:DataForm x:Name="myDataForm"
             AutoEdit="False"
             CommandButtonsVisibility="All"
             Grid.Row="1"
             Width="400"
             Height="300"
             Margin="10"
             HorizontalAlignment="Left"
             VerticalAlignment="Top" >
</df:DataForm>
</Grid>
```

4. Add a new class named `Person` to the Silverlight project having `ID`, `FirstName`, `LastName`, and `DateOfBirth` as its properties. This class is shown in the following code. We will visualize an instance of the `Person` class using the `DataForm`.

```
public class Person
{
   public int ID { get; set; }
   public string FirstName { get; set; }
   public string LastName { get; set; }
   public DateTime DateOfBirth { get; set; }
}
```

5. Open `MainPage.xaml.cs` and add a `person` property of the `Person` type to it. Also, create a method named `InitializePerson` in which we'll initialize this property as shown in the following code:

```
public Person person { get; set; }
private void InitializePerson()
{
   person = new Person()
   {
      ID = 1,
      FirstName = "Kevin",
      LastName = "Dockx",
      DateOfBirth = new DateTime(1981, 5, 5)
   };
}
```

6. Add a call to `InitializePerson` in the constructor of `MainPage.xaml.cs` and set the `CurrentItem` property of the `DataForm` to a `person` as shown in the following code:

```
InitializePerson();
myDataForm.CurrentItem = person;
```

7. You can now build and run your solution. When you do this, you'll see a `DataForm` that has automatically generated the necessary fields in order to display a person. This can be seen in the following screenshot:

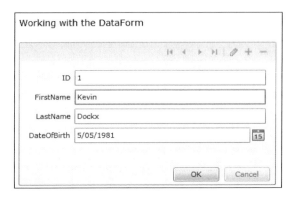

How it works...

To start off, we needed something to display in our DataForm: a `Person` entity. This is why we've created the `Person` class: it will be bound to the `DataForm` by setting the `CurrentItem` property to an object of type `Person`.

Doing this will make sure that the `DataForm` automatically generates the necessary fields. It looks at all the public properties of our `Person` object and generates the correct control depending on the type. A string will be displayed as a `TextBox`, a Boolean value will be displayed as a `CheckBox`, and so on.

As we have set the `CommandButtonsVisibility` property on the `DataForm` to `All`, we get an **Edit** icon in the command bar at the top of the `DataForm`. (Setting `AutoEdit` to `False` makes sure that we start in the display mode, rather than the edit mode). When you click on the **Edit** icon, the `DataForm` shows the person in the editable mode (using the `EditItemTemplate`) and an **OK** button appears. Clicking on the **OK** button will revert the form to the regular displaying mode. Do keep in mind that the changes you make to the person are persisted immediately in memory (in the case of a `TextBox`, when it loses focus).

If necessary, you can write extra code to persist the `Person` object from the memory to an underlying datastore by handling the `ItemEditEnded` event on the `DataForm`.

There's more...

At this moment, we've got a `DataForm` displaying a single item that you can either view or edit. But what if you want to cancel your edit? As of now, the **Cancel** button appears to be disabled. As the changes you make in the `DataForm` are immediately persisted to the underlying object in the memory, cancelling the edit would require some extra business logic. Luckily, it's not hard to do.

First of all, you'll want to implement the `IEditableObject` interface on the `Person` class, which will make sure that cancelling is possible. As a result, the **Cancel** button will no longer be disabled. The following code is used to implement this:

```
public class Person : IEditableObject
{
  public int ID { get; set; }
  public string FirstName { get; set; }
  public string LastName { get; set; }
  public DateTime DateOfBirth { get; set; }
  public void BeginEdit()
  {}
  public void CancelEdit()
  {}
  public void EndEdit()
  {}
}
```

This interface exposes three methods: `BeginEdit`, `CancelEdit`, and `EndEdit`. If needed, you can write extra business logic in these methods, which is exactly what we need to do. For most applications, you might want to implement only `CancelEdit`, which would then refetch the person from the underlying data store. In our example, we're going to solve this problem by using a different approach. (You can use this approach if you haven't got an underlying database from which your data can be refetched, or if you don't want to access the database again.) In the `BeginEdit` method, we save the current property values of the person. When the edit has been cancelled, we put them back to the way they were before. This is shown in the following code:

```
public void BeginEdit()
{
  // save current values
  tmpPerson = new Person()
  {
    ID = this.ID,
    FirstName = this.FirstName,
    LastName = this.LastName,
    DateOfBirth = this.DateOfBirth
  };
```

```
  }
  public void CancelEdit()
  {
    // reset values
    ID = tmpPerson.ID;
    FirstName = tmpPerson.FirstName;
    LastName = tmpPerson.LastName;
    DateOfBirth = tmpPerson.DateOfBirth;
  }
```

Now, cancelling an edit is possible and it actually reverts to the previous property values.

More on DataForm behavior

The `DataForm` exposes various events such as `BeginningEdit` (when you begin to edit an item), `EditEnding` (occurs just before an item is saved), and `EditEnded` (occurs after an item has been saved). It also exposes properties that you can use to define how the `DataForm` behaves.

Validating a DataForm or a DataGrid

As you might have noticed, the `DataForm` includes validation on your fields automatically. For example, try inputting a string value into the **ID** field. You'll see that an error message appears. This is beyond the scope of this recipe, but more on this will be discussed in the *Validating the DataForm* recipe.

Managing the editing of an object on different levels

There are different levels of managing the editing of an object. You can manage this on the control level itself by handling events such as `BeginningEdit` or `ItemEditEnded` in the `DataForm`. Besides that, you can also handle editing on a business level by implementing the `IEditableObject` interface and providing custom code for the `BeginEdit`, `CancelEdit`, or `EndEdit` methods in the class itself. Depending on the requirements of your application, you can use either of the levels or even both together.

See also

In this recipe, we've seen how the `DataForm` is created automatically. For most applications, you require more control over how your fields, for example, are displayed. The `DataForm` is highly customizable, both on a template level (through template customization) and on how the data is generated (through data annotations). To learn more about customizing the template of a `DataForm`, you can refer to the *Customizing the DataForm template* recipe. For more information about customizing the way the `DataForm` is generated, have a look at the *Customizing the DataForm using Data Annotations* and the *Customizing the DataForm using a custom DataTemplate* recipes. If you want to learn about using the `DataForm` to display or edit a list of items rather than just one, have a look at the next recipe, *Displaying and editing a collection using the DataForm*.

Displaying and editing a collection using the DataForm

In the previous recipe, you learned how to work with the basic features of the DataForm. You can now visualize and edit an entity. But in most applications, this isn't enough. Often, you'll want to have an application that shows you a list of items with the ability to add a new item or delete an item from the list. You'll want the application to allow you to edit every item and provide an easy way of navigating between them. A good example of this would be an application that allows you to manage a list of employees.

The DataForm can do all of this and most of it is built-in. In this recipe, you'll learn how to achieve this.

Getting ready

For this recipe, we're starting with the basic setup that we completed in the previous recipe. If you didn't complete that recipe, you can find a starter solution in the Chapter05/Dataform_Collection_Starter folder in the code bundle that is available on the Packt website. The finished solution for this recipe can be found in the Chapter05/Dataform_Collection_Completed folder.

In any case, you'll need to install the Silverlight Toolkit as the assemblies containing the DataForm are offered through it. You can download and install it from http://www.codeplex.com/Silverlight/.

How to do it...

We're going to create an application that visualizes a list of people using the DataForm. In order to achieve this, carry out the following steps. (If you're starting from a blank solution, you'll need to add a DataForm to your MainPage and create a Person class having ID, FirstName, LastName, and DateOfBirth as its properties.)

1. Open MainPage.xaml.cs and add a new property called lstPerson of the ObservableCollection type of Person to it. This is shown in the following line of code:

```
public ObservableCollection<Person> lstPerson { get; set; }
```

2. Create a new method called `InitializePersons()`, which is used to initialize `lstPerson`. This is shown in the following code:

```
private void InitializePersons()
{
  lstPerson = new ObservableCollection<Person>()
  {
    new Person()
    {
      ID=1,
      FirstName="Kevin",
      LastName="Dockx",
      DateOfBirth = new DateTime(1981, 5, 5)
    },
    new Person()
    {
      ID=2,
      FirstName="Gill",
      LastName="Cleeren",
      DateOfBirth = new DateTime(2009, 1, 1)
    },
    new Person()
    {
      ID=3,
      FirstName="Judy",
      LastName="Garland",
      DateOfBirth = new DateTime(1922, 6, 10)
    }
  };
}
```

3. In the `MainPage` constructor, call the `InitializePersons()` method and set the `ItemsSource` property of `myDataForm` to `lstPerson` as shown in the following code:

```
public MainPage()
{
  InitializeComponent();
  InitializePersons();
  myDataForm.ItemsSource = lstPerson;
}
```

4. You can now build and run the solution. You'll notice that you can navigate through the list of persons in the `DataForm` by using the navigation buttons at the top of the `DataForm`. This can be seen in the following screenshot:

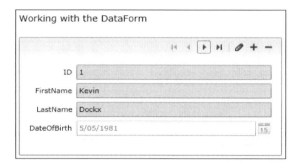

How it works...

In the previous recipe, we set the `CurrentItem` property of the `DataForm` to a `Person` object. This recipe builds on that, but instead of setting the `CurrentItem` property, we bind the `ItemsSource` property to our `ObservableCollection` of `Person`. While doing this, the `DataForm` will automatically generate navigation buttons to navigate through the collection and will also generate an **Add** and a **Delete** button. In order to access the current item, you can refer to the `CurrentItem` property, which will change automatically while navigating through the list.

There's more...

In order to change the behavior of the `DataForm`, you can set a variety of its properties on the `DataForm`. `AutoCommit` makes sure changes are saved if the user navigates through the list without clicking on the **OK** button, while `AutoEdit` makes sure the `DataForm` automatically goes in **Edit** mode when the user selects a record. `CancelButtonContent` sets the content for the **Cancel** button. (You need to implement `IEditableObject` on your `Person` class for this button to be enabled. Have a look at the previous recipe for more information on this.) `CommitButtonContent` sets the content for the **OK** button.

In order to change the ability to add or delete items, you can easily change the `CommandButtonsVisibility` property to show or hide the corresponding buttons.

Along with that, the `DataForm` exposes a few events specifically for use while binding to collections. `AddingNewItem` is fired just before an item is added to the collection, `DeletingItem` is fired just before an item is deleted, and `CurrentItemChanged` is fired when the current item has been changed (which happens when you navigate through the list of items, or when you add or delete an item).

See also

In this recipe, we've used an `ObservableCollection` that is bound to the `ItemsSource` property of the `DataForm`. To learn more about this `ObservableCollection` and binding in general, have a look at Chapter 2 and Chapter 3.

For most applications, you'll require more control over how your fields (for example) are displayed. The `DataForm` is highly customizable, both on a template level (through template customization) and on how the data is generated (through Data Annotations). In order to learn more about customizing the template of a `DataForm`, you can refer to the *Customizing the DataForm template* recipe in this chapter. For more information about customizing the way the `DataForm` is generated, have a look at the *Customizing the DataForm using a custom DataTemplate* and *Customizing the DataForm using Data Annotations*.

Customizing the DataForm using Data Annotations

In the previous recipes, we looked at how to easily display an object or a collection of objects using a `DataForm`, which includes a lot of functionalities out of the box. However, as you might have noticed, the generated fields aren't always the way you'd want them to be. The labels could be more descriptive or user-friendly, a field could be invisible or read-only, and so on. To achieve this, you can use helpers—**Data Annotations**. They will define how the `DataForm` should be generated.

In this recipe, we'll use helpers in the form of Data Annotations to change the auto-generation of our `DataForm`.

Getting ready

We're starting from the solution that we completed in the previous recipe. If you didn't finish that recipe, you can find a starter solution in the `Chapter05\Dataform_DataAnnotations_Starter` folder in the code bundle that is available on the Packt website. The finished solution for this recipe can be found in the `Chapter05\Dataform_DataAnnotations_Completed` folder.

In any case, you'll need to install the Silverlight Toolkit as the assemblies containing the `DataForm` are offered through it. You can download and install it from `http://www.codeplex.com/Silverlight/`.

How to do it...

If you're starting from a blank solution, you'll need to add a `DataForm` to your `MainPage` and create a `Person` class having `ID`, `FirstName`, `LastName`, and `DateOfBirth` as its properties. The `DataForm` on the `MainPage` should be bound to an `ObservableCollection` of `Person`.

We're going to change the way our `DataForm` is generated by using Data Annotations. In order to achieve this, carry out the following steps:

1. Add a reference to `System.ComponentModel.DataAnnotations` in your Silverlight project.

2. Open the `Person.cs` file and add a `using` directive to include the newly added `System.ComponentModel.DataAnnotations` namespace. This is shown in the following line of code:

    ```
    using System.ComponentModel.DataAnnotations;
    ```

3. Add the following Data Annotations to the properties of your `Person` class:

    ```
    [Editable(false)]
    [Display(Description="Internal identification of this record")]
    public int ID { get; set; }
    [Display(Name="First name", Description="The first name of this
        person")]
    public string FirstName { get; set; }
    [Display(Name = "Last name", Description = "The last name of this
        person")]
    public string LastName { get; set; }
    [Display(Name = "Date of birth", Description = "The date of birth
        of this person")]
    public DateTime DateOfBirth { get; set; }
    ```

4. You can now build and run your application. You'll notice that the `ID` property isn't editable anymore, the generated `TextBlocks` are more user-friendly, and a tooltip appears where applicable. This can be seen in the following screenshot:

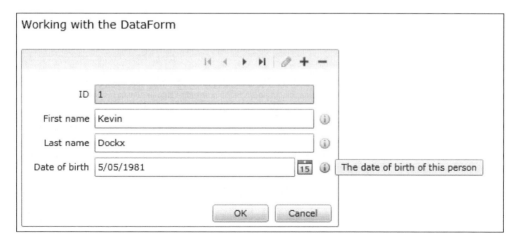

How it works...

In order to customize our `DataForm`, we've added Data Annotations to the properties of the class that represents a `Person`. When the `DataForm` is generated, it will look at the public properties and the Data Annotations on those properties to find out how it should be generated.

On the `ID` property, we've added an `Editable` attribute telling it that it shouldn't be editable. This makes sure that the property is read-only, even in the edit mode.

Besides that, we've added a `Display` attribute that defines how the field should be displayed. We've made sure that friendly names are used instead of property identifiers by setting the `Name` property as well as the `Description` property in the `Display` attribute. We've also defined the Tooltip that appears next to the `TextBox`.

There's more...

More Data Annotation options exist to further customize our `DataForm`. For example, while `DataType` allows you to specify a particular type of data for your property, `DisplayFormat` allows you to specify a format string to apply to your property. For a full and up-to-date list, you can have a look at `http://msdn.microsoft.com/en-us/library/dd901590(VS.95).aspx`.

Using Data Annotations for validation

Data Annotations are also used to define how validation should occur while using the `DataForm`. This is covered in the *Validating the DataForm* recipe of this chapter.

See also

In order to learn more about customizing the `DataForm`, have a look at the next recipe, *Customizing the DataForm using a custom DataTemplate*. To learn more about how to use Data Annotations to validate a `DataForm`, refer the *Validating the DataForm* recipe in this chapter.

Customizing the DataForm using a custom DataTemplate

In order to customize the `DataForm`, you can use helpers in the form of Data Annotations as seen in the *Customizing the DataForm using Data Annotations* recipe. But sometimes this isn't sufficient. You might have a requirement where generating the fields automatically, even with the use of Data Annotations , isn't sufficient: you need more control. But at the same time, you'd still like to use the built-in navigation capabilities, read/edit-mode, and so on of the `DataForm`.

In this recipe, you'll learn how to do just that. You'll learn to completely customize the way the `DataForm` shows your data by disabling automatic generation and defining the `DataTemplate` yourself.

Getting ready

We're starting from the solution that we completed in the *Displaying and editing a collection using the DataForm* recipe. If you didn't complete that recipe, you can find a starter solution located in the `Chapter05\Dataform_CustomDataTemplate_Starter` folder in the code bundle that is available on the Packt website. The finished solution for this recipe can be found in the `Chapter05\Dataform_CustomTemplate_Completed` folder.

In any case, you'll need to install the Silverlight Toolkit as the assemblies containing the `DataForm` are offered through it. You can download and install it from `http://www.codeplex.com/Silverlight/`.

How to do it...

If you're starting from a blank solution, you'll need to add a `DataForm` to your `MainPage` and create a `Person` class having `ID`, `FirstName`, `LastName`, and `DateOfBirth` as its properties. The `DataForm` on the `MainPage` should be bound to an `ObservableCollection` of `Person`.

We're going to change the appearance of our `DataForm` by turning the auto-generation off and defining the `DataTemplate` ourselves. In order to achieve this, carry out the following steps:

1. Open the `Person.cs` class and implement the `INotifyPropertyChanged` interface on it as shown in the following code:

```
public class Person : IEditableObject, INotifyPropertyChanged
{
  public event PropertyChangedEventHandler PropertyChanged;
  protected virtual void OnPropertyChanged(string propName)
  {
    if (PropertyChanged != null)
    {
      PropertyChanged(this, new
        PropertyChangedEventArgs(propName));
    }
  }
}
```

2. Change the properties in the `Person` class so that they call `OnPropertyChanged` in their `set` function. This is shown in the following code:

```
private int pID;
public int  ID
{
  get
  {
    return pID;
  }
  set
  {
    pID = value;
    OnPropertyChanged("ID");
  }
}
private string pFirstName;
public string FirstName
{
  get
  {
    return pFirstName;
  }
  set
  {
    pFirstName = value;
    OnPropertyChanged("FirstName");
  }
}
private string pLastName;
public string LastName
{
  get
  {
    return pLastName;
  }
  set
  {
    pLastName = value;
    OnPropertyChanged("LastName");
  }
}
private DateTime pDateOfBirth;
public DateTime DateOfBirth
{
  get
  {
    return pDateOfBirth;
  }
  set
```

```
      {
          pDateOfBirth = value;
          OnPropertyChanged("DateOfBirth");
      }
   }
```

3. Open `MainPage.xaml` and set `AutoGenerateFields` in the `DataForm` to `False` as shown in the following code:

```xml
<df:DataForm x:Name="myDataForm"
             AutoEdit="False"
             CommandButtonsVisibility="All"
             AutoGenerateFields="False"
             Grid.Row="1"
             Width="400"
             Height="300"
             Margin="10"
             HorizontalAlignment="Left"
             VerticalAlignment="Top" >
```

4. Define a `ReadOnlyTemplate` on your `DataForm` and add the `DataField` elements that are bound to the properties of a `Person` object to it. This is shown in the following code:

```xml
<df:DataForm.ReadOnlyTemplate>
  <DataTemplate>
    <Grid>
      <Grid.RowDefinitions>
        <RowDefinition Height="30"></RowDefinition>
        <RowDefinition Height="30"></RowDefinition>
        <RowDefinition Height="30"></RowDefinition>
        <RowDefinition Height="30"></RowDefinition>
      </Grid.RowDefinitions>
      <df:DataField Label="First name"
                    LabelPosition="Left">
        <TextBlock Text="{Binding FirstName}">
        </TextBlock>
      </df:DataField>
      <df:DataField Label="Last name"
                    LabelPosition="Left"
                    Grid.Row="1">
        <TextBlock Text="{Binding LastName}">
        </TextBlock>
      </df:DataField>
      <df:DataField Label="Date of birth"
                    LabelPosition="Left"
                    Grid.Row="2">
```

```
            <TextBlock Text="{Binding DateOfBirth}">
            </TextBlock>
        </df:DataField>
        <df:DataField Label="ID"
                      LabelPosition="Left"
                      Grid.Row="3">
            <TextBlock Text="{Binding ID}">
            </TextBlock>
        </df:DataField>
      </Grid>
    </DataTemplate>
</df:DataForm.ReadOnlyTemplate>
```

5   In the same way, define an `EditTemplate` on your DataForm. Use a `DatePicker` control for the date of birth property and use a `NumericUpDown` control (from the Silverlight Toolkit you've already installed) for the ID property. This is shown in the following code:

```
<df:DataForm.EditTemplate>
  <DataTemplate>
    <Grid>
      <Grid.RowDefinitions>
        <RowDefinition Height="30"></RowDefinition>
        <RowDefinition Height="30"></RowDefinition>
        <RowDefinition Height="30"></RowDefinition>
        <RowDefinition Height="30"></RowDefinition>
      </Grid.RowDefinitions>
      <df:DataField Label="First name"
                    LabelPosition="Left">
        <TextBox Text="{Binding FirstName, Mode=TwoWay}" />
      </df:DataField>
      <df:DataField Label="Last name"
                    LabelPosition="Left"
                    Grid.Row="1">
        <TextBox Text="{Binding LastName, Mode=TwoWay}" />
      </df:DataField>
      <df:DataField Label="Date of birth"
                    LabelPosition="Left"
                    Grid.Row="2">
        <controls:DatePicker SelectedDate="{Binding DateOfBirth,
                             Mode=TwoWay}"/>
      </df:DataField>
      <df:DataField Label="ID"
                    LabelPosition="Left"
                    Grid.Row="3">
        <inputToolkit:NumericUpDown Value="{Binding ID,
                                    Mode=TwoWay}" />
      </df:DataField>
    </Grid>
  </DataTemplate>
</df:DataForm.EditTemplate>
```

6. You can now build and run your solution. You'll notice that you've still got all the functionalities offered by a `DataForm`. However, you've completely customized the way your `DataForm` looks. This can be seen in the following screenshot:

How it works...

In the first two steps of this recipe, we've changed the `Person` class so that the `PropertyChanged` event gets fired when the `Person` properties are set. When you're defining a custom `DataTemplate` for the `DataForm`, this is necessary because we need it to make sure that we can correctly use `TwoWay` bindings. If you're not customizing the `DataTemplate`, this isn't necessary. The `DataForm` automatically fires the required event when it's allowed to generate the fields.

Next, we turn off the auto-generation of fields on the `DataForm` by setting the `AutoGenerateFields` property to `False`. This will make sure that the `DataTemplate` isn't generated automatically anymore. Due to this, we now need to define the `DataTemplate` ourselves.

A `DataForm` has different modes. The records can be viewed as well as edited. You'll want different templates for this quite frequently. For example, you might want a bunch of `TextBlocks` showing your data when the records are viewed, but you might want the controls to be different while editing—a `DatePicker` for date values, a `NumericUpDown` control for integer values, and so on. In order to allow for this separation, the `DataForm` includes different customizable `DataTemplate` elements. By defining the `ReadOnlyTemplate`, you define how your data will look when the user is viewing it, whereas by defining the `EditTemplate`, you define how it will look when the user is editing it.

In this recipe, we've created both these `DataTemplate` elements. Of course, you'll also need to be able to show the data in the controls you've added. The `DataField` elements are used in order to do this. These are fields that act as containers for other controls, which can then be bound to the properties of whichever object is bound to the `DataForm`. In our case, the `ItemsSource` of the `DataForm` is a collection of `Person`. This means that one `DataForm` item is a `Person`, so we can bind to the `Person` properties. In the `EditTemplate`, we're allowing the user to edit the data. So we need to make sure that the changes they make in the UI element are persisted to the underlying `Person`. We do this using the `TwoWay` binding syntax.

By bringing all of this together, we've ended up with a functional, yet completely customized `DataForm`.

There's more...

It is possible to carry out more customization on the `DataField`. If you want, you can define a custom style for the labels by setting the `LabelStyle` property. Along with that, you can also add a description for the `DataField` by setting the `Description` property. You can align or style it using the `DescriptionViewerPosition` and the `DescriptionViewerStyle` properties. Of course, other templating/styling abilities exist in line with what you can do with other Silverlight controls.

In this recipe, we've created a custom `EditTemplate` and a `ReadOnlyTemplate`. If you're allowing your user to add new items, you can also define a custom `NewItemTemplate` in the same way.

See also

In order to know more about some other way of customizing the `DataForm`, have a look at the previous recipe, *Customizing the DataForm using Data Annotations*.

Customizing the DataForm template

In the previous recipes, we've covered various ways of customizing the way the data is shown on the `DataForm`. The `DataForm` still looks like a `DataForm` and for most applications, this isn't what you'd want. You'd want the `DataForm` to conform to the general look and feel of your application.

You can completely customize the way the `DataForm` looks , just as you can with all the other Silverlight controls. In this recipe, you'll learn how it can be done.

Getting ready

We're starting from the solution that we completed in the *Displaying and editing a collection using the DataForm* recipe. If you didn't complete that recipe, you can find a starter solution in the `Chapter05\Dataform_CustomTemplate_Starter` folder in the code bundle that is available on the Packt website. However, we're only using the previously created solution to make sure that we have some dummy data on the screen. In order to customize the template of a `DataForm`, all that you really need is a Silverlight project with a `UserControl` containing an empty `DataForm`.

In any case, you'll need to install the Silverlight Toolkit as the assemblies containing the `DataForm` are offered through it. You can download and install it from `http://www.codeplex.com/Silverlight/`.

How to do it...

We're going to customize our `DataForm` using Expression Blend. To achieve this, carry out the following steps:

1. Open `MainPage.xaml` in Expression Blend. Locate the `DataForm` (named `myDataForm`), right-click on it, and select **Edit Template | Edit a Copy...** as shown in the following screenshot. When prompted for a name, name the style as **myDataFormStyle** and select **define in this document:**.

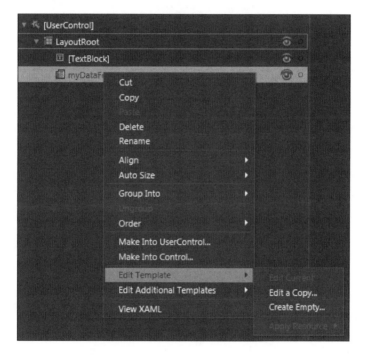

2. On the left-hand side, you'll see a window with the structure of the DataForm template. Select **DataFormBorder** and change the Background to a nice gradient. Select the **[Grid]** surrounding the controls on top of the DataForm and change its Background as well. This can be seen in the following screenshot:

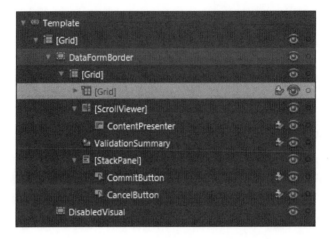

3. You can now build and run your solution. You'll notice that the DataForm looks similar to the way we've defined it in Blend. Now, the background is gray in color and there's a nice gradient on the bar containing the navigation, which shows you how easy it is to customize the look and feel of the DataForm.

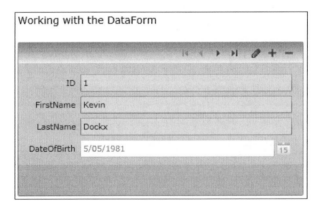

How it works...

The way the DataForm looks is highly customizable just like any control in Silverlight. Typically, this is done by changing the various templates. In this recipe, we used Blend to achieve this (as it provides a visual and easy way of customizing the templates, thereby generating the accompanying XAML for us). But you might just as well write the XAML code yourself.

Each control has a default template that defines the way it looks. In this case, we've created a copy of this template and changed that copy. The modified copy is (in this case) stored in the `UserControl` resources and bound to the `Style` property of our `DataForm` in `MainPage.xaml`. This can be seen in the following code:

```
<df:DataForm x:Name="myDataForm"
             AutoEdit="False"
             CommandButtonsVisibility="All"
             Grid.Row="1"
             Width="400"
             Height="300"
             Margin="10"
             HorizontalAlignment="Left"
             VerticalAlignment="Top"
             Style="{StaticResource myDataFormStyle}" />
```

When the application is running, Silverlight will look for `myDataFormStyle` and use this template to define the look of the `DataForm`, instead of the default template.

There's more...

In this recipe, we've only changed a few `Background` properties to redefine the way the `DataForm` looks. However, a lot more customization is possible. The `DataForm` consists of various parts: various buttons, a header, a `ValidationSummary`, all customizable in the same way using the same logic we've used in this recipe.

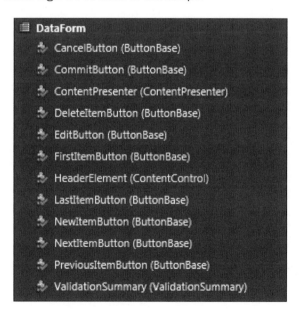

Getting the default template of a control

Each control has a default template. You can have a look at this template by editing a copy of the template of the current control using Expression Blend. This will create an editable copy of the default template.

Alternatively, free tools are available to view the default templates of the controls without using Expression Blend. One of these tools is Delay's Silverlight Default Style Browser, which can be installed from `http://delay.members.winisp.net/SilverlightDefaultStyleBrowser/SilverlightDefaultStyleBrowser.application`.

See also

In order to learn more about working with Expression Blend, have a look at the first chapter of this book.

Validating the DataForm

Validation of your data is a requirement for almost every application to make sure that no invalid input is possible. If you're using a `DataForm`, you can easily implement validation by using Data Annotations on your classes or properties. This control picks up these validation rules automatically and even provides visual feedback. In this recipe, you'll learn how to implement this kind of validation for a `DataForm`.

Getting ready

We're starting from the solution that we competed in the *Displaying and editing a collection using the DataForm* recipe. If you didn't complete that recipe, you can find a starter solution located in the `Chapter05\Dataform_Validation_Starter` folder in the code bundle that is available on the Packt website. The finished solution for this recipe can be found in the `Chapter05\Dataform_Validation_Completed` folder.

In any case, you'll need to install the Silverlight Toolkit as the assemblies containing the `DataForm` are offered through it. You can download and install it from `http://www.codeplex.com/Silverlight/`.

How to do it...

If you're starting from a blank solution, you'll need to add a `DataForm` to your `MainPage` and create a `Person` class having `ID`, `FirstName`, `LastName`, and `DateOfBirth` as its properties. The `DataForm` on the `MainPage` should be bound to an `ObservableCollection` of `Person`.

We're going to make sure that the `DataForm` reacts to the validation attributes we'll add to the `Person` class. To achieve this, carry out the following steps:

1. Add a reference to `System.ComponentModel.DataAnnotations` in your Silverlight project.

2. Open the `Person` class and add the following attributes to the `FirstName` property of this class:

    ```
    [StringLength(30, MinimumLength=3,
        ErrorMessage="First name should have between 3 and 30
        characters")]
    [Required(ErrorMessage="First name is required")]
    public string FirstName { get; set; }
    ```

3. We can now build and run our solution. When you enter invalid data in the **FirstName** field, you notice that you get visual feedback for these validation errors and you aren't able to persist your changes unless they are valid. This can be seen in the following screenshot:

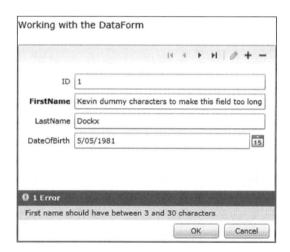

How it works...

We've added Data Annotations such as the `RequiredAttribute` and the `StringLengthAttribute` to the `FirstName` property in the `Person` class. These Data Annotations respectively tell any control that can interpret them that the `FirstName` is required and it should have between 3 and 30 characters. We've also added a custom error message for both the Data Annotations by filling out the `ErrorMessage NamedParameter`.

As a `DataForm` is able to look for these validation rules automatically, it will show validation errors if the validation fails. This feature comes out of the box with a `DataForm`, without you having to do any of the work. Therefore, you can easily enable validation by just using Data Annotations.

By using named parameters in the constructors of your attributes, you can further customize how the attribute should behave. For example, `ErrorMessage` enables you to customize the message that is shown when validation fails.

There's more...

In this recipe, we've used just a few of the possible data annotations. `DataTypeAttribute`, `RangeAttribute`, `RegularExpressionAttribute`, `RequiredAttribute`, `StringLengthAttribute`, and `CustomValidationAttribute` are all of the data annotations at your disposal.

For all of these attributes, named parameters are possible in order to further customize the way validation should occur. `ErrorMessage`, `ErrorMessageResourceName`, and `ErrorMessageResourceType` are available on all attributes, but many more are available depending on the attribute you use. You can check them by looking at the IntelliSense tooltip you get on the attribute constructor.

Other uses of Data Annotations

In the other recipes of this chapter, you've already noticed that other non-validating data attributes exist such as the display attributes and the mode attributes. These attributes are used to control how certain information should be displayed or how certain properties should relate to each other.

RIA Services and Data Annotations

Data Annotations are heavily used in combination with WCF RIA Services. You can learn more about this by referring to Chapter 9, *Talking to WCF RIA Services*.

See also

If you want to learn more about the various uses of Data Annotations, have a look at Chapter 9, *Talking to WCF RIA Services*. You can also have a look at the *Customizing the DataForm using Data Annotations* recipe, where Data Annotations are used to customize the way the `DataForm` is generated. If you want to learn more about working with the `DataGrid`, have a look at the previous chapter, *The Data Grid*.

6

Talking to Services

In this chapter, we will cover:

- ▶ Connecting and reading from a standardized service
- ▶ Persisting data using a standardized service
- ▶ Configuring cross-domain calls
- ▶ Working cross-domain from a trusted application
- ▶ Reading XML using HttpWebRequest
- ▶ Reading out an RSS feed
- ▶ Aggregating RSS feeds
- ▶ Talking with services in the Windows Azure cloud
- ▶ Persisting data to and reading data from the Windows Azure cloud
- ▶ Using socket communication

Introduction

Looking at the namespaces and classes in the Silverlight assemblies, it's easy to see that there are no ADO.NET-related classes available in Silverlight. Silverlight does not contain a `DataReader`, a `DataSet` or any option to connect to a database directly. Thus, it's not possible to define a connection string for a database and let Silverlight applications connect with that database directly.

The solution adds a layer on top of the database in the form of services. The services that talk directly to a database (or, more preferably, to a business and data access layer) can expose the data so that Silverlight can work with it. However, the data that's exposed in this way does not always have to come from a database. It can come from a third-party service through, by reading a file, or be the result of an intensive calculation executed on the server.

Silverlight has a wide range of options to connect with services. This is important as it's the main way of getting data into our applications. In this chapter, we'll look at the concepts of connecting with several types of services and external data. In Chapter 7 and Chapter 8, we'll take a detailed look at communicating with WCF and REST services respectively, which are the most widely used types of services when working with Silverlight.

We'll start our journey by looking at how Silverlight connects and works with a regular service. We'll see that the concepts we use here recur for other types of service communications as well. One of these concepts is cross-domain service access. In other words, this means accessing a service on a domain that is different from the one where the Silverlight application is hosted. We'll see why Microsoft has implemented cross-domain restrictions in Silverlight and what we need to do to access externally hosted services.

Silverlight includes various classes to make it easy to work with **RSS feeds**. However, the same cross-domain service access restrictions apply. In this chapter, we'll look at reading out RSS feeds and saving RSS feeds to a publicly accessible file on your web server.

Next, we'll talk about the **Microsoft Windows Azure Platform**. More specifically, we'll talk about how we can get our Silverlight application to talk to services that are hosted in the cloud, how we can store data to and read data from the cloud, and even how we can host our Silverlight application in the cloud.

Finally, we'll finish this chapter by looking at **socket communication**. This type of communication is rare and chances are you'll never have to use it. However, if your application needs the fastest possible access to data, sockets may provide the answer.

Connecting and reading from a standardized service

If we need data inside a Silverlight application, chances are that this data resides in a database or another data store on the server. Silverlight is a client-side technology, so when we need to connect to data sources, we need to rely on services. Silverlight has a broad spectrum of services to which it can connect.

In this recipe, we'll look at the concepts of connecting with services, which are usually very similar for all types of services Silverlight can connect with. We'll start by creating an ASMX webservice—in other words, a regular web service. We'll then connect to this service from the Silverlight application and invoke and read its response after connecting to it.

Getting ready

In this recipe we'll build the application from scratch. However, the completed code for this recipe can be found in the `Chapter06/SilverlightJackpot_Read_Completed` folder in the code bundle that is available on the Packt website.

How to do it...

We'll start to explore the usage of services with Silverlight using the following scenario. Imagine we are building a small game application in which a unique code belonging to a user needs to be checked to find out whether or not it is a winning code for some online lottery. The collection of winning codes is present on the server, perhaps in a database or an XML file. We'll create and invoke a service that will allow us to validate the user's code with the collection on the server. The following are the steps we need to follow:

1. We'll build this application from scratch. Our first step is creating a new Silverlight application called **SilverlightJackpot**. As always, let Visual Studio create a hosting website for the Silverlight client by selecting the **Host the Silverlight application in a new Web site** checkbox in the **New Silverlight Application** dialog box. This will ensure that we have a website created for us in which we can create the service as well.

2. We need to start by creating a service. For the sake of simplicity, we'll create a basic ASMX web service. To do so, right-click on the project node in the `SilverlightJackpot.Web` project and select **Add | New Item...** in the menu. In the **Add New Item** dialog, select the **Web Service** item. We'll call the new service **JackpotService**. Visual Studio creates an ASMX file (`JackpotService.asmx`) and a code-behind file (`JackpotService.asmx.cs`).

3. To keep things simple, we'll mock the data retrieval by hardcoding the winning numbers. We'll do so by creating a new class called `CodesRepository.cs` in the web project. This class returns a list of winning codes. In real-world scenarios, this code would go out to a database and get the list of winning codes from there. The code in this class is very easy. The following is the code for this class:

```
public class CodesRepository
{
    private List<string> winningCodes;
    public CodesRepository()
    {
        FillWinningCodes();
    }
    private void FillWinningCodes()
    {
        if (winningCodes == null)
        {
            winningCodes = new List<string>();
```

```
          winningCodes.Add("12345abc");
          winningCodes.Add("azertyse");
          winningCodes.Add("abcdefgh");
          winningCodes.Add("helloall");
          winningCodes.Add("ohnice11");
          winningCodes.Add("yesigot1");
          winningCodes.Add("superwin");
        }
    }
    public List<string> WinningCodes
    {
      get
      {
        return winningCodes;
      }
    }
}
```

4. At this point, we need only one method in our service. This method should accept the
    code sent from the Silverlight application, check it with the list of winning codes and
    return whether or not the user has a lucky day. Only the methods that are marked with
    the `WebMethod` attribute are made available over the service. The following is the code
    for our service:

```
[WebService(Namespace = "http://tempuri.org/")]
[WebServiceBinding(ConformsTo = WsiProfiles.BasicProfile1_1)]
[System.ComponentModel.ToolboxItem(false)]
public class JackpotService : System.Web.Services.WebService
{
  List<string> winningCodes;
  public JackpotService()
  {
    winningCodes = new CodesRepository().WinningCodes;
  }
  [WebMethod]
  public bool IsWinningCode(string code)
  {
    if(winningCodes.Contains(code))
      return true;
    return false;
  }
}
```

5. Build the solution at this point to ensure that our service will compile and can be connected from the client side.

6. Now that the service is ready and waiting to be invoked, let's focus on the Silverlight application. To make the service known to our application, we need to add a reference to it. This is done by right-clicking on the `SilverlightJackpot` project node and selecting the **Add Service Reference...** item.

7. In the dialog that appears, we have the option to enter the address of the service ourselves. However, we can click on the **Discover** button as the service lives in the same solution as the Silverlight application. Visual Studio will search the solution for the available services. If there are no errors, our freshly created service should show up in the list. Select it and rename the **Namespace:** as **JackpotService** as shown in the following screenshot. Visual Studio will now create a proxy class.

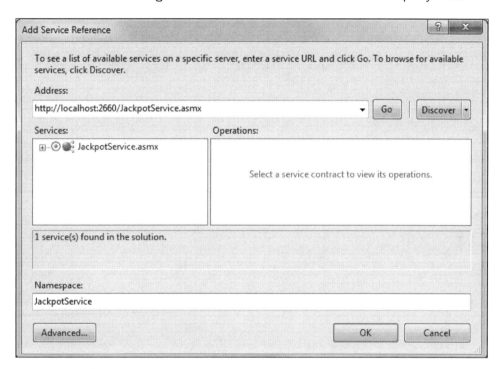

8. The UI for the application is kept quite simple. A screenshot of the UI can be seen a little further ahead. It contains a `TextBox` where the user can enter a code, a `Button` that will invoke a check, and a `TextBlock` that will display the result. This can be seen in the following code:

```
<TextBox x:Name="CodeTextBox"
         Width="100"
         Height="20">
</TextBox>
```

```
<Button x:Name="CheckForWinButton"
        Content="Check if I'm a winner!"
        Click="CheckForWinButton_Click">
</Button>
<TextBlock x:Name="ResultTextBlock">
</TextBlock>
```

9. In the `Click` event handler, we'll create an instance of the proxy class that was created by Visual Studio as shown in the following code:

```
private void CheckForWinButton_Click(object sender,
  RoutedEventArgs e)
{
  JackpotService.JackpotServiceSoapClient client = new
    SilverlightJackpot.JackpotService.JackpotServiceSoapClient();
}
```

10 All service communications in Silverlight happen asynchronously. Therefore, we need to provide a callback method that will be invoked when the service returns:

```
client.IsWinningCodeCompleted += new EventHandler
 <SilverlightJackpot.JackpotService.IsWinningCodeCompletedEventArgs>
 (client_IsWinningCodeCompleted);
```

11. To actually invoke the service, we need to call the `IsWinningCodeAsync` method as shown in the following line of code. This method will make the actual call to the service. We pass in the value that the user entered.

```
client.IsWinningCodeAsync(CodeTextBox.Text);
```

12. Finally, in the callback method, we can work with the result of the service via the `Result` property of the `IsWinningCodeCompletedEventArgs` instance. Based on the value, we display another message as shown in the following code:

```
void client_IsWinningCodeCompleted(object sender,
  SilverlightJackpot.JackpotService.
  IsWinningCodeCompletedEventArgs e)
{
  bool result = e.Result;
  if (result)
    ResultTextBlock.Text = "You are a winner! Enter your data
      below and we will contact you!";
  else
    ResultTextBlock.Text = "You lose... Better luck next time!";
}
```

We now have a fully working Silverlight application that uses a service for its data needs. The following screenshot shows the result on entering a valid code:

How it works...

As it stands, the current version of Silverlight does not have support for using a local database. Silverlight thus needs to rely on external services for getting external data. Even if we had local database support, we would still need to use services in many scenarios. The sample used in this recipe is a good example of data that would need to reside on a secure location (meaning, on the server). In any case, we should never store the winning codes in a local database that would be downloaded to the client side.

Silverlight has the necessary plumbing on board to connect with the most common types of services. Services such as ASMX, WCF, REST, RSS and so on don't pose a problem for Silverlight. While the implementation of connecting with different types of services differs, the concepts are similar.

In this recipe, we used a plain old web service. Only the methods that are attributed with the `WebMethodAttribute` are made available over the service. This means that even if we create a public method on the service, it won't be available to clients if it's not marked as a `WebMethod`. In this case, we only create a single method called `IsWinningCode`, which retrieves a list of winning codes from a class called `CodesRepository`. In real-world applications, this data could be read from a database or an XML file. Thus, this service is the entry point to the data.

For Silverlight to work with the service, we need to add a reference to it. When doing so, Visual Studio will create a proxy class. Visual Studio can do this for us because the service exposes a Web Service Description Language (WSDL) file. This file contains an overview of the methods supported by the service. A proxy can be considered as being a copy of the server-side service class, but without the implementations. Instead, each copied method contains a call to the actual service method. The proxy creation process carried out by Visual Studio is the same as adding a service reference in a regular .NET application.

However, invoking the service is somewhat different. All communication with services in Silverlight is carried out asynchronously. If this wasn't the case, Silverlight would have had to wait for the service to return its result. In the meantime, the UI thread would be blocked and no interaction with the rest of the application would be possible.

To support the asynchronous service call inside the proxy, the `IsWinningCodeAsync` method as well as the `IsWinningCodeCompleted` event is generated. The `IsWinningCodeAsync` method is used to make the actual call to the service. To get access to the results of a service call, we need to define a callback method. This is where the `IsWinningCodeCompleted` event comes in. Using this event, we define which method should be called when the service returns (in our case, the `client_IsWinningCodeCompleted` method). Inside this method, we have access to the results through the `Result` parameter, which is always of the same type as the return type of the service method.

See also

Apart from reading data, we also have to persist data. In the next recipe, *Persisting data using a standardized service*, we'll do exactly that.

Persisting data using a standardized service

In the previous recipe, we connected with the service and read out the result of the service call. However, we can also send data back to the service as a type known by the service. If a type is used as the type for a parameter or as the return type for a service method, that type will be exposed by the service as well. Through the proxy generation, we have access to this type inside the Silverlight application as well.

In this recipe, we'll add another method to the web service that uses a custom type as the type for its parameter.

Getting ready

This recipe builds on the code from the previous recipe. If you want to follow along with this recipe, you can either continue using your code or use the provided starter solution located in the `Chapter06/SilverlightJackpot_Persist_Starter` folder in in the code bundle that is available on the Packt site. The finished solution for this recipe can be found in the `Chapter06/SilverlightJackpot_Persist_Completed` folder.

How to do it...

We'll extend the Silverlight Jackpot solution we built in the previous recipe. When the user enters a valid code, a registration form appears that allows the user to enter his or her credentials. We'll extend the service as well so that it accepts this data and stores it accordingly. Let's look at the way this is done in the following steps:

1. We'll start by adding a new class called `Winner` in the web project. This class will be used to store the information about a winner.

```
public class Winner
{
  public string FirstName { get; set; }
  public string LastName { get; set; }
  public string Email { get; set; }
}
```

2. We'll also create another class called `WinnerRepository`. This class would allow us to store all the winners in a static `List<Winner>`. Just as the previous recipe, this data would be stored in a database in real-world scenarios.

```
public static class WinnerRepository
{
  private static List<Winner> winners = new List<Winner>();
  public static void AddWinner(Winner newWinner)
  {
    winners.Add(newWinner);
  }
}
```

3. We can now extend the service (`JackpotService.asmx.cs`) so that it includes a method (again marked as `WebMethod`) that accepts a `Winner` and stores it in the `List<Winner>` of the `WinnerRepository` class. This is shown in the following code:

```
[WebMethod]
public void SaveWinner(Winner winner)
{
  WinnerRepository.AddWinner(winner);
}
```

4. Build the solution to make sure that the service works correctly.

5. To make the new method available in the Silverlight application, we need to right-click on the **JackpotService** node within the Silverlight project in the **Solution Explorer** and select the **Update Service Reference** item. Visual Studio will reconnect to the service and rebuild the proxy. It will also include our extra method.

6. We need to add some XAML code to add the fields to collect the required information. For the complete listing, refer to the `MainPage.xaml` file in the sample code. The following is the most relevant part of the XAML code as it contains the fields in which the user can enter his/her details:

```
<TextBlock x:Name="NameTextBlock"
           Text="Name: ">
</TextBlock>
<TextBox x:Name="NameTextBox">
</TextBox>
<TextBlock x:Name="FirstNameTextBlock">
</TextBlock>
<TextBox x:Name="FirstNameTextBox">
</TextBox>
<TextBlock x:Name="EmailTextBlock">
</TextBlock>
<TextBox x:Name="EmailTextBox">
</TextBox>
<Button x:Name="SubmitButton"
        Click="SubmitButton_Click">
</Button>
<TextBlock x:Name="SubmissionResultTextBlock">
</TextBlock>
```

7. In the `Click` event handler, we start off by creating an instance of the proxy similar to the previous recipe. We'll define the callback method when the service call completes, as well as make the asynchronous call. However, the latter requires an instance of the `Winner` class, which was originally created on the server. This instance is now sent to the service. In the callback method, we'll update the user interface so that the result of the service call is shown.

```
private void SubmitButton_Click(object sender, RoutedEventArgs e)
{
  JackpotService.JackpotServiceSoapClient client = new
    SilverlightJackpot.JackpotService.JackpotServiceSoapClient();
  client.SaveWinnerCompleted += new
    EventHandler<System.ComponentModel.AsyncCompletedEventArgs>
    (client_SaveWinnerCompleted);
  client.SaveWinnerAsync(
    new JackpotService.Winner()
    {
      FirstName = FirstNameTextBox.Text,
      LastName = NameTextBox.Text,
      Email = EmailTextBox.Text
    }
  );
}
```

```
void client_SaveWinnerCompleted(object sender,
  System.ComponentModel.AsyncCompletedEventArgs e)
{
  if (e.Error == null)
  {
    ResultTextBlock.Text = string.Empty;
    SubmissionResultTextBlock.Text = "Submission successful!";
    UserDetailGrid.Visibility = Visibility.Collapsed;
  }
}
```

After completing these steps, we have successfully allowed the user to send data from the Silverlight application to the service. In turn, the service can store this data in any data store. The following screenshot shows the expanded fields. The application will bundle the entered information into a `Winner` object and send it to the service.

How it works...

Apart from reading data, we also need to send data back to a service. Behind this service façade, code can be used that stores this data into a database or any other data store. An important thing to understand here is that persisting data can be carried out by passing in values for the parameters of a service method.

When the service uses a particular class (such as the `Winner` class in this recipe) as a parameter type, this class gets sent down the wire to the Silverlight application as well. On generating the proxy based on the WSDL file, a local copy of this class will be generated in the Silverlight application as well. This class can be used in the same way as a normal class. In this sample, we have created an instance of this class using the following code:

```
client.SaveWinnerAsync(new JackpotService.Winner()
  { FirstName = FirstNameTextBox.Text, LastName = NameTextBox.Text,
  Email = EmailTextBox.Text });
```

This instance is then serialized in a SOAP message (because of the ASMX service) and sent to the service. On the service side, the instance is rebuilt and used as a parameter for the service method through deserialization.

See also

We have looked at connecting with a service and reading data from it in the first recipe of this chapter, *Connecting and reading from a standardized service*.

Configuring cross-domain calls

In the previous recipes, we have used services that were hosted within the same website (and consequently the same domain) as the Silverlight application itself. However, more often than not, this will not be the case in real-world scenarios. We may need to connect to a third-party service (such as Flickr's API services) from Silverlight. Even if we wrote the service layer ourselves, it may be hosted on a different domain.

Silverlight imposes restrictions on communication with external services. However, Silverlight allows services to opt-in to allow being connected to from a Silverlight application. In this recipe, we'll look at the actions we need to take to make it possible to connect to a self-written service that is hosted in a different domain.

Getting ready

To follow along with this recipe, a starter solution is provided in the `Chapter06/SilverlightCrossDomain_Starter` folder in the code bundle that is available on the Packt site. The finished solution for this recipe can be found in the `Chapter06/SilverlightCrossDomain_Completed` folder.

How to do it...

In this recipe, we'll build a Silverlight application that shows flight information based on the values entered by the user. However, this information is located in a service hosted by the airline companies, which means it runs externally and on a different domain than our Silverlight application. In the following steps, we'll first create the application and see what we need to do to make it work. In other words, we'll see what we need to change so that Silverlight can access externally hosted services:

1. We'll start this recipe from scratch, so begin by creating a new Silverlight application called **SilverlightCrossDomain**.

2. In this solution, add a new **ASP.NET Web Application** and name it as **FlightInformation**. You can do this by right-clicking on the solution in the **Solution Explorer** and selecting **Add | New Project...**. In the dialog that appears, select **ASP. NET Web Application** under the **Visual C# | Web** node.

3. We'll create a WCF service in this web application. Add a new **WCF service** called **FlightInformationService.svc**. Visual Studio will create the `FlightInformationService.svc` file, the `IFlightInformationService.cs` interface, and the concrete implementation—`FlightInformationService.svc. cs`. (Note that we'll be using more WCF services in Chapter 7.)

4. To make the service accessible from Silverlight, we need to change the binding type from `wsHttpBinding` to `basicHttpBinding` in the `web.config` of the project. The change we need to make is shown in the following code:

```
<endpoint address=""
          binding="basicHttpBinding"
          contract="FlightInformation.IFlightInformationService">
  <identity>
    <dns value="localhost" />
  </identity>
</endpoint>
```

5. Let's now define the contract of the service in the `IFlightInformationService` interface. We'll keep it simple by making it possible for the service to return only a list of `Flight` instances.

```
[ServiceContract]
public interface IFlightInformationService
{
  [OperationContract]
  List<Flight> GetFlights(string fromAirport, string toAirport,
    DateTime date);
}
```

6. The `Flight` class is not yet defined, so we should go ahead and create this class as shown in the following code:

```
[DataContract]
public class Flight
{
  [DataMember]
  public string Airway { get; set; }
  [DataMember]
  public DateTime DepartureTime { get; set; }
  [DataMember]
  public DateTime ArrivalTime { get; set; }
  [DataMember]
  public double Price { get; set; }
}
```

7. We can now add the implementation method for the service in the `FlightInformationService` class. For now, we'll create a hardcoded list of `Flight` instances. In real-world scenarios, this data would come from a real data store such as a database. The following is the code for the service:

```
public class FlightInformationService : IFlightInformationService
{
  public List<Flight> GetFlights(string fromAirport, string
    toAirport, DateTime date)
  {
    //some data access code here...
    return new List<Flight>()
    {
      new Flight()
      {
        Airway = "Silverlight Airways",
        DepartureTime = DateTime.Now,
        ArrivalTime = DateTime.Now.AddHours(3),
        Price=300
      },
      new Flight()
      {
        Airway = "Packt Airways",
        DepartureTime = DateTime.Now.AddHours(5),
        ArrivalTime = DateTime.Now.AddHours(10),
        Price=1000
      },
```

```
      new Flight()
      {
        Airway = "New Airways",
        DepartureTime = DateTime.Now,
        ArrivalTime = DateTime.Now.AddHours(9),
        Price=1200
      },
      new Flight()
      {
        Airway = "Silverlight Airways",
        DepartureTime = DateTime.Now.AddHours(3),
        ArrivalTime = DateTime.Now.AddHours(5),
        Price=200
      }
    };
  }
}
```

8. Build the solution at this point.

9. Now that the external service is ready, we can use it from our Silverlight application. Or can we? Let's try and see how it goes! Add a service reference in the Silverlight application by right-clicking on the Silverlight project in the **Solution Explorer** and selecting **Add Service Reference....** In the dialog, search for the `FlightInformationService` using the **Discover** button. Once it's located, set `FlightInformationService` as the namespace.

10. In the Silverlight application, we create a basic UI (shown in the screenshot a bit later in this recipe). The most important element of the UI is a `ListBox` control, which we'll use to bind the flight information. The UI also contains a `Button` that will trigger a request to the service. Refer to the sample code for the complete listing.

11. In the `Click` event of the `Button`, we perform an asynchronous call to the service. This is shown in the following code:

```
private void SearchButton_Click(object sender, RoutedEventArgs e)
{
  FlightInformationService.FlightInformationServiceClient proxy =
    new SilverlightCrossDomain.FlightInformationService.
    FlightInformationServiceClient();
  proxy.GetFlightsCompleted += new
    EventHandler<SilverlightCrossDomain.
    FlightInformationService.GetFlightsCompletedEventArgs>
    (proxy_GetFlightsCompleted);
  proxy.GetFlightsAsync("Brussels", "New York",
    DateTime.Now.Date);
}
```

12. In the `proxy_GetFlightsCompleted` event handler, we can read the results from the `e.Result` property and bind them to the `ListBox` as shown in the following code:

```
void proxy_GetFlightsCompleted(object sender,
  SilverlightCrossDomain.FlightInformationService.
  GetFlightsCompletedEventArgs e)
{
  FlightListBox.ItemsSource = e.Result;
}
```

13. On running this code now, we'll get an exception telling us that we're most likely trying to do a cross-domain service call. The exception is of the `CommunicationException` type.

14. To solve this, we need to add a file called `clientaccesspolicy.xml` to our web project (the project where the service resides). Silverlight will check for the existence of this file in the root of the service domain when performing a cross-domain call. The content of this file is shown in the following code:

```
<?xml version="1.0" encoding="utf-8"?>
<access-policy>
  <cross-domain-access>
    <policy>
      <allow-from http-request-headers="*">
        <domain uri="*"/>
      </allow-from>
      <grant-to>
        <resource path="/" include-subpaths="true"/>
      </grant-to>
    </policy>
  </cross-domain-access>
</access-policy>
```

When trying to run the code again, Silverlight will make the call to the service and the results are displayed as shown in the following screenshot:

Find your flight with Silverlight

From: New York

To: London

Search Flights

Silverlight Airways Price: $900.00
Departure Arrival
23:51 6:51

Packt Airways Price: $1,000.00
Departure Arrival
4:51 10:51

New Airways Price: $1,200.00
Departure Arrival
23:51 5:51

Silverlight Airways Price: $1,200.00
Departure Arrival
5:51 11:51

How it works...

When talking to services that are not hosted in the same domain as the Silverlight application, Silverlight is quite restrictive. By default, it does not allow so-called cross-domain calls. This is purely for security reasons. Let's look at what would happen if Silverlight would allow making cross-domain calls.

Let's assume that a website hosted on `SomeFriendlySite.com` requires the user to log in. The credentials are stored on the user's PC, so that on the next visit they wouldn't need to log in again. This site also exposes a service that contains secret information about the user, which is only accessible when logged in to the site.

An attacker could create a Silverlight application that would try to retrieve this secret information and host this application on `SomeFakeSite.com`. Unaware of any danger, the user accesses the Silverlight application on `SomeFakeSite.com` and thereby installs the hacker's Silverlight application on his machine. This application can now try to make a request to the `SomeFriendlySite.com` service using the stored credentials and can send the secret information to `BadAttackerSite.com`. Worst of all, the user would not even know of all this happening as it would take place behind the scenes. This type of attack from Silverlight is comparable to a cross-site scripting attack, in which the same technique is used. To make it impossible for these kinds of attacks to occur, Silverlight does not make a request to an external service; that is, unless this service explicitly allows us to do so (usually because it does not expose any sensitive data).

When making a call to such an external service, Silverlight will first check the existence of a file called `clientaccesspolicy.xml`. If this file exists, it will be analyzed by Silverlight. If the file allows all domains to call the service (`domain uri="*"`), or if the domain in which the Silverlight application is running is in the specified list, Silverlight will make the service call. The following listing shows a `clientaccesspolicy.xml` file, which allows only some domains to call it:

```
<?xml version="1.0" encoding="utf-8"?>
<access-policy>
  <cross-domain-access>
    <policy>
      <allow-from http-request-headers="*">
        <domain uri="http://www.snowball.be"/>
        <domain uri="http://api.snowball.be"/>
        <domain uri="http://www.codeflakes.com"/>
      </allow-from>
      <grant-to>
        <resource path="/" include-subpaths="true"/>
      </grant-to>
    </policy>
  </cross-domain-access>
</access-policy>
```

The approach that Silverlight uses here is similar to what Flash does. Flash also does not allow cross-domain calls. When making a request to an external service, it will check for the existence of a file called `crossdomain.xml`. The following is a sample `crossdomain.xml` file:

```
<?xml version="1.0" encoding="utf-8"?>
<cross-domain-policy>
  <allow-access-from domain="*" />
</cross-domain-policy>
```

Silverlight can work with both `clientaccesspolicy.xml` as well as `crossdomain.xml`. When calling a service, Silverlight will first check if `clientaccesspolicy.xml` exists at the root of the domain. If it does not, it will check if `crossdomain.xml` is located at the root. If neither of the files is present, the request is blocked. The following screenshot shows that Silverlight searched for `clientaccesspolicy.xml` before allowing the call to the service.

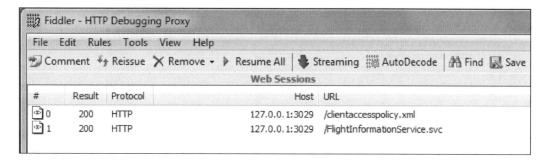

Of course, the need for one of these two files is bad news when we are creating mashups. They are often composed of data coming from different services. However, the good news is that several services (such as Flickr) expose a file that allows cross-domain calls. That said, some services do not, while others are restrictive (such as Twitter). Nothing is lost in this case, but we are required to do some additional work. We need to create an extra service layer in the same domain as the one in which the Silverlight application is hosted. These services can connect with every service (as this is not a cross-domain call from a client). Thus, when calling the external service, we would actually call the local service from Silverlight, which would in turn call the external service. The local service acts as a pass-through for data. Note that while this is a good solution, it will put extra load on the server as every service call will pass by that server. In Chapter 8, the *Talking to Twitter* recipe looks at how to do this using the Twitter API.

Working cross-domain from a trusted Silverlight application

In the previous recipe, we looked at the restrictions enforced by the Silverlight runtime when accessing services that do not live in the same domain as the Silverlight application. These are called cross-domain restrictions. To access a service that lives in another domain, a cross-domain policy file should be in place. If not, the service won't be accessed.

Silverlight 4 brings an exception to this rule. In this version, the notion of so-called trusted applications is added. A trusted application or an application with elevated permissions is similar to an out-of-browser application. However, it gets more permissions on the system. One of these permissions is accessing services in a cross-domain manner without requiring a cross-domain file to be in place.

In this recipe, we'll make cross-domain calls from a trusted Silverlight application.

Getting ready

For this recipe, you can use any of the other Silverlight applications. In the following steps, we use the starter solution for this recipe that can be found in the `Chapter06/Silverlight_TrustedCrossDomain_Starter` folder in the code bundle that is available on the Packt site. The completed solution can be found in the `Chapter06/Silverlight_TrustedCrossDomain_Completed` folder.

How to do it...

To allow a Silverlight application to make cross-domain calls without having a cross-domain file in place, the application should run as an out-of-browser application having elevated permissions. The following are the steps we need to perform to get this working:

1. Open a Silverlight project (starter solution or your own project) as outlined in the *Getting ready* section of this recipe.

2. Right-click on the **SilverlightCrossDomain** project and select the **Properties** item to open the **Project Properties** window.

3. In this window, select the **Enable running application out of the browser** option. This will allow us to install the application locally so that it can run as a standalone application and will not require a browser to be opened.

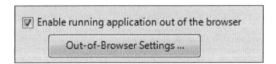

4. Running without a browser is not enough; the application should run with elevated permissions. To enable this, click on the **Out-of-Browser Settings...** button as shown in the previous screenshot and mark the **Require elevated trust when running outside the browser** option in the dialog box that appears. This is shown in the following screenshot:

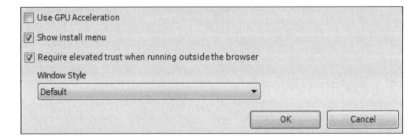

5. In the `FlightInformation` project, we don't need the `clientaccesspolicy.xml` anymore. It can be deleted from the project.

6. You can now run the application. Before interacting with it, right-click on the interface and choose the second option—**Install SilverlightCrossDomain Application onto this computer**. As shown in the following screenshot, Silverlight will display a prompt warning that the application requires elevated permissions and thus has access to system resources. Click on the **Install** button to finish installing the application on the local machine.

Our application now runs as a trusted application and can access the service located on another domain without cross-domain restrictions preventing us from accessing this service. The running application is shown in the following screenshot:

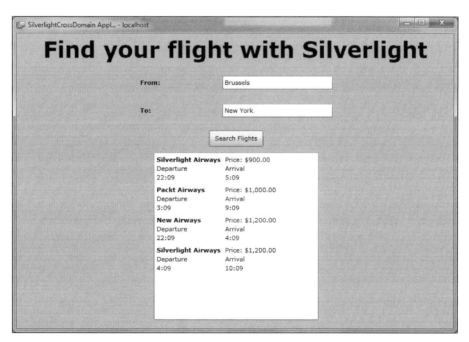

How it works...

The default behavior of Silverlight is the same in both Silverlight 3 as well as Silverlight 4 when accessing services that are hosted on a domain different from the one the Silverlight application itself is hosted on. As explained in depth in the previous recipe, Silverlight will check for the existence of a cross-domain policy file.

Silverlight 4 does add something new—a variant of the out-of-browser application that runs with elevated permissions. This so-called trusted application has permissions that regular in-browser or regular out-of-browser Silverlight applications don't have. It can access the local file system, perform COM interop (interoperability with Word, Excel, and so on), and also perform cross-domain service access without checking for the policy file.

See also

In the previous recipe, we looked at the default cross-domain behavior, where Silverlight restricts the access to services that are not hosted in the same domain. In the *Talking to Twitter from a non-trusted application* recipe in Chapter 8, we apply the concepts learned in this recipe by communicating with Twitter.

Reading XML using HttpWebRequest

The services we used in the first two recipes of this chapter were self-describing services. By this we mean that the service itself exposes information about its methods and data types by means of a WSDL file.

However, often we might need to access data that is not exposed by such a service. For example, we may need to read out XML data. This data could be available as a physical file on the server. It could perhaps be dumped by a process on a specific location. Alternatively, while sending a request to a specific URL, some services such as REST services return XML data. Communicating with REST services is the topic of Chapter 8.

Whether the XML comes from a REST service or lives in a file on the server, reading out XML is done using the `WebClient` class most of the time. We'll use this class extensively in Chapter 8. However, if we need a fine-grained control over the call, we should use the `HttpWebRequest` class. Everything we can do with the `WebClient` class can also be done using the `HttpWebRequest` class, but not vice-versa.

In this recipe, we'll look at how we can use the `HttpWebRequest` class to read out the XML data returned by a handler file.

Getting ready

If you want to follow along with this recipe, you can use the starter solution located in the `Chapter06/SilverlightHttpWebRequest_Starter` folder in the code bundle that is available on the Packt site. The completed solution for this recipe can be found in the `Chapter06/SilverlightHttpWebRequest_Completed` folder.

How to do it...

To find out how to work using the `HttpWebRequest` class, we'll develop a handler that generates an XML string containing news items. Our Silverlight client will create an `HttpWebRequest` instance to request news items newer than a specified date from the handler and receive a response, being the XML literal. We can use such a literal in a data binding scenario by parsing it using LINQ to XML. The following are the steps we need to execute to get the `HttpWebRequest` class working:

1. Open the starter solution as outlined in the *Getting Ready* section of this recipe. In the web project, add a new **Generic Handler** in the **Add new item** dialog named **NewsHandler.ashx**. A handler can be recognized by its .ASHX file extension and is comparable to an ASP.NET webform as both implement the `IHttpHandler` interface and act like an endpoint. The `IHttpHandler` interface defines one method (`ProcessRequest`) and one Boolean property (`IsReusable`). The `ProcessRequest` method will be executed when sending a request to the handler.

2. Before we add the code to the handler, let's create a class named `NewsRepository` that represents a data access layer containing some hardcoded data (which is news items here). This class is located in the `NewsRepository.cs` file in the web project and can be found in the samples. The most relevant part is shown in the following code. It contains the `GetNewsAsXml` method, which accepts the start date parameter. The method will carry out a LINQ query to retrieve the news items and return them in an XML format using the `XElement` class (part of LINQ To XML). The rest of the code for this class can be found in the completed solution of the code bundle.

```
public string GetNewsAsXml(DateTime startDate)
{
  XElement element = new XElement("news");
  var result = from n in CreateNews()
               where n.DatePosted > startDate
               select n;
  foreach (var newsItem in result.ToList())
  {
    element.Add(new XElement("newsitem",
      new XElement("newsitemid", newsItem.NewsItemId),
      new XElement("title", newsItem.Title),
      new XElement("content", newsItem.Content),
      new XElement("dateposted", newsItem.DatePosted),
```

```
         new XElement("image", newsItem.Image)
         ));
    }
    return element.ToString();
}
```

For compiling this code, a reference has to be made to the
`System.Xml.Linq` assembly.

3. Let's now look back at the handler. In the `ProcessRequest` method, we'll call
   the previous method, which required a parameter of DateTime type. We can get
   access to objects such as `Server` and `Request` using the context parameter of
   the `ProcessRequest` method. In this case, we'll use it to get the value sent from
   the client. In the following steps, we'll write the code that passes a `DateTime` object.
   Finally, we'll use the same `Context` instance to send the result back to the caller
   in an XML format. All this can be achieved using the following code:

```
public void ProcessRequest(HttpContext context)
{
    string news;
    using (System.IO.StreamReader reader = new
        System.IO.StreamReader(context.Request.InputStream))
    {
        string input = reader.ReadToEnd();
        DateTime startDate = DateTime.Parse(input);
        news = new NewsRepository().GetNewsAsXml(startDate);
    }
    context.Response.ContentType = "text/xml";
    context.Response.Write(news);
}
```

4. That's all for the server side! The next stop is the client side. The UI for the
   application is quite simple. The code can be found in the `MainPage.xaml` file
   of the code bundle. It mainly contains a `Button` that will load the news items into a
   `ListBox` when clicked. The `ListBox` has a `DataTemplate` applied to it which uses
   data binding features to tie the items to the template.

5. When clicking on the button, we need to send a request to the URI of the
   handler and later work with the response. We can use the `Create` method of
   the `HttpWebRequest` class to create the request. This method accepts a URI as
   a parameter and returns a `WebRequest` instance. We can use this instance to call
   the service. The following code creates a `WebRequest` using the `Create` method
   of the `HttpWebRequest` class:

```
private void LoadButton_Click(object sender, RoutedEventArgs e)
{
    WebRequest request = HttpWebRequest.Create(new
```

```
    Uri("http://localhost:61639/NewsHandler.ashx",
    UriKind.Absolute));
}
```

6. We need a stream to send data to a service (being the start date). Getting this stream is carried out asynchronously using the `BeginGetRequestStream` method of the request. We also need to specify that we'll be sending data, so we need to set the `Method` to POST. This is shown in the following code:

```
request.ContentType = "text/xml";
request.Method = "POST";
request.BeginGetRequestStream(RequestCallback, request);
```

7. The callback method implements the `AsyncCallback` delegate. It has an `IAsyncResult` parameter. The `AsyncState` property of the `IAsyncResult` instance is cast to `HttpWebRequest`. Using this instance, we retrieve the `EndGetRequestStream` method to get the request stream. We use a `StreamWriter` instance to write the current date as shown in the following code:

```
void RequestCallback(IAsyncResult result)
{
    HttpWebRequest request = result.AsyncState as HttpWebRequest;
    Stream stream = request.EndGetRequestStream(result);
    using (StreamWriter writer = new StreamWriter(stream))
    {
        writer.Write(new DateTime(2009, 12, 1));
    }
}
```

8. We can now use the request to invoke the service and get its result asynchronously. This is done using the `BeginGetResponse` method. The invocation is carried out using the following line of code, which again specifies a callback method—`ResponseCallback`:

```
request.BeginGetResponse(ResponseCallback, request);
```

9. The `ResponseCallback` method is similar to the `RequestCallback`. It has the same `IAsyncResult` parameter as the `RequestCallback` had. We get access to the `HttpWebRequest` object again using the `AsyncState` property of the `IAsyncResult`. On this instance, we call the `EndGetResponse` to get an `HttpWebResponse` instance. This is shown in the following code:

```
void ResponseCallback(IAsyncResult result)
{
    HttpWebRequest request = result.AsyncState as HttpWebRequest;
    HttpWebResponse response = request.EndGetResponse(result) as
        HttpWebResponse;
}
```

10. We invoke the `GetResponseStream` method on the `HttpWebResponse` instance. This call returns a `Stream` that can be used in combination with a `StreamReader` to read out the response from the service. This is shown in the following lines of code:

```
using(StreamReader reader = new
   StreamReader(response.GetResponseStream()))
{
   string responseMessage = reader.ReadToEnd();
}
```

11. This string now contains the XML data as returned from the service. We can parse it and generate instances of a custom class called `NewsItem` using LINQ to XML. This is shown in the following code:

```
public class NewsItem
{
   public int NewsItemId { get; set; }
   public string Title { get; set; }
   public string Content { get; set; }
   public DateTime DatePosted { get; set; }
   public string NewsImage { get; set; }
}
```

12. The parsing of the XML code generates a `List<NewsItem>`. The code uses the `XDocument` and the `XElement` classes that are located in the `System.Xml.Linq` namespace. This namespace lives in the corresponding `System.Xml.Linq` assembly to which we need to create a reference. The parsing process is shown in the following lines of code:

```
XDocument document = XDocument.Parse(responseMessage);
var query = from n in document.Descendants("newsitem")
               select n;
List<NewsItem> newsItems = new List<NewsItem>();
foreach (XElement element in query)
{
   NewsItem newsItem = new NewsItem();
   newsItem.NewsItemId = int.Parse
      (element.Descendants("newsitemid").First().Value);
   newsItem.Title = element.Descendants("title").First().Value;
   newsItem.Content = element.Descendants("content").First().Value;
   newsItem.DatePosted = DateTime.Parse
      (element.Descendants("dateposted").First().Value);
   newsItem.NewsImage= element.Descendants("image").First().Value;
   newsItems.Add(newsItem);
}
```

13. Now that we have a collection of items, we want to display them in a `ListBox`. However, the asynchronous service call operates in the background thread and thus cannot directly access the controls in the UI that live in the UI thread. However, we can use the `Dispatcher` class to invoke the code in the UI thread from the background thread as shown in the following line of code:

```
this.Dispatcher.BeginInvoke(() => NewsListBox.ItemsSource =
    newsItems);
```

At this point, we have successfully communicated with a service using the `HttpWebRequest` class.

How it works...

Silverlight can connect with several types of services. They can be categorized into two types—services that describe themselves and services that do not describe themselves. The latter can be used from Silverlight by using either the `WebClient` class or the `HttpWebRequest` class. Most of the time, the more easy-to-use `WebClient` class will suffice. It contains all that is needed to carry out communication with most services. However, if more control is needed over the call to the service, the `HttpWebRequest` class can be used. It has more options than the `WebClient` class. In spite of that, the `WebClient` class does use the `HttpWebRequest` class under the hood. In Chapter 8, we will be using the `WebClient` class where we will discuss communication with REST services. However, all those samples can be performed using the `HttpWebRequest` class as well.

All calls carried out using the `HttpWebRequest` class take place asynchronously. Using the `HttpWebRequest` class, we can send data to the service using the request as well as read out data using the response.

The request

A `WebRequest` instance is created using the `Create` method of the `HttpWebRequest` class. This method accepts one parameter, which is the URI of the service. On the created `WebRequest` instance, we can specify the HTTP verb. Silverlight's `HttpWebRequest` class supports the `GET` and the `POST` methods. If we want to send data to the service (for example a search term), we need to get the request stream. This can be done using the `BeginGetRequestStream` method of the `HttpWebRequest` class, which starts an asynchronous call to get the request. This method requires two parameters—a callback method and a state. The callback method is executed when the request stream is ready. For the state, we pass in the request itself so that we have access to it in the callback.

In the callback method, we can get the request by casting the `AsyncResult` property of the `IAsyncState` interface back into the `HttpWebRequest` class. On this instance, we can call the `EndGetRequestStream` method that gives us access to the request stream. We can write to this stream using a `StreamWriter`.

The response

The request instance can be used to invoke a service and get back its result. To carry out this invocation, we use the `BeginGetResponse` method on the request, which is, quite logically, also asynchronous. In the specified callback, we can use the `EndGetResponse` method, which will give us an `HttpWebResponse` instance. On this instance, we can use the `GetResponseStream` method, which returns a stream. This stream can then be used to read the textual response from the server.

Threading headaches

Calls using the `HttpWebRequest` class take place on the background thread. The code that runs in this thread has no access to the UI and its controls. This means that we can't update the UI from the callback method. Luckily, we can use the `Dispatcher` class. Using the `Dispatcher`, we can cross threads quite easily by means of the `BeginInvoke` method. The `Dispatcher.BeginInvoke` method allows us to call from the background thread code that will be executed on the UI thread.

See also

In Chapter 8, we'll use the `WebClient` class intensively while working with REST services.

Reading out an RSS feed

Most modern, regularly updated websites (such as news sites, blogs, and so on) allow the users of these sites to subscribe to a **Really Simple Syndication** (**RSS**) feed (which is in fact an XML file that follows a certain schema), which will typically contain excerpts of site updates. A lot of people use specialized RSS readers for this (such as Google Reader) or integrate the RSS feeds into applications that they use on a day-to-day basis (such as Outlook).

Silverlight includes a few classes to make it very easy to write your own RSS reader. In this recipe, we'll learn how to achieve this.

Getting ready

We'll need to start from a Silverlight solution that contains a few sample feeds and some code to show the feeds you're going to read on screen. You can find a starter solution in the `Chapter06\Reading_RSS_Starter` folder in the code bundle that is available on the Packt site. The completed solution can be found in the `Chapter06\Reading_RSS_Completed` folder.

How to do it...

We're going to add code to our Silverlight project to read out and show an RSS feed. To achieve this, carry out the following steps:

1. Open `MainPage.xaml` and have a look at the code. This file contains the code for a `ListBox` with data binding that will be used to visualize the RSS feed. Also, familiarize yourself with the project layout. It contains the RSS XML files that will be parsed, which contain the RSS updates.

2. Add a new class to the Silverlight project and name it as `SimpleSyndicationItem.cs`.

3. Add the following code to this new class:

    ```
    public class SimpleSyndicationItem
    {
        public DateTimeOffset Date { get; set; }
        public string Title { get; set; }
        public Uri Link { get; set; }
        public SimpleSyndicationItem(DateTimeOffset Date, string Title,
          Uri Link)
        {
            this.Date = Date;
            this.Title = Title;
            this.Link = Link;
        }
    }
    ```

4. Open `MainPage.xaml.cs` and add a new property to it, which will be used to store a collection of `SimpleSyndicationItem`. This is shown in the following line of code:

    ```
    public ObservableCollection<SimpleSyndicationItem>
      lstSimpleItems { get; set; }
    ```

5. Locate the `FetchItems()` method and add the following code to the method body:

    ```
    XmlReader reader = XmlReader.Create("rssicecream.xml");
    SyndicationFeed feed = new SyndicationFeed();
    feed = SyndicationFeed.Load(reader);
    lstSimpleItems = new
      ObservableCollection<SimpleSyndicationItem>();
    foreach (var item in feed.Items)
    {
        lstSimpleItems.Add(new SimpleSyndicationItem(item.PublishDate,
          item.Title.Text, item.Links[0].Uri));
    }
    lstbxRSS.ItemsSource = lstSimpleItems;
    ```

6. You can now build and run the application. You'll notice a `ListBox` having all the updates from our RSS file. This can be seen in the following screenshot:

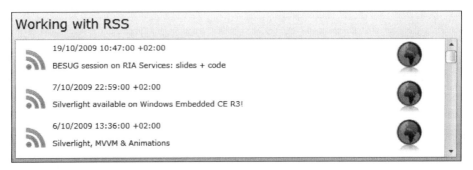

How it works...

Silverlight contains classes that make it very easy to work with RSS feeds. These classes are contained in the `System.ServiceModel.Syndication` assembly. The Silverlight project requires a reference to this assembly.

One of these useful classes is the `SyndicationFeed` class. With this class, you can easily load RSS feeds and work with them. The statement used to do this is `SyndicationFeed.Load`. This statement accepts an `XmlReader`. So we created an `XmlReader` that points to the RSS feed XML we want to parse, and passed this reader to the `SyndicationFeed.Load` method.

Now, our `SyndicationFeed` instance contains all the items from the RSS feed, which are nicely organized. We run through this collection to create `SimpleSyndicationItem` objects (which are simplified objects that contain only the data we want to visualize) and add these items to an `ObservableCollection` of `SimpleSyndicationItem`.

Finally, we set this collection as an `ItemsSource` of our `ListBox`. Our collection is now nicely visualized because of Silverlight's data binding abilities.

There's more...

You can't just read out any RSS feed (XML file). Silverlight doesn't allow you to access any domain you want. The owner of the domain has to allow you to access files/services on it by publishing a `clientaccesspolicy.xml` or a `crossdomain.xml` file in which the owner can describe who has access to what. If this file is missing, Silverlight will not be able to communicate with the requested service.

A way to work around this would be to design an RSS reader that doesn't communicate with RSS feeds directly, but communicates with a service that in turn talks to the RSS feeds. The service, which you'd write yourself, can then be published on your own web server along with a `clientaccesspolicy.xml` or a `crossdomain.xml` file to allow your Silverlight application to access your service , if this service lives in a different domain than the Silverlight application.

RSS versions

There are different versions of RSS available. But luckily, most of these versions are supported by most RSS readers. You can find out more about these different versions at http://en.wikipedia.org/wiki/RSS#Variants.

See also

If you want to learn how to aggregate different RSS feeds into one feed (and publish this feed), you might want to have a look at the next recipe, *Aggregating RSS feeds*.

Aggregating RSS feeds

Most modern, regularly updated websites (such as news sites, blogs, and so on) allow the users of these sites to subscribe to an RSS feed (which is in fact an XML file that follows a certain schema), which will typically contain excerpts of site updates. As we've learned in the previous recipe, we can easily access RSS feeds from Silverlight.

However, sometimes you might want to publish your own RSS feed. In this recipe, we'll build an application that aggregates a few RSS feeds into one new feed, which is then published so that people can subscribe to it.

Getting ready

We're starting from the solution we completed in the previous recipe. If you didn't complete that recipe, you can find a starter solution located in the code bundle that is available on the Packt site. You can find this starter solution in the Chapter06\Aggregating_RSS_Starter folder. The completed solution can be found in the Chapter06\Aggregating_RSS_Completed folder.

How to do it...

We're going to modify the starter solution so that it reads two different RSS files. We'll aggregate them and write the aggregated file to a new XML file. To achieve this, carry out the following steps:

1. Open `MainPage.xaml.cs`, locate the `FetchItems()` method, and modify it as shown in the following code:

```
private void FetchItems()
{
    // read and load an RSS xml, using SyndicationFeed
    XmlReader readerFirst = XmlReader.Create("rssicecream.xml");
    XmlReader readerSecond = XmlReader.Create("rsssnowball.xml");
    SyndicationFeed feedFirst = new SyndicationFeed();
```

```
feedFirst = SyndicationFeed.Load(readerFirst);
SyndicationFeed feedSecond = new SyndicationFeed();
feedSecond = SyndicationFeed.Load(readerSecond);
// transform to simpler objects for this example
// In real life, this should include lots of checks.
// => for simplicity, we assume.
lstSimpleItems = new
  ObservableCollection<SimpleSyndicationItem>();
foreach (var item in feedFirst.Items)
{
  lstSimpleItems.Add(new SimpleSyndicationItem(item.PublishDate,
    item.Title.Text, item.Links[0].Uri));
}
foreach (var item in feedSecond.Items)
{
  lstSimpleItems.Add(new SimpleSyndicationItem(item.PublishDate,
    item.Title.Text, item.Links[0].Uri));
}
lstbxRSS.ItemsSource = lstSimpleItems.OrderByDescending(i =>
  i.Date);
}
```

2. Add a new method that will create a new feed consisting of the aggregated items and write it to an XML file. This is shown in the following code:

```
private void WriteNewFeed()
{
  SyndicationFeed feedNew = new SyndicationFeed();
  List<SyndicationItem> items = new List<SyndicationItem>();
  foreach (var oneItem in lstSimpleItems)
  {
    items.Add(new SyndicationItem(oneItem.Title, "",
      oneItem.Link){ PublishDate = oneItem.Date});
  }
  feedNew.Items = items;
  IsolatedStorageFile isoStore =
    IsolatedStorageFile.GetUserStoreForApplication();
  IsolatedStorageFileStream isoStream = new
    IsolatedStorageFileStream("rss.xml", FileMode.Create,
    isoStore);
  XmlWriter rssWriter = XmlWriter.Create(isoStream);
  Rss20FeedFormatter rssFormatter = new
    Rss20FeedFormatter(feedNew);
  rssFormatter.WriteTo(rssWriter);
  rssWriter.Flush();
  rssWriter.Close();
  isoStream.Close();
}
```

3. Add the following code to the top of `MainPage.xaml.cs`:

```
using System.IO.IsolatedStorage;
using System.IO;
```

4. Modify the constructor by adding the following code at the end of the constructor so that it calls `WriteNewFeed()`:

```
public MainPage()
{
    InitializeComponent();
    FetchItems();
    WriteNewFeed();
}
```

5. You can now build and run your application. Both feeds will be aggregated and the aggregated feed will be written to the Isolated Storage on the client PC.

How it works...

The `System.ServiceModel.Syndication` assembly contains classes so that it can easily work with RSS feeds. One of these useful classes is the `SyndicationFeed` class. With this class, you can easily load RSS feeds and work with them. The statement used to do this is `SyndicationFeed.Load`. This statement accepts an `XmlReader` type. So we create an `XmlReader` instance that points to the RSS feed XML we want to parse and pass this reader to the `SyndicationFeed.Load` method. We do this twice, once for the first file and once for the second one.

Now, we run through both the `SyndicationFeed` instances and create `SimpleSyndicationItem` objects (which are simplified objects that contain only the data we want to visualize), which are then added to an `ObservableCollection` of `SimpleSyndicationItem`. This collection now contains `SimpleSyndicationItem` objects coming from both the feeds we parsed.

We now set this collection (ordered by date) as the `ItemsSource` of our `Listbox`, which results in a nicely visualized list of `SimpleSyndicationItems`.

To write a new feed, we need to first create a new `SyndicationFeed` object and pass a list of `SyndicationItem` instances to it. In the `WriteNewFeed()` method, we need to run through the `ObservableCollection` of `SimpleSyndicationItem` and create a `SyndicationItem` for each `SimpleSyndicationItem`.

The next step is to effectively save this `SyndicationFeed` object to a file. We're saving it to the Isolated Storage on the client PC, so we create a new `IsolatedStorageFileStream` instance. An `XmlWriter` is created for this stream and we use an `Rss20FeedFormatter` object to serialize our new aggregated `SyndicationFeed`. The serialization is executed by calling the `Flush()` method and the aggregated feed is saved.

There's more...

As you might have noticed, this recipe shows you how to write your RSS feed to the Isolated Storage. As your Silverlight application runs on the client, it cannot directly save your RSS feed to, for example, a web server where it is publicly accessible. Luckily, there's an easy way to achieve this. Use a service to save your RSS feed to a web server. To do this, you'd want to pass the RSS (typically as a string) from your Silverlight application to a service method. (The service can be created using any service type such as REST, WCF, a simple ASMX web service, and so on.) This service method can then save your feed to a location on the web server.

See also

If you want to find out more information about reading RSS feeds, you might want to have a look at the previous recipe, *Reading out an RSS feed*.

Talking with services in the Windows Azure cloud

The Microsoft Azure platform that consists of Windows Azure (an operating system as a service), SQL Azure (a fully relational database in the cloud), and .NET Services (consumable web-based services that provide secure connectivity and federated access control for applications) is the talk of the town these days. It allows you to host your applications, services, and so on in the cloud instead of your own servers and automatically offers you scalability and data reliability, so you don't have to worry about these things anymore. Silverlight applications can talk to services in the cloud or can even be hosted as cloud applications themselves.

In this recipe, we'll learn how to achieve this.

Getting ready

To begin this recipe, you'll need to install the Windows Azure SDK & Tools (which requires IIS7). You can find this SDK along with all the pre-requirements at `http://www.microsoft.com/windowsazure/getstarted/#develop`.

In addition to allowing you to develop Windows Azure applications, this SDK also includes a "local cloud" that allows you to test your applications and services before publishing them. In the next recipes, we'll run our applications on this local cloud.

You can find the completed solution in the `Chapter06\CloudService_Completed` folder in the code bundle that is available on the Packt site.

How to do it...

We're going to create a Silverlight application that is hosted in the cloud, which talks to a cloud service. After you've installed the SDK & Tools, start up Visual Studio and carry out the following steps:

1.   Select **File| New | Project...** and create a new **Windows Azure Cloud Service** project. Name this project as **CloudServiceExample** as shown in the following screenshot:

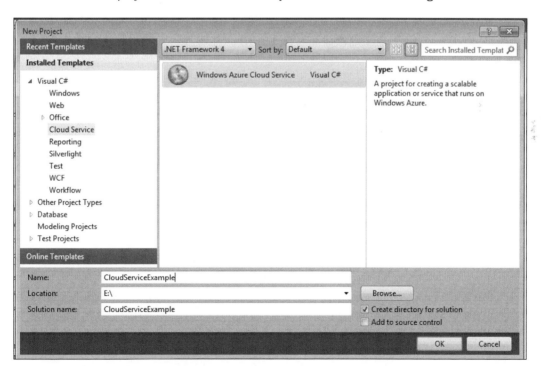

2. As shown in the next screenshot, a popup will appear that will allow you to select an **ASP .NET Web Role** application, a **WCF Service Web Role** application, and a **Worker Role** application. Add one of each of these applications:

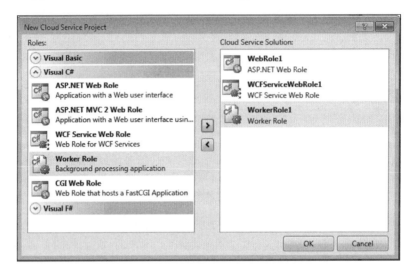

3. A solution is created that contains a `WebRole1` project, a `WCFServiceWebRole1` project, a `WorkerRole1` project, and a project containing the configuration files for our cloud service. A service is created by default in the `WCFServiceWebRole1` project, but we're going to add a new one with a better name. Add a **Silverlight-enabled WCF service** to the `WCFServiceWebRole1` application (which is hosted in the cloud). To achieve this, right-click on the `WCFServiceWebRole1` project, select **Add | New Item...**, select a **Silverlight-enabled WCF Service**, and name it as `MyCloudHostedWCFService`. This can be seen in the following screenshot:

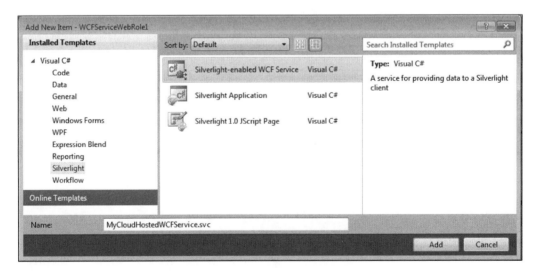

4. Open the `MyCloudHostedWCFService.svc.cs` file, remove the automatically created `DoWork` method, and add the following code:

```
[OperationContract]
public string GetDataFromService()
{
  return DateTime.Now.ToString();
}
```

5. Add a valid `clientaccesspolicy.xml` file as shown in the following code:

```
<?xml version="1.0" encoding="utf-8"?>
<access-policy>
  <cross-domain-access>
    <policy>
      <allow-from http-request-headers="*">
        <domain uri="http://*" />
        <domain uri="https://*" />
      </allow-from>
      <grant-to>
        <resource path="/" include-subpaths="true"/>
      </grant-to>
    </policy>
  </cross-domain-access>
</access-policy>
```

6. Build the application. We've now got a cloud-hosted WCF service. We'll have to add a Silverlight application that will consume this WCF service. Select **File | Add | New Project...**, choose the **Silverlight Application** project template, name your application as **MyCloudHostedSilverlightApplication**, and host it in the `WebRole1` project.

7. Open the `MainPage.xaml` file and add the following code:

```
<Grid x:Name="LayoutRoot">
  <Grid.RowDefinitions>
    <RowDefinition Height="Auto"></RowDefinition>
    <RowDefinition></RowDefinition>
  </Grid.RowDefinitions>
  <TextBlock Height="30"
            Text="Silverlight and the Azure Cloud" />
  <StackPanel Grid.Row="1"
            Orientation="Horizontal">
    <TextBlock Text="Data from cloud service: " ></TextBlock>
    <TextBlock Text="{Binding Result}" ></TextBlock>
  </StackPanel>
</Grid>
```

8. Add a service reference to the Silverlight application referencing `MyCloudHostedWCFService.Svc` and name it as `MyCloudServiceReference`.

9. Replace the constructor of `MainPage.xaml.cs` with the following code:

```
public class Dummy
{
  public string Result { get; set; }
}
public MainPage()
{
  InitializeComponent();
  CallService();
}
private void CallService()
{
  MyCloudServiceReference.MyCloudHostedWCFServiceClient client =
    new MyCloudHostedSilverlightApplication
    .MyCloudServiceReference.MyCloudHostedWCFServiceClient
    (new BasicHttpBinding(), new EndpointAddress
    (string.Format("http://{0}:{1}/MyCloudHostedWCFService.svc",
    HtmlPage.Document.DocumentUri.Host, "8080")));
  client.GetDataFromServiceCompleted += new
    EventHandler<MyCloudServiceReference
    .GetDataFromServiceCompletedEventArgs>
    (client_GetDataFromServiceCompleted);
  client.GetDataFromServiceAsync();
}
void client_GetDataFromServiceCompleted(object sender,
  MyCloudServiceReference.GetDataFromServiceCompletedEventArgs e)
{
  if (e.Error == null)
  {
    Dummy dummy = new Dummy() { Result = e.Result };
    this.DataContext = dummy;
  }
}
```

10. You can now build and run your application. Your Silverlight application will display the status current date and it will be automatically hosted in the cloud, talking to a cloud hosted service.

> Silverlight and the Azure Cloud
>
> Data from cloud service: 31/01/2010 14:58:35

How it works...

When you're working with the Microsoft Azure platform, you're essentially using the cloud infrastructure to host your applications and services using the Windows Azure application platform. In this recipe, we're using Windows Azure (not SQL Azure or .NET Services, which are also a part of the Microsoft Azure platform) which provides a Windows-based environment for running applications and storing data on servers in the Microsoft data centers.

An application typically has multiple instances, each running a copy (all or part) of the application's code. To create an application, we use a Web Role and/or a Worker Role instance (or instances). A Web Role can be implemented using any technology that works with IIS (such as ASP.NET, WCF, Silverlight, and so on). Windows Azure provides built-in load balancing to spread requests across Web Role instances that are a part of the same application. It essentially accepts incoming requests via IIS 7. If you want to view the Web Role as an analogy to the regular, non-cloud hosted solutions, you could compare a Web Role instance to a web server. A nice thing about the cloud is that when the load gets high, you can easily increase the Web Role instances to keep your application running fluidly. In this example, we've added an extra role—WCF Service Role. Due to this, our services run separately from our web application.

On the other hand, the Worker Role cannot directly accept requests from the outside world. It typically gets input via a queue in Windows Azure storage that might have come from a Web Role instance. The Worker Role can send the output to another queue (or to the outside world). Thus, a worker role is essentially a batch process and is typically used by your Web Role for communication.

Project templates for Web Roles, Worker Roles, and others are provided when you install the SDK. This makes the development of the Microsoft Azure Platform look much like building a traditional application.

If we look at our Silverlight application, this is immediately noticeable. We've added a Web Role, a WCF Service Role, and a Worker Role (the Worker Role is used in the next recipe, which builds on the solution you've created in this recipe). They look just like regular projects. However, everything you program in the Web Role is automatically hosted in the cloud.

In step 3, we added a simple WCF service to the WCF Service Role application. This is actually a standard, cloud-hosted web application project type that is used to host WCF services in the cloud. In step 6, we added a Silverlight application to our solution and used the Web Role application to host it in. By doing this, we automatically host our Silverlight application in the cloud.

All the other steps in the recipe are standard Silverlight programming principles. We've added a reference to the WCF service, thus generating proxy classes. Also, we're showing the data the WCF service returns to us on the screen. The only difference is that we're passing in the address of the endpoint manually as we're not actually hosting on the localhost. We're hosting our service on port 8080 (by default) in the cloud.

There's more...

Besides Windows Azure, the Microsoft Azure Platform consists of SQL Azure and Windows Azure AppFabric. These specific technologies aren't used in this book, but more information on them can be found at `http://www.microsoft.com/windowsazure/getstarted`.

What about other cloudservices?

The Windows Azure cloud is just one of the cloud services available to you. When developing in a Microsoft environment, it seems like a logical choice because of the tight integration with Visual Studio. However, both Amazon and Google offer their own cloud service solutions. You can find out more about them at `http://aws.amazon.com/ec2/` and `http://code.google.com/appengine/`.

See also

To find out more information about how to read and persist data from/in the cloud, have a look at the next recipe.

Persisting data to and reading data from the Windows Azure cloud

In the previous recipe, we've learned how to host a service and a Silverlight application in the Windows Azure cloud, and how to talk to that service from our Silverlight application. However, you'll quickly run into other requirements. Most applications need some kind of mechanism to access data from or to persist data to a datastore.

In this recipe, we'll learn how to read data that has been persisted in the cloud and how to persist data to the cloud ourselves.

Getting ready

To begin this recipe, you'll need to install the Windows Azure SDK & Tools. You can find this SDK along with all the requirements at `http://www.microsoft.com/windowsazure/getstarted/#develop`. In addition to allowing you to develop Windows Azure applications, this SDK also includes a "local cloud" that allows you to test your applications and services before publishing them. In this recipe, we'll run our application on this local cloud.

We're starting from the solution we completed in the previous recipe. If you didn't complete that recipe, you can find a starter solution located in the `Chapter06\CloudServicePersistingAndReading_Starter` folder in the code bundle that is available on the Packt site. The completed solution can be found in the `Chapter06\CloudServicePersistingAndReading_Completed` folder.

How to do it...

We're going to persist data to and read data from the cloud using a Table Storage through a WCF Service Role. To achieve this, carry out the following steps:

1. We'll need to make sure that the table storage uses the development environment. To do this, right-click on **WCFServiceWebRole1**, select **Settings**, and add a configuration setting called **DataConnectionString**. For this setting, select the **Type** as **ConnectionString** and enter the **Value** as **UseDevelopmentStorage=true** as shown in the following screenshot:

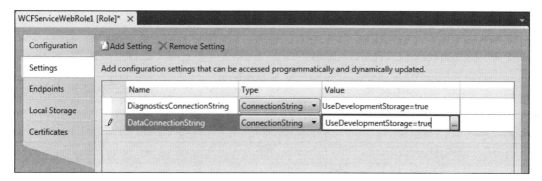

2. Add a reference to `System.Data.Services.Client` in the `WCFServiceWebRole1`.

3. Add a new class called `Person`, and let it inherit `TableServiceEntity` (`Microsoft.WindowsAzure.StorageClient` namespace). It can be implemented using the following code:

```
public class Person : TableServiceEntity
{
  public string Name { get; set; }
  public DateTime DateOfBirth { get; set; }
  public Person()
  {
    PartitionKey = DateOfBirth.ToString();
  }
}
```

4. Add a new class called `SerializablePerson` and implement it as shown in the following code:

```
public class SerializablePerson
{
  public string Name { get; set; }
  public DateTime DateOfBirth { get; set; }
  public SerializablePerson()
```

```
    {}
    public SerializablePerson(string name, DateTime dateofbirth)
    {
      this.Name = name;
      this.DateOfBirth = dateofbirth;
    }
  }
```

5. Add a new class called `PersonServiceContext`, let it inherit `TableServiceContext`, and implement it as shown in the following code:

```
using System;
using System.Collections.Generic;
using System.Linq;
using System.Web;
using Microsoft.WindowsAzure.StorageClient;
using Microsoft.WindowsAzure;
namespace WCFServiceWebRole1
{
  public class PersonServiceContext : TableServiceContext
  {
    public IQueryable<Person> Persons
    {
      get
      {
        return this.CreateQuery<Person>("Persons");
      }
    }
    public PersonServiceContext(string baseAddress,
      StorageCredentials credentials)
      : base(baseAddress, credentials)
    {
    }
    public void AddPerson(string name, DateTime dateofbirth)
    {
      this.AddObject("Persons", new Person() { Name = name,
        DateOfBirth = dateofbirth });
      this.SaveChanges();
    }
  }
}
```

6. Open the `WebRole.cs` file and replace the OnStart method with the following code:

```csharp
public override bool OnStart()
{
    DiagnosticMonitor.Start("DiagnosticsConnectionString");
    RoleEnvironment.Changing += RoleEnvironmentChanging;
    // This code sets up a handler to update CloudStorageAccount
    // instances when their configuration settings
    // change in the service config file
    CloudStorageAccount.SetConfigurationSettingPublisher
        ((configName, configSetter) =>
    {
        // Provide configSetter with initial value
        configSetter(RoleEnvironment.GetConfigurationSettingValue
            (configName));
        RoleEnvironment.Changed += (anotherSender, arg) =>
        {
            if (arg.Changes.OfType<RoleEnvironmentConfiguration
                SettingChange>().Any((change) =>
                (change.ConfigurationSettingName == configName)))
            {
                // The corresponding configuration setting has changed
                if (!configSetter(RoleEnvironment
                    .GetConfigurationSettingValue(configName)))
                {
                    // Role needs to be recycled in order to use
                    // the latest settings.
                    RoleEnvironment.RequestRecycle();
                }
            }
        };
    });
    // It is recommended the data tables should be only created
    // once. It is typically done as a
    // provisioning step and rarely in application code.
    var account = CloudStorageAccount.FromConfigurationSetting
        ("DataConnectionString");
    // dynamically create the tables
    CloudTableClient.CreateTablesFromModel
        (typeof(PersonServiceContext), account.TableEndpoint
        .AbsoluteUri, account.Credentials);
    return base.OnStart();
}
```

7. Open the `MyCloudHostedWCFService.svc.cs` file and add the following methods to it:

```
[OperationContract]
public List<Person> GetPersons()
{
  var account = CloudStorageAccount.FromConfigurationSetting
    ("DataConnectionString");
  var context = new PersonServiceContext(account.TableEndpoint
    .ToString(), account.Credentials);
  return new List<Person>(context.Persons);
}
[OperationContract]
public void AddPerson(string name, DateTime dateofbirth)
{
  var account = CloudStorageAccount.FromConfigurationSetting
    ("DataConnectionString");
  var context = new PersonServiceContext(account.TableEndpoint
    .ToString(), account.Credentials);
  context.AddPerson(name, dateofbirth);
}
```

8. Open the Silverlight application and add the following code to `MainPage.xaml`:

```
<Grid x:Name="LayoutRoot">
  <Grid.RowDefinitions>
    <RowDefinition Height="Auto"></RowDefinition>
    <RowDefinition Height="Auto"></RowDefinition>
    <RowDefinition Height="Auto"></RowDefinition>
    <RowDefinition></RowDefinition>
  </Grid.RowDefinitions>
  <TextBlock Text="Silverlight and the Azure Cloud"
            FontSize="20" />
  <ListBox Grid.Row="1"
          Width="400"
          Height="200"
          HorizontalAlignment="Left">
    <ListBox.ItemTemplate>
      <DataTemplate>
        <StackPanel Orientation="Horizontal">
          <TextBlock Text="{Binding Name}"></TextBlock>
          <TextBlock Text=", "></TextBlock>
          <TextBlock Text="{Binding DateOfBirth}"></TextBlock>
        </StackPanel>
```

```xml
        </DataTemplate>
      </ListBox.ItemTemplate>
    </ListBox>
    <TextBlock Text="Add person"
               FontSize="16"
               Margin="0,10,0,10"
               Grid.Row="2"></TextBlock>
    <StackPanel Orientation="Vertical"
                Grid.Row="3">
      <StackPanel Orientation="Horizontal">
        <TextBlock Width="200"
                   Text="Name: "></TextBlock>
        <TextBox x:Name="txtName"
                 Width="200"></TextBox>
      </StackPanel>
      <StackPanel Orientation="Horizontal">
        <TextBlock Width="200"
                   Text="Date of birth: "></TextBlock>
        <my:DatePicker x:Name="dtpDateOfBirth"
                       Width="200"></my:DatePicker>
      </StackPanel>
      <Button x:Name="btnAdd"
              Content="Add person"
              Width="150"
              Click="btnAdd_Click"
              Margin="0,10,0,0"
              HorizontalAlignment="Right" ></Button>
    </StackPanel>
  </Grid>
```

9. Open `MainPage.xaml.cs` and replace the code with the following code:

```csharp
public partial class MainPage : UserControl
{
  public ObservableCollection<SerializablePerson> Persons { get;
    set; }
  public MainPage()
  {
    InitializeComponent();
    CallService();
  }
  private void CallService()
  {
    MyCloudServiceReference.MyCloudHostedWCFServiceClient client =
      new MyCloudHostedSilverlightApplication.MyCloudService
```

```
        Reference.MyCloudHostedWCFServiceClient(new
        BasicHttpBinding(), new EndpointAddress(string.Format
        ("http://{0}:{1}/MyCloudHostedWCFService.svc",
        HtmlPage.Document.DocumentUri.Host, "8080")));
    client.GetPersonsCompleted += new
        EventHandler<GetPersonsCompletedEventArgs>
        (client_GetPersonsCompleted);
    client.GetPersonsAsync();
}
void client_GetPersonsCompleted(object sender,
    GetPersonsCompletedEventArgs e)
{
    if (e.Error == null)
    {
        Persons = e.Result;
    }
}

private void btnAdd_Click(object sender, RoutedEventArgs e)
{
    MyCloudServiceReference.MyCloudHostedWCFServiceClient client =
        new MyCloudHostedSilverlightApplication.MyCloudService
        Reference.MyCloudHostedWCFServiceClient(new
        BasicHttpBinding(), new EndpointAddress(string.Format
        ("http://{0}:{1}/MyCloudHostedWCFService.svc",
        HtmlPage.Document.DocumentUri.Host, "8080")));
    client.AddPersonCompleted += new EventHandler
        <System.ComponentModel.AsyncCompletedEventArgs>
        (client_AddPersonCompleted);
    client.AddPersonAsync(txtName.Text.Trim(),
        Convert.ToDateTime(dtpDateOfBirth.SelectedDate));
}
void client_AddPersonCompleted(object sender,
    System.ComponentModel.AsyncCompletedEventArgs e)
{
    CallService();
}
}
```

10. Update the `MyCloudServiceReference` service reference by right-clicking on it and selecting **Update Service Reference**.

11. You can now build and run your application. Every time you add a person, the list will be reloaded and the complete list of persons will be visualized on your Silverlight application.

Silverlight and the Azure Cloud
Kevin, 5/5/1981 12:00:00 AM
Add person
Name:
Date of birth: `<d/MM/yyyy>` [15]
Add person

How it works...

Windows Azure allows access to its Table Storage through an HTTP-based, REST-style interface (or by using WCF Data Services). To get started, we need to make sure that the development environment is used for table storage. This is configured in the first step. The DataConnectionString is the connection string to the Windows Azure account (in our case, local) and is used by the StorageClient to access the table storage.

To use table storage, we need to have a class that contains a few required properties such as a Timestamp, a RowKey, and a PartitionKey. Our class should also contain the DataServiceKey attribute. This is why we let our Person class inherit the TableServiceEntity class (found in the Microsoft.WindowsAzure.StorageClient namespace), which already defines these required properties and decoration.

Windows Azure Storage uses the PartitionKey if it needs to store data across different storage nodes. Items having the same PartitionKey will be stored in the same node, which can be useful from the performance point of view. In this case, we've set the PartitionKey to DateOfBirth. This means that all persons having the same birth date will be stored in the same node. RowKey represents the unique identification of an entity in the partition to which it belongs. We've not set it in this recipe. Thus, we've allowed Windows Azure Storage to decide this for us.

In the next step, we've created a context to communicate with the table storage. The PersonServiceContext class inherits TableServiceContext and we've added methods to it to fetch data as well as persist data. Visual Studio will automatically identify any property that returns an IQueryable<T> (where T identifies the class that models the table schema) and create a table in the local development storage according to this property. This means that in our case, we'll have a table called Persons that will contain all the persons we add.

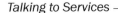

In step 6, we made sure that the table storage tables are created if they're not available. This needs to be done only once (for each environment).

After this, we added two methods to our WCF Service. These methods will be called from the Silverlight application. They are used to fetch data from and persist data to the table storage using the `PersonServiceContext` class we created before. We don't pass `Person` objects back to the Silverlight application as they inherit `TableServiceEntity` and can't be serialized. Instead, we return a list of `SerializablePerson`. As you might have noticed, this way of working really resembles how we work with the Entity Framework or the RIA Services' `DomainContext`.

All that is left now is building the UI in our Silverlight application and calling the WCF service operations on loading the data and on submitting a new person. This is explained thoroughly in the other recipes throughout this book. All the Azure-related magic takes place behind the service methods.

There's more...

In this recipe, we've used tables to store data in the cloud. There are two other built-in options in Windows Azure to store data—blobs and queues. A blob is the simplest way of storing data in the cloud. It's generally unstructured data such as a JPEG or an MP3 file. Blobs can have a large file size (each up to 50 GB) and can be subdivided into blocks to make transferring more efficient.

Queues are also available along with blobs and tables. They essentially provide a way for the Web Role instances to communicate with the Worker Role instances. You can learn more about them at `http://www.microsoft.com/windowsazure/getstarted/`.

What about relational data storage?

We're using tables to store data in the cloud. However, these aren't relational tables. They actually contain data stored in a set of entities with properties. If you're looking for relational data storage, you should refer the SQL Azure at `http://www.microsoft.com/windowsazure/getstarted/#sql`.

See also

For a more general overview of the Windows Azure cloud, have a look at the previous recipe.

Using socket communication in Silverlight

Until now, all the communication with services has been initialized by the client. The Silverlight application makes a call to a service, which can be a WCF service, an ASMX service, or an RSS feed. After receiving the call, the service will start working by sending the response back to the Silverlight application. Such kind of communication is typically carried out by HTTP, which is based on a request model. A response will be sent based on a request.

Sometimes, we need the opposite. The initiative needs to be taken by the server by pushing data to its client(s). Initially, this client should register with the server, but from then on, the server can decide when it needs to send data to the connected applications.

This type of communication can be achieved using sockets in Silverlight. Sockets are the endpoints on both sides. The server and the client can both send data to an endpoint, making it possible for the server to push data back into the socket on the client side.

Sockets aren't used often (we'll take a look at the reason for this in the *How it works...* section), but they have their advantages such as speed, less overhead, bi-directional communication, and so on. In this recipe, we'll take a look at what we need to do to get sockets working in a Silverlight application.

Getting ready

We're building the entire application in this recipe from scratch. The finished code for this recipe can be found in the `Chapter06/SilverlightStockSocket_Completed` folder in the code bundle that is available on the Packt site.

How to do it...

In this recipe, we'll build a service that sends up-to-date stock information and is similar to a stock ticker. It's possible that more than one client is connected simultaneously. In this case, all connected clients will receive updates from the server. We'll see that some of the techniques we used to communicate with a socket service are similar to connecting with a regular service such as WCF. However, some are entirely different. For example, socket services also require a `clientaccesspolicy.xml` to be present. On the other hand, socket services can push data to the clients, which is typical for this type of communication.

We need to carry out the following steps to get a working socket service and client:

1. We'll start from scratch and build the application. Create a new Silverlight solution in Visual Studio called **SilverlightStockSocket**.

2. Every Silverlight application (unless it runs as a trusted application having elevated permissions) that calls a service in a domain other than the one in which it is hosted requires a `clientaccesspolicy.xml` or a `crossdomain.xml` file (as we saw in the *Configuring cross-domain calls* recipe). The same holds true for a socket-based application. When dealing with services hosted by a web server, serving the `clientaccesspolicy.xml` is handled by the server software itself. This isn't the case with a socket server. Thus, our first task will be to build a policy server, which is a piece of software that will open a socket and serve the `clientaccesspolicy.xml` when requested. We'll build the policy server as a Console application. To do this, add a new Console application to the solution and name it as **StockSocketPolicyServer**.

3. In this new project, we'll first include the policy file itself. Add a new XML file to the project and name it as `clientaccesspolicy.xml`. In the **Properties** window, set its **Build Action** to **None** and **Copy to Output Directory** to **Copy Always**. Due to this, while building, the XML file is copied to the same directory as the executable of the application. The following code represents the content of the file:

```xml
<?xml version="1.0" encoding ="utf-8"?>
<access-policy>
  <cross-domain-access>
    <policy>
      <allow-from>
        <domain uri="*" />
      </allow-from>
      <grant-to>
        <socket-resource port="4530" protocol="tcp" />
      </grant-to>
    </policy>
  </cross-domain-access>
</access-policy>
```

4. To serve this file, we need a policy server containing the code that reads out the file and sends its contents to the connecting Silverlight application. The policy server's main task is to listen for incoming connections and respond with the contents of the policy file. Add a new class called `PolicyServer.cs` to the project.

5. The policy server reads the content of the XML file when it starts up. The content is loaded into a byte array as shown in the following code:

```csharp
public class PolicyServer
{
  private byte[] clientaccesspolicy;
  public void StartPolicyServer()
  {
    using (FileStream stream = new
      FileStream("clientaccesspolicy.xml", FileMode.Open))
    {
      clientaccesspolicy = new byte[stream.Length];
      stream.Read(clientaccesspolicy, 0,
        clientaccesspolicy.Length);
    }
  }
}
```

6. After reading out the content, the policy server has to start listening for incoming requests for the policy file. A `TcpListener` object is required to do this. These requests will always be sent to port 943. So we configure the `TcpListener` instance to listen to that port. As shown in the following code, the `BeginAcceptTcpClient` method starts a new thread on which the actual listening is done. Thus, it returns immediately.

```
private TcpListener tcpListener;
public void StartPolicyServer()
{
    ...

    tcpListener = new TcpListener(IPAddress.Any, 943);
    tcpListener.Start();
    tcpListener.BeginAcceptTcpClient(new AsyncCallback
        (OnBeginAcceptTcpClient), null);
}
```

7. When a client eventually connects, the `OnBeginAcceptTcpClient` callback will be invoked. In this method, we begin the process of receiving data asynchronously using the resulting `TcpClient` instance. The data that will be sent by the client is the request for the policy file.

```
private TcpClient tcpClient;
private byte[] receivedBytes;
private static string policyRequestString =
    "<policy-file-request/>";
private void OnBeginAcceptTcpClient(IAsyncResult ar)
{
    receivedBytes = new byte[policyRequestString.Length];
    tcpClient = tcpListener.EndAcceptTcpClient(ar);
    tcpClient.Client.BeginReceive(receivedBytes, 0,
        policyRequestString.Length, SocketFlags.None,
        new AsyncCallback(OnReceive), null);
}
```

8. The `OnReceive` callback is invoked when the operation is complete. In this method, we check if the received string data is equal to `<policy-file-request/>`. This string data is a request for the policy file. Now, we find out that the request was a policy request and we start sending the content of the `clientaccesspolicy.xml` file. Finally, we need to start listening again for new incoming requests. This is shown in the following code:

```
private void OnReceive(IAsyncResult ar)
{
    int receivedLength = tcpClient.Client.EndReceive(ar);
    string policyRequest = Encoding.UTF8.GetString
        (receivedBytes, 0, receivedLength);
```

```
      if (policyRequest.Equals(policyRequestString))
      {
        tcpClient.Client.BeginSend(clientaccesspolicy, 0,
          clientaccesspolicy.Length, SocketFlags.None,
          new AsyncCallback(OnSend), null);
      }
      tcpListener.BeginAcceptTcpClient(new
        AsyncCallback(OnBeginAcceptTcpClient), null);
    }
    private void OnSend(IAsyncResult ar)
    {
      tcpClient.Client.Close();
    }
```

9. The policy server also needs to close at some point. The Stop method is used for this as shown in the following code:

```
public void StopPolicyServer()
{
  tcpListener.Stop();
}
```

10. Managing the policy server (starting and stopping) can be carried out from the Main method in the Program.cs file that was added automatically when we created the project. This is shown in the following code:

```
class Program
{
  static void Main(string[] args)
  {
    Console.WriteLine("Starting policy server");
    PolicyServer policyServer = new PolicyServer();
    policyServer.StartPolicyServer();
    Console.WriteLine("Policy server successfully started");
    Console.WriteLine("Press any key to exit the server");
    Console.ReadLine();
    policyServer.StopPolicyServer();
  }
}
```

11. Now that the policy server is in place, it's time to build the real socket server. The code for this is quite similar to the code of the policy server. Add another Console application to the solution and name it as **StockSocketServer**. Add a new class to this project called **SocketServer**.

12. A client connects to the socket server to receive updates on stock quotes. We'll simulate this using a `Timer` that sends new, random stock data to all connected clients every two seconds. Also, all the clients that are connected to the socket server at any given point of time need to be stored by the server. As shown in the following code, we create a `List<StreamWriter>` to achieve this:

```
Timer stockTimer;
List<StreamWriter> clientConnections;
public SocketServer()
{
    stockTimer = new Timer();
    clientConnections = new List<StreamWriter>();
}
public string GetStockInfo()
{
    double randomStockValue =
        30 + Math.Round(10 * new Random().NextDouble(), 2);
    return "MSFT: " + randomStockValue.ToString();
}
```

13. Just like the policy server, the socket server will listen for incoming requests using the `TcpListener`. However, here the listener needs to work on a port between 4502 and 4532. Instantiating and starting the listener is carried out in the `StartSocketServer` method. We also configure the `Timer` instance in this method as shown in the following code:

```
private TcpListener tcpListener;
public void StartSocketServer()
{
    stockTimer.Interval = 2000;
    stockTimer.Enabled = true;
    stockTimer.Elapsed += new
        ElapsedEventHandler(stockTimer_Elapsed);
    stockTimer.Start();
    tcpListener = new TcpListener(IPAddress.Any, 4530);
    tcpListener.Start();
    tcpListener.BeginAcceptTcpClient
        (OnBeginAcceptTcpClient, null);
}
```

14. In the `BeginAcceptTcpClient` callback, we access the stream associated with the client connection. This stream is first stored in the previously mentioned `List<StreamWriter>`. We push data from the server to the client using the `Write` method. Finally, we start listening for new incoming requests. All this is shown in the following code:

```
private TcpClient tcpClient;
public void OnBeginAcceptTcpClient(IAsyncResult ar)
{
  Console.WriteLine("Client connected successfully");
  tcpClient = tcpListener.EndAcceptTcpClient(ar);
  StreamWriter streamWriter = new
    StreamWriter(tcpClient.GetStream());
  clientConnections.Add(streamWriter);
  streamWriter.AutoFlush = true;
  streamWriter.Write(GetStockInfo());
  //wait again for new connection
  tcpListener.BeginAcceptTcpClient(OnBeginAcceptTcpClient,
    null);
}
```

15. When the `Elapsed` event of the `Timer` triggers, we want to update all clients by sending new data. To do this, we loop over the `List<StreamWriter>` and call the `Write` method again, thereby passing new data to the clients. This is shown in the following code:

```
void stockTimer_Elapsed(object sender, ElapsedEventArgs e)
{
  if (clientConnections != null)
  {
    foreach (var clientConnection in clientConnections)
    {
      if (clientConnection != null)
        clientConnection.Write(GetStockInfo());
    }
  }
}
```

16. Closing the socket server consists of two things—closing each `StreamWriter` instance followed by stopping the listener as shown in the following code:

```
public void StopSocketServer()
{
  foreach (var streamWriter in clientConnections)
  {
    streamWriter.Close();
  }
  tcpListener.Stop();
}
```

17. Similar to the policy server, the socket server is managed from the `Main` method in the `Program.cs` file as shown in the following code:

```
class Program
{
  static void Main(string[] args)
  {
    Console.WriteLine("Starting socket server");
    SocketServer socketServer = new SocketServer();
    socketServer.StartSocketServer();
    Console.WriteLine("Socket server successfully started");
    Console.WriteLine("Press any key to exit the server");
    Console.ReadLine();
    socketServer.StopSocketServer();
  }
}
```

18. Finally, we have created both the policy server and the socket server. Let's now turn our attention to the Silverlight application that needs to connect with this socket server. The UI layout is pretty straightforward and can be found in the code bundle. Its primary components are a `Button` and a `TextBlock`. We want to connect with the socket server once the `Button` has been clicked. The results sent back from the server should be shown in the `TextBlock`.

19. In the `Click` event of the `Button`, we start by defining the socket endpoint using the `DnsEndPoint` class. Due to this, the Silverlight application knows where the host is located. It then creates the `Socket` object as well as the `SocketAsyncEventArgs` instance as shown in the following code. The latter represents the asynchronous operation with the socket.

```
private void StartButton_Click(object sender, RoutedEventArgs e)
{
  DnsEndPoint endPoint = new DnsEndPoint
    (Application.Current.Host.Source.DnsSafeHost, 4530);
  Socket socket = new Socket(AddressFamily.InterNetwork,
    SocketType.Stream, ProtocolType.Tcp);
  SocketAsyncEventArgs args = new SocketAsyncEventArgs();
  args.UserToken = socket;
  args.RemoteEndPoint = endPoint;
  args.Completed += new
    EventHandler<SocketAsyncEventArgs>(OnSocketConnected);
  socket.ConnectAsync(args);
}
```

20. The `OnSocketConnected` callback is fired when the client has finished attempting to connect with the server socket. In this method, we check if the connection was a success. If it was, we create a buffer that will contain the received data and start the receiving process using the `ReceiveAsync` method. This is shown in the following code:

```
private void OnSocketConnected(object sender,
    SocketAsyncEventArgs e)
{
  if (e.SocketError == SocketError.Success)
  {
    byte[] response = new byte[1024];
    e.SetBuffer(response, 0, response.Length);
    e.Completed -= new
      EventHandler<SocketAsyncEventArgs>(OnSocketConnected);
    e.Completed += new
      EventHandler<SocketAsyncEventArgs>(OnSocketStartReceive);
    Socket socket = (Socket)e.UserToken;
    socket.ReceiveAsync(e);
  }
}
```

21. We can access the received data in the `OnSocketStartReceive` callback. We can't update the UI directly as the code is now executing on a background thread. Therefore, we need to use `Dispatcher.BeginInvoke` to get access to the UI thread. To register to receive new updates coming from the server, we call the `ReceiveAsync` again as shown in the following code:

```
private void OnSocketStartReceive(object sender,
    SocketAsyncEventArgs e)
{
  string data = Encoding.UTF8.GetString(e.Buffer, e.Offset,
    e.BytesTransferred);
  Dispatcher.BeginInvoke(() => StockTickingTextBlock.Text = data);
  Socket socket = (Socket)e.UserToken;
  socket.ReceiveAsync(e);
}
```

22. We have now arrived at a point where we can test the application. To test the application, we need to start the Silverlight application, the policy server, and the socket server. Starting these two servers is necessary because they run as separate projects and need to be available so that the Silverlight application can connect with them. To achieve this, first start the application by setting the web project as a **Startup project** and running it by pressing the *F5* key. Secondly, right-click on both the policy server and the socket server projects in the **Solution Explorer** and select **Debug | Start new instance**.

The following screenshot shows the Silverlight application as well as both the server applications running:

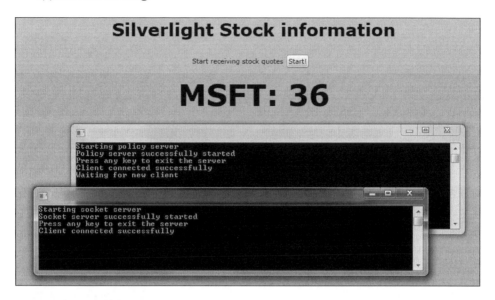

How it works...

When we need a type of service that is able to push data from the server to the client, a socket-based application might be a good solution. Socket-based applications can also be considered as an option when pure speed for communicating with a service is our top priority. This can be explained by the TCP protocol they use. All other services use HTTP, which is a higher layer on top of TCP. HTTP is slower than pure TCP and it can't push data back to the client as it requires a request for every response that goes out.

When would we actually need this increased performance or this bi-directional, push-enabled communication? If raw data is all that passes over a wire and it needs to move fast, a socket can be used. A stock ticker is a great example of this. The client (some application) registers with the socket server and starts receiving updates from then on without asking!

The policy server

Just like other service communications, Silverlight needs to know that the server allows connecting from another domain. In other words, it will check for cross-domain restrictions. For example, when connecting to a WCF service, Silverlight will send a request for the `clientaccesspolicy.xml` file to the web server. If not found, it will request for the `crossdomain.xml` file. If neither of these files is found or the file enforces restrictions on who can access the service (only requests from specific domains are allowed), Silverlight will not allow the call to the service. Otherwise, it will go ahead and let us communicate with the service.

In the case of a socket-based application, the server can be any type of application ranging from a console application to a Windows service. These types of applications aren't web servers that will automatically serve the policy file when requested. Therefore, we need to write a policy server.

This policy server uses a `TcpListener` to listen for incoming requests. Policy requests always arrive at port 943. So this port needs to be specified when creating the `TcpListener` instance.

The `BeginAcceptTcpClient` method of the `TcpListener` class actually starts the listening process on another thread. That is why this method returns immediately and then waits for a client to connect. Once data is received, it is checked to see if the request is really a policy request. If it is so, the contents of the `clientaccesspolicy.xml` file is sent back to the requesting application (in our case, a Silverlight application). In this way, Silverlight can determine if the application can access the service.

The socket server

The actual socket-based communication will take place between the Silverlight application and the socket server application. Just like the policy server, this server will also listen for incoming requests using the `TcpListener` class. Multiple client applications can connect to the server. To manage this, the server uses a `List<StreamWriter>`. In this list, we store a `StreamWriter` that references the network stream to the connected client application. Whenever new data needs to be sent to the client(s), we move through the list and data is sent over each encountered writer.

The socket server can listen for incoming requests on any port varying between 4502 and 4532. It's important that whenever a new client has connected, we start listening for new incoming requests using the following line of code:

```
tcpListener.BeginAcceptTcpClient(OnBeginAcceptTcpClient, null);
```

Connecting the Silverlight application

When connecting to the socket server from the client side, we can basically perform three tasks: connect to the server, send data, and receive data. We can do this using the `ConnectAsync`, `SendAsync`, and `ReceiveAsync` methods respectively. In this sample, we haven't sent data to the server. However, it's similar to receiving data. We can't work with the `TcpClient` as it's not available in Silverlight. We need to use the `Socket` class directly.

A `SocketAsyncEventArgs` instance is required to communicate with the socket server. With this instance, we can store a reference to the socket and the endpoint for the connection, stored as a `DnsEndPoint`.

The `ConnectAsync` method on the `Socket` instance will make the actual call connecting with the server using the `SocketAsyncEventArgs` instance. The connection call is carried out asynchronously and when it returns, we can check if the attempt to connect with the server has succeeded. If it does succeed, we can create a buffer so that some received data can be stored inside it.

Using the following code:

```
Socket socket = (Socket)e.UserToken;
socket.ReceiveAsync(e);
```

We can tell the client to start listening for any incoming messages from the server. The callback method is invoked whenever a message is received. As we're now in a different thread than the UI thread, we can no longer access the UI elements such as the `TextBlock` control. Thus, we need to use `Dispatcher.BeginInvoke`. This allows us to execute the specified delegate on the thread that is associated with the `Dispatcher` (in this case, the UI thread). The delegate is simply a call for updating the value of the `TextBlock` control.

7
Talking to WCF and ASMX Services

In this chapter, we will cover:

- ▶ Invoking a service that exposes data
- ▶ Invoking a service such as Bing.com
- ▶ Handling faults when calling a service
- ▶ Optimizing performance using binary XML
- ▶ Using duplex communication
- ▶ Using duplex communication with the net.tcp protocol
- ▶ Debugging WCF service errors with Silverlight
- ▶ Ensuring that data is encrypted
- ▶ Securing service communication using message-based security
- ▶ Uploading files to a WCF service
- ▶ Displaying images as a stream from a WCF service
- ▶ Hooking into proxy creation using slsvcutil.exe
- ▶ Calling a WCF service from Silverlight using ChannelFactory

Introduction

When building services in .NET, most developers will choose WCF (Windows Communication Foundation). WCF was introduced with .NET 3.0 as an API that eased building service-oriented applications. It aims at unifying several communication APIs such as remoting, "classic" web services, and so on.

Due to its wide adoption, it's easy to understand that Microsoft included support for communication with WCF services in Silverlight. At this point, the combination of Silverlight and WCF has the most options when it comes to communicating with services from Silverlight. When starting the development of an enterprise, WCF would probably be your choice.

ASMX or classic web services are widely used as well. We can also connect with classic services from Silverlight, although not all options available with WCF are possible with these types of services.

In this chapter, we'll look at communicating with services we create ourselves as well as third-party services. Sites such as Bing offer an API that includes service endpoints.

We'll also look at duplex communication in this chapter. Silverlight 2 already included support for duplex communication using a WCF service. Though it was possible, it was quite hard to do. With Silverlight 3, duplex communication using WCF over HTTP became much simpler. Silverlight 4 added support for the `net.tcp` protocol. We can perform unidirectional as well as bidirectional communication with much better performance using `net.tcp` binding in WCF.

Speaking of performance, Silverlight 3 added support for binary encoding of the exchanged information, resulting in faster data transfer. Also, Silverlight now supports fault handling. Until the introduction of Silverlight 3, faults thrown by the service were not visible in Silverlight. This resulted in a bad debugging experience. In this chapter, we'll see how we can leverage these features.

One of the important things to keep in mind when working with services is securing them, either by making sure the data is sent over the wire in an encrypted format or by ensuring only certain users can access the service methods. This chapter includes recipes to help you achieve both.

Services aren't limited to sending and receiving textual data. Silverlight can send or receive an image from a service. In this case, the image is being sent as binary data. We'll look at how we can create a service that is capable of this type of communication and how Silverlight can work with it.

Invoking a service that exposes data

When working on a Silverlight project that involves services, WCF is the preferred choice for building a service if we have to create both the service and the Silverlight client application that will use it. Using WCF gives us a complete control over what types will be sent to the client and for each type. We can also specify whether or not a field should be included in the client-side copy of the type.

When we want to build a Silverlight application that works with the data available on the service (perhaps coming from a database or another external service), we need to ask ourselves two questions. How should we design the service that exposes the data so that it can be accessible from Silverlight? And secondly, how should we go about designing the Silverlight application so that it communicates with the service?

In this recipe, we'll take a look at finding answers to both these questions.

Getting ready

We'll build the application in this recipe from scratch. However, the complete code for this recipe can be found in the `Chapter07/SilverlightEmployeeBrowser` folder in the code bundle that is available on the Packt site.

How to do it...

To show how we can connect from Silverlight to a WCF service that exposes data, we'll start quite logically with designing the service itself. For this recipe, we'll assume that we are building an easy employee overview screen, where the user can see all the employee information. The employee data is exposed by the service. The Silverlight application will connect to the service and work with the data on the client side. The following are the steps we need to execute to get this working:

1. For this recipe, we'll start from an empty Silverlight application. Create a new Silverlight solution in Visual Studio and name it as `SilverlightEmployeeBrowser`. As usual, Visual Studio will create a solution containing both a Silverlight application called `SilverlightEmployeeBrowser` and a hosting website called `SilverlightEmployeeBrowser.Web`.

2. Let's first focus on the web application. The data we want to expose consists of employee data. The following class diagram shows the relation. Add all the classes and the `CarType` enumeration in a folder called `Model` within the project. Note that `Employee` is an abstract base class.

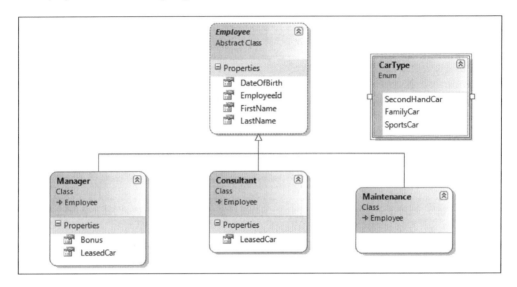

The following is the code for the `Employee` class. Note the attributes added to the class. By specifying the `DataContractAttribute`, we state that this type can be sent over the wire. Also, we have marked all fields with the `DataMemberAttribute`. Every field that is attributed with the `DataMemberAttribute` will be included in the type being sent over the wire to the client side. Finally, we also add the `KnownTypeAttribute` in the base class. This attribute marks the types that should be included in the serialization process.

```
[DataContract]
[KnownType(typeof(Manager))]
[KnownType(typeof(Consultant))]
[KnownType(typeof(Maintenance))]
public abstract class Employee
{
    [DataMember]
    public int EmployeeId { get; set; }
    [DataMember]
    public string FirstName { get; set; }
    [DataMember]
    public string LastName { get; set; }
    [DataMember]
    public DateTime DateOfBirth { get; set; }
}
```

The following is the code for the `Manager` class that inherits from `Employee`:

```
public class Manager : Employee
{
  [DataMember]
  public CarType LeasedCar { get; set; }
  [DataMember]
  public double Bonus { get; set; }
}
```

The other classes in the hierarchy are similar and can be found in the completed sample.

3. This step consists of creating a class called `EmployeeRepository` that will load in the sample data. In a real-world scenario, we would load data from a database or an external service. The following is the code for this class. It uses a static `List<Employee>` that is filled upon first creation of the `EmployeeRepository` class:

```
public class EmployeeRepository
{
  private static List<Employee> allEmployees;
  public EmployeeRepository()
  {
    FillEmployees();
  }
  private void FillEmployees()
  {
    if(allEmployees == null)
    {
      allEmployees = new List<Employee>()
      {
        new Manager()
        {
          EmployeeId=1,
          FirstName="Gill",
          LastName="Cleeren",
          LeasedCar=CarType.SportsCar,
          Bonus=10000.00,
          DateOfBirth=new DateTime(1980, 1, 1)
        },
        new Consultant()
        {
          EmployeeId=2,
          FirstName="John",
```

```
            LastName="Smith",
            LeasedCar=CarType.FamilyCar,
            DateOfBirth=new DateTime(1976, 11, 9)
        },
        new Consultant()
        {
          EmployeeId=3,
          FirstName="Jeff",
          LastName="Jones",
          LeasedCar=CarType.SecondHandCar,
          DateOfBirth=new DateTime(1983, 3, 12)
        },
        new Consultant()
        {
          EmployeeId=4,
          FirstName="Lindsey",
          LastName="Clarks",
          LeasedCar=CarType.FamilyCar,
          DateOfBirth=new DateTime(1984, 6, 7)
        },
        new Maintenance()
        {
          EmployeeId=5,
          FirstName="Clay",
          LastName="Richards",
          DateOfBirth=new DateTime(1960, 9, 22)
        },
        new Maintenance()
        {
          EmployeeId=6,
          FirstName="Marie",
          LastName="Smith",
          DateOfBirth=new DateTime(1963, 2, 19)
        },
      };
    }
  }
  public List<Employee> AllEmployees
  {
    get
    {
      return allEmployees;
    }
  }
}
```

4. Now that we have the model and the repository, we're ready to add a WCF service to this project. Right-click on the **SilverlighttEmployeeBrowser.Web** project node in the **Solution Explorer** and select **Add | New Item…**. In the **Add New Item** dialog, we have two options for adding a WCF service—a regular **WCF Service** and a **Silverlight-enabled WCF Service**. Select the latter and name the service as **EmployeeService**. Visual Studio will add a *.svc file, a *.svc.cs file, and make some configuration changes to make the service accessible.

5. The service exposes two methods. The first one retrieves all employees, while the second one retrieves an employee based on the employee's ID. Each method or operation that should be available on the client side needs to be attributed with the OperationContract attribute. In a WCF scenario, the service itself should be attributed with the ServiceContract attribute. The service with its two methods is shown in the following code:

```
[ServiceContract(Namespace = "")]
[AspNetCompatibilityRequirements(RequirementsMode =
  AspNetCompatibilityRequirementsMode.Allowed)]
public class EmployeeService
{
  [OperationContract]
  public List<Employee> GetAllEmployees()
  {
    return new Model.EmployeeRepository().AllEmployees;
  }
  [OperationContract]
  public Employee GetEmployeeById(int employeeId)
  {
    return new Model.EmployeeRepository().AllEmployees.Where
      (e => e.EmployeeId == employeeId).FirstOrDefault();
  }
}
```

6. We're now ready on the server side. Build the project before continuing.

7. In the Silverlight application, right-click on the project node in the **Solution Explorer** and select **Add Service Reference....** In the dialog box that appears, click on the **Discover** button and if the service can be connected to without errors, it will appear in the list as shown in the following screenshot. Select the service and enter **EmployeeService** in the **Namespace:** field. An error will occur if the service wasn't built. After clicking on the **OK** button, Visual Studio will attempt to build a proxy that is roughly a client-side copy of the service class.

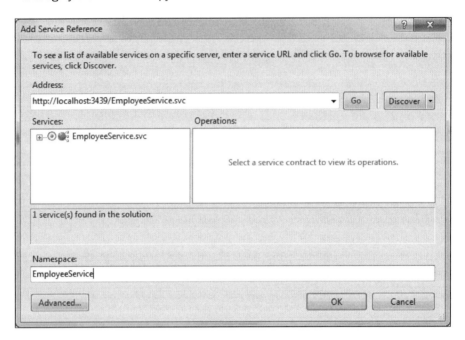

8. The UI of the application is very simple. The complete code list can be found in the code bundles. As shown a bit later in this recipe, it contains a `TextBox` and a `Button`, which should trigger a call to the `GetEmployeeId` service operation. The retrieved details are to be shown in a detailed grid. Also, while loading the application for the first time, a call to the `GetAllEmployees` method should be triggered and the result of this call should be shown in the `DataGrid`. Here we'll focus on the latter.

9. When the control has loaded, a call to the `LoadEmployees` method is invoked. In this method, we create an instance of the proxy class, which was generated by Visual Studio when we connected with the service. Next, we specify the callback method. Communication with a WCF service, similar to all other types of service connections, will take place asynchronously. Finally, we perform the actual invocation of the service method. All this is shown in the following code:

```
private void UserControl_Loaded(object sender, RoutedEventArgs e)
```

```
{
  LoadAllEmployees();
}
private void LoadAllEmployees()
{
  EmployeeService.EmployeeServiceClient proxy = new
    SilverlightEmployeeBrowser.EmployeeService
    .EmployeeServiceClient();
  proxy.GetAllEmployeesCompleted +=
    proxy_GetAllEmployeesCompleted;
  proxy.GetAllEmployeesAsync();
}
```

10. If no errors occurred in the callback method, we get access to the result of the service call via the `Result` property of the `SilverlighttEmployeeBrowser.EmployeeService.GetAllEmployeesCompletedEventArgs` parameter. This property is of the same type as returned by the service method (in this case a `List<SilverlighttEmployeeBrowser.EmployeeService.Employee>`). For the `DataGrid`, we set the list as `ItemsSource` as shown in the following code:

```
void proxy_GetAllEmployeesCompleted(object sender,
  SilverlightEmployeeBrowser.EmployeeService
  .GetAllEmployeesCompletedEventArgs e)
{
  if (e.Error == null)
    EmployeeDataGrid.ItemsSource = e.Result;
  else
    ErrorTextBlock.Text = "An error occurred while communicating
      to the service";
}
```

All employees should now be shown in the `DataGrid`, as shown in the next screenshot. Calling the `GetEmployeeById` operation is similar. The code for this can be found in the code bundles.

How it works...

WCF services are a preferred way of authoring services in the .NET framework. From the Silverlight point of view, the WCF services are also the best choice. Let's take a look at the specifics for both the service and the Silverlight application connecting to the service.

The WCF service

Adding a WCF service is possible using one of the two item templates available in Visual Studio—the **WCF Service** template or the **Silverlight-enabled WCF Service** template. The first one configures the service to use `wsHttpBinding`, which is the default for WCF. However, Silverlight can't work with this type of binding. So, if we choose to use this template, we need to configure the `web.config` manually so that the service uses `basicHttpBinding` as shown in the following code:

```
<system.serviceModel>
  <services>
    <service behaviorConfiguration="SilverlightEmployeeBrowser
             .Web.EmployeeServiceBehavior"
          name="SilverlightEmployeeBrowser.Web.EmployeeService">
      <endpoint address=""
                binding="basicHttpBinding"
                contract="SilverlightEmployeeBrowser
                  .Web.IEmployeeService">
        <identity>
          <dns value="localhost" />
        </identity>
      </endpoint>
    </service>
  </services>
</system.serviceModel>
```

However, if we use the **Silverlight-enabled WCF Service** template, the service will get configured automatically so that it'll work when accessed from a Silverlight application. This is shown in the following code snippet:

```
<system.serviceModel>
  <behaviors>
    ...
  </behaviors>
  <bindings>
    <customBinding>
      <binding name="customBinding0">
        <binaryMessageEncoding/>
        <httpTransport>
          <extendedProtectionPolicy policyEnforcement="Never"/>
```

```
            </httpTransport>
          </binding>
        </customBinding>
      </bindings>
      <serviceHostingEnvironment aspNetCompatibilityEnabled="true"/>
      <services>
        <service behaviorConfiguration="SilverlighttEmployeeBrowser
                  .Web.EmployeeServiceBehavior"
                 name="SilverlighttEmployeeBrowser.Web.EmployeeService">
          <endpoint address=""
                    binding="customBinding"
                    bindingConfiguration="customBinding0"
                    contract="SilverlighttEmployeeBrowser.Web
                      .EmployeeService"/>
          <endpoint address="mex"
                    binding="mexHttpBinding"
                    contract="IMetadataExchange"/>
        </service>
      </services>
    </system.serviceModel>
```

Note that the service is using binary message encoding by default so that the data will get compressed when sent over the wire, resulting in quicker transfers.

When creating a WCF service, we need to specify what will be exposed over the service. In more detail, we need to specify the operations that can be invoked on the service through the use of a service contract and the types that will be sent over the wire for the client application to use. Each class that should be available on the client side needs to be marked with the `DataContract` attribute. In these classes, we can specify which fields should go over the wire. Only those fields marked with the `DataMemberAttribute` will be sent to the client. Thus, we have granular control over what will and what will not be sent to the client-side application.

Connecting to the service

Once the service is in place, we can connect to it from the Silverlight application. This can be done using the **Add Service Reference** dialog box. Visual Studio will create a proxy class when the connection is made. This class contains a client-side copy of the types exposed by the service (for example, the `Employee` and the `Manager` class) and a copy of the service methods among others. However, code is generated for each service method that makes it possible to call the service asynchronously. The actual service code is not copied to the proxy. To view this code, click on the **Show All Files** button located at the top of the **Solution Explorer**. Then, select the **+** sign in front of the service reference and expand it so that the `Reference.cs` file is shown, which contains the code for the proxy class.

The requirement of calling the service asynchronously can also be seen in the code that's written in the Silverlight application itself. We start by instantiating the proxy class. On this instance, we define the callback method for the XXX_Completed event. Finally, we perform the service invocation by calling the XXX_Async method, which launches the request to the service. If the call is not carried out asynchronously, the application will cause the UI thread to hang until the service returns.

The callback method is invoked once the service returns. In this method, we have access to the result via the e.Result property. This property will be of the same type as returned by the service method (using the client-side copy of the data contracts).

See also

The communication with a WCF service is not very different from the general pattern used for communicating with a service in Silverlight. Take a look at the *Connecting and reading from a standardized service* recipe in the previous chapter where we discussed all general aspects of this topic.

Invoking a service such as Bing.com

Many (large) websites expose services that we can use in our applications. Some of these expose a WSDL file and thus expose metadata that we can use to develop an application around them. One of these sites is Bing (www.bing.com), the search engine from Microsoft. The Bing API allows us to connect in several ways and interact with its services using many protocols. It also exposes a WSDL file to which we can connect from Visual Studio.

In this recipe, we'll build a Silverlight application that incorporates the services in Bing.

Getting ready

In this recipe, we're building the sample application from scratch. The finished solution for this recipe can be found in the Chapter07/SilverBing folder.

How to do it...

We can integrate search functionalities into our Silverlight applications using the Bing API. Bing exposes a WSDL file to which we can connect from Visual Studio. Visual Studio can create a proxy based on the metadata in this file. Thus, we get IntelliSense on the types and methods exposed by the service. The following are the steps we need to perform to get this working:

1. We need an API key to interact with the Bing API. This key is required so that Bing can check that the request has arrived from a registered developer. A key can be obtained for free at http://www.bing.com/developers/createapp.aspx.

2. To build the actual application, we'll start from a clean slate. Create a new Silverlight application in Visual Studio and name it as `SilverBing`.

3. We don't need to create a service ourselves; we just have to connect with the service from Bing. To do this, right-click on the Silverlight project node in the **Solution Explorer** and select **Add Service Reference....** In the dialog box that appears, enter the URI `http://api.search.live.net/search.wsdl?AppID=XXX` for the WSDL file where XXX needs to be replaced with the obtained API key. Enter **BingService** in the **Namespace:** field. Visual Studio will create the proxy after you click on the **OK** button.

4. The UI of the application consists of a search `TextBox`, a `Button`, and a templated `ListBox`. The complete XAML listing can be found in the code bundles.

5. When clicking on the above-mentioned `Button`, in the event handler, we need to create a request for sending to Bing. The request is encapsulated in a `SearchRequest` object, which is a type exposed by the service for us to use in our application. It contains the parameters we need to pass to the service (such as the API key) and the type of search we want to conduct. After constructing the `SearchRequest` instance, we define the callback method that should be executed when the service call returns. Finally, we perform the search asynchronously. The following code is used to illustrate this:

```
private void SearchButton_Click(object sender, RoutedEventArgs e)
{
  BingService.LiveSearchPortTypeClient soapClient =
    new SilverBing.BingService.LiveSearchPortTypeClient();
  SearchRequest request = new SearchRequest();
  request.AppId = "PERSONAL API KEY GOES HERE";
  request.Sources = new SourceType[] { SourceType.Web };
  if (SearchTextBox.Text != string.Empty)
  {
    request.Query = SearchTextBox.Text;
    soapClient.SearchCompleted +=
      new EventHandler<SearchCompletedEventArgs>
      (soapClient_SearchCompleted);
    soapClient.SearchAsync(request);
  }
}
```

6. We define a data-only class called `BingSearchResult` in the Silverlight project in order to work with the results. This class is shown in the following code:

```
public class BingSearchResult
{
  public string Title { get; set; }
  public string Uri { get; set; }
  public string Description { get; set; }
}
```

7. When the service returns, the results are packaged in a `SearchResponse`, which is a type defined by Bing's service. We can loop through the results using a LINQ query and build `BingSearchResult` instances as shown in the following code:

```
void soapClient_SearchCompleted(object sender,
  SearchCompletedEventArgs e)
{
  SearchResponse response = e.Result;
  if (response.Web.Results.Count() > 0)
  {
    var results = from result in response.Web.Results
                  select new BingSearchResult
    {
      Title = result.Title,
      Uri = result.Url,
      Description = result.Description
    };
    ResultListBox.ItemsSource = results.ToList();
  }
}
```

The results are now shown in a `ListBox` with a `DataTemplate` applied to it. The following screenshot shows the results obtained on searching for "Silverlight":

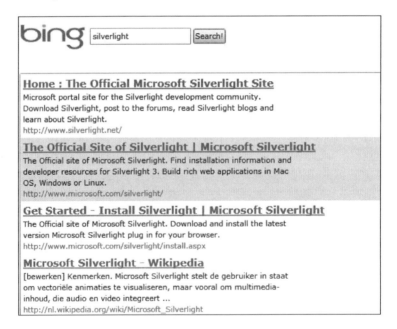

How it works...

Publicly accessible services such as the services from Bing allow us to integrate functionality into our Silverlight applications. Some services expose a REST API (refer to Chapter 8 for more information about REST access), while some expose SOAP services. Bing exposes both and we used the latter option in this recipe. If a service exposes both, using SOAP is recommended. We have full IntelliSense because Visual Studio can generate a proxy in the project based on the WSDL file. This proxy also contains all types and enumerations exposed by the service. Another advantage is that we get deserializing of the SOAP response done automatically and it does not require us to do manual processing of XML.

The entire API for Bing can be found at `http://www.bing.com/developers/s/API%20 Basics.pdf`. Working with the API requires an API key, based on which Bing can track if the request is authorized. We can find the address of the WSDL file in the documentation as well.

To perform a search, we need to instantiate an object of the `SearchRequest` class. This class is exposed by the service and is available on the client side because of the proxy generation. When Visual Studio connects with the service, it reads the exposed metadata (in the form of a WSDL file) and generates the client-side proxy. The `SearchRequest` class is used to pass parameters to the service such as the API key and the search term. Invoking the service is done asynchronously, as with all other services.

The callback method is invoked once the service request is complete and the result is available. The result is of the `SearchResponse` type. Looping through the `Web.Results` property of the `SearchResponse` allows us to retrieve the results as returned by Bing.

There's more...

Bing exposes a `SourceType` enumeration that can be used to specify if we want to perform a regular web search, an image search, a news search, and so on. Bing exposes a specific type for some of the options of the enumerations. For example, it exposes the `ImageRequest` class for `SourceType.Image`. This class exposes more specific properties related to image searching. This `ImageRequest` can then be linked with the original request using its `Image` property.

See also

Communicating with Bing's service is similar to what we did in the previous recipe of this chapter.

Handling faults when calling a service

When you're developing an application that relies on service calls from your client to your server, you'll probably want to have some kind of mechanism in place to allow feedback to the client when something goes wrong. You'll probably also want to know what went wrong so that you can take the necessary action on your client.

For this purpose, Silverlight supports Fault Exceptions when working with WCF services. In this recipe, we'll learn how to get this to work.

Getting ready

To follow along with this recipe, you can use the starter solution located in the `Chapter07/HandlingFaults_Starter` folder in the code bundle that is available on the Packt site. The finished solution for this recipe can be found in the `Chapter07/HandlingFaults_Completed` folder.

How to do it...

To look at how we can handle faults, we're starting from a simple Silverlight solution that includes a Silverlight project that calls a WCF service method. This method returns a `Person` object and shows it on the screen. We're going to make sure that our client is aware of errors that might occur when calling services. To achieve this, carry out the following steps:

1. Open the starter solution as outlined in the *Getting ready* section.

2. Add a new class to the web application project and name it as `MyFaultBehaviour`. Let this class inherit from `BehaviorExtensionElement` and implement the `IEndpointBehavior` interface as shown in the following code:

```
public class MyFaultBehaviour : BehaviorExtensionElement,
  IEndpointBehavior
{
  public void ApplyDispatchBehavior(ServiceEndpoint endpoint,
    EndpointDispatcher endpointDispatcher)
  {
    SilverlightFaultMessageInspector inspector = new
      SilverlightFaultMessageInspector();
    endpointDispatcher.DispatchRuntime.MessageInspectors
      .Add(inspector);
  }
  public class SilverlightFaultMessageInspector :
    IDispatchMessageInspector
  {
    public void BeforeSendReply(ref Message reply, object
```

```
          correlationState)
      {
        if (reply.IsFault)
        {
          HttpResponseMessageProperty property = new
            HttpResponseMessageProperty();
          // Change response code to 200 (default: 500)
          property.StatusCode = System.Net.HttpStatusCode.OK;
          reply.Properties[HttpResponseMessageProperty.Name] =
            property;
        }
      }
      public object AfterReceiveRequest(ref Message request,
        IClientChannel channel, InstanceContext instanceContext)
      {
        return null;
      }
    }
    public void AddBindingParameters(ServiceEndpoint endpoint,
      BindingParameterCollection bindingParameters)
    {}
    public void ApplyClientBehavior(ServiceEndpoint endpoint,
      ClientRuntime clientRuntime)
    {}
    public void Validate(ServiceEndpoint endpoint)
    {}
    public override System.Type BehaviorType
    {
      get { return typeof(MyFaultBehaviour); }
    }
    protected override object CreateBehavior()
    {
      return new MyFaultBehaviour();
    }
  }
```

3. Add the following `using` statements to this file to import the correct namespaces:

```
using System.ServiceModel.Description;
using System.ServiceModel.Dispatcher;
using System.ServiceModel.Channels;
using System.ServiceModel;
using System.ServiceModel.Configuration;
```

4. Modify the `web.config` file so that the WCF Endpoint uses this behavior, and exception details are included in the faults. This is shown in the following code:

```
<system.serviceModel>
  <extensions>
    <behaviorExtensions>
      <add name="silverlightFaults"
           type="HandlingFaults.Web.MyFaultBehaviour,
             HandlingFaults.Web, Version=1.0.0.0, Culture=neutral,
             PublicKeyToken=null"/>
    </behaviorExtensions>
  </extensions>
  <behaviors>
    <serviceBehaviors>
      <behavior name="">
        <serviceMetadata httpGetEnabled="true" />
        <serviceDebug includeExceptionDetailInFaults="true" />
      </behavior>
    </serviceBehaviors>
    <endpointBehaviors>
      <behavior name="SilverlightFaultBehavior">
        <silverlightFaults/>
      </behavior>
    </endpointBehaviors>
  </behaviors>
  <bindings>
    <customBinding>
      <binding name="HandlingFaults.Web.MyWCFService
                 .customBinding0">
        <binaryMessageEncoding />
        <httpTransport />
      </binding>
    </customBinding>
  </bindings>
  <serviceHostingEnvironment aspNetCompatibilityEnabled="true" />
  <services>
    <service name="HandlingFaults.Web.MyWCFService">
      <endpoint address=""
                binding="customBinding"
                bindingConfiguration="HandlingFaults.Web
                  .MyWCFService.customBinding0"
                contract="HandlingFaults.Web.MyWCFService"
                behaviorConfiguration="SilverlightFaultBehavior"/>
      <endpoint address="mex"
                binding="mexHttpBinding"
                contract="IMetadataExchange" />
    </service>
  </services>
</system.serviceModel>
```

5. Open `MainPage.xaml.cs` and add the following code to the completed handler of the service call to show the faults in our application:

```
void client_GetPersonCompleted(object sender,
  MyWCFServiceReference.GetPersonCompletedEventArgs e)
{
  if (e.Error == null)
  {
    this.DataContext = e.Result;
  }
  else if (e.Error is FaultException<ExceptionDetail>)
  {
    FaultException<ExceptionDetail> fault = e.Error as
      FaultException<ExceptionDetail>;
    txtError.Text = fault.Message;
  }
}
```

6. Open `MyWCFService.cs` and modify the `GetPerson` method to throw an `Exception` before trying to return a `Person` object. This can be seen in the following code:

```
[OperationContract]
public Person GetPerson()
{
  throw new Exception("Exception from WCF Service, transferred as
    Fault.");
  return new Person("Dockx", "Kevin");
}
```

7. You can now build and run your solution. You'll notice that the `Exception` gets thrown and is accessible in the client side through `FaultException`. This can be seen in the following screenshot:

Handling Faults

Firstname:

Name:

Error: Exception from WCF Service, transferred as Fault.

How it works...

Typically, when a fault occurs on the server, Silverlight would get it back from WCF as a standard HTTP 500 response error. There would be no way to know exactly what the exception was because WCF returns fault messages this way by default. So the first thing we need to do is to make sure that WCF returns fault messages with an HTTP 200 response code, thus enabling Silverlight to read the fault.

We do this by defining a WCF endpoint behavior for Silverlight faults (`SilverlightFaultBehavior`) in which we change this response code.

We must then make sure that this behavior is used by our endpoint. We do this by adding the behavior as an extension in the WCF service configuration file, adding it to the behaviors collection, and setting it as a `behaviorConfiguration` of our endpoint.

Faults are accessible to Silverlight clients after this has been done. When exceptions occur on the service, they are automatically converted into SOAP faults, are sent back to the client, and are converted into fault expressions after being received. This way, our Silverlight client can easily take the required action by looking at the properties of the fault expression.

There's one more thing to do in our configuration file. We need to make sure that the exception details are sent when a fault is thrown. This is done by setting `includeExceptionDetailInFaults` to `true` in the `serviceDebug` configuration element.

All that's left is to make sure that we handle these faults on our client. We do this by adding code to the callback of the WCF service method call on our Silverlight client.

There's more...

There are two types of faults: undeclared faults and declared faults. In our example, we've used an undeclared fault. These are faults that aren't specified in the contract for an operation and are typically used when debugging a service.

Declared faults are the faults in which an operation has a `FaultContract` attribute that specifies a custom fault type. These types of faults can include custom properties and are typically used in production environments, in which you have to take specific action depending on the type of fault you receive.

To get declared faults to work in our example, we need to make the following changes:

- We need to define the fault in our WCF service.
- We need to mark the operation in which this fault can occur with the `FaultContract` attribute. This makes sure that WCF exposes the type.

Instead of catching `FaultException<ExceptionDetail>`, we can now catch a `FaultException` of our defined fault type (after having updated the service reference so that the proxy gets regenerated) and can access the public properties we've defined in this type on our client.

Optimizing performance using binary XML

When working with data in Silverlight, you'll typically get your data through some kind of service call. This means that this data has to be sent over the wire. In some cases, the data that is to be sent back and forth is relatively small, but in other cases, the amount of transported data can become quite large, which means more bandwidth consumption and a longer wait for the user.

When using WCF services with Silverlight, it's possible to compress this data, thus ensuring lower bandwidth consumption. In this recipe, you'll learn how to achieve this.

Getting ready

If you want to follow along with this recipe, you can use the provided starter solution located in the `Chapter07/UsingBinaryXML_Starter` folder in the code bundle that is available on the Packt site. The completed solution can be found in the `Chapter07/UsingBinaryXML_Completed` folder.

How to do it...

To look at how binary XML works, we're starting from a simple Silverlight solution that includes a Silverlight project that calls a WCF service method. This method returns a `Person` object and shows it on the screen. This starter solution uses `basicHttpBinding`. We're going to encode our data to binary, so the bandwidth consumption is smaller. To achieve this, complete the following steps:

1. Start by opening the solution as outlined in the *Getting ready* section of this recipe.

2. Open the `web.config` file and locate the endpoint exposed by `MyWCFService`. At the moment, this endpoint uses a `basicHttpBinding`. Change this endpoint to use a custom binding to encode the data to binary as shown in the following code:

```
<bindings>
  <customBinding>
    <binding name="UsingBinaryXML.Web.MyWCFService
      .customBinding0">
      <binaryMessageEncoding />
      <httpTransport />
    </binding>
  </customBinding>
```

```
        </bindings>
        <serviceHostingEnvironment aspNetCompatibilityEnabled="true" />
        <services>
          <service name="UsingBinaryXML.Web.MyWCFService">
            <endpoint address=""
                        binding="customBinding"
                        bindingConfiguration="UsingBinaryXML.Web
                          .MyWCFService.customBinding0"
                        contract="UsingBinaryXML.Web.MyWCFService" />
            <endpoint address="mex"
                        binding="mexHttpBinding"
                        contract="IMetadataExchange" />
          </service>
        </services>
```

3. Open the Silverlight application and update the Service Reference by right-clicking on **MyWCFServiceReference** and selecting **Update Service Reference**.

4. You can now build and run the solution. The data will be sent over the wire binary encoded.

How it works...

When using a WCF service, changing the way data is encoded is a matter of defining the correct binding in the corresponding config files. WCF takes care of the rest.

In the second step of this recipe, we've added a `customBinding` that defines the `binaryMessageEncoding` element. This binding is then used by our endpoint (instead of `basicHttpBinding`) to make sure that binary encoding will be used. In the third step, we make sure that the correct corresponding client-side endpoint configuration is generated in `ServiceReferences.ClientConfig` by updating the Service Reference.

The code doesn't have to be changed to achieve binary encoding.

The default configuration is different depending on the version of Silverlight you're using

In Silverlight 3 and higher, a custom binding that provides binary encoding is automatically generated. So you don't need to execute the previous steps to get the advantages of binary encoding.

Using binary encoding is not a security measure

Although the data sent over the wire isn't as easily readable as plain text, it's not that hard to write a decoder. Thus, binary encoding should be used as a means of lowering your bandwidth consumption, but never as a security measure.

As mentioned before, using binary encoding is not a security measure. To learn how to secure your communication, have a look at the *Ensuring data is encrypted* and *Securing service communication using message-based security* recipes.

Using duplex communication

Most types of communication between a client and a server are initiated by the client. The client sends a request to the server and the server sends its response back to the client. However, we may sometimes need to inform the client of changes that take place in the service. This will then be a server-initiated request to the client as the server needs to push information to the client. This leads us to the fact that sometimes we may need so-called duplex communication, in which both the server and the client side can initiate the communication. This isn't possible out of the box because of the HTTP stack. HTTP is based on a client-initiated request, on which the server can react.

The `PollingDuplexBinding` was introduced to mimic this duplex communication. In this type of binding, the client will almost continuously poll for new messages on the server, creating the illusion of a duplex communication channel.

Silverlight 2 already had basic support for duplex communication. However, Silverlight 3 extended this model and dramatically reduced its complexity. It's now very easy to create duplex communication using WCF.

Getting ready

We'll build the application in this recipe from scratch. To follow along with this recipe, a starter solution is provided in the `Chapter07/DuplexStockService_Starter` folder in the code bundle that is available on the Packt site. This solution contains some images that are used in the application code. The finished solution can be found in the `Chapter07/DuplexStockService_Completed` folder.

How to do it...

We'll build a stock ticker in this recipe. A stock ticker is a typical scenario in which the server should be able to send new information to the client when the value of a stock has changed. We'll start by building the service and afterwards, we'll connect the Silverlight application with the newly created service. Using the `PollingDuplexBinding`, the client will receive updates as they happen on the server. The following are the steps we need to complete to make duplex communication work:

1. We'll build the entire application from scratch, both the service and the client-side Silverlight application. Create a new Silverlight solution in Visual Studio and call it `DuplexStockService`.

2. Let's first focus on the service. The support for duplex communication both on the server and the client side is provided by two assemblies that are automatically installed with the Silverlight SDK. For the server side, there's the `System.ServiceModel.PollingDuplex.dll` assembly that is located in the `%ProgramFiles%\Microsoft SDKs\Silverlight\v4.0\Libraries\Server` directory. Note that when using a 64-bit OS such as Windows 7 64 bit, this file will be located in the`%ProgramFiles(x86)%\Microsoft SDKs\Silverlight\v4.0\Libraries\Server` directory. Add a reference to this assembly in the web project of the solution.

3. To add the service, right-click on the web project and add a **Silverlight-enabled WCF Service**. Name this service as `StockService`.

4. We need to make some modifications to the service so that it can work as a duplex service. First, add a new interface to the project by right-clicking on the web project and selecting the **Interface** item in the dialog. Name this interface as `IStockService`.

5. In this interface, we will define the `contract` the service exposes. In this case, the service exposes one operation called `Connect`, which will be invoked from the client application, passing in the stock symbol that we want to receive updates from. However, we also have to specify a client callback interface called `IStockServiceClient`. This is shown in the following code:

```
[ServiceContract(Namespace = "Silverlight", CallbackContract =
   typeof(IStockServiceClient))]
public interface IStockService
{
   [OperationContract(IsOneWay = true)]
   void Connect(string stockSymbol);
}
```

Note that the `OperationContract` was defined with the `IsOneWay` parameter set to `true`. This indicates that the operation will not return a reply message and the updates will be pushed to the client.

6. In the `IStockService.cs` file, we still need to define the client interface called `IStockServiceClient`. This interface defines that we can send a message of the `Update` type to the client (we'll add the `Update` class in the next step). This is shown in the following code:

```
[ServiceContract]
public interface IStockServiceClient
{
   [OperationContract(IsOneWay = true)]
   void SendUpdate(Update update);
}
```

7. The `Update` class contains information about the stock such as the new value, the change percentage, and an indication whether it increased or decreased. The status of the stock is wrapped as an enumeration type called `UpdateType` as shown in the following code:

```
public class Update
{
  public double Amount { get; set; }
  public UpdateType UpdateType { get; set; }
  public double Percentage { get; set; }
}
public enum UpdateType
{
  Increase,
  Decrease,
  NoChange
}
```

8. Let's now implement the `IStockService` interface. The implementation should be added to the `StockService.svc.cs` file. We'll introduce a `Timer` (of the `System.Threading` namespace) that will simulate new stock values coming in. Using the `OperationContext.Current.GetCallbackChannel`, we get access to the client callback interface. This instance is then used to send updates using the `SendUpdate` method in the `Tick` event of the `Timer` as shown in the following code:

```
public class StockService : IStockService
{
  private IStockServiceClient client;
  private Timer updateTimer;
  private Update update;
  private Update previousUpdate;
  public void Connect(string stockSymbol)
  {
    client = OperationContext.Current.GetCallbackChannel
      <IStockServiceClient>();
    updateTimer = new Timer(new TimerCallback(TimerTick),
      null, 500, 5000);
  }
  void TimerTick(object state)
  {
    if (client != null)
    {
      try
      {
```

```
              RefreshUpdate();
              client.SendUpdate(update);
          }
          catch (Exception)
          {
              client = null;
              updateTimer.Dispose();
          }
      }
  }
  private void RefreshUpdate()
  {
    Random r = new Random();
    double value = Math.Round(30 + 10 * r.NextDouble(), 2);
    if (update == null)
    {
      update = new Update()
      {
        Amount = value,
        UpdateType = UpdateType.NoChange,
        Percentage = 0.0
      };
      previousUpdate = update;
    }
    else
    {
      //calculate difference
      double diff = value > previousUpdate.Amount ? value -
        previousUpdate.Amount : previousUpdate.Amount - value;
      double percentage = diff / previousUpdate.Amount*100;
      UpdateType updateType = value > previousUpdate.Amount ?
        UpdateType.Increase : UpdateType.Decrease;
      update = new Update()
      {
        Amount = value,
        UpdateType = updateType,
        Percentage = Math.Round(percentage, 2)
      };
      previousUpdate = update;
    }
  }
}
```

9. The last step for the service is changing its configuration. In the `web.config`, in the `system.serviceModel` node, we need to specify that the service will be using polling duplex communication. The code for the configuration is as follows:

```
<system.serviceModel>
  <extensions>
    <bindingExtensions>
      <add name="pollingDuplexHttpBinding"
          type="System.ServiceModel.Configuration
            .PollingDuplexHttpBindingCollectionElement,
            System.ServiceModel.PollingDuplex, Version=4.0.0.0,
            Culture=neutral, PublicKeyToken=31bf3856ad364e35"/>
    </bindingExtensions>
  </extensions>
  <behaviors>
    <serviceBehaviors>
      <behavior name="DuplexStockService.Web
                .StockServiceBehavior">
        <serviceMetadata httpGetEnabled="true"/>
        <serviceDebug includeExceptionDetailInFaults="false"/>
      </behavior>
    </serviceBehaviors>
  </behaviors>
  <bindings>
    <pollingDuplexHttpBinding>
    </pollingDuplexHttpBinding>
  </bindings>
  <serviceHostingEnvironment aspNetCompatibilityEnabled="false"/>
  <services>
    <service behaviorConfiguration="DuplexStockService.Web
                .StockServiceBehavior"
            name="DuplexStockService.Web.StockService">
      <endpoint address=""
                binding="pollingDuplexHttpBinding"
                contract="DuplexStockService.Web.IStockService"/>
      <endpoint address="mex"
                binding="mexHttpBinding"
                contract="IMetadataExchange"/>
    </service>
  </services>
</system.serviceModel>
```

10. Working with a duplex service from a client-side perspective is not very different from working with a regular WCF service. The biggest difference is that for the time being, there's no support for working with `*.config` files when working with duplex services. This results in some more manual work that needs to be done. Start by adding a service reference to the service. To do this, right-click on the **Service References** node in the Silverlight project and select **Add Service Reference....** In the dialog box that appears, we can find the service using the **Discover** button as it's located in the same solution as the Silverlight project itself. Enter **StockService** into the **Namespace:** field. This process is entirely similar to a non-duplex service.

11. Similar to the service, we also need to add a reference to the `System.ServiceModel.PollingDuplex.dll` file in the Silverlight application. This file can be found in `%ProgramFiles%\Microsoft SDKs\Silverlight\v4.0\Libraries\Client` (or `%ProgramFiles(x86)%\Microsoft SDKs\Silverlight\v4.0\Libraries\Client` in the case of a 64-bit OS).

12. The UI for the application is simple and contains a few basic controls. The screenshot is shown a bit further, whereas the code can be found in the code bundle.

13. We want to receive updates when the user enters a stock symbol and clicks on the `Button`. We start by creating an `EndPointAddress` instance that points to the URI of the service. After that, we create an instance of the `CustomBinding` class to make communication with the service possible. The rest of the code consists of instantiating the proxy, attaching the callback method, and invoking the `Connect` operation using the `ConnectAsync` method. Note that the `Connect` will not return a message and the callback is registered for the `SendUpdateReceived` event. This is shown in the following code:

```
private StockService.StockServiceClient proxy;
private void StartButton_Click(object sender, RoutedEventArgs e)
{
  StockSymbolTextBlock.Text = StockSymbolTextBox.Text + ":";
  EndpointAddress address = new EndpointAddress
    ("http://localhost:6138/StockService.svc");
  CustomBinding binding = new CustomBinding
    (new PollingDuplexBindingElement(),
     new BinaryMessageEncodingBindingElement(),
     new HttpTransportBindingElement());
  proxy = new DuplexStockService.StockService
    .StockServiceClient(binding, address);
  proxy.SendUpdateReceived += new EventHandler<DuplexStockService
    .StockService.SendUpdateReceivedEventArgs>
    (proxy_SendUpdateReceived);
  proxy.ConnectAsync(StockSymbolTextBox.Text);
}
```

Note that the port number (`localhost:6138`) may be different in your own project.

14. We have access to the UI from the callback (so no crossing threads is needed here). We can update the UI with a new value for every message that comes from the server. This can be achieved using the following code:

```
void proxy_SendUpdateReceived(object sender, DuplexStockService
  .StockService.SendUpdateReceivedEventArgs e)
{
   this.DataContext = e.update;
}
```

We have now created a service that allows duplex communication with a Silverlight application. The result is shown in the following screenshot:

How it works...

To explain how duplex communication works, we need to cover several items. Let's start with what really happens behind the scenes.

The PollingDuplexBinding: polling, binding, and assemblies

There's a real need of supporting two-way communication in real-world applications. In some scenarios, in addition to requesting data from the client, the server must be capable of initiating the action itself and sending data to the client side. In Silverlight 3, two options are available: using sockets (which is explained in the *Using socket communication* in Silverlight recipe in Chapter 6) and using duplex bindings. (In fact, a third option is added in Silverlight 4, namely the net.tcp binding, which is the subject of the following recipe.) While sockets can be a great solution, they have their disadvantages as well. They communicate over an exotic range of ports, which may not always be accessible through firewalls, making it impossible to use them.

However, duplex communication is implemented through the PollingDuplexBinding in WCF. By looking at the name of this binding, it's easy to see that it's implemented using some sort of polling, sometimes referred as smart polling. The reason for this name is the following. Writing a polling client is something we could do ourselves as well. In that case, the Silverlight client application would contact the server quite often for new information. However, this would have its complications. Finding a perfect poll interval would be rather difficult. If we set the interval too small, we'll bring down the server. If we set it too large, we won't be notified about updates in time. This solution would also be unscalable, resulting in server overload when too many clients start polling.

Due to this, Microsoft introduced the smart polling technique. Based on polling, it's much more lightweight when it is at its core. The client has to contact the server to initiate the communication. The reason for this is that we're working over HTTP and HTTP first requires a request to start the communication. If the communication had taken place over TCP, this wouldn't have been the case as TCP is a duplex protocol. Once a connection is made, the `PollingDuplexBinding` allows a channel to remain connected until a timeout occurs, disconnecting only to refresh the channel or to send received messages to the client. In between that time, the client polls the service almost continuously. The timeout is defined by the `PollTimeout` property on the `PollingDuplexBindingElement` and defaults to five minutes. When the timeout occurs, no exceptions are thrown if the client and the server haven't aborted the session. If they have, a `TimeoutException` is raised. When the channel needs to refresh, no exception is thrown; an empty response is returned, and the channel is opened up again. As a result, the polling starts again. If messages are created within this period, they are stored on the server and are sent to the client on the first poll.

A second type of timeout called the `InactivityTimeout` is also available. It defines the interval of time that can pass without activity from either the client or the server. It has a default value of ten minutes, after which the channel is set to a faulted state.

To support duplex binding both on the server and the client side, we need to add a reference to an assembly that provides support for duplex binding. This assembly is named `System. ServiceModel.PollingDuplex.dll` on both sides. On the server side, this assembly is located by default at `%ProgramFiles%\Microsoft SDKs\Silverlight\v3.0\ Libraries\Server`. On the client side, it is located at `%ProgramFiles%\Microsoft SDKs\Silverlight\v3.0\Libraries\Client`.

The service

The service does not differ that much from a WCF service written for one-way communication. However, some specifics need to be taken into account to make duplex bindings work. Let's take a look at them. In the service contract (both `IStockService` and `IStockServiceClient`), we specified the `IsOneWay` property as `true` in the `OperationContract` attribute. The result of setting this value is that the client will not wait for the service to return, which it would normally do in a one-way scenario. In this case, the client calls the method, but returns immediately and does not wait for the service code to execute. Due to this, the operations need to have `void` as the return type as no value can be returned.

The service contract is attributed with the `CallbackContract` attribute. The specified contract—`IStockServiceClient`—is used as a callback contract. This allows client applications to listen to the incoming operation calls sent independently by the service.

Using the `GetCallbackChannel` method in the service, we get access to the client instance that made the call to the service. This instance is of the `IstockServiceClient` type and the interface is defined as a callback contract. Due to this, we can call the `SendUpdate` method on it, thus triggering the operation on the client side.

Finally, the service needs its configuration. In this configuration, we specify that the service will be communicating using duplex communication. The most important part in this is the addition of `pollingDuplexHttpBinding` in the `bindings` collection.

```
<bindings>
  <pollingDuplexHttpBinding>
  </pollingDuplexHttpBinding>
</bindings>
```

This binding is then used as the binding for the endpoint of the service using the following code:

```
<endpoint address=""
          binding="pollingDuplexHttpBinding"
          contract="DuplexStockService.Web.IStockService"/>
```

The client

With the service in place, one or more clients can connect to the service. We need to define an `EndPointAddress` instance in the client code. The `EndPointAddress` class contains the address of the service endpoint that will be used for duplex communication. We need to create the binding instance manually. To do this, we use `CustomBinding`. This instance is initialized with a list of binding elements that define the binding when taken together.

The actual communication is carried out using a proxy similar to a normal service. However, there are a few differences. The first one is the instantiation of the proxy. It requires both the `EndPointAddress` and the `CustomBinding` instance to be passed in. Secondly, the method we call asynchronously is not the same as the one we register to receive callbacks from. This is quite logical. The asynchronously called method is used in this example to connect to the service. The callbacks are received when the service invokes the client operations.

See also

Duplex services are one way to perform duplex communication. Another way are socket services way, which are discussed in the *Using socket communication in Silverlight* recipe in Chapter 6.

Using duplex communication with the WCF net.tcp binding

So far, we have looked at two technologies that allow us to perform duplex communication. In the previous chapter, we looked at how we could set this up using TCP sockets communication. The biggest advantage of using sockets is their speed. The second option is duplex WCF services, which is the focus of the previous recipe. Being WCF services, the programming model is much simpler. Based on contracts, we get typed access to the objects with which we're working. However, they rely on HTTP for their communication, resulting in slower speeds.

Silverlight 4 has added a new option that brings the best of both worlds—WCF net.tcp binding. We can still use the same simple programming model from WCF and benefit from better transport speed. However, note that net.tcp isn't targeted only at duplex communication. We can also use this binding for regular service communications.

In this recipe, we'll see how we can change the WCF duplex communication sample created in the previous recipe to use the net.tcp binding.

Getting ready

This recipe will change the code created in the previous recipe to use the WCF net.tcp binding. However, it's advisable to use the starter solution located in the `Chapter07/DuplexCommunication_NetTcp_Starter` folder in the code bundle that is available on the Packt website. The finished solution for this recipe can be found in the `Chapter07/DuplexCommunication_NetTcp_Completed` folder.

How to do it...

In this recipe, we'll start from the sample we created in the previous recipe that uses WCF duplex communication over HTTP. Changing the application to use net.tcp instead of HTTP for its communication in itself boils down to changing the configuration code within `web.config`. However, we also need to make some changes in the way the services are hosted. The following are the steps we need to perform:

1. Open the solution as outlined in the *Getting ready* section of this recipe.

2. To set up a net.tcp communication, we need to make some changes on the web server software. The built-in ASP.NET Web Server of Visual Studio does not support net.tcp communication. So we'll need to use **Internet Information Services (IIS)** for this.

3. Deploying the hosting site to IIS can be carried out in several ways. In this recipe, we'll take the manual route. Open **IIS** and create a new application under the **Default Web Site** node. Name this application as **StockService**. The result is shown in the following screenshot:

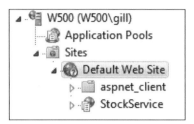

4. When hosting WCF services with net.tcp in IIS 7, we need to enable **Windows Process Activation Service** (**WAS**). Web applications are normally activated based on incoming HTTP requests. With net.tcp communication, a web application will be activated by a net.tcp request. This feature is not enabled on IIS by default. To enable it, go to **Windows Features** and under **Microsoft .NET Framework 3.5.1**, check on **Windows Communication Foundation Non-HTTP Activation**. This is shown in the following screenshot:

5. In the IIS, we have to enable the `net.tcp` protocol. To do this, right-click on the **StockService** application in the **IIS Manager** and select **Manage Application | Advanced settings**. In the **Enabled Protocols** field, add **http,net.tcp** as shown in the following screenshot:

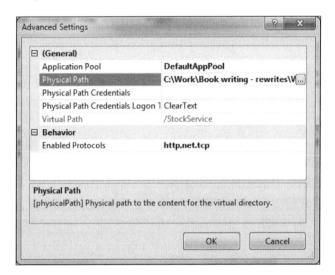

6. We should also open the port for communication over net.tcp. The available ports are the same as with TCP communication. To do this, right-click on the website hosting the application (in our case **Default Web Site**) and select **Edit bindings**. In the dialog box that appears, add the port **4502** (lowest available port number) for the **net.tcp** binding type as shown in the following screenshot:

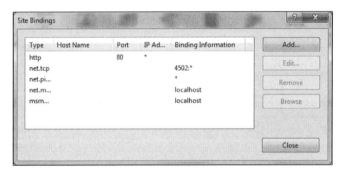

7. Now that we have IIS configured, we need to specify in Visual Studio that the `DuplexCommunication.Web` website should start from this IIS site instead of the built-in ASP.NET server. To do this, right-click on the hosting website in the **Solution Explorer** and select **Properties**. In the properties window, under the **Web** tab, select the **Use Local IIS Web server** option and point to the web application in IIS (for example `http://localhost/StockService`).

8. We have to make changes to `web.config` so that the service will support the net.tcp binding. To do this, change the code in `web.config` as follows:

```
<system.serviceModel>
  <extensions>
    <bindingExtensions>
      <add name="pollingDuplexBinding"
           type="System.ServiceModel.Configuration
             .PollingDuplexHttpBindingCollectionElement,
             System.ServiceModel.PollingDuplex"/>
    </bindingExtensions>
  </extensions>
  <behaviors>
    <serviceBehaviors>
      <behavior name="DuplexCommunicationNetTcpBehavior">
        <serviceMetadata httpGetEnabled="true"/>
        <serviceDebug includeExceptionDetailInFaults="true"/>
      </behavior>
    </serviceBehaviors>
  </behaviors>
  <bindings>
    <pollingDuplexBinding>
      <binding name="DuplexNetTcpBinding"
               useTextEncoding="true"/>
    </pollingDuplexBinding>
    <netTcpBinding>
      <binding name="DuplexNetTcpBinding">
        <security mode="None"/>
      </binding>
    </netTcpBinding>
  </bindings>
  <services>
    <service behaviorConfiguration="DuplexCommunication
               NetTcpBehavior"
             name="DuplexCommunication.Web.StockService">
      <endpoint address=""
                binding="pollingDuplexBinding"
                bindingConfiguration="DuplexNetTcpBinding"
                contract="DuplexCommunication.Web.IStockService"/>
      <endpoint address=""
                binding="netTcpBinding"
                bindingConfiguration="DuplexNetTcpBinding"
                contract="DuplexCommunication.Web.IStockService"/>
      <endpoint address="mex"
                binding="mexHttpBinding"
                contract="IMetadataExchange"/>
    </service>
  </services>
</system.serviceModel>
```

9. The service code (the `IStockService` contract and the `StockService.svc.cs` implementation) doesn't need any changes. However, the `Update` class does need a few changes as shown in the following code:

```
[MessageContract]
public class Update
{
  [MessageBodyMember]
  public double Amount { get; set; }
  [MessageBodyMember]
  public double Percentage { get; set; }
}
```

10. Just like TCP socket communication (refer to Chapter 6 for more information), net.tcp communication needs a policy server. The code for this is not included in this recipe. However, it can be found in the `PolicyServer` project in the code bundle of this recipe.

11. As we're now ready with the service, we can build the solution.

12. As we're communicating with a WCF service, we can create a proxy class using the **Add Service Reference...** option inside the Silverlight application. Along with the proxy generation, configuration code is also generated in the `ServiceReferences.ClientConfig` code. The generated code refers to the service using net.tcp. It is shown in the following code:

```
<configuration>
  <system.serviceModel>
    <bindings>
      <customBinding>
        <binding name="NetTcpBinding_IStockService">
          <binaryMessageEncoding />
          <tcpTransport maxReceivedMessageSize="2147483647"
                        maxBufferSize="2147483647" />
        </binding>
      </customBinding>
    </bindings>
    <client>
      <endpoint address="net.tcp://localhost:4502/StockService/
                StockService.svc"
                binding="customBinding"
                bindingConfiguration="NetTcpBinding_IStockService"
                contract="StockService.IStockService"
                name="NetTcpBinding_IStockService" />
    </client>
  </system.serviceModel>
</configuration>
```

13. The Silverlight client code can be made easier than the code with regular duplex WCF services. We can create an instance of the proxy by passing in the name of the binding. This can be seen in the following code:

```
private void StartButton_Click(object sender, RoutedEventArgs e)
{
  StockService.StockServiceClient client = new
    StockService.StockServiceClient("NetTcpBinding
    _IStockService");
  client.SendUpdateReceived += new EventHandler
    <StockService.SendUpdateReceivedEventArgs>
    (client_SendUpdateReceived);
  client.ConnectAsync("MSFT");
}
void client_SendUpdateReceived(object sender,
  StockService.SendUpdateReceivedEventArgs e)
{
  AmountTextBlock.Text = (e.request as Update).Amount.ToString();
  PercentageTextBlock.Text = (e.request as
    Update).Percentage.ToString();
}
```

We have now completed the switch of the application to use net.tcp binding instead of duplex communication over HTTP.

How it works...

With Silverlight 2 and Silverlight 3, we were basically limited to use the `BasicHttpBinding`. Silverlight 4 adds support for the net.tcp binding. The major benefit of this binding is improved performance while still using the easy programming model offered by WCF.

Another advantage is the fact that it can also perform duplex communication. This results in Silverlight 4 having the following three ways to perform two-way communication between a service and a client:

▶ **Duplex WCF communication**: Uses HTTP for its communication, but benefits from the easy programming model of WCF.

▶ **TCP communication**: Fast communication because of TCP. It's more complex to work with.

▶ **Net.tcp**: Combines the speed of TCP with the easy programming model of WCF.

Net.tcp builds `System.Net.Sockets` underneath the covers. Due to this, it has the same restrictions. Silverlight can connect to TCP services only on ports between 4502 and 4534. The same holds true for net.tcp. Due to this, just like TCP, net.tcp is a good fit for intranet applications and not for internet applications. Also, just as for TCP, when connecting with net.tcp services, Silverlight requires the presence of a policy server.

On the client side, we can use the **Add Service Reference...** dialog box to build a proxy class. The use of the net.tcp binding is detected and the configuration code is generated as well. The actual code to perform the call to the service uses the same model as used for communication with other services. By specifying the name of the binding in the client configuration code, we can instantiate the proxy using the following code:

```
StockService.StockServiceClient client = new
    StockService.StockServiceClient("NetTcpBinding_IStockService");
```

Setup requirements

When working with net.tcp, we can't use the ASP.NET Development Server (built-in with Visual Studio). It doesn't support the `net.tcp` protocol. Due to this, we need to host the website containing the services in IIS. As outlined in the recipe steps, IIS itself needs some configuration done to it.

See also

This recipe used the net.tcp binding for its communication and we used it for building a duplex communication mechanism. In the *Using duplex communication* recipe, we built the same application using duplex communication over HTTP. In the *Using socket communication in Silverlight* recipe in Chapter 6, we used TCP for this two-way communication.

Debugging a service in Silverlight

One of the things that were missing in Silverlight 2 when it came to working with services was the ability to debug them. In the event of an error occurring in the service code, it was not possible to get information about this error in the Silverlight client application. The only information we got when something went wrong was "The remote server returned an error: NotFound" and that was it. The user wasn't provided with any inner exception with a clue about the real error on the service, any messages, and so on. While this was a problem during development, it was a worse a problem that we could not give any indication to the end user on what he/she should do to solve the issue. This was because we could not distinguish let's say a divide-by-zero error from an error caused by the database being down inside the Silverlight application.

If we are developing both the service and the Silverlight application, we can still debug the service code and find out the eventual errors. However, it's a real show-stopper when working with external, perhaps third-party services to which we don't have access as we can't see what's happening on the service side.

Luckily, Silverlight has evolved quite a lot since version 2, as it now includes the option to debug the service by displaying the returned error from the service side. In this recipe, we'll look at how to set this up.

Getting ready

To try out this sample, a starter solution is provided in the `Chapter07/ SilverlightServiceDebugging_Starter` folder in the code bundle available on the Packt website. The finished solution can be found in the `Chapter07/ SilverlightServiceDebugging_Completed` folder.

How to do it...

To explain the way Silverlight makes it possible to debug a service, we'll start from an application that could have been easily created in Silverlight 2 and we'll follow the changes we need to make to both the service and the Silverlight application. We do this so that we can debug the service and get error information in the Silverlight client.

The scenario is very simple. The application allows us to search for an employee or a list of employees in a directory based on username. If a result is found, a `DataGrid` is shown containing the results. Let's take a look at the steps we need to perform to make it possible to debug this application:

 Note that this recipe requires either Fiddler or Web Development Helper to view the traffic from and to the service. See Appendix XXX for more info on these. We'll use Fiddler in this recipe.

1. Open the solution located in the `Chapter07/SilverlightServiceDebugging_ Starter` folder in the code bindle and take a look at the `SilverlightEmployeeLookup.Web/EmployeeLookupService.svc.cs` file. The `RetrieveEmployeesByUserName(string userName)` method that has a bug resides in this class. If no `Employee` items are found, we still try to retrieve the first item. Of course, this will generate an error. The following code shows the faulty code:

```
if (results.Count<Employee>() == 0)
{
   Employee employee = results.First();
}
```

2. Let's try if we can see in the Silverlight application what went wrong. Run the application and search for **George**. Visual Studio will show the **Sequence contains no elements** error inside the service code. However, on the client side, the error information is not available anymore and the dreaded **NotFound** exception is thrown as shown in the following screenshot:

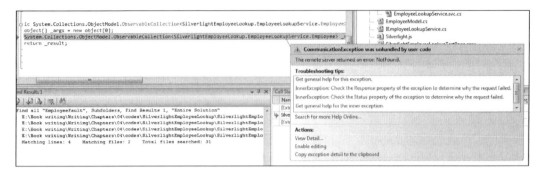

3. At this point, even Fiddler is of no help. Let's run the application with Fiddler open again. When the error occurs, a message with status 500 is shown as well as the following result being shown, containing no information about the error:

```
<s:Envelope xmlns:s="http://schemas.xmlsoap.org/soap/envelope/">
  <s:Body>
    <s:Fault>
      <faultcode xmlns:a="http://schemas.microsoft.com/
          net/2005/12/windowscommunicationfoundation/dispatcher">
        a:InternalServiceFault
      </faultcode>
      <faultstring xml:lang="nl-BE">
        The server was unable to process the request due to
        an internal error.  For more information about the
        error, either turn on IncludeExceptionDetailInFaults
        (either from ServiceBehaviorAttribute or from the
        &lt;serviceDebug&gt; configuration behavior) on the
        server in order to send the exception information back to
        the client, or turn on tracing as per the Microsoft .NET
        Framework 3.0 SDK documentation and inspect the server
        trace logs.
      </faultstring>
    </s:Fault>
  </s:Body>
</s:Envelope>
```

The previous message says that we need to turn on `IncludeExceptionDetailInFaults` to receive information about the error. We'll come to this later.

4. The reason that Silverlight can't read the error is that the message has a status 500. Due to the browser networking stack that Silverlight uses under the covers, plugins such as Silverlight don't get access to this message. Hence, we should try to change the status to 200 so that Silverlight can access the error. This change can be brought about by creating a WCF endpoint behavior for Silverlight faults. This will do the conversion from HTTP status 500 to HTTP status 200.

5. We'll create this behavior in a class in a separate project. To do this, create a new class library (not a Silverlight class library as this library will be used by the web project, not the Silverlight project). Name the new project as `FaultBehavior`.

6. In this new project, we create a class containing the new behavior. The complete code for this behavior can be found at `http://msdn.microsoft.com/en-us/library/dd470096(VS.95).aspx` as well as in the code bundle. The most relevant part, which does the status conversion, is shown in the following code:

```
public void BeforeSendReply(ref Message reply,
    object correlationState)
{
  if (reply.IsFault)
  {
    HttpResponseMessageProperty property =
      new HttpResponseMessageProperty();
    // Here the response code is changed to 200.
    property.StatusCode = System.Net.HttpStatusCode.OK;
    reply.Properties[HttpResponseMessageProperty.Name] =
      property;
  }
}
```

7. Build the class library and reference the project from the `SilverlightEmployeeLookup.Web` web project.

8. We need to make some configuration changes in the `web.config` file so that our service can use the newly created behavior. Change the code in the `web.config` file as shown in the following code (note that `includeExceptionDetailInFaults` is set to `true` in this code):

```
<system.serviceModel>
  <extensions>
    <behaviorExtensions>
      <add name="silverlightFaults"
          type="FaultBehavior.SilverlightFaultBehavior,
            FaultBehavior, Version=1.0.0.0, Culture=neutral,
            PublicKeyToken=null" />
    </behaviorExtensions>
  </extensions>
  <behaviors>
```

```
<endpointBehaviors>
  <behavior name="SilverlightFaultBehavior">
    <silverlightFaults />
  </behavior>
</endpointBehaviors>
<serviceBehaviors>
  <behavior name="SilverlightEmployeeLookup.Web
              .EmployeeLookupServiceBehavior">
    <serviceMetadata httpGetEnabled="true"/>
    <serviceDebug includeExceptionDetailInFaults="true"/>
  </behavior>
</serviceBehaviors>
</behaviors>
<services>
  <service behaviorConfiguration="SilverlightEmployeeLookup.Web
              .EmployeeLookupServiceBehavior"
            name="SilverlightEmployeeLookup.Web
              .EmployeeLookupService">
    <endpoint address=""
            binding="basicHttpBinding"
            behaviorConfiguration="SilverlightFaultBehavior"
            contract="SilverlightEmployeeLookup.Web
              .IEmployeeLookupService">
      <identity>
        <dns value="localhost"/>
      </identity>
    </endpoint>
    <endpoint address="mex"
            binding="mexHttpBinding"
            contract="IMetadataExchange"/>
  </service>
</services>
</system.serviceModel>
```

9. Now that all the plumbing is done, we can focus on the service again. Let's start by adding a new class called `EmployeeFault`. This class will contain information on the error that occurred. The following code specifies our own fault type called `EmployeeFault`. It contains two properties that will be filled with data when an error occurs.

```
public class EmployeeFault
{
  public string Message { get; set; }
  public string AdditionalInfo { get; set; }
}
```

10. In the contract of the `IEmployeeLookupService`, we need to add the `FaultContract` attribute. This is shown in the following code:

```
[ServiceContract]
public interface IEmployeeLookupService
{
   [OperationContract]
   [FaultContract(typeof(EmployeeFault))]
   List<Employee> RetrieveEmployeesByUserName(string userName);
}
```

11. In the service implementation, we can now create an instance of the `EmployeeFault` when an exception occurs. In the following code, we check if there are no results and if so, we return an instance of the `EmployeeFault` that contains information regarding the results.

```
if (results.Count<Employee>() == 0)
{
   EmployeeFault fault = new EmployeeFault();
   fault.Message = "No results found.";
   fault.AdditionalInfo = "Perhaps try a different search term.";
   throw new FaultException<EmployeeFault>(fault,
      "Bad search term");
}
```

12. Build the solution again. We also need to update the service reference so that the client-side proxy code is recreated. To do this, right-click on the service reference and select **Update Service Reference**. The generated code in the proxy class will now also include the `EmployeeFault`.

13. In the callback method of the Silverlight application, we can now check if the result contains an error, and if it does, we can check the type of the returned fault. This fault also includes relevant information that we can use to display to the user.

```
if (e.Error == null)
{
   EmployeesDataGrid.ItemsSource = e.Result;
}
else if (e.Error is FaultException<EmployeeFault>)
{
   FaultException<EmployeeFault> serviceFault =
      e.Error as FaultException<EmployeeFault>;
   ErrorTextBlock.Text = serviceFault.Detail.Message + " " +
      serviceFault.Detail.AdditionalInfo;
}
```

If we run the application now and search for a non-existing employee, we see the information contained in the fault returned by the service as shown in the following screenshot:

How it works...

When a service encounters an error, it returns an HTTP status code 500. Silverlight can't receive these responses because of the browser networking stack. Due to this, when working with services, we often encounter the "The remote server returned an error: NotFound error" error message. This isn't very helpful because no information on what really went wrong is included.

To make it possible for Silverlight to read service faults, we need to change the status code from 500 to 200. This can be achieved by adding a behavior that will do this for our WCF service. When using this behavior on a service, we also need to make configuration changes in the web.config file of the service project.

After this change, service faults are accessible in Silverlight. The fault—a SOAP fault—needs to be translated into managed code. Silverlight 2 could not do this. However, this changed with the introduction of Silverlight 3 and remained the same for Silverlight 4 as well. This way, error information sent by the service can be translated into a managed exception that can be inspected and used for error-handling purposes.

Types of faults

There are two types of faults that can be sent by a service—a declared fault and an undeclared fault.

Declared faults

Declared faults are the type of faults we should use in a production environment. These define a custom type that will be sent back to the client-side application, containing information on the error that occurred. Declared faults occur in operations annotated with the FaultContractAttribute. By annotating an operation with this attribute, we specify that this operation may throw this type of exception and if it does, the resulting fault instance should be sent to the client.

When building the proxy, the custom fault type will be generated on the client side as well. This way, we can build code that will check if the returned error is an instance of the custom fault type. If it is, we can get the error information from the instance.

Undeclared faults

During development, we often want all the information about an error that occurs. Remember the error message we got earlier in this recipe using Fiddler (in step 3)? Hidden in the response of the service, it was mentioned that we could get more information on the error that occurred by setting `IncludeExceptionDetailInFaults` to `true` in the service configuration. This is shown in the following line of code:

```
<serviceDebug includeExceptionDetailInFaults="true"/>
```

Doing this (and thus not using the declared faults) results in the original error being sent over the wire. Silverlight will also be able to pick up this type of fault (assuming we still have the behavior in place that converts status 500 to status 200). The following code can be used to capture undeclared faults:

```
void proxy_RetrieveEmployeesByUserNameCompleted(object sender,
    SilverlightEmployeeLookup.EmployeeLookupService
    .RetrieveEmployeesByUserNameCompletedEventArgs e)
{
    if (e.Error == null)
    {
        EmployeesDataGrid.ItemsSource = e.Result;
    }
    else if (e.Error is FaultException<ExceptionDetail>)
    {
        FaultException<ExceptionDetail> serviceFault =
            e.Error as FaultException<ExceptionDetail>;
        ErrorTextBlock.Text = serviceFault.Detail.Message;
    }
}
```

If we run this code, the Silverlight application will show the error message as it was sent when the error occurred on the service.

The main reason to favor declared faults for production code is that we don't want to show real service errors to the end users. These might even include sensitive information such as database passwords.

Ensuring data is encrypted

In Silverlight, you'll typically work service oriented through WCF services, REST services, and so on. However, this implies that your data is sent over the wire in an unencrypted format. This is not much of a problem in most controlled environments. But what if the data is sent through an uncontrolled environment (for example the internet)? It could be easily intercepted by someone with bad intentions. While that's bad when you're sending confidential data, it's even worse when your message header includes a username/password combination.

In this recipe, you'll learn how to make sure that the data sent over the wire is encrypted using **Secure Socket Layer communication** (**SSL**).

Getting ready...

This recipe is mainly about configuring IIS and WCF and it's much less about writing code. What you need is a simple Silverlight application calling a WCF service and a correctly configured/installed IIS web server where your Silverlight application and service host are hosted. A starter solution is located in the `Chapter07/EnsuringDataIsEncrypted_Starter` folder in the code bundle available on the Packt website. The completed solution can be found in the `Chapter07/EnsuringDataIsEncrypted_Completed\` folder.

How to do it...

We're going to set up a website in IIS 7.0 to use SSL through a self-signed certificate. After this, we're going to make sure that our WCF service is hosted on this website and securely callable from Silverlight. To achieve this, carry out the following steps:

1. Open **Internet Information Services (IIS) Manager** and create a new website by right-clicking on **Sites** on the left side of the IIS Manager and selecting **Add Web Site**. We'll name this website as **SSLServiceHost**. This can be seen in the following screenshot:

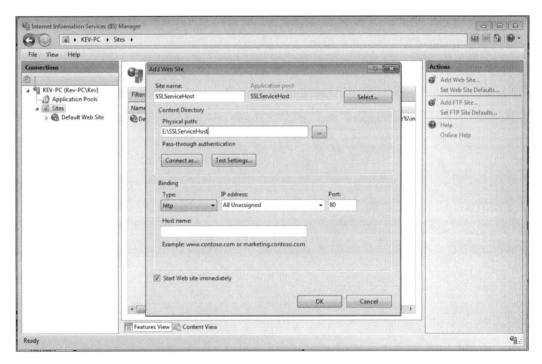

2. We're going to need a security certificate to use with the SSL binding. You might want to get one from one of the many vendors on the internet (for example Verisign), but in this example, we're going to create a self-signed one for testing purposes. Click on the root machine node on the left side of your IIS Manager and double-click on **Server Certificates**. This is shown in the following screenshot:

3. In the right-hand pane, click on **Create Self-Signed Certificate** and complete the wizard by providing **SilverlightTestCertificate** as a friendly name for this certificate. This can be seen in the following screenshot:

4. Click on **SSLServiceHost** on the left side of your IIS Manager, click on **Bindings...** on the right-hand pane, and add an SSL binding for this website using our freshly created security certificate.

5. Our website is now set up for secure communication over https. We're now going to host our WCF service on this site. Open the provided starter solution and navigate to the **Web** tab in the project properties of the `EnsuringDataIsEncrypted.Web` application. Select **Use Local IIS Web server** and make sure that the **Project Url:** refers to the website (https) we've created in the previous steps. Refer to the website by the server name and not using "localhost". If you use "localhost", the certificate will throw a warning ("computer name does not match" because "localhost" isn't the same as your server name) and you won't be able to access your service.

6. Open the `web.config` file, locate the custom binding with the name `EnsuringDataIsEncrypted.Web.MyWCFService.customBinding0`, and change the `HttpTransport` element to an `HttpsTransport` element.

7. Open your Silverlight application, add a Service Reference to `MyWCFService`, and name it as `MyWCFServiceReference`. If you get a warning concerning the security certificate, ignore it (as this is a self-signed certificate).

8. Locate the `btnCall_Click` handler in `MainPage.xaml.cs` and replace it with the following code:

```
private void btnCall_Click(object sender, RoutedEventArgs e)
{
  MyWCFServiceReference.MyWCFServiceClient client = new
    MyWCFServiceReference.MyWCFServiceClient();
  client.GetPersonCompleted += new EventHandler
    <MyWCFServiceReference.GetPersonCompletedEventArgs>
    (client_GetPersonCompleted);
  client.GetPersonAsync();
}
void client_GetPersonCompleted(object sender,
  MyWCFServiceReference.GetPersonCompletedEventArgs e)
{
  if (e.Error == null)
  {
    this.DataContext = e.Result;
  }
}
```

9. You can now build and run your application. Your application will securely call the WCF service over HTTPS.

How it works...

Making sure that communication is secure is about completing two steps. The first one is creating a website in IIS set up to use a certificate, either one you bought (for production sites) or one you've created yourself (for testing purposes). This is done in steps 1 to 4.

When that's done, we need to configure our application to use this website and the correct bindings. Configuring the application to use this website is done through the project properties window. By changing the web server to our previously created virtual directory instead of the development server, we ensure SSL communication is possible. It's impossible to use SSL with the built-in Visual Studio development server.

Starting from step 6, we make changes to our application. To be able to use transport security (SSL), we need to tell WCF to use this. This is done in step 6. We make sure that communication with our endpoint is possible only through SSL (https) and not through regular http by changing the transport element in the `web.config` to `HttpsTransport`.

Let's now go back to the Silverlight application. As we've done in previous recipes, we're adding a service reference to the service at the https endpoint. When we do this, Visual Studio generates the accompanying proxy classes as well as generates the correct bindings in `ServiceReferences.ClientConfig`. If you look at this file, you'll notice that the generated binding is enabled for `HttpsTransport` security.

All that's left now is adding code to call the `GetPerson()` service operation. This is done in step 8. If you build and run your solution now, all communication will be done through SSL and your messages will be encrypted.

See also

If you want to learn how to use message-based security (through SSL), have a look at the next recipe.

Securing service communication using message-based security

Service-oriented solutions typically require the services to know which user is accessing them, if this user is authenticated or not, and even if this user is authorized or not. If you don't implement these checks and if your services are hosted in a publicly available, uncontrolled environment, everyone will be able to access them. This is definitely something you don't want especially if confidential data is fetched or even edited using service calls.

So we need to make sure that certain service methods are accessible only to certain persons. A typical way of doing this is by using message-based security, which in this case means that you'd include the username/password combination in every message that's being sent to the service, where the received combination is then checked. If the combination is valid, the service operation can be executed. If not, typically a fault is returned.

Note that it's not possible to implement full message-based security as defined by the WS Security specification as Silverlight does not support this. Passing the credentials in the message header is the furthest we can go.

In this recipe, you'll learn how to do this with your Silverlight application using WCF services.

Getting ready

We're starting from a simple Silverlight solution that includes a Silverlight project that calls a WCF service method through HTTPS. Make sure that you've set up your IIS for HTTPS as explained in the previous recipe, because this recipe uses the website you've created in that recipe for hosting your WCF Service. If you want to follow along with this recipe, you can find a starter solution located in the `Chapter07/MessageBasedSecurity_Starter` folder in the code bundle available on the Packt website. The completed solution for this recipe can be found in the `Chapter07/MessageBasedSecurity_Completed` folder.

How to do it...

We're going to modify the starter solution to ensure that credentials are passed to the server and are checked before allowing further execution of the service method. To achieve this, complete the following steps:

1. Navigate to the **Web** tab in the project properties of the web application and change the virtual directory to a valid, SSL-enabled virtual directory on your computer.

2. Add a reference to `System.IdentityModel` and `System.IdentityModel.Selectors` to the web application.

3. Open the web application and add a new class. Name this class as `UsernamePWValidator`, let it inherit `UsernamePasswordValidator`, and implement it as shown in the following code:

```
using System;
using System.Collections.Generic;
using System.Linq;
using System.Web;
using System.ServiceModel;
using System.IdentityModel.Selectors;
namespace MessageBasedSecurity.Web
{
  public class UsernamePWValidator : UserNamePasswordValidator
  {
    public UsernamePWValidator()
```

```
      {
      }
      public override void Validate(string userName,
        string password)
      {
        if (userName != "Kevin" || password != "Dockx")
        {
          throw new FaultException("The provided credentials
            are invalid.");
        }
      }
    }
  }
}
```

4. Open the `web.config` file, locate the included service behavior, and change it to the following code:

```
<behavior name="MyServiceBehaviour">
<serviceMetadata httpGetEnabled="true" />
<serviceDebug includeExceptionDetailInFaults="false" />
  <serviceCredentials>
    <userNameAuthentication userNamePasswordValidationMode=
                            "Custom"
                            customUserNamePasswordValidatorType=
                            "MessageBasedSecurity.Web
                            .UsernamePWValidator,
                            MessageBasedSecurity.Web" />
  </serviceCredentials>
</behavior>
```

5. In the same file, locate the custom binding called `MessageBasedSecurity.Web.MyWCFService.customBinding0` and change the code as follows:

```
<customBinding>
  <binding name="MessageBasedSecurity.Web.MyWCFService
            .customBinding0">
    <security authenticationMode="UserNameOverTransport"/>
    <binaryMessageEncoding />
    <httpsTransport />
  </binding>
</customBinding>
```

6. In the same file, locate the service endpoint and change it as follows (remember to replace the `baseAddress` with your local IIS server name):

```
<service name="MessageBasedSecurity.Web.MyWCFService"
         behaviorConfiguration="MyServiceBehaviour">
```

```
<host>
  <baseAddresses>
    <add baseAddress="https://kev-pc"/>
  </baseAddresses>
</host>
<endpoint address=""
          binding="customBinding"
          bindingConfiguration="MessageBasedSecurity.Web
            .MyWCFService.customBinding0"
          contract="MessageBasedSecurity.Web.MyWCFService" />
<endpoint address="mex"
          binding="mexHttpBinding"
          contract="IMetadataExchange" />
</service>
```

7. In your Silverlight project, add a service reference to `MyWCFService` and name it as `MyWCFServiceReference`.

8. Replace the `Click` handler of the `btnWrongCredentials` button with the following code:

```
private void btnWrongCredentials_Click(object sender,
  RoutedEventArgs e)
{
  WebRequest.RegisterPrefix("https://",
    WebRequestCreator.ClientHttp);
  this.DataContext = null;
  MyWCFServiceReference.MyWCFServiceClient client = new
    MyWCFServiceReference.MyWCFServiceClient();
  client.GetPersonCompleted += new EventHandler
    <MyWCFServiceReference.GetPersonCompletedEventArgs>
    (client_GetPersonCompleted);
  client.ClientCredentials.UserName.UserName = "WrongUsername";
  client.ClientCredentials.UserName.Password = "WrongPassword";
  client.GetPersonAsync();
}
void client_GetPersonCompleted(object sender,
  MyWCFServiceReference.GetPersonCompletedEventArgs e)
{
  if (e.Error == null)
  {
    this.DataContext = e.Result;
  }
  else
  {
    MessageBox.Show(e.Error.Message);
  }
}
```

9. Replace the `Click` handler of the `btnCredentials` button with the following code:

```
private void btnCredentials_Click(object sender,
  RoutedEventArgs e)
{
  WebRequest.RegisterPrefix("https://",
    WebRequestCreator.ClientHttp);
  this.DataContext = null;
  MyWCFServiceReference.MyWCFServiceClient client = new
    MyWCFServiceReference.MyWCFServiceClient();
  client.GetPersonCompleted += new EventHandler
    <MyWCFServiceReference.GetPersonCompletedEventArgs>
    (client_GetPersonCompletedWithCredentials);
  client.ClientCredentials.UserName.UserName = "Kevin";
  client.ClientCredentials.UserName.Password = "Dockx";
  client.GetPersonAsync();
}
void client_GetPersonCompletedWithCredentials(object sender,
  MyWCFServiceReference.GetPersonCompletedEventArgs e)
{
  if (e.Error == null)
  {
    this.DataContext = e.Result;
  }
  else
  {
    MessageBox.Show(e.Error.Message);
  }
}
```

10. You can now build and run your solution. Depending on which button you click, the right credentials will be sent and your service call will either succeed or fail.

How it works...

As you've noticed, most of the work is done through WCF configuration and not through code changes. We want to make sure that our WCF service expects credentials and we need to provide a way to validate these credentials.

In step 4, we've changed the behavior our endpoint uses to expect credentials. This is done through the `userNameAuthentication` element. By providing this element, we make sure that any endpoint using this behavior expects client credentials in the form of a username/ password combination.

As well as that, we define the way these credentials must be validated by setting the value of the `customUserNamePasswordValidatorType` attribute to a custom validator. This custom validator is the one we've created in step 3. It must inherit the `UserNamePasswordValidator` class and we override the `Validate` method to define our own validation. In this specific example, validation will succeed when the username/password combination is Kevin/Dockx. All other combinations will fail and will prevent the service method from being executed. Of course, you can write your own way of validating by changing the `Validate` method. For example, you could check your own custom user tables in an underlying database.

We've already defined our custom behavior. What's next is defining the custom binding to be used by our service endpoint. This is done in step 5. The binding is changed to expect the `UserNameOverTransport` authentication and to use `HttpsTransport` (SSL).

We now need to bring this together, which is done in step 6. Our service is configured to use the custom behavior we created in step 4 by setting the `BehaviorConfiguration` attribute on the service element to our custom behavior. The endpoint is configured to use our custom binding by setting the `bindingConfiguration` attribute on the endpoint element.

After this, everything that is to be done on the service side of our application is done. Next up is the client side. First, a service reference is added that will generate the necessary proxy classes and a client config file. The two different buttons in our application are set to include client credentials on the client proxy instance (this has to be done only once per proxy instance). In the first button handler, the wrong credentials are set. In the second handler, the correct credentials will be passed to the service.

When you call the `GetPerson()` service method, the client credentials are securely sent over the wire in the message header (through SSL) and they're automatically checked by the `Validate` method of our custom validator. Only if they check out will the method be executed.

Transport security is required

Due to security measures, Silverlight doesn't allow a binding as used in this recipe (with credentials sent over the wire) to be used over regular HTTP. Allowing this would mean that the credentials would be sent in clear text. When you're using a binding that expects client credentials, you're obligated to use SSL (as defined by the `HttpsTransport` element in the `web.config` file).

See also

To learn how to secure your communication using SSL, have a look at the previous recipe.

Uploading files to a WCF service

While most of the time we'll want to download files such as images from a server, sometimes a scenario may arise where we might need to send files to a server. For example, imagine we are building a Silverlight image editor where the user is editing an image locally. After completion, the user may want to save this image on the server, perhaps in a folder or even in a SharePoint library. In this case, the locally created file (in this case an image) somehow needs to be transmitted to the server.

WCF services can help in implementing this scenario. At its heart, a file is nothing more than binary data that can be sent to a service endpoint. In this recipe, we'll build such a service and a client application that uses this service.

Getting ready

We'll build the application in this recipe from scratch. However, the finished solution can be found in the `Chapter07/SilverlightImageUpload` folder in the code bundle available on the Packt website.

How to do it...

To start sending files to the server, we need to create a service that is capable of receiving binary data. The service can take care of converting the binary data into a physical file that it can store on the local file system. The client-side Silverlight application can then send data to the service. The following are the steps we need to perform to complete this task:

1. We'll start from an empty Silverlight application in this recipe. Create a new Silverlight solution in Visual Studio and name it as `SilverlightImageUpload`.

2. Let's first take a look at how to create a service. In the `SilverlightImageUpload.Web` web project, add a new WCF service by right-clicking on the project and selecting the **Add | New Item...** option. In the dialog box that appears, select the regular **WCF service** template and name the service as `ImageUploadService.svc`. Visual Studio creates the `ImageUploadService.svc`, the `ImageUploadService.svc.cs`, and the `IImageUploadService.cs` files. The latter contains the service contract.

3. The service contract in the `IImageUploadService.cs` file is quite simple, containing only one operation. This is shown in the following code. The operation accepts one parameter, namely an instance of the `ImageUpload` class that we'll create in the next step.

```
[ServiceContract]
public interface IImageUploadService
{
    [OperationContract]
```

```
    bool Upload(ImageUpload imageUpload);
}
```

4. The `ImageUpload` class that is attributed with the `DataContract` attribute contains a byte array as one of its members. This is shown in the following code:

```
[DataContract]
public class ImageUpload
{
    [DataMember]
    public string ImageName { get; set; }
    [DataMember]
    public byte[] Image { get; set; }
}
```

5. Of course, we need to implement the service as well. The following code will convert the byte array sent by the client application into a file. The code relies on classes in the `System.IO` namespace such as `FileStream` and `BinaryWriter`. Note that we also add the `AspNetCompatibilityRequirementsAttribute` to this service. Setting this attribute results in the service running in an ASP.NET compatibility mode. This in turn results in the WCF service behaving like an ASMX service for some ASP.NET features.

```
[AspNetCompatibilityRequirements(RequirementsMode =
    AspNetCompatibilityRequirementsMode.Required)]
public class ImageUploadService : IImageUploadService
{
    public bool Upload(ImageUpload imageUpload)
    {
        FileStream fileStream = null;
        BinaryWriter writer = null;
        string imagePath;
        try
        {
            imagePath = HttpContext.Current.Server.MapPath(".") +
                ConfigurationManager.AppSettings["ImageUploadDirectory"] +
                imageUpload.ImageName;
            if (imageUpload.ImageName != string.Empty)
            {
                fileStream = File.Open(imagePath, FileMode.Create);
                writer = new BinaryWriter(fileStream);
                writer.Write(imageUpload.Image);
            }
            return true;
        }
```

```
      catch (Exception)
      {
        return false;
      }
      finally
      {
        if (fileStream != null)
          fileStream.Close();
          if (writer != null)
            writer.Close();
      }
    }
  }
}
```

6. In the previous step, we used `ConfigurationManager.AppSettings["Imag eUploadDirectory"]`. This line of code refers to an entry in the `appSettings` collection in the `web.config` file where we store settings that are specific to the application. Add the following code in the `web.config` file (note that it is to be inserted between the opening and closing `appSettings` tags):

```
<appSettings>
  <add key="ImageUploadDirectory"
       value="/Images/"/>
</appSettings>
```

7. Finally, we need to tweak the configuration of the service to make it possible to receive larger than normal messages. In the `web.config` file, change the `system. ServiceModel` node so that it reflects the following code changes:

```
<system.serviceModel>
  <serviceHostingEnvironment aspNetCompatibilityEnabled="true"/>
  <bindings>
    <basicHttpBinding>
      <binding name="ImageUploadBinding"
               maxReceivedMessageSize="2000000"
               maxBufferSize="2000000">
        <readerQuotas maxArrayLength="2000000"
                      maxStringContentLength="2000000"/>
      </binding>
    </basicHttpBinding>
  </bindings>
  <behaviors>
    ...
  </behaviors>
  <services>
    <service behaviorConfiguration="SilverlightImageUpload.Web
             .ImageUploadServiceBehavior"
             name="SilverlightImageUpload.Web.ImageUploadService">
      <endpoint address=""
                binding="basicHttpBinding"
                bindingConfiguration="ImageUploadBinding"
```

```
                    contract="SilverlightImageUpload.Web
                     .IImageUploadService">
          . . .
      </service>
    </services>
  </system.serviceModel>
```

Note that the binding of the service is also set to basicHttpBinding.

8. Now that the service is ready, build it.

9. Add a service reference to the Silverlight application by right-clicking on the project node and selecting the **Add Service Reference...** option. In the dialog box that appears, click on the **Discover** button. Visual Studio should find the service. Set the namespace as ImageUploadService.

10. The UI of the application is very simple. The most important element is a Button. The complete code can be found in the code bundle.

11. In the event handler of the Click event of the Button, an OpenFileDialog is presented to the user in which he or she can select an image file (only *.jpg files are allowed in our scenario). The image is then converted into a byte array. This array along with a filename is used for the creation of an ImageUpload instance. Finally, an instance of the proxy class is created and a service call is made asynchronously, passing in the ImageUpload instance. This is shown in the following code:

```
private void UploadButton_Click(object sender, RoutedEventArgs e)
{
  OpenFileDialog openFileDialog = new OpenFileDialog();
  openFileDialog.Filter = "JPEG files|*.jpg";
  if (openFileDialog.ShowDialog() == true)
  {
    Stream stream = (Stream)openFileDialog.File.OpenRead();
    byte[] bytes = new byte[stream.Length];
    stream.Read(bytes, 0, (int)stream.Length);
    string fileName = openFileDialog.File.Name;
    ImageUploadService.ImageUpload imageUpload = new
      SilverlightImageUpload.ImageUploadService.ImageUpload();
    imageUpload.ImageName = fileName;
    imageUpload.Image = bytes;
    ImageUploadService.ImageUploadServiceClient proxy =
      new SilverlightImageUpload.ImageUploadService
      .ImageUploadServiceClient();
    proxy.UploadCompleted += new EventHandler
      <SilverlightImageUpload.ImageUploadService
      .UploadCompletedEventArgs>(proxy_UploadCompleted);
    proxy.UploadAsync(imageUpload);
  }
}
```

12. In the callback method, we have access to the result. We use this result to give feedback to the user as shown in the following code:

```
void proxy_UploadCompleted(object sender, SilverlightImageUpload
  .ImageUploadService.UploadCompletedEventArgs e)
{
  if (e.Error == null)
  {
    if (e.Result)
    {
      ResultTextBlock.Text = "Image uploaded successfully!";
    }
    else
    {
      ResultTextBlock.Text = "An error occurred while uploading
        the image";
    }
  }
}
```

13. We have now successfully uploaded the image to the server using the WCF service. The next screenshot shows the interface with the `OpenFileDialog` open, thus allowing the user to select an image. The selected image will then be uploaded to the service.

How it works...

To upload files to the server, WCF services can be the solution. The process is actually quite simple. We need to create a service that accepts a byte array. In the service code, this byte array can then be converted into a file. In this recipe, we have used images, but the process explained works for all types of files (a Word document, an Excel file, and so on).

By default, a WCF service does not accept incoming messages larger than 65536 bytes. This is an issue when sending files because most files will be larger than this limit. Due to this, we need to configure the binding in the web.config file of the service so that larger messages aren't blocked. In our recipe, we specified the maximum file size to be 2 megabytes.

The client application can open a file on the user's hard drive by using the OpenFileDialog. We get a read-only stream to the file. This resulting stream can then be used to create a byte array that is then passed to the service.

See also

In the next recipe, we carry out a similar operation, namely displaying images sent to the Silverlight application as binary data.

Displaying images as a stream from a WCF service

In the previous recipe, we looked at how we could send files to a server using a WCF service that lies in between. The data is sent in that scenario as a stream of bytes.

Instead of uploading files, we may also come across a situation where a service sends data such as images in the form of binary data (instead of just sending a link to the file). This can be the case if the files are stored in a database in binary format. In this recipe, we'll look at exactly this.

Getting ready

A starter solution containing some sample images is provided in the code bundle available on the Packt website. This solution can be found in the Chapter07/ SilverlightImageDownload_Starter directory. The complete code for this recipe can be found in the Chapter07/SilverlightImageDownload_Completed directory.

How to do it...

In this recipe, we'll build a simple image search application in which the user can enter a value to find an image. This service will search for an image in a specific directory and if found, it will return this image as binary data. This way, we can send images to the Silverlight application that live on the server and not in a web folder. The following are the steps we need to perform to get this working:

1. Open the starter solution as outlined in the *Getting ready* section of this recipe.

2. Let's first focus on the server side. Add a new regular **WCF service** and name it as `ImageDownloadService.svc`. Visual Studio will add three files: the service endpoint (`ImageDownloadService.svc`), the service contract (`IImageDownloadService.cs`), and the service implementation (`ImageDownloadService.cs`).

3. The service contract defines the `Download` method that returns an `ImageDownload` instance and accepts one parameter of the `string` type. This is the name of the image the user is searching for. This method is also attributed with the `OperationContract` attribute as shown in the following code:

```
[ServiceContract]
public interface IImageDownloadService
{
    [OperationContract]
    ImageDownload Download(string imageName);
}
```

4. The `ImageDownload` class contains a string and a byte array. This is the data contract for the service and is attributed as shown in the following code:

```
[DataContract]
public class ImageDownload
{
    [DataMember]
    public string ImageName { get; set; }
    [DataMember]
    public byte[] Image { get; set; ý
}
```

5. The service implementation searches for an image with a specific name in a specified directory. If found, the image file is read and the bytes are placed in a byte array. This byte array is then wrapped into an `ImageDownload` instance that can be returned to the client side. The following code allows us to do this:

```
[AspNetCompatibilityRequirements(RequirementsMode =
    AspNetCompatibilityRequirementsMode.Required)]
public class ImageDownloadService : IImageDownloadService
{
    public ImageDownload Download(string imageName)
```

```
    {
      FileStream fileStream = null;
      BinaryReader reader = null;
      string imagePath;
      byte[] imageBytes;
      try
      {
        imagePath = HttpContext.Current.Server.MapPath(".") +
          ConfigurationManager.AppSettings["ImageDirectory"] +
        imageName + ".jpg";
        if (File.Exists(imagePath))
        {
          fileStream = new FileStream(imagePath, FileMode.Open,
            FileAccess.Read);
          reader = new BinaryReader(fileStream);
          imageBytes = reader.ReadBytes((int)fileStream.Length);
          return new ImageDownload() { ImageName = imageName,
            Image = imageBytes };
        }
        return null;
      }
      catch (Exception)
      {
        return null;
      }
    }
  }
```

Note that the service is attributed with the
`AspNetCompatibilityRequirementsAttribute`. This is done
as we're using ASP.NET-specific features such as `HttpContext`.

6. We have used `ConfigurationManager.AppSettings["ImageDirectory"]`
    in step 5. This line of code refers to an entry in the `appSettings` collection in the
    `web.config` file where we store settings that are specific to the application. Add
    the following code in the `web.config` file (note that it is to be inserted in between
    the opening and closing `appSettings` tags):

```
<appSettings>
  <add key="ImageDirectory"
      value="/Images/"/>
</appSettings>
```

Create the `Image` directory as a subdirectory within the web application.

7. As the service runs in ASP.NET Compatibility mode, we need to allow this from the configuration code. This is done by adding the following code in the `web.config` file:

```
<system.serviceModel>
  <serviceHostingEnvironment aspNetCompatibilityEnabled="true"/>
  ...
</system.serviceModel>
```

8. Finally, we need to change the type of binding for the server side. As we used a regular **WCF Service** as opposed to a **Silverlight-enabled WCF Service**, the binding added in the configuration was a `wsHttpBinding`. Silverlight can't work with this binding, so we need to change it to a `basicHttpBinding`. This is shown in the following code:

```
<endpoint address=""
          binding="basicHttpBinding"
          contract="SilverlightImageDownload.Web
            .IImageDownloadService">
```

9. Compile the project so that the service can be connected to it.

10. In the Silverlight project, add a service reference to the newly created service. If the service was created correctly, Visual Studio will go ahead and add a proxy to the Silverlight project. Set the namespace as `ImageDownloadService`.

11. The UI of the application is intentionally kept simple. It can be seen a bit further in this recipe. It allows the user to enter a search term. In the `Click` event of the `Button`, the service will be called and the image will be shown, if found. The code for this UI can be found in the code bundle.

12. We instantiate the proxy in the `Click` event. In the asynchronous call, we pass in the search term entered by the user. This is shown in the following code:

```
private void SearchButton_Click(object sender, RoutedEventArgs e)
{
  ImageDownloadService.ImageDownloadServiceClient proxy =
    new SilverlightImageDownload.ImageDownloadService
    .ImageDownloadServiceClient();
  proxy.DownloadCompleted += new EventHandler
    <SilverlightImageDownload.ImageDownloadService
    .DownloadCompletedEventArgs>(proxy_DownloadCompleted);
  proxy.DownloadAsync(SearchImageTextBox.Text);
}
```

13. In the code of the callback method, we have access to the image in binary format (if one was returned by the service). The byte array in which the image data resides is loaded into the memory using a `MemoryStream` instance. We then create a `BitmapImage` and set its source to a loaded stream using the `SetSource` method. This `BitmapImage` is finally set as the `Source` for the image. The code for this is as follows:

```
void proxy_DownloadCompleted(object sender,
    SilverlightImageDownload.ImageDownloadService
    .DownloadCompletedEventArgs e)
{
    NoImageTextBlock.Visibility = Visibility.Collapsed;
    BitmapImage image = new BitmapImage();
    if (e.Error == null)
    {
        if (e.Result != null)
        {
            ImageDownloadService.ImageDownload imageDownload = e.Result;
            MemoryStream stream = new MemoryStream(imageDownload.Image);
            image.SetSource(stream);
            ResultImage.Source = image;
        }
        else
        {
            NoImageTextBlock.Visibility = Visibility.Visible;
        }
    }
}
```

As shown in the following screenshot, when searching for a specific image, it is loaded from the service and displayed in an `Image` control.

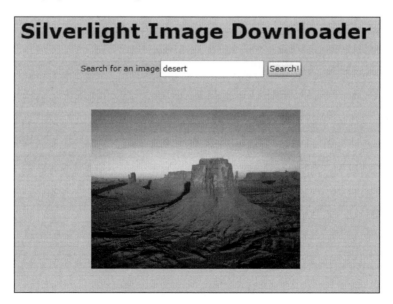

How it works...

When images are stored in a non-accessible location on the server (meaning there's no URL through which we can access them) or when an image is stored in a database, a service that returns an image to the client as an array of bytes might be available. WCF services can handle this type of traffic without problems.

Silverlight applications can capture this incoming binary data and recreate the original image from that byte array. For this, it can create a stream from the bytes. This stream can be used in combination with the `BitmapImage` class. The latter can then be used to set the `Source` for an `Image` control from the code-behind.

See also

In the previous recipe, we uploaded images as binary data to the service.

Hooking into proxy creation using slsvcutil.exe

Adding a service reference is straightforward because of Visual Studio. The IDE searches for available services and when found, adds the service reference in the Silverlight application. It is also capable of generating the proxy class and it offers several choices for this generation such as the used collection type.

However, we may not always have Visual Studio available for this task. Luckily, the Silverlight SDK contains a command-line tool called the **Silverlight Metadata Utility Tool** (`slsvcutil.exe`) that is also capable of generating a proxy. It offers a wide range of parameters that can help us to customize how the generated code should look. In this recipe, we'll look at the tool and some of its parameters.

Getting ready

The sample code in the `Chapter07/WorkingWithSlSvcUtil` directory contains a service that can be used to try out the proxy generation. However, the process is similar for every other WCF service.

How to do it...

To use the `slsvcutil.exe` tool, the Silverlight SDK must be installed. Visual Studio is not required for this. We'll take a look at how we can create a proxy and its accompanying configuration code for a service. To achieve this, we'll need to perform the following steps:

1. Open the `WorkingWithSlSvcUtil` solution from the code bundle available on the Packt website.

2. In the web application, a service called `EmployeeService.svc` already exists that returns a list of `Employee` instances.

3. Open a command prompt and navigate to `%PROGRAMFILES%\Microsoft SDKs\ Silverlight\v4.0\Tools` (or `%PROGRAMFILES(x86)%\Microsoft SDKs\ Silverlight\v4.0\Tools` on a 64-bit machine).

4. Execute the following command:

```
C:\Program Files\Microsoft SDKs\Silverlight\v4.0
\Tools>SlSvcUtil.exe http://localhost:10020/
EmployeeService.svc /directory:C:\temp
```

On a 64-bit machine, the following command needs to be executed:

```
C:\Program Files (x86)\Microsoft SDKs\Silverlight\v4.0
\Tools>SlSvcUtil.exe http://localhost:10020/
EmployeeService.svc /directory:C:\temp
```

5. After completion, the tool will have generated two files inside the `C:\temp` directory: a proxy (`*.cs`) and a configuration file (`ServiceReferences.ClientConfig`). Add both generated files to the Silverlight project in the opened solution.

We have now successfully created the two files needed for service communication using the Silverlight Metadata Utility Tool, thus without the help of Visual Studio.

How it works...

The Silverlight Metadata Utility Tool has two main purposes. First, it can be used to generate a proxy when Visual Studio isn't available. Second, it offers a wide range of parameters to tailor the proxy generation according to specific needs. The following table contains a list of the most commonly used parameters. The full list can be found at `http://msdn.microsoft.com/ en-us/library/dd470117(VS.95).aspx`.

Parameter	Function
`/directory:<directory>`	Specifies a directory in which the generated files are placed; by default, this is the home directory of the `slsvcutil. exe` tool.
`/collectionType:<type>`	Specifies the collection type (`List`, `ObservableCollection`, and so on) used by a proxy.
`/enableDataBinding`	Specifies that the proxy class will implement the `INotifyPropertyChanged` parameter so that we can use the results in data binding scenarios.
`/language:<language>`	Specifies the language (C#, VB.NET, and so on) in which the proxy class should be defined. C# is the default.

Calling a WCF service from Silverlight using ChannelFactory

A lot of Silverlight applications using services are typically developed using the **Add Service Reference** dialog box to add service references that generate the client-side proxy classes. However, this isn't sufficient or advisable for some applications or pieces of code. You might want to call variable endpoints or you might be developing a library or a framework in which you wouldn't want to have service references for pluggability or for extension purposes (for example: through a provider pattern).

This is where a `ChannelFactory` comes in handy. Through a `ChannelFactory`, you can combine a binding and an address from code with a contract to open a channel to a service endpoint that implements a matching contract. This can be done without ever using the **Add Service Reference** dialog box.

In this recipe, we'll learn how to achieve this.

Getting ready

We're starting from a simple Silverlight solution that includes a Silverlight project containing our UI and a WCF service in a hosting web application project. If you want to follow along with this recipe, you can use the provided starter solution located in the `Chapter07/UsingChannelFactory_Starter` folder in the code bundle available on the Packt website. The completed solution can be found in the `Chapter07/UsingChannelFactory_Completed` folder.

How to do it...

We're going to modify the starter solution to make sure that we can call WCF service using a Channel Factory. To achieve this, complete the following steps:

1. We're going to start by adding a new interface called the `IPersonServiceClient` to the Silverlight application. This is an asynchronous representation of the synchronous server-side `IPersonService` contract. Implement it as shown in the following code:

```
[ServiceContract(Name = "IPersonService")]
public interface IPersonServiceClient
{
    [OperationContract(AsyncPattern = true)]
    IAsyncResult BeginGetPerson(int ID, AsyncCallback callback,
      Object state);
    Person EndGetPerson(IAsyncResult result);
}
```

2. Next, we'll add a `Person` class to the Silverlight application that contains the following code:

```
public class Person
{
   public int ID { get; set; }
   public string Name { get; set; }
   public string FirstName { get; set; }
}
```

3. Locate the `Click` handler for `btnFetch` and implement it as shown in the following code:

```
private void btnFetch_Click(object sender, RoutedEventArgs e)
{
   BasicHttpBinding basicHttpBinding = new BasicHttpBinding();
   EndpointAddress endpointAddress = new EndpointAddress
     ("http://localhost:2967/PersonService.svc");
   IPersonServiceClient personService =new ChannelFactory
     <IPersonServiceClient>(basicHttpBinding,
     endpointAddress).CreateChannel();
   var y = personService.BeginGetPerson(Convert.ToInt32(txtID.Text)
     , (asyncResult) =>
     {
       this.Dispatcher.BeginInvoke(delegate
       {
         var returnedPerson = personService
           .EndGetPerson(asyncResult);
         this.DataContext = returnedPerson;
       });
     }
     , null);
}
```

4. We can now build and run the application. When a user inputs a value in the textbox and clicks on the **Fetch** button, the `GetPerson` service method is called using a channel factory. The result can be observed in the following screenshot:

How it works...

We're starting from a solution that includes a WCF Service exposing an endpoint using a `basicHttpBinding` and the `IPersonService` service contract. When we want to use a channel factory to access this service, we need to pass in the contract when we create the channel factory. As Silverlight makes its service calls asynchronously, we just can't copy or use the same `IPersonService` service contract as this doesn't include asynchronous methods. We need to define a new `ServiceContract` that consists of asynchronous method signatures matching the synchronous GetPerson method and that can be matched to the server-side `IPersonService` contract.

We do this by defining a `BeginGetPerson` method (that accepts an ID parameter, callback, and state, returns an `IAsyncResult`, and is decorated with the `[OperationContract(AsyncPattern = true)]` attribute), an `EndGetPerson` method (that accepts an `IAsyncResult` and returns a `Person`), and by setting the contract name as `IPersonService`. This way, we can link our newly created asynchronous contract to its matching synchronous contract, allowing us to create a channel factory using the asynchronous, client-side `IPersonServiceClient` contract to communicate with a service implementing the synchronous `IPersonService` contract.

Next, we've created a `Person` class in the Silverlight application, which is a type returned by the service method. There's one important thing to notice here. The `Person` class in the Silverlight application and the `Person` class in the web application are essentially the same. They exist in the same namespace and have a same name. You can check this by having a look at the `Person` class in the web application. You'll notice that the namespace refers to `UsingChannelFactory` and not to `UsingChannelFactory.Web` as you'd expect. If you don't match these namespaces, the returned object will be null as .NET does not know how to cast a `UsingChannelFactory.Web.Person` class to a `UsingChannelFactory.Person` class (you could alternatively extend your class to make it implicitly convertible).

The pieces are in place now, so all that's left to do is actually creating the channel and calling the service method. This is done in the `Click` handler of the **Fetch** button.

As you can see, the channel is created using the `CreateChannel()` method. Once this is done, we can call the `BeginGetPerson` method and pass in the ID to fetch the correct person. What's important is that we have to make a call to `EndGetPerson` in the callback. The callback will be executed after the service method has run and `EndGetPerson` will return the value the service method returns (in this case a `Person`).

Another important fact to notice is that the callback makes a call to `Dispatcher.BeginInvoke`. We do this because we're accessing the UI thread (setting the `DataContext`) in the callback. If we omit this, we'll get an invalid cross-thread access exception.

See also

To learn about other ways of communicating with WCF Services, have a look at the other recipes in this chapter.

8
Talking to REST and WCF Data Services

In this chapter, we will cover:

- ▶ Reading data from a REST service
- ▶ Parsing REST results with LINQ-To-XML
- ▶ Persisting data using a REST service
- ▶ Working with the ClientHttpStack
- ▶ Communicating with a REST service using JSON
- ▶ Using WCF Data Services from Silverlight
- ▶ Reading data from WCF Data Services
- ▶ Persisting data using WCF Data Services
- ▶ Talking to Flickr
- ▶ Talking to Twitter from a non-trusted application
- ▶ Passing credentials and cross-domain access to Twitter from a trusted Silverlight application

Introduction

While WCF and ASMX services are very powerful and can address almost every situation, these services might be overkill for some scenarios. Sometimes, a simple exchange of textual information, preferably in XML or JSON (JavaScript Object Notation—an easy-to-read data exchange format), might be enough.

The protocol used for this type of communication is REST (REpresentational State Transfer). Compared to web services (WCF or ASMX), REST has some advantages that can be significant in the case of Silverlight. The exchanged information is human-readable text, mostly in the XML format. The XML is clean, meaning there is not a lot of XML markup being added. SOAP messages—the format for web services—are also XML, but a lot of extra overhead is added in the so-called SOAP envelope. Using REST will result in less data being sent over the wire, resulting in better performance from a bandwidth perspective. In general, REST is easier to use and entirely platform independent. It does not require any extra software as it relies on standard HTTP methods.

Are **RESTful** services (a service that follows REST principles is often referred to as being RESTful) a trend? It's safe to say so. Today, many large web applications such as Flickr, FaceBook, Twitter, YouTube and so on offer (part of) their functionality using a RESTful API (a collection of REST services). In .NET, creating RESTful services is fully supported. Moreover, Silverlight can easily connect to REST services.

In this chapter, we'll first look at talking with REST services from Silverlight. Secondly, we'll look at how to work with WCF Data Services (formerly known as ADO.NET Data Services), which are also pure REST services at their base. However, through the use of the client-side library available for use with Silverlight, a lot of plumbing code (necessary to work with RESTful services) is abstracted away and we get typed access to the entities made available over the service. In other words, it provides a wrapper around REST-based access.

Throughout this chapter, all recipes (except where we use Flickr or Twitter) use the same scenario—the Computer Inventory application. This application could be used by an internal IT department of an organization to keep track of PCs, laptops, and so on as well as by the users registered on a particular system. It consists of two parts—the **User Management**, which we'll build using pure REST services, and the **Computer Management**, which will be built through the use of WCF Data Services. The following image is the schema for the database used. It shows that a Computer is of a certain ComputerType and has a Manufacturer. Each Computer can be registered with one or more User instances.

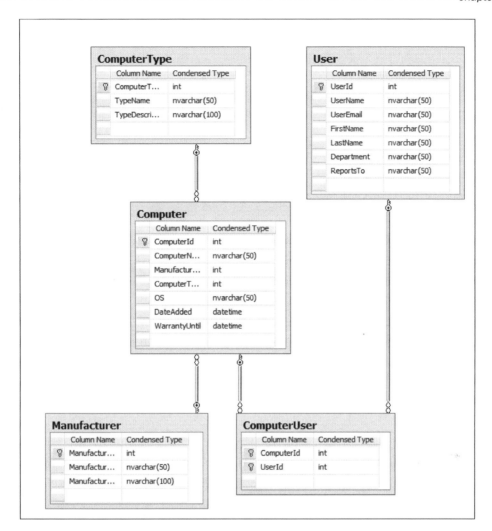

Reading data from a REST service

Let's assume that we are writing a Silverlight application that needs to work with data exposed by a RESTful service. The first question that comes to mind is: how can we communicate with such a service and read out the data returned by the service?

This recipe focuses on the communication aspect of REST services, such as how we can connect to a RESTful service from Silverlight and get data into our application.

In this recipe, we'll retrieve a list of all users in the Users table using a REST service. For now, we'll show the results in the same format as they are returned, which is plain XML.

Getting ready

The finished solution for this recipe can be found in the `Chapter08/` `TalkingToSimpleRESTServices_ReadingFromRest_Completed` folder in the code bundle available on the Packt website. To follow along with this recipe, the starter solution located in the `Chapter08/TalkingToSimpleRESTServices_ReadingFromRest_` `Starter` folder can be used.

In this recipe, we're working with a local REST service. The good thing is that building REST services ourselves using WCF is pretty easy. In the sample code, some REST services have already been constructed, such as a service that returns all users (`GetAllUsers`), a service that retrieves a user based on the passed-in user ID (`GetUserById`) and a service that searches for a user based on his/her username (`GetUserByUserName`). These services can be found in the `TalkingToSimpleRESTServices.Services` project in both the starter and the completed solution.

To find out how to create REST services from WCF, please refer to Appendix A.

For this sample (as well as the samples of the other recipes in this chapter) to work, we need the `ComputerInventory` database. This database is included both as a **Microsoft SQL Server Database File** (**MDF**) file (`CompterInventory.mdf`) and as a `*.sql` script file. Both the files are located in the `Chapter08` folder. For an explanation on how to install them, refer to Appendix B.

How to do it...

This recipe will mainly focus on the aspect of communication with REST services. We'll call the RESTful service that returns all users and display the result in its original format—plain XML. The UI of this recipe is kept very basic, containing just enough to trigger a call to the service and show the results, so it won't be in our way while exploring the communication features. The following screenshot shows the application containing a `TextBox` that displays the result of a REST service call, namely an XML string. (Don't worry about any formatting. We'll look at working with XML in the next recipe.)

In order to begin reading data from a REST service, we'll need to complete the following steps:

1. Open the solution file in the `Chapter08/TalkingToSimpleRESTServices_ ReadingFromRest_Starter` folder. It will open a solution containing a Silverlight application, a hosting website (`TalkingToSimpleRESTServices.Web`), and a website where the REST services are located (`TalkingToSimpleRESTServices. Services`).

2. The easiest way to communicate with a RESTful service is through the use of the `WebClient` class. This class is part of the `System.Net` namespace which resides in the `System.Net` assembly. If you're working with Visual Studio 2010 (either with Silverlight 3 or 4), a reference to this assembly should be added automatically. If you're working with Visual Studio 2008 in combination with Silverlight 3, this assembly reference has to be created manually. To do so, right-click on the Silverlight project, select **Add reference**. In the dialog that appears, on the tab titled **.NET**, **select System.Net**.

3. Let's add some XAML code to `MainPage.xaml` to build the necessary UI for the Silverlight application. We'll add a button that will trigger the call to the service. We'll also add a non-editable textbox in which the results will be shown as plain text. This can be achieved using the following code:

```
<Grid x:Name="LayoutRoot"
      Background="LightGray">
  <Grid.RowDefinitions>
    <RowDefinition Height="50"></RowDefinition>
    <RowDefinition Height="40"></RowDefinition>
    <RowDefinition ></RowDefinition>
  </Grid.RowDefinitions>
  <TextBlock x:Name="TitleTextBlock"
```

```
              Text="Computer Inventory - User Management"
              FontSize="30"
              FontWeight="Bold"
              HorizontalAlignment="Left"
              Margin="5">
    </TextBlock>
    <StackPanel Grid.Row="1"
                Orientation="Horizontal" >
        <TextBlock x:Name="ControlsTextBlock"
                Text="Controls: "
                Margin="3"
                VerticalAlignment="Center">
        </TextBlock>
        <Button x:Name="ReLoadButton"
                Content="Reload data"
                Click="ReLoadButton_Click"
                HorizontalAlignment="Left"
                Margin="3"
                VerticalAlignment="Center">
        </Button>
    </StackPanel>
    <TextBox x:Name="ResultTextBox"
                Grid.Row="2"
                VerticalScrollBarVisibility="Visible"
                TextWrapping="Wrap"
                Width="600"
                IsReadOnly="True">
    </TextBox>
</Grid>
```

4. Let's now look at the service that will be called. The contract for this service is located in the `TalkingToSimpleRESTServices.Services` project in the `IUserManagementService.svc.cs` file. Calling a RESTful service is nothing more than sending a request to the URI of the service and reading the returned response. In this case, we're sending a request to our own service. In fact, we're sending a request to a method of the service, each method of which has its own address (a unique URI). The format of this URI is defined by the `UriTemplate`. For the `GetAllUsers` method, the value of the `UriTemplate` is set to `userlist` as shown in the following code:

```
[OperationContract]
[WebGet(UriTemplate = "userlist",
  BodyStyle = WebMessageBodyStyle.Bare,
  RequestFormat = WebMessageFormat.Xml)]
List<DTO.User> GetAllUsers();.
```

5. In our Silverlight code, we need to match this format. The URI is composed of the base URI (the address of the service itself, assigned to the `serviceBaseUrl` variable in the following code), appended with the `userlist` suffix (defined in the previous code as the value for the `UriTemplate` and assigned to the `getAllUser` variable in the following code). In our case, the complete URI will be `http://localhost:23960/UserManagementService.svc/userlist` (note that the port number, here 23960, may vary on your machine).

```
string serviceBaseUrl =
  "http://localhost:23960/UserManagementService.svc/";
string getAllUser = "userlist";
```

Ideally, in real-world applications, this URL would be stored in a configuration file.

6. Now that we have the URI, we need to actually make a call to it. For this, we use the `WebClient` class. In the **Reload** button's `Click` event handler, we first create an instance of this type. Just like any other service calls, REST service calls are asynchronous. Therefore, we need to register an event handler for the `DownloadStringCompleted` event, which will be called whenever the service returns. Finally, we perform the call by using the `DownloadStringAsync` method, passing in the URI as the parameter. This is shown in the following code:

```
private void ReLoadButton_Click(object sender, RoutedEventArgs e)
{
  WebClient client = new WebClient();
  client.DownloadStringCompleted += new
    DownloadStringCompletedEventHandler
    (DownloadAllUsersCompleted);
  client.DownloadStringAsync(new Uri
    (serviceBaseUrl + getAllUser, UriKind.Absolute));
}
```

7. When the service call returns, the event handler defined in the previous step will be called automatically. In this event handler, we have access to the result of the call via the `Result` property on the instance of the `DownloadStringCompletedEventArgs` named e. The response is plain XML. Each returned `User` instance is serialized before being sent. If errors have occurred, we can see them here as well. This is shown in the following code:

```
void DownloadAllUsersCompleted(object sender,
  DownloadStringCompletedEventArgs e)
{
  ResultTextBox.Text = e.Result;
}
```

How it works...

Let's first take a look at some particulars of REST. One of the most important principles in REST is the concept of resources. A resource is a container of information. Each resource can be uniquely identified by a URI. One of the best examples of the REST architecture is the World Wide Web itself. A page is a resource and it has a unique URI to access it.

While SOAP mainly uses the HTTP POST verb, RESTful services use GET, POST, PUT, and DELETE. With the default HTTP stack (also known as `BrowserHttpStack`), Silverlight can work only with GET and POST because of the limitations of the browser networking APIs it uses internally. In Silverlight 3, a second stack was introduced—the `ClientHttpStack` (we'll be looking at the `ClientHttpStack` in a later recipe in this chapter).

Communicating with REST services differs from communicating with SOAP-based services as REST services don't expose a WSDL file that contains the functionalities of the service. We can't add a reference to these kind of services in Visual Studio. So there will be no proxy generation and no IntelliSense available.

The solution uses the `WebClient` class that is part of the full .NET framework as well. The `WebClient` class has two important ways of requesting data—DownloadString and OpenRead. DownloadString (which we used in this recipe) can be used when we're reading textual information such as XML returned by a REST service. OpenRead can be used when we want to read the result into a stream. The `WebClient` class defines a pair of an asynchronous method and a Completed event for both these ways of requesting data. This Completed event is fired on the UI thread, which means that to update UI elements in the event handler, we can do so directly and don't have to cross threads.

Instead of using the `WebClient` class, we can also use the `HttpWebRequest` class. This class should be our choice if we need more control over the call to the service. The `WebClient` class uses the `HttpWebRequest` class internally. We looked at working with `HttpWebRequest` in the *Reading XML using HttpWebRequest* recipe in Chapter 6.

Calling REST services is possible only in an asynchronous way. Silverlight allows only this type of calls. This asynchronous behavior is reflected in both the actual call to the service (`DownloadStringAsync`) and the registration of the event handler (`DownloadStringCompleted`), which is called whenever the service returns.

Communication with REST services can be summarized as a three-step process:

- ▶ Create a URI to which a request needs to be sent
- ▶ Send the request
- ▶ Get in the results and work with them (parsing and so on)

The format of the URI is defined by the service itself. Each URI corresponds to a specific method that will return data. The actual sending of a request is done in the `DownloadStringAsync` method of the `WebClient` class. When the service returns, the callback is invoked and the response is available through the `Result` property of `DownloadStringCompletedEventArgs`.

See also

In the next recipe, we're going to work with the results of the service through the use of LINQ-To-XML. The asynchronous way of working with services in general is explained in the *Connecting and reading from a standardized service recipe* in Chapter 6.

Parsing REST results with LINQ-To-XML

We have successfully connected to a REST service from a Silverlight application in the previous recipe. The response from the service is XML. Most of the time, showing pure XML to the end user is not the goal of an application, so we'll want to parse the XML. Silverlight contains several options to work with XML, which include XmlReader/XmlWriter, XmlSerializer, and LINQ-To-XML (also known as XLinq). The latter is a preferred way to parse XML.

In this recipe, we'll look at how we can use LINQ-To-XML to transform XML into real data. The raw user data (originally in XML) will be transformed in `User` objects.

Getting ready

This recipe builds on the code created in the previous recipe, so you can continue using that solution. Alternatively, you can use the starter solution for this recipe located in the `Chapter08/TalkingToSimpleRESTServices_LinqToXml_Starter` folder in the code bundle available on the Packt website. The finished solution for this recipe can be found in the `Chapter08/TalkingToSimpleRESTServices_LinqToXml_Completed` folder.

How to do it...

In this recipe, we'll transform the plain XML returned by a RESTful service into real, meaningful data. The XML will be parsed using LINQ-To-XML. Without a doubt, LINQ-To-XML is the easiest and most efficient way for this task. To begin parsing the XML, we'll complete the following steps:

1. Either continue working on the solution created in the previous recipe or use the provided solution as outlined in the *Getting ready* section.

2. The assembly needed to use LINQ-To-XML in Silverlight applications is not added by default. Therefore, we need to add a reference to the `System.Xml.Linq` assembly in the Silverlight project. The basic features of LINQ, such as the `select` statement, live in the `System.Linq` assembly that is added by default. (Note that the `System.Xml.Linq` assembly is about 120KB in file size.)

3. As Visual Studio can't create a proxy for a REST service, we don't get types to work with on the client side, although this would be a lot easier. Therefore, we'll manually create a `User` class ourselves in the `TalkingToSimpleRESTServices` Silverlight project that will contain the object representation of the XML data. This is a data-only type. The `User` class is shown in the following code:

```
public class User
{
  public int UserId { get; set; }
  public string UserName { get; set; }
  public string FirstName { get; set; }
  public string LastName { get; set; }
  public string Email { get; set; }
  public string Department { get; set; }
  public string ReportsTo { get; set; }
}
```

4. Next, in the `DownloadAllUsersCompleted` callback method located in the code-behind of `MainPage.xaml`, we'll need to load the XML into an `XDocument` using the `Parse` method. An `XDocument` is able to load in the entire XML stream given to it. With a query, we search for all `User` descendants of the root node using the `Descendants` method. As we don't want to work with the `XElement` instances in our client code, we read each `User` `XElement` and load its values into a new instance of the `User` class. Note that we can use the `Element` or `Descendants` methods. Both methods have the same result. This is shown in the following code:

```
void DownloadAllUsersCompleted(object sender,
  DownloadStringCompletedEventArgs e)
{
  XDocument xml = XDocument.Parse(e.Result);
  var users = from results in xml.Descendants("User")
                select new User
  {
    UserId = Int32.Parse(results.Element("UserId")
      .Value.ToString()),
    UserName = results.Descendants("UserName").First().Value,
    FirstName = results.Descendants("FirstName").First().Value,
    LastName = results.Descendants("LastName").First().Value,
    Department = results.Element("Department").Value.ToString(),
    Email = results.Element("Email").Value.ToString(),
    ReportsTo = results.Element("ReportsTo").Value.ToString()
  };
}
```

5. We will then need to replace the **ResultTextBox** in `MainPage.xaml` with a `DataGrid` called **UsersDataGrid**. The code for this control is as follows:

```
<sdk:DataGrid x:Name="UsersDataGrid"
              Grid.Row="2"
              AutoGenerateColumns="False"
              Width="600"
              Height="500"
              HorizontalAlignment="Left"
              VerticalAlignment="Top"
              Margin="3">
  <sdk:DataGrid.Columns>
    <sdk:DataGridTextColumn Binding="{Binding UserId}"
                            Header="UserId" />
    <sdk:DataGridTextColumn Binding="{Binding UserName}"
                            Header="User name" />
    <sdk:DataGridTextColumn Binding="{Binding FirstName}"
                            Header="First name" />
    <sdk:DataGridTextColumn Binding="{Binding LastName}"
                            Header="Last name" />
  </sdk:DataGrid.Columns>
</sdk:DataGrid>
```

6. Finally, we can use the data in our application. We can now bind the generic `List<User>` to the `DataGrid` by setting it as the value of the `ItemsSource` property. This is shown in the following code:

```
void DownloadAllUsersCompleted(object sender,
  DownloadStringCompletedEventArgs e)
{
  ...
  UsersDataGrid.ItemsSource = users.ToList();
}
```

The following screenshot shows the `User` instances bound to the `DataGrid`:

How it works...

When working with data coming from a RESTful service, most of the time it's important to look at the schema of the XML. Here, the data is quite simple as it's created through serialization of an object on the server side. Serialization is the process of converting an object into a stream so that it can be easily sent over the wire. In our case, we are serializing instances of a class called `User` that is located in the `TalkingToSimpleRestServices.DTO` project. Each property of this class is translated into XML as shown in the following code:

```
<ArrayOfUser>
  <User>
    <Department />
    <Email />
    <FirstName />
    <LastName />
    <ReportsTo />
    <UserId />
    <UserName />
  </User>
</ArrayOfUser>
```

While RESTful services may respond with more complicated XML code, LINQ-To-XML contains everything needed to parse the data easily. We should always start by loading the entire XML into an `XDocument` or an `XElement`. `XElement` may even be a better fit here as we're not using any particularities of the root node. Using the `Descendants` method and passing in the name of the node we want to retrieve, we get a list of all the `XElement` instances matching the requested pattern. As this is a list, we can perform a query on it. In this query, for each encountered `XElement`, we create a new `User` instance by passing in the retrieved values of the XML.

With this, we have successfully loaded data from a REST service into the types on the client side. This data can now be used in all scenarios we want, for example, data binding.

See also

The previous recipe explains how to get the XML data into the application. In the next recipe, we explore the options to send data from Silverlight to a REST service. In the *Communicating with a REST service using JSON* recipe, we'll look at how we can work with a REST service that returns JSON.

We used very simple data binding here, but if you'd like to explore this topic further, refer to Chapter 2 and Chapter 3.

Persisting data using a REST service

Some REST services accept data that we send to them as well, so this data can then be persisted back into a database. In this recipe, we'll make it possible to add, update, or delete a user in the Computer Inventory application where we're working on the User Management.

Getting ready

This recipe builds on the code created in the previous two recipes. If you want to follow along with the steps in this recipe, you can also use the starter solution located in the `Chapter08/TalkingToSimpleRESTServices_PersistingData_Starter` folder in the code bundle available on the Packt website. The finished solution for this recipe can be found in the `Chapter08/TalkingToSimpleRESTServices_PersistingData_Completed` folder.

How to do it...

Persisting data to a REST service is actually the opposite of reading. We'll use the same class, namely the `WebClient`. However, instead of downloading data, we'll serialize client-side data and send it back to the service. To begin persisting data to the REST service, we'll complete the following steps:

1. As outlined in the *Getting ready* section, use either the solution from the previous recipe or the provided solution in the sample code.

2. We'll be using the `WebClient` class that resides in the `System.Net` namespace. If not yet added, add a reference to this assembly in your Silverlight project. To do so, right-click on the **TalkingToSimpleRESTServices** project, select **Add reference**, and select the required assembly in the dialog box that appears. Visual Studio 2010 creates this assembly reference automatically.

3. In this recipe, we'll use a detail window to add, update or delete a user. The following is the XAML code for this user control. This code is placed inside a new Silverlight child window. To add a child window to the project, right-click on the Silverlight project node in the **Solution Explorer**, select **Add | New item...**, and select **Silverlight Child Window** in the template selection dialog box. Name this new file **UserDetailEdit**. Such a child window contains out of the box zoom-in or zoom-out effects when initiated or closed respectively.

    Note that we're going to use data binding to show a `User` instance or to get the changes back into the object when the values have changed. `TwoWay` bindings are used so that the bound CLR object will update automatically as well. The complete XAML code for this child window can be found in the code bundle. The following code shows the most relevant parts:

    ```
    <Grid x:Name="LayoutRoot" Margin="2">
      <Grid.RowDefinitions>
        <RowDefinition />
    ```

```xml
      <RowDefinition Height="Auto" />
    </Grid.RowDefinitions>
  <Grid Grid.Row="0" x:Name="UserDetailGrid" >
    <Grid.RowDefinitions>
      <RowDefinition></RowDefinition>

      ...

    </Grid.RowDefinitions>
    <Grid.ColumnDefinitions>

      ...

    </Grid.ColumnDefinitions>
    <TextBlock Text="User ID: "
              Grid.Row="0"
              Grid.Column="0"
              VerticalAlignment="Top">
    </TextBlock>
    <TextBlock x:Name="UserIdTextBlock"
              Grid.Row="0"
              Grid.Column="1"
              Text="{Binding UserId}"
              VerticalAlignment="Top">
    </TextBlock>
    <TextBlock Text="User name: "
              Grid.Row="1"
              Grid.Column="0"
              VerticalAlignment="Top">
    </TextBlock>
    <TextBox x:Name="UserNameTextBox"
            Grid.Row="1"
            Grid.Column="1"
            Text="{Binding UserName, Mode=TwoWay}"
            VerticalAlignment="Top">
    </TextBox>
    <!-- Similar code omitted-->
  </Grid>
  <Button x:Name="DeleteButton"
          Content="Delete"
          Click="DeleteButton_Click"
          Width="75"
          Height="23"
          HorizontalAlignment="Right"
          Margin="0,12,79,0"
          Grid.Row="1" />
  <Button x:Name="CancelButton"
          Content="Cancel"
          Click="CancelButton_Click"
```

```
            Width="75"
            Height="23"
            HorizontalAlignment="Right"
            Margin="0,12,0,0"
            Grid.Row="1" />
    <Button x:Name="SaveButton"
            Content="Save"
            Click="SaveButton_Click"
            Width="75"
            Height="23"
            HorizontalAlignment="Right"
            Margin="0,12,158,0"
            Grid.Row="1" />
</Grid>
```

4. Similar to reading from a REST service, we need a URI to send a request, as dictated by the service itself. Each action (add, update, or delete) has a different address. We'll combine these specific addresses with the base address of the service to get the correct URI based on the required action. This is shown in the following code:

```
string serviceBaseUrl =
    "http://localhost:23960/UserManagementService.svc/";
string getUserById = "user/{0}";
string addUser = "user/add";
string updateUser = "user/update";
string deleteUser = "user/delete";
```

Note that the port number (here 23960) may be different on your machine.

5. Let's now look at the actions required to add a new User. We first need to change the client-side User class in the Silverlight project. The class itself needs to be decorated with a DataContract attribute and the members we want to send over need a DataMember attribute. The updated class is shown in the following code. Note that we define the Namespace to be empty.

```
[DataContract(Name = "User", Namespace = "")]
public class User
{
    [DataMember]
    public int UserId { get; set; }
    [DataMember]
    public string UserName { get; set; }
    [DataMember]
    public string FirstName { get; set; }
    [DataMember]
    public string LastName { get; set; }
    [DataMember]
    public string Email { get; set; }
```

```
      [DataMember]
      public string Department { get; set; }
      [DataMember]
      public string ReportsTo { get; set; }
  }
```

6. Upon constructing the `UserDetailEdit` instance, we can check which action the window is supposed to be performing. This can be either editing an existing `User` or adding a new `User`. These actions are reflected in a new enumeration called `EditingModes` that we add to the Silverlight project. This is shown in the following code:

```
public enum EditingModes
{
  New,
  Edit
}
```

7. This enumeration is now used as a parameter type in the constructor. When we add a `User`, a new instance is created and is set as the value for the `DataContext` property of the `UserDetailGrid`:

```
private User user;
private int userId;
private EditingModes editingMode;
public UserDetailEdit(int userId, EditingModes editingMode)
{
  InitializeComponent();
  this.userId = userId;
  this.editingMode = editingMode;
  if (editingMode == EditingModes.New)
  {
    user = new User();
    UserDetailGrid.DataContext = user;
    DeleteButton.IsEnabled = false;
  }
}
```

8. When the user clicks on the **Save** button, we need to send the `User` instance to the RESTful service. However, this can be done only after serializing the object. This can be done through the use of the `DataContractSerializer` type as shown in the following code:

```
private void SaveButton_Click(object sender, RoutedEventArgs e)
{
  WebClient client = new WebClient();
```

```
Uri uri = new Uri(serviceBaseUrl + addUser);
DataContractSerializer dataContractSerializer = new
    DataContractSerializer(typeof(User));
MemoryStream memoryStream = new MemoryStream();
dataContractSerializer.WriteObject(memoryStream, user);
string xmlData = Encoding.UTF8.GetString(memoryStream.ToArray(),
    0, (int)memoryStream.Length);
}
```

9. Now that we have the XML available, we need to send it. This will be done through the use of the `WebClient`, but instead of using the `DownloadString` method, we'll use the `UploadString` method. It's required to set the content-type. It should be set to `application/xml` as shown in the following code. Also, in the `UploadStringAsync` method, we're using `POST` as the method for the HTTP request and are adding data:

```
client.UploadStringCompleted += new
    UploadStringCompletedEventHandler(UploadCompleted);
client.Headers[HttpRequestHeader.ContentType] = "application/xml";
client.UploadStringAsync(uri, "POST", xmlData);
```

10. In the `UploadCompleted` event handler for the callback, we can check if the upload went well using the `Error` property of the `UploadStringCompletedEventArgs` event arguments. This is shown in the following code:

```
private void UploadCompleted(object sender,
    UploadStringCompletedEventArgs e)
{
    if (e.Error == null)
        this.DialogResult = true;
    else
        MessageBox.Show(e.Error.Message);
}
```

11. At this point, the child window is ready. The only thing left to do is calling it from `MainPage.xaml`. To do so, start by adding a new `Button` called `NewUserButton` in the `StackPanel` within `MainPage.xaml`. This is shown in the following code:

```
<Button x:Name="NewUserButton"
        Content="Add user"
        Click="NewUserButton_Click"
        HorizontalAlignment="Left"
        Margin="3"
        VerticalAlignment="Center">
</Button>
```

12. In the `Click` event handler, we instantiate the `UserDetail` child window as shown in the following code:

```
private void NewUserButton_Click(object sender, RoutedEventArgs e)
{
    UserDetailEdit editView = new
        UserDetailEdit(0, EditingModes.New);
    editView.Show();
}
```

With that, we've created all the necessary code to allow the persisting of `User` instances over the REST service. In the following screenshot, the child window is shown in its "New" editing mode:

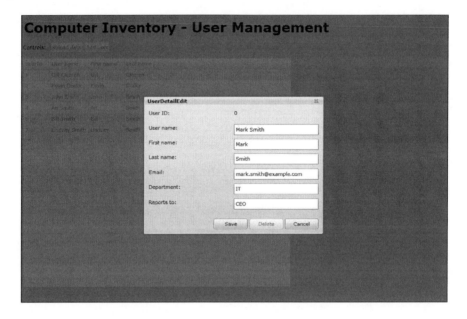

Updating and deleting `User` instances are similar. The sample code contains all the logic for these actions as well.

How it works...

When persisting data to a RESTful service, the first concern is getting the data on the service. Data is almost always available on the client side in the form of objects. We can't just go sending the objects straight away; they have to be serialized first. For the service and the client to understand one another, the XML should be in a correct format. Hence, the `DataContract` and the `DataMember` attributes are used in the `User` class on the client side. The client-side and the server-side objects must have the same names for their properties, otherwise the (de)serialization will fail.

The process of serialization from and to XML has often been the job of the XmlSerializer class and it has been included since NET 1.0. When WCF arrived, a new serializer called the DataContractSerializer was included, in the first place intended for use with WCF. However, as seen in this recipe, it can be used for any serialization purpose.

Since version 3, Silverlight contains has contained two network stacks—the browser stack used in this sample and the ClientHttpStack. The browser stack is named so because Silverlight internally uses the browser networking APIs. Through this stack, only HTTP GET and POST are supported. In the sample code, you can see that we use a POST request to perform an add, an update, or a delete. Another way of using PUT and DELETE is through POST by passing in the real HTTP value as a custom header. This technique isn't perfectly RESTful either, because the request method and what we want to achieve don't match, which is a tenet of the REST principle. This technique is also used in WCF Data Services. The ClientHttpStack does allow Silverlight to use real PUT or DELETE messages.

There's more...

For the serialization process, we could have used the XmlSerializer class. While this class also does the job and is included in Silverlight, the DataContractSerializer is easier to use (as you have more control over the namespace, and so on). The sample code also contains some code where the XmlSerializer class is used.

See also

Reading and persisting data using REST services is very similar. Read both the *Reading data from a REST service* and *Parsing REST results with LINQ-To-XML* recipes in this chapter and notice the link between the two.

Working with the ClientHttpStack

When communicating with a REST service, Silverlight uses the BrowserHttpStack by default. Due to this, Silverlight can't use all HTTP verbs such as PUT and DELETE. Silverlight 3 added a new option, namely the ClientHttpStack. This new stack bypasses the browser stack and performs its communication directly through the operating system.

In this recipe, we'll look at the changes we need to make to use this networking stack.

Getting ready

To follow along with this recipe, you can use the code created in the previous recipe. Alternatively, you can use the starter solution located in the Chapter08/ TalkingToSimpleRESTServices_ClientHttp_Starter folder in the code bundle available on the Packt website. The completed solution can be found in the Chapter08/ TalkingToSimpleRESTServices_ClientHttp_Completed folder.

How to do it...

To make a Silverlight application that talks with REST services use the `ClientHttpStack` instead of the `BrowserHttpStack`, we need to perform a few simple steps. We'll use the application built in the previous recipes (Computer Inventory) to use the new stack. Let's take a look at what we need to do:

To make an application use the `ClientHttpStack`, we need to tell Silverlight to do so. The easiest way is telling Silverlight that all traffic for addresses beginning with `http://` has to use this stack. This can be done using the following code:

```
public MainPage()
{
  InitializeComponent();
  HttpWebRequest.RegisterPrefix("http://",
    WebRequestCreator.ClientHttp);
}
```

With the previous code executed, all calls will be executed over the `ClientHttpStack`.

How it works...

The REST protocol specifies that we can identify any resource with a unique URL. This resource can be any information on the Web, for example, a user instance in the application. Using REST, we can get this user with the GET command, create or update the user using the PUT command, use the POST command to create a new instance, delete the user using the DELETE command, and so on.

Silverlight supports communication with REST services, but as it works by default through the browser stack, it's limited to use only GET and POST. With Silverlight 3, a new stack was introduced, namely the `ClientHttpStack`.

Working with this new stack requires almost no changes to existing applications as the API is identical. The only thing we need to do is let Silverlight know that we want to use this stack. This can be done by saying that all requests starting with `http://` should use the `ClientHttpStack`. This is shown in the following line of code:

```
HttpWebRequest.RegisterPrefix("http://",
  WebRequestCreator.ClientHttp);
```

If we have requests over HTTPS and want these to happen over the client stack as well, we need to register them using the following line of code:

```
HttpWebRequest.RegisterPrefix("https://",
  WebRequestCreator.ClientHttp);
```

We can also be more specific. For example, assume we have an application that communicates with `http://www.snowball.be` and `http://www.packtpub.com`. If we want the REST communication with `http://www.snowball.be` to go over the `ClientHttpStack` and `http://www.packtpub.com` to use the default browser stack, we can specify this using the following code:

```
HttpWebRequest.RegisterPrefix("http://www.snowball.be",
    WebRequestCreator.ClientHttp);
```

Advantages of ClientHttpStack

Using the `ClientHttpStack` has some advantages over using the `BrowserHttpStack`. As already mentioned, it supports more HTTP verbs (GET, POST, PUT, and DELETE). It does not support other HTTP verbs such as CONNECT, TRACE and so on. However, the service can be limited in the keywords it supports. It's possible to specify in the client access policy file (`clientaccesspolicy.xml`) which verbs are supported and which aren't.

The error messages when using the `BrowserHttpStack` are limited. With this stack, we have access to only 200 and 404. The `ClientHttpStack` supports all error messages, making it easier to see what's wrong with the service.

Starting with Silverlight 4, it's also possible to perform authentication using the `ClientHttpStack` (we'll look at this in the *Passing credentials and cross-domain access to Twitter from a trusted Silverlight application* recipe later in this chapter).

When we download an image with the `BrowserHttpStack`, it's automatically cached by the browser as it is its default behavior. However, when working with the `ClientHttpStack`, the browser won't cache it; it simply won't see the image passing by. In Silverlight 3, there was no option to cache using the ClientHttpStack. Silverlight 4 adds support for caching though.

The same goes for cookies. When using the `BrowserHttpStack`, all cookies coming in from a site or going out to a site are managed by the browser. Due to this, when we're logged in to a site based on cookies (the way ASP.NET works), the requests made to that same site from a Silverlight application are also authenticated. With the `ClientHttpStack`, again this won't work. With the `ClientHttpStack`, we can work with cookies, but this is manual work and can be done using the `CookieContainer`.

See also

In the previous recipes of this chapter, we looked at the specifics of working with REST services from Silverlight.

Communicating with a REST service using JSON

When we work with REST services, data is sent over the wire in XML by default. However, REST services can also send back their information in another format such as **JavaScript Object Notation** (**JSON**). This can be the case if the service has also got to be accessible from JavaScript code or if the transferred data is to be very compact.

In this recipe, we'll look at how to communicate from Silverlight with a REST service in the JSON format.

Getting ready

This recipe builds on the code created in the previous recipes, so you can continue using your own code for this recipe. Alternatively, you can also use the provided starter solution located in the Chapter08/TalkingToSimpleRESTServices_ReadingWithJSON_Starter folder in the code bundle available on the Packt website. The finished solution for this recipe can be found in the Chapter08/TalkingToSimpleRESTServices_ReadingWithJSON_Completed folder.

How to do it...

Communicating with a REST service using JSON data is a matter of changing the format of the data sent over the wire and parsing this data using a JsonArray. To do this, we have to complete following steps:

1. Open the solution as outlined in the *Getting ready* section and locate the project containing your services called TalkingToSimpleRESTServices.Services. In this project, find the IUserManagementService interface and add the following code to it. Notice that the RequestFormat and the ResponseFormat NamedParameters are set to Json as shown in the following code:

```
[OperationContract]
[WebGet(UriTemplate = "userlistjson",
    BodyStyle = WebMessageBodyStyle.Bare,
    RequestFormat = WebMessageFormat.Json),
    ResponseFormat = WebMessageFormat.Json)])]
List<DTO.User> GetAllUsersJson();
```

2. We can now implement this method. To do so, add the following code to the `UserManagementService` class:

```
public List<DTO.User> GetAllUsersJson()
{
   List<DTO.User> dtoUserList = new List<DTO.User>();
   List<User> userList = new UserRepository().GetAllUsers();
   foreach (var user in userList)
   {
      DTO.User dtoUser = ConvertUserToDTOUser(user);
      dtoUserList.Add(dtoUser);
   }
   return dtoUserList;
}
```

3. In the Silverlight project, we need to add a reference to `System.Json`.

4. We'll now try to retrieve all users using JSON, instead of XML. In the UI, add a new `Button` to the `StackPanel` as shown in the following code:

```
<Button x:Name="NewUserButton"
        Content="Create new"
        Click="NewUserButton_Click"
        HorizontalAlignment="Left"
        Margin="3"
        VerticalAlignment="Center">
</Button>
```

5. In the event handler of this `Button`, we can perform a call to the `GetAllUsersJson` method using the following code:

```
private void JsonButton_Click(object sender, RoutedEventArgs e)
{
   WebClient client = new WebClient();
   client.OpenReadCompleted += new
     OpenReadCompletedEventHandler(client_OpenReadCompleted);
   client.OpenReadAsync(new Uri(serviceBaseUrl + "userlistjson",
     UriKind.Absolute));
}
```

6. Add the following code to handle the `OpenReadCompleted` event of our JSON request. In this method, we're parsing the result of the request.

```
void client_OpenReadCompleted(object sender,
  OpenReadCompletedEventArgs e)
{
   if (e.Error == null)
   {
      JsonArray items = (JsonArray)JsonArray.Load(e.Result);
```

```
            var query = from user in items
                        select new User
        {
          Department = user["Department"],
          Email = user["Email"],
          FirstName = user["FirstName"],
          LastName = user["LastName"],
          ReportsTo = user["ReportsTo"],
          UserId = user["UserId"],
          UserName = user["UserName"]
        };
        UsersDataGrid.ItemsSource = query.ToList();
      }
    }
```

Build and run your application. If we place a breakpoint in the returning method, we can see that the data is effectively returned in a JSON format.

How it works...

By setting the `RequestFormat` and the `ResponseFormat` NamedParameters to `WebMessageFormat.Json` in our `OperationContract`, we're telling our service that it should use JSON as the data format while transferring data for both requests and responses. Whenever we send or receive data using this `OperationContract`, everything is done using JSON.

To easily parse this result, Silverlight includes classes to easily handle JSON data. They're located in the `System.Json` namespace. By calling `JsonArray.Load` in the response stream, we can load the response into a `JsonArray` object. This represents a collection of `JsonValue`. In this example, each `JsonValue` is a `User`, so all that's left to do is convert these items into `User` objects and set the `ItemsSource` collection of the `DataGrid`.

See also

To get data in the XML format rather than the JSON format, have a look at the *Reading data from a REST service* recipe in this chapter.

Using WCF Data Services with Silverlight

Above our data layer, we may have an entity model that exposes entities (for example, created using the ADO.NET Entity Framework) for our application to use. **WCF Data Services** allows exposing these entities over REST-based services. In this recipe, we'll look at how we can use WCF Data Services from Silverlight.

WCF Data Services is the new name for ADO.NET Data Services. This name change was made in the .NET Framework 4 timeframe.

In the previous recipes, we worked on the User Management part of the Computer Inventory application. In this and the following two recipes, we'll work on the Computer Management.

Getting ready

This recipe, along with the following two recipes, uses the same database called ComputerInventory as used in the RESTful services recipes. This database is included as a Microsoft SQL Server Database File (MDF) in the code bundle available on the Packt website. Refer to Appendix B for installation instructions.

This recipe starts from an empty Silverlight application. Refer to Chapter 1 for more information on how to do so.

How to do it...

We'll first set up WCF Data Services and then build a model using Entity Framework. In the following recipes, we'll connect to these services from a Silverlight client application. The following are the steps we need to perform to get this working:

1. We'll build the entire application from scratch. Create a new Silverlight solution and select **ASP.NET Web Application** as the type for the hosting website. The latter is needed to create the model and host the service. If you have an existing Silverlight solution to which you want to add a WCF Data Service, you can add the model in the hosting web application.

2. WCF Data Services work on a model, not directly on a database. Add a new Entity Framework Model by right-clicking on the web project, selecting **Add | New Item...**, and selecting **ADO.NET Entity Data Model**. Name the model as **ComputerInventory.edmx**.

3. In the wizard that appears, select **Generate from Database** in the first dialog box. This indicates that we want to start creating the model based on the tables in the database.

4. The next step allows us to configure the connection to the database by clicking on the **New Connection** button. Leave the checkbox checked to allow storing the connection string in the `web.config` file.

5. The final step in the wizard allows us to select which items from the database we want to make part of the model. Select **all tables**, excluding the **sysdiagrams**. When we click on **Finish**, Visual Studio generates the model as shown in the following screenshot:

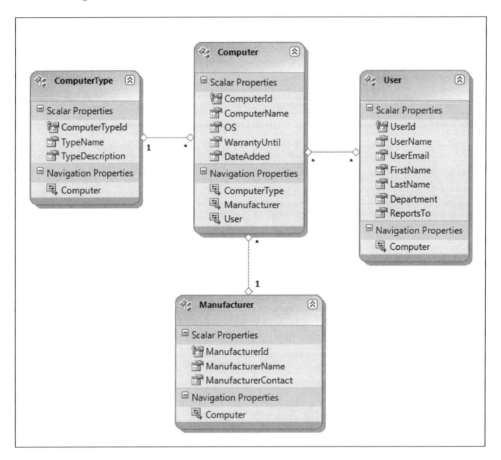

6. Next, we create the actual WCF Data Service. To do so, add an **WCF Data Service** called `ComputerInventoryService.svc` to your web project.

The generated code needs some changes done to it. A link needs to be created between the model and the data service by making the latter inherit from `DataService<ComputerInventoryEntities>`. The `ComputerInventoryEntities` type parameter is often referred to as the context or context object representing the model.

7. In the `InitializeService` method, we need to explicitly allow access-specific entities by using the `EntitySetRights` enumeration. In the following code, we are saying that all rights are allowed on the specified entities:

```
public static void InitializeService(DataServiceConfiguration
   config)
{
   config.UseVerboseErrors = true;
   config.SetEntitySetAccessRule("Computer", EntitySetRights.All);
   config.SetEntitySetAccessRule("User", EntitySetRights.All);
   config.SetEntitySetAccessRule("ComputerType",
      EntitySetRights.All);
   config.SetEntitySetAccessRule("Manufacturer",
      EntitySetRights.All);
}
```

8. Go to the Silverlight application and add a service reference to the `*.svc` file by right-clicking on the Silverlight application and selecting **Add Service Reference...**. Then, click on the **Discover** button in the **Add Service Reference** dialog box. Change the namespace to **ComputerInventoryService**. Visual Studio will now generate a proxy for this service and a reference to `System.Data.Services.Client` will be automatically added. You now have typed access to the entities exposed by the service, although we're in the background and using REST to communicate with the service.

How it works...

WCF Data Services is a server-side technology that allows making entities of a model available on the web. Underlying, it uses REST as its communication platform. So, it's possible to connect to the services using the `WebClient` class or the `HttpWebRequest` class. Each entity of the model is exposed as a resource and can be connected to via a unique URI. However, the data source used has to have an `IQueryable` interface for exposing the entities. If we want updates to be sent to the data, the `IUpdatable` interface should be implemented as well. A good example of this is the ADO.NET Entity Framework, which exposes such a data source through the Entity Model. Note that you can create your own data source and attach WCF Data Services to it as well.

One important thing to understand is that WCF Data Services have nothing to do with the actual data access itself. It works with entities exposed by a model (in this example, the model from Entity Framework).

It's easy to see that WCF Data Services actually use REST under the hood. To get data, we need to send a request to a specifically formed URI, combined with one of the standard HTTP keywords such as GET, POST, PUT, or DELETE. Sounds familiar? Indeed, it is exactly the same way of working as we did with REST in the previous recipes.

The URIs created by WCF Data Services to expose the entities are simple to understand. In the following example, which will retrieve a `Computer` entity with ID equal to 1, we can see that the URI is composed of the name of the service, followed by the name of the entity (`Computer`), and the ID we want to retrieve `http://localhost:12345/ComputerInventoryService.svc/Computer(1)`.

The resulting response can be sent in an XML or JSON format. XML, in the form of AtomPub, is the default format and is actually easiest to read. The **Atom Publishing Protocol** (**AtomPub**) is a protocol based on HTTP that allows creating and publishing web resources. The response sent when invoking the above URI is shown in the following code:

```xml
<?xml version="1.0" encoding="utf-8" standalone="yes" ?>
<entry
    xml:base="http://localhost:8624/ComputerInventoryService.svc/"
    xmlns:d="http://schemas.microsoft.com/ado/2007/08/dataservices"
    xmlns:m="http://schemas.microsoft.com/ado/2007/08/dataservices/
       metadata"
    xmlns="http://www.w3.org/2005/Atom">
 <id>http://localhost:8624/ComputerInventoryService.svc/Computer(1)
 </id>
 <title type="text" />
 <updated>2009-07-19T12:37:26Z</updated>
 <author>
   <name />
 </author>
 <link rel="edit" title="Computer" href="Computer(1)" />
 <link rel="http://schemas.microsoft.com/ado/2007/08/dataservices
         /related/ComputerType"
       type="application/atom+xml;type=entry" title="ComputerType"
       href="Computer(1)/ComputerType" />
 <link rel="http://schemas.microsoft.com/ado/2007/08/dataservices/
related/Manufacturer" type="application/atom+xml;type=entry"
title="Manufacturer" href="Computer(1)/Manufacturer" />
 <link rel="http://schemas.microsoft.com/ado/2007/08/dataservices
         /related/User"
       type="application/atom+xml;type=feed" title="User"
       href="Computer(1)/User" />
 <category term="ComputerInventoryModel.Computer" scheme="http://
schemas.microsoft.com/ado/2007/08/dataservices/scheme" />
 - <content type="application/xml">
   - <m:properties>
     <d:ComputerId m:type="Edm.Int32">1</d:ComputerId>
     <d:ComputerName>Lenovo W500</d:ComputerName>
     <d:OS>Windows 7</d:OS>
     <d:WarrantyUntil m:type="Edm.DateTime">2012-07-01T00:00:00</
```

```
d:WarrantyUntil>
      <d:DateAdded m:type="Edm.DateTime">2009-07-01T00:00:00</
d:DateAdded>
    </m:properties>
  </content>
</entry>
```

The big difference in working with plain REST services is the existence of the WCF Data Service Client library in Silverlight. It frees us from manually having to create the URIs to request data and writing XML parsing code to read out the response. It's basically a large wrapper around these tasks, allowing us to work with data on the client as if the service barrier isn't there.

This is achieved through code-generation. It's possible to add a service reference to an WCF. Data Service in your Silverlight project. This will result in the creation of client-side data classes and a class derived from `DataServiceContext` that represents the service itself. All these classes are located in the `reference.cs` file. The following screenshot shows where all this generated code is located:

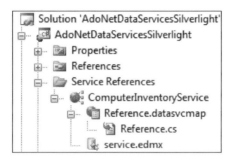

Also, the required assembly—`System.Data.Services.Client.dll`—is added to the Silverlight project. Finally, a client-side version of the server-side entity model (`*.edmx`) is generated that contains the structure of the entity model.

We can write LINQ queries in the Silverlight application that are translated into a URI to which a request is sent. The response is parsed for us and available as objects of the generated classes. Thus, we have full IntelliSense inside Visual Studio as well, which makes coding a lot easier. We'll look at writing queries to get and update data in the next two recipes.

Locked-down services

WCF Data Services are completely locked down by default. Access is not permitted to the entities automatically. Due to this, in the `InitializeService` method of the `DataService` class, we have to configure this access using the `DataServiceConfiguration` instance. Several options exist to give more or less permissions to the entities such as All, AllRead, None, and so on. Go to `http://msdn.microsoft.com/en-us/library/system.data.services.entitysetrights.aspx` for a complete overview of this enumeration.

See also

In the next recipe, we'll build further on this recipe by showing how we can read data from services. The *Persisting data using WCF Data Services* recipe will show how we can perform create, update, and delete operations on the data.

Reading data using WCF Data Services

Let's assume we have decided that WCF Data Services is going to be the technology to get data inside our Silverlight application, which admittedly is a great choice. In the previous recipe, we saw how we can set up Silverlight to use WCF Data Services. However, we didn't actually exchange any data with the service (which is quite ironic for a data service).

In this recipe, we'll perform read operations on the data by building on the code created in the previous recipe. This time, we'll focus on the `Computer` data in the database.

Getting ready

This recipe continues on the code created in the previous recipe. If you want to follow along, you can continue using your code or use the provided starter solution located in the `Chapter08/WorkingWithWcfDataServices_Reading_Starter` folder in the code bundle available on the Packt website. The finished solution for this recipe can be found in the `Chapter08/WorkingWithWcfDataServices_Reading_Completed` folder.

How to do it...

In the previous recipe, we introduced the client library that dramatically reduces the amount of code we need to write compared to plain REST services. Using this library, we can load data in several formats such as an entire list, a single object with or without related entities, and so on. We'll build an application that shows a list of computers. The details of each computer can be seen using a detail screen. Perform the following steps to start reading data from WCF Data Services:

1. The XAML for the application is similar to the XAML we used in the previous recipes. The application's UI mainly consists of a `DataGrid` with defined columns. The code for this `DataGrid` can be found in the code bundle.

    Thanks to the client library, we have the possibility to write LINQ queries. These LINQ queries are executed using an instance of the **context**, so creating this `context` instance should be our first step. Note that the `context` instance accepts a URI to the `.svc` file of the service as a parameter. After this, we can write a LINQ query in which we load all `Computer` entities. A little caution though: WCF Data Services wouldn't load the related `Manufacturer` objects by default, although we want to show this information as well in the `DataGrid`. Therefore, we specify this using the `Expand` method as shown in the following code:

```
ComputerInventoryEntities context =
  new ComputerInventoryEntities(new
  Uri("ComputerInventoryService.svc", UriKind.Relative));
public MainPage()
{
  InitializeComponent();
}
private void UserControl_Loaded(object sender, RoutedEventArgs e)
{
  ComputerLoadStart();
}
private void ComputerLoadStart()
{
  var query = from c in context.Computer.Expand("Manufacturer")
              select c;
}
```

2. While the query looks rather normal, do keep in mind that all Silverlight's service requests are carried out asynchronously. Therefore, the query is cast to a `DataServiceQuery<T>` (in this case, the return type `T` is `Computer`). On this instance, the `BeginExecute` method is called, which triggers an asynchronous call to the service. Similar to other asynchronous calls, a callback method is passed in. The query itself is also passed in, so we have access to it in the callback method. This is shown in the following code:

```
private void ComputerLoadStart()
{
  ...
  DataServiceQuery<Computer> dsq =
    (DataServiceQuery<Computer>)query;
  dsq.BeginExecute(ComputerLoadCompleted, dsq);
}
```

3. When the service is ready, the `ComputerLoadCompleted` callback method is invoked. This method receives an `IAsyncResult` instance as parameter, which contains the `DataServiceQuery<T>`. By calling the `EndExecute` method on this instance, we get access to the returned `Computer` instances. We place these instances in an `ObservableCollection` called `computerCollection` for data binding purposes. The collection is bound to the `DataGrid` using the `ItemsSource` property as shown in the following code:

```
ObservableCollection<Computer> computerCollection =
  new ObservableCollection<Computer>();
private void ComputerLoadCompleted(IAsyncResult asr)
{
```

```
DataServiceQuery<Computer> dsq =
    (DataServiceQuery<Computer>)asr.AsyncState;
foreach (var computer in dsq.EndExecute(asr).ToList())
{
    computerCollection.Add(computer);
}
ComputersDataGrid.ItemsSource = computerCollection;
}
```

The result is a list of computers as shown on the following screenshot:

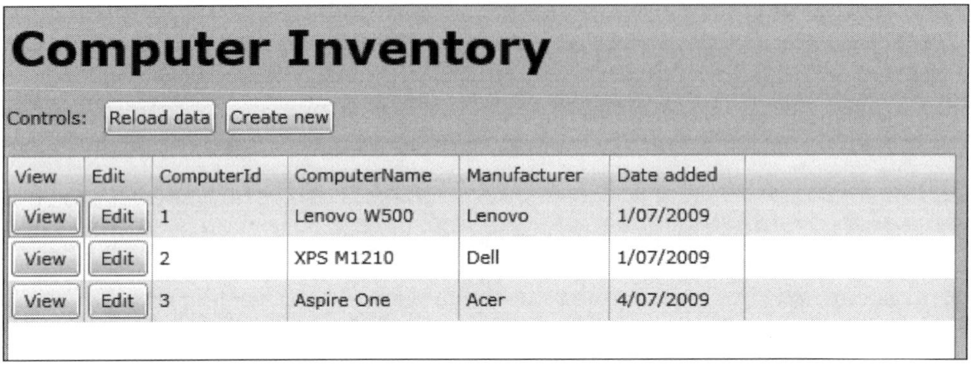

Computer Inventory

Controls: [Reload data] [Create new]

View	Edit	ComputerId	ComputerName	Manufacturer	Date added	
[View]	[Edit]	1	Lenovo W500	Lenovo	1/07/2009	
[View]	[Edit]	2	XPS M1210	Dell	1/07/2009	
[View]	[Edit]	3	Aspire One	Acer	4/07/2009	

4. Let's now take a look at the detail page. When clicking on a **View** button in the grid, we load a Silverlight Child Window named `ComputerDetailView.xaml` that features a nice zoom-in effect when opened. The XAML for this window is straightforward and can be found in the code bundle.

5. To show the details of the selected computer in the `DataGrid`, we pass the `context` as well as the `computerID` of the selected computer via the constructor. This is shown in the following code:

```
private ComputerInventoryEntities context;
private int computerId;
private Computer computer;
public ComputerDetailView(ComputerInventoryEntities context,
    int computerId)
{
    InitializeComponent();
    this.context = context;
    this.computerId = computerId;
    LoadComputer();
}
```

6. In the `LoadComputer` method, we load the details of the selected computer. However, the computer is already being tracked by the `context` because of the list display, but not all the data we need is loaded (the computer type is omitted in the list). Thus, we need to explicitly tell the `context` that it has to reload the computer using the `OverWriteChanges` of the `MergeOption` enumeration. The following code shows this loading process:

```
private void LoadComputer()
{
   context.MergeOption = MergeOption.OverwriteChanges;
   var query = from c in context.Computer.Expand("ComputerType")
               where c.ComputerId == computerId
               select c;
   DataServiceQuery<Computer> dsq =
      (DataServiceQuery<Computer>)query;
   dsq.BeginExecute(ComputerLoadCompleted, dsq);
}
private void ComputerLoadCompleted(IAsyncResult asr)
{
   DataServiceQuery<Computer> dsq =
      (DataServiceQuery<Computer>)asr.AsyncState;
   computer = dsq.EndExecute(asr).FirstOrDefault<Computer>();
   ComputerDetailGrid.DataContext = computer;
}
```

After all the previous code is added, we have successfully created a master-detail implementation based on WCF Data Services. The detail screen is shown in the following screenshot:

How it works...

The most important part of this recipe is the LINQ query. When executing a LINQ query against an WCF Data Service, the query is translated into a format that the service understands—a URI. All the options we specify in the query are translated into the URI. The URI to which a request is sent is `http://127.0.0.1:8624/ComputerInventoryService.svc/Computer()?$expand=Manufacturer`. (This can be seen using Fiddler2. More information on this tool can be found in Appendix C.)

Note that the `Expand` option instructs the service to retrieve all `Computer` instances and expand the results to include the related `Manufacturer` instances for each `Computer` instance. This process is called eager loading. In this process, we explicitly ask to load the related entities initially. If we omit eager loading, the property will have a null value.

To see what the AtomPub (XML) response of the service looks like, simply copy/paste the previously mentioned URI in your browser or view it in Fiddler2.

The **context** is the real workhorse in this recipe. It keeps track of all the loaded items (this is called object tracking). However, sometimes we need to ask for a complete reload. In the example at hand, we need to do so in the detail screen. We have the `MergeOption` enumeration at our disposal for this. The `OverwriteChanges` explicitly tells the **context** that it should replace the item loaded in the context.

There's more...

We might know that there are related entities, but not want to load them initially. We can load on demand using the `LoadProperty` method. This method is used in the detail screen of the application. When loading, the allowed users are not retrieved automatically (for example not to stress the database). By clicking on the **Load** button, we load them asynchronously on demand using the `LoadProperty` method. The result is that the `Computer` entity will have its property filled with the related `User` entities. This is shown in the following code:

```
private void LoadUsersButton_Click(object sender, RoutedEventArgs e)
{
  context.BeginLoadProperty(computer, "User", UsersLoadCompleted,
    null);
}
private void UsersLoadCompleted(IAsyncResult asr)
{
  context.EndLoadProperty(asr);
  // do something with the loaded values here
}
```

See also

In the *Reading data from ADO.NET Data Services* recipe, we create the ADO.NET Data Service and set up communication with it.

Persisting data using WCF Data Services

In the previous recipe, we saw how to read data from WCF Data Services. Apart from reading data, we should be able to persist data using these services. In other words, adding, updating, and deleting data to make the **CRUD** story complete (**CRUD: Create, Read, Update, and Delete**, this term is often used to refer to the four basic operations on data).

This recipe will add a new screen to the application built in the previous two recipes to make it possible to create new computers and to update and delete the existing ones. The screen in the following screenshot is similar to the View screenshot, but it has editable fields and some extra buttons:

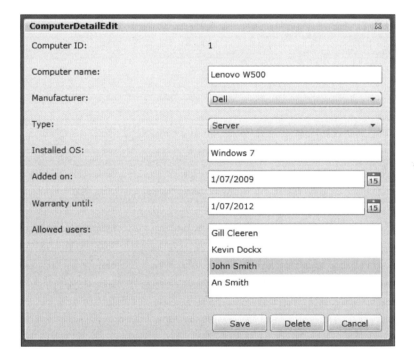

Getting ready

This recipe builds on the code created in the previous two recipes. This means that you can continue using your own solution to follow along with this recipe. Alternatively, you can use the starter solution located in the `Chapter08/WorkingWithWcfDataServices_Persisting_Starter` folder in the code bundle available on the Packt website. The finished solution for this recipe can be found in the `Chapter08/WorkingWithWcfDataServices_Persisting_Completed` folder.

How to do it...

We'll follow a small scenario, where we'll create a new computer object, update it, and finally remove it from the database. Along the way, we'll come across the specifics of each operation. In order to do this, we'll need to complete the following steps:

1. As this screen is used for both adding new items and editing existing ones, we add an enumeration to the Silverlight application called `EditingModes` to see in which state we are. This is shown in the following code:

    ```
    public enum EditingModes
    {
        New,
        Edit
    }
    ```

2. The UI contains two `ComboBox` controls that allow the user to select a `Manufacturer` and a `Type`. Also, all `Users` should be loaded in the `ListBox` at the bottom of the screen. Loading data into these controls is similar. The code to load the `Manufacturer` objects is as follows:

    ```
    public ComputerDetailEdit(ComputerInventoryEntities context,
        int computerId, EditingModes editingMode)
    {
        InitializeComponent();
        ...
        ManufacturerLoadStart();
    }
    private void ManufacturerLoadStart()
    {
        var query = from m in context.Manufacturer
                    select m;
        DataServiceQuery<Manufacturer> dsq =
            (DataServiceQuery<Manufacturer>)query;
        dsq.BeginExecute(ManufacturerLoadCompleted, dsq);
    }
    ```

```
private void ManufacturerLoadCompleted(IAsyncResult asr)
{
  DataServiceQuery<Manufacturer> dsq =
    (DataServiceQuery<Manufacturer>)asr.AsyncState;
  ComputerManufacturerComboBox.ItemsSource = dsq.EndExecute(asr);
  ComputerManufacturerComboBox.DisplayMemberPath =
    "ManufacturerName";
}
```

3. Let's now look at how we can add an item. We create a new instance of the `Computer` class and set it as the `DataContext` of the main grid—`ComputerDetailGrid`. As this is a new object, the context doesn't know it yet, so we make the context track it using the `AddObject` method. This is shown in the following code:

```
Computer computer = new Computer();
ComputerDetailGrid.DataContext = computer;
context.AddObject("Computer", computer);
```

4. The selected `ComputerType` and `Manufacturer` should be linked to the `Computer` object so that the context can track this link. Also, every selected user in the listbox should be linked to the computer. It's important that the context knows which links exist between objects. When persisting, it needs to know which relations in the database need to be created. This is shown in the following code:

```
private void SaveButton_Click(object sender, RoutedEventArgs e)
{
  context.SetLink(computer, "ComputerType",
    computer.ComputerType);
  context.SetLink(computer, "Manufacturer",
    computer.Manufacturer);
  foreach (var user in ComputerUsersListBox.SelectedItems)
  {
    context.AddLink(computer, "User", (User)user);
  }
}
```

5. Once the user clicks on the **Save** button, the actual save operation should start. Again, this is done asynchronously by making use of the `BeginSaveChanges` method available on the context. We pass in a callback method that will be called when the service returns. This is shown in the following code:

```
context.BeginSaveChanges(SaveChangesOptions.None, new
  AsyncCallback(PersistChanges), null);
```

6. In the callback, we use the `EndSaveChanges` method, which returns a `DataServiceResponse` object, containing the response of the server. If errors were encountered, we can retrieve them by looping over this object. This is shown in the following code:

```
private void PersistChanges(IAsyncResult asr)
{
  try
  {
    DataServiceResponse dataServiceResponse =
      (DataServiceResponse)context.EndSaveChanges(asr);
    foreach (OperationResponse operationResponse in
      dataServiceResponse)
    {
      if (operationResponse.Error != null)
      {
        //do something with the error
      }
    }
    if (errorsOccurred)
      MessageBox.Show(builder.ToString());
  }
  catch (Exception ex)
  {
    MessageBox.Show(ex.Message);
  }
}
```

7. When we want to update the instance, the code is quite similar. As shown in the following code, we call the `UpdateObject` method to mark the object as `Modified`. The same callback is used as when adding new items:

```
context.UpdateObject(computer);
context.BeginSaveChanges(SaveChangesOptions.Batch, new
  AsyncCallback(PersistChanges), null);
```

8. Finally, deleting the object is done using the `DeleteObject` method. This is shown in the following line of code:

```
context.DeleteObject(computer);
```

Take a look at the sample code where the full code listing is available.

How it works...

When creating a new instance, we immediately set it as the `DataContext` for the main grid of the user control. This way, all changes done by the user on the text boxes that are bound using the `TwoWay` binding are propagated back into the object. However, as this object is new, it is unknown to the context. It's not yet being tracked by the context, so we need to add it to the collection of tracked objects.

The `Computer` class has links to other classes, namely the `ComputerType`, the `Manufacturer`, and the `User`. Thus, we need to create links in the context using `SetLink` (for links with multiplicity = 1) or `AddLink` (for links with multiplicity > 1). Links also need to be made or recreated when updating or deleted when deleting a `Computer` instance.

Just like all other operations towards services, the actual save operation is asynchronous. That's why we use the `BeginSaveChanges` method and specify the callback method in one go. Saving is actually sending data to one or more specific URIs. In the callback method, we use the `EndSaveChanges` method, which returns a `DataServiceResponse` object. This object contains the responses for all calls made to the service (one for saving the actual object, one for linking, and so on). If an operation fails, we can get the error information from the `DataServiceResponse` object as well.

Updating and deleting are very similar. All changes are done initially on the objects tracked by the context. Afterwards, the changes are persisted using exactly the same code as for adding new objects.

There's more...

When calling the `BeginSaveChanges` method, we have the option to pass along how we want the subsequent operations to be executed through the `SaveChangeOptions` enumeration. We can use the `Batch` option, which creates a unit of work containing all operations. This can be compared to working with a transaction—either all operations work or they all fail. Other options include None and ContinueOnError. More information on this enumeration can be found at `http://msdn.microsoft.com/en-us/library/system.data.services.client.savechangesoptions.aspx`.

Talking to Flickr

There are quite a few large websites out there that expose (part of) their functionality through services, most of the time through the use of RESTful services. A great example is **Flickr** (`www.flickr.com`). Flickr exposes many services that allow searching for pictures, tagging existing pictures, uploading pictures, and so on. We can leverage all the goodness that Flickr provides inside our applications to provide more functionality to our end users.

Flickr is a popular website where people can upload and share images and videos. Apart from viewing this content on the site, Flickr offers a wide range of services for interaction with its content. Currently, Flickr has millions of users sharing several billion images!

One thing that is very important is the open `crossdomain.xml` file Flickr exposes. It allows connecting from every domain (so also from a Silverlight application running locally). This is why we can connect directly from Silverlight to Flickr. However, most Web 2.0 websites aren't that open, for example, Twitter. Communication with such a service from Silverlight is explained in the following recipe.

Note that not all code for this sample is printed in this book. Refer to the code in the downloadable samples for this.

Getting ready

Most sites that expose public services, such as Flickr, Amazon, Digg and so on allow us free access to their services, however you'll often need to register to get a key/identification. This is then used by the issuing site to track where the call came from. Some services allow only a limited number of calls for a particular key within a certain time span to discourage overuse. For the code in this recipe, you'll need a Flickr API key, which can be obtained for free from `http://www.flickr.com/services/api/keys/`. This key can be pasted in the sample code that can be downloaded for this book.

The recipe uses a `WrapPanel`—a control that's part of the Silverlight Control Toolkit. The toolkit is a collection of controls and extensions on Silverlight. This can be obtained from `www.codeplex.com/silverlight`. See Appendix D from more information on the Silverlight Control Toolkit.

To follow along with this recipe, a starter solution has been provided in the `Chapter08/SilverFlickr_Starter` folder in the code bundle available on the Packt website. The completed solution for this recipe can be found in the `Chapter08/SilverFlickr_Completed` folder.

How to do it...

In this recipe, we'll build a simple application that allows us to search for photos based on a search term the user can enter. On clicking on one of the results, the details of the photo are shown. For this, the application uses two of the many methods available from Flickr, namely `flickr.photos.search` and `flickr.photos.getinfo`. These methods allow searching for photos matching a search string and getting more information on a photo respectively. To begin building this application, we'll need to complete the following steps:

1. We start from an empty Silverlight application. Therefore, create a new Silverlight solution called **SilverFlickr**.

2. As we are going to use REST services, we'll be making use of the `WebClient` class. This class resides in the System.Net namespace, which is part of the System. Net assembly. If you're using Visual Studio 2008, you need to add a reference to this assembly yourself. Visual Studio 2010 refers this assembly by default for new projects for both Silverlight 3 and 4 projects.

3. The XAML code for the UI of the application is quite easy to understand. A `StackPanel` resides at the top of the page, containing an `Image`, a `TextBox` to enter the search query and a `Button`. The page also contains a `ScrollViewer` with a `WrapPanel` (part of the Silverlight Control Toolkit, refer to the *Getting ready* section of this recipe) on the left. The XAML code for this is as follows:

```xml
<Grid x:Name="LayoutRoot"
      Background="White">
  <Grid.RowDefinitions>
    <RowDefinition Height="50"></RowDefinition>
    <RowDefinition></RowDefinition>
  </Grid.RowDefinitions>
  <Grid.ColumnDefinitions>
    <ColumnDefinition Width="300"></ColumnDefinition>
    <ColumnDefinition></ColumnDefinition>
  </Grid.ColumnDefinitions>
  <StackPanel Grid.Row="0"
              Grid.Column="0"
              HorizontalAlignment="Left"
              Orientation="Horizontal"
              Grid.ColumnSpan="2">
    <Image Source="flickr.png"
           Stretch="None"
           Margin="3 0 0 0" >
    </Image>
    <TextBox x:Name="SearchTextBox"
             Width="200"
             Height="30"
             Margin="5">
    </TextBox>
    <Button x:Name="SearchButton"
            Content="Search Flickr"
            Click="SearchButton_Click"
            HorizontalAlignment="Center"
            VerticalAlignment="Center"
            Margin="5">
    </Button>
  </StackPanel>
```

```
<ScrollViewer Grid.Row="1"
              Grid.Column="0"
              Background="DarkGray">
   <toolkit:WrapPanel x:Name="ResultPanel"
                          HorizontalAlignment="Center">
   </toolkit:WrapPanel>
   </ScrollViewer>
</Grid>
```

4. As mentioned before, Flickr's API is a REST API. Thus, we need to send a request to a specific URI and read out the response being sent back. Let's first take a look at the URI. As defined by Flickr, this URI needs to be in a specific format. As we'll be doing a search, we'll use the `flickr.photos.search` method. It requires two parameters: your personal API key and the search term entered in the search field. This is shown in the following code:

```
string api_key = "123456";//TODO: replace with your own key
string searchUrl = "http://api.flickr.com/services/rest
   /?method=flickr.photos.search&api_key={0}&text={1}";
```

5. We now have the URI; we can use it to send a request to. To send this request, we'll use the `WebClient` class again. In the `Click` event handler of the button, we'll create an instance of this class. We need to register the callback method via `DownloadStringCompleted` and send the request using `DownloadStringAsync`, passing in the URI as a parameter. As with other services, these calls are asynchronous. This is shown in the following code:

```
private void SearchButton_Click(object sender, RoutedEventArgs e)
{
   WebClient client = new WebClient();
   client.DownloadStringCompleted +=
     new DownloadStringCompletedEventHandler
     (client_DownloadStringCompleted);
   client.DownloadStringAsync(new Uri(string.Format(searchUrl,
     api_key, SearchTextBox.Text)));
}
```

6. In the callback, we have access to the result of the call via the `Result` property on the instance of the `DownloadStringCompletedEventArgs`. The response is plain XML, formatted by Flickr in a specific format. We'll use LINQ-To-XML to parse this XML code and create a list of `ImageInfo` objects (shown in the following code), a custom type defined to have typed access to our data in the Silverlight application. Note that the `ImageUrl` implementation creates the link to the image as used by Flickr. Add the following class to the Silverlight project:

```
public class ImageInfo
{
   public string ImageId { get; set; }
```

```
public string FarmId { get; set; }
public string ServerId { get; set; }
public string Secret { get; set; }
public string ImageUrl
{
  get
  {
    return string.Format
      ("http://farm{0}.static.flickr.com/{1}/{2}_{3}_m.jpg",
      FarmId, ServerId, ImageId, Secret);
  }
}
}
```

7. Add a reference to the `System.Xml.Linq` assembly inside the Silverlight project.

8. Finally, each `ImageInfo` instance is used to dynamically create an image and add it to the `WrapPanel`. Every image also gets a click event attached to it, which is used to open the detail page. This is shown in the following code:

```
void client_DownloadStringCompleted(object sender,
  DownloadStringCompletedEventArgs e)
{
  XDocument xml = XDocument.Parse(e.Result);
  var photos = from results in xml.Descendants("photo")
               select new ImageInfo
  {
    ImageId = results.Attribute("id").Value.ToString(),
    FarmId = results.Attribute("farm").Value.ToString(),
    ServerId = results.Attribute("server").Value.ToString(),
    Secret = results.Attribute("secret").Value.ToString()
  };
  foreach (var image in photos)
  {
    Image img = new Image();
    BitmapImage bmi = new BitmapImage(new
      Uri(image.ImageUrl, UriKind.Absolute));
    img.Source = bmi;
    img.Width = 200;
    img.Height = 200;
    img.Stretch = Stretch.Uniform;
    img.Tag = image;
    img.Margin = new Thickness(3);
    img.HorizontalAlignment = HorizontalAlignment.Center;
    ResultPanel.Children.Add(img);
  }
}
```

At this point, we can search Flickr for images. The following screenshot shows the finished application. Note that this final application includes extra code that allows clicking an image and viewing its details. However, the code for this is very similar and can be found in the code bundle.

How it works...

Communicating with Flickr's REST services is, in fact, no different from communicating with a self-created REST service, as was done in the beginning of this chapter.

The URI is created according to the specifications given by the Flickr API. At http://www.flickr.com/services/api, you can find an overview of all the methods exposed by Flickr, varying from searching for pictures and reading out comments on a picture to finding pictures based on a location. For this recipe, we use the flickr.photos.search and flickr.photos.getinfo methods. Both require the API key sent as a parameter, apart from the specific parameters depending on the method.

The format of the XML sent by Flickr's services is fixed. It's safe to build our code around this API as the format can be considered to be a contract between the service and the client application. The service will always return the response formatted according to this specification. The following is the XML structure used by Flickr:

```
<rsp>
  <photos>
    <photo id="1234567890"
           secret="0987654321"
           server="1234"
           farm="1" />
  </photos>
</rsp>
```

There's more...

Communication with the services exposed by Flickr from Silverlight is possible because Flickr has a `crossdomain.xml` file in place that allows calls from any domain, as explained in the introduction of the recipe. The following is the complete `crossdomain.xml` (`http://api.flickr.com/crossdomain.xml`) file of Flickr. Refer to the *Configuring cross-domain calls* recipe in Chapter 6 for more information on the concept of cross-domain calls.

```
<?xml version="1.0" ?>
  <!DOCTYPE cross-domain-policy (View Source for full doctype...)>
  <cross-domain-policy>
    <allow-access-from domain="*" secure="true" />
    <site-control permitted-cross-domain-policies="master-only" />
  </cross-domain-policy>
```

However, other sites don't open up their API as much as Flickr does. A good example is Twitter (`http://twitter.com/crossdomain.xml`), which allows calls only from particular domains. This can be seen in the following code:

```
<?xml version="1.0" encoding="UTF-8" ?>
  <cross-domain-policy xmlns:xsi="http://www.w3.org/2001/
                       XMLSchema-instance"
                       xsi:noNamespaceSchemaLocation=
                       "http://www.adobe.com/xml/schemas/
                       PolicyFile.xsd">
    <allow-access-from domain="twitter.com" />
    <allow-access-from domain="api.twitter.com" />
    <allow-access-from domain="search.twitter.com" />
    <allow-access-from domain="static.twitter.com" />
    <site-control permitted-cross-domain-policies="master-only" />
    <allow-http-request-headers-from domain="*.twitter.com"
      headers="*" secure="true" />
  </cross-domain-policy>
```

The consequence of such a `crossdomain.xml` file is that Silverlight can't connect directly with these services. The solution is creating an extra service on the same domain as the Silverlight application, which will in turn call the REST services. Your application then only has to connect with the new service, which shouldn't be a problem. We'll look at this scenario in the following recipe. A second possible solution is building a Trusted Silverlight application, which we'll look at in the last recipe of this chapter..

Flickr... more information

The accompanying code for this book also contains the code to create the detail screen. For this, we can use another method, namely `flickr.photos.getinfo` to retrieve more information about an image based on the photo ID.

Displaying the values is done through the use of data binding. The `DataContext` property of the grid, located in the Details portion of the interface, is set to an instance of another type called `ImageDetail`.

One particularity is certainly worth mentioning here, that is, data binding the image is done through the use of a converter. The link to the image is stored as a `Uri` in the instance of `ImageDetail`. However, binding in XAML expects a `BitmapImage`. The conversion of type A to type B is done through the use of a converter—a class that implements the `IValueConverter` interface. This interface has two methods—`Convert` and `ConvertBack`. This is shown in the following code:

```
public class ImageConverter:IValueConverter
{
  public object Convert(object value, Type targetType, object
    parameter, System.Globalization.CultureInfo culture)
  {
    if (value != null)
      return new BitmapImage((Uri)value);
    else
      return "";//can be link to a "NoImage.png" of some kind
  }
  public object ConvertBack(object value, Type targetType, object
    parameter, System.Globalization.CultureInfo culture)
  {
    . . .
  }
}
```

See also

In the *Reading data from a REST service* and *Parsing REST results with LINQ-To-XML* recipes from this chapter, we go deeper into the details of communication with a REST service. The following recipe shows the scenario to connect with services that don't allow cross-domain calls.

For more information on data binding, refer to the recipes in Chapter 2 and Chapter 3.

Talking to Twitter over REST

Like Flickr, Twitter has a great API that allows us to build applications incorporating its functionality.

> Twitter is a social networking site where people can post small messages of up to 140 characters, also known as tweets. These messages are shared with people that follow you, meaning they're interested in what you're doing. Twitter is often referred to as being a micro-blogging site. Using Twitter is free.

However, as explained in the *There's more...* section of the previous recipe, where we compared the `crossdomain.xml` files of Flickr and Twitter, Twitter is much more locked down. It doesn't allow client-side applications built in Silverlight to make cross-domain calls. In this recipe, which can be generalized for all types of REST services that don't have an open cross-domain file, we'll look at how we can still succeed in communicating with the service.

Getting ready

To work with the application built in this sample, you'll need an account on Twitter. Twitter is free and you can register at `www.twitter.com`. Unlike Flickr, you don't have an API key. In this recipe, we'll start from an empty Silverlight application. Refer to Chapter 1 for more information on this.

A starter solution for this chapter is provided in the `Chapter08/SilverWitter_Starter` folder in the code bundle available on the Packt website. The finished solution for this recipe can be found in the `Chapter08/SilverWitter_Completed` folder.

How to do it...

The way we architect the application that will work with Twitter is quite important, as we can't call the Twitter services from Silverlight directly. However, services that run on a server don't mind cross-domain restrictions. They can call Twitter's REST services without a problem. The solution for the problem is adding an extra service layer in our architecture. The Silverlight application will communicate with our own services and in turn, these services can talk to Twitter. The following screenshot demonstrates this idea clearly:

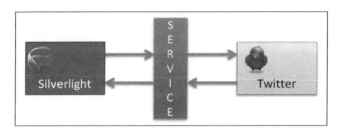

To get up and running, we'll need to complete the following steps:

1. Open the starter solution as outlined in the *Getting ready* section, containing an ASP. NET Web Application.

2. Add another ASP.NET web application to the solution called **SilverWitter.Services**.

3. In this web application, add a WCF service called **TwitterService.svc**. Thus, you'll have three projects in your solution: the Silverlight application, the hosting web application, and an extra website containing a WCF service.

4. Silverlight will communicate only with the WCF service and the service will communicate with Twitter. Only the functionality we expose on our own service will be available for the Silverlight application. Let's first define the contract, an interface, of our WCF service in the `ITwitterService.svc.cs` file. We want to be able to validate user credentials, get all tweets from the public time line, get all tweets from a specified user and his/her friends and finally add a tweet (a small message). Note that this is a WCF service, and not a REST service, although we could create a REST service if we wanted to. The following code shows the contract:

```
[ServiceContract]
public interface ITwitterService
{
  [OperationContract]
  List<TwitterUpdate> GetPublicTimeLine();
  [OperationContract]
  List<TwitterUpdate> GetUserTimeLine(string twitterUser,
    string userName, string userPassword);
  [OperationContract]
  List<TwitterUpdate> GetFriendsTimeLine(string twitterUser,
    string userName, string userPassword);
```

```
[OperationContract]
string AddMessage(string message, string userName,
  string userPassword);
[OperationContract]
bool CheckCredentials(string userName, string userPassword);
}
```

5. We use the `TwitterUpdate` class in some of the above methods. This class should be added to the services project—`SilverWitter.Services`. As instances of this class will be sent over the wire (to the Silverlight application), this class should be attributed with the `DataContractAttribute`. Its members have the `DataMemberAttribute` applied to them. This class is shown as follows:

```
[DataContract]
public class TwitterUpdate
{
  [DataMember]
  public string Message { get; set; }
  [DataMember]
  public string User { get; set; }
  [DataMember]
  public string Location { get; set; }
}
```

6. In the implementations of these methods, in the `TwitterService.cs` file, we'll write the code to talk with Twitter. Twitter's API is REST based and can communicate using XML, JSON, RSS, and ATOM. This means that we have to send a request to a particular URI and capture the results sent back by Twitter. This result can then be parsed using LINQ-To-XML and mapped to the CLR objects.

   Let's take a look at the code we need to write in the service method implementations. We'll implement the `GetUserTimeLine` method here; the other ones are similar and can be found in the code bundle available on the Packt website. As the service is a REST service, we need to use a specific URL, as defined by Twitter.

```
public List<TwitterUpdate> GetUserTimeLine(string twitterUser,
  string userName, string userPassword)
{
  try
  {
    string userTimeLine =
      "http://twitter.com/statuses/user_timeline/"
      + twitterUser + ".xml";
  }
  catch (Exception)
  {
    return null;
  }
}
```

7. Although we're not writing Silverlight code here to access Twitter (we're writing a WCF service implementation), the concepts are the same. We can use the `WebClient` class to perform the call to the service. One big difference here is that service communication can be done synchronously. Note that Twitter requires that we pass in credentials to access this service method.

```
WebClient client = new WebClient();
client.Credentials = new
  NetworkCredential(userName, userPassword);
ServicePointManager.Expect100Continue = false;
string result = client.DownloadString(
  string.Format(userTimeLine, twitterUser));
```

8. Once the result is available, we'll parse it using LINQ-To-XML as shown in the following code. On parsing the XML, we are creating a `List<TwitterUpdate>`.

```
XDocument document = XDocument.Parse(result);
List<TwitterUpdate> twitterData =
  (from status in document.Descendants("status")
  select new TwitterUpdate
  {
    Message = status.Element("text").Value.Trim(),
    User = status.Element("user").Element("name").Value.Trim()
  }).ToList();
return twitterData;
```

9. As this service is in another site than the Silverlight application, Silverlight will need to perform a cross-domain call to it. To allow this, we have to add a policy file. Add a new XML file called `clientaccesspolicy.xml` to the services site and insert the following code:

```
<?xml version="1.0" encoding="utf-8"?>
<access-policy>
  <cross-domain-access>
    <policy>
      <allow-from http-request-headers="*">
        <domain uri="*"/>
      </allow-from>
      <grant-to>
        <resource path="/" include-subpaths="true"/>
      </grant-to>
    </policy>
  </cross-domain-access>
</access-policy>
```

10. After having implemented the methods on the WCF service, let's focus on the Silverlight application. First, in the Silverlight project, add a service reference to the `TwitterService` WCF service. Set the service namespace to `TwitterService`.

11. The UI of the application built in this sample is shown in the following screenshot. The XAML code can be found in the code bundle. When opening the application, the statuses of the public timeline are shown as they don't require any credentials. The user can log in to Twitter, and when authenticated, add a tweet and view his/her tweets and those of his/her friends as the following screenshot demonstrates:

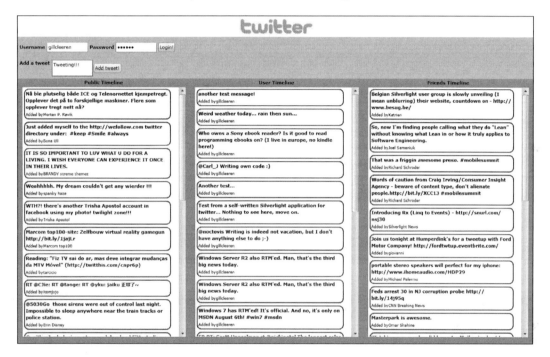

12. The Silverlight application now talks to our own service. In the following code, we are asynchronously invoking the service to get the time line (status updates) of the user:

```
private void LoadUserTimeLine()
{
    TwitterService.TwitterServiceClient client = new
        SilverWitter.TwitterService.TwitterServiceClient();
    client.GetUserTimeLineCompleted += new EventHandler
        <SilverWitter.TwitterService.GetUserTimeLineCompleted
        EventArgs>(client_GetUserTimeLineCompleted);
    client.GetUserTimeLineAsync(UserNameTextBox.Text,
        UserNameTextBox.Text, PasswordTextBox.Password);
}
```

```
void client_GetUserTimeLineCompleted(object sender,
    SilverWitter.TwitterService.GetUserTimeLineCompletedEventArgs e)
{
  if (e.Result != null)
  {
    UserTimeLineListBox.ItemsSource = e.Result;
  }
}
```

The other methods are similar and can be found in the sample code.

How it works...

As previously explained, Twitter, along with most Web 2.0-type applications, has a locked-down cross-domain file. Silverlight's cross-domain restrictions prohibit us from directly calling the REST API from Silverlight. Therefore, we need to build a service layer in between the Silverlight application and the REST service. As services themselves don't mind cross-domain restrictions, we can call whatever type of REST services (or other types) we want. Our own service will act as a pass-through for data in both directions.

See also

To understand why Twitter and Flickr need such a different approach, read the previous recipe *in this chapter*. In the following recipe, we'll see how trusted Silverlight applications can talk directly to Twitter as they aren't tied to cross-domain restrictions.

Passing credentials and cross-domain access to Twitter from a trusted Silverlight application

Whenever we need to communicate with a service that is not hosted in the same domain as the Silverlight application, we need to think of cross-domain restrictions. Silverlight will check if a cross-domain policy file is in place at the root of the domain.

Silverlight 4 applications can not only run out-of-browser (a capability added with Silverlight 3 that allows applications to run as a standalone application instead of in the browser), they can also run as a Trusted Application. Such an application runs with elevated permissions. On the agreement of the user, the application is installed and has more permissions on the local system and other capabilities than the in-browser or regular out-of-browser applications. One of these capabilities is accessing cross-domain services without restrictions, meaning that the service will be accessible from Silverlight even if there's no policy file present.

Another added feature with Silverlight 4 is the ability to send credentials to a service when using a `WebClient` instance.

The combination of these two new features in Silverlight 4 makes it possible to write a standalone Twitter client that does not need the intermediary service layer, like we used in the previous recipe. Instead, we can now directly communicate with Twitter's API from Silverlight because there are no cross-domain restrictions. To authorize on the services of Twitter, we need to be able to send credentials, which has also become possible. In this recipe, we'll change the SilverWitter client to run as a trusted, out-of-browser application.

Getting ready

To follow along with this recipe, you can use your code created with the previous recipe. Alternatively, a starter solution is provided with the samples for the book in the `Chapter08/TrustedSilverWitter_Starter` folder. The finished solution for this recipe can be found in the `Chapter08/TrustedSilverWitter_Completed` folder.

How to do it...

In the previous recipe, we have already built SilverWitter as an in-browser Silverlight application. Due to this, we required a service layer. Silverlight communicates with this service layer and the service layer in turn communicates with the API of Twitter. If we create the application as a trusted application (that is, with elevated permissions), this service layer becomes obsolete as there are no cross-domain restrictions. We also need to authenticate with Twitter. We'll do so by sending credentials over the service. The following are the steps we need to follow to create this application:

1. While the UI of the application is similar to the one created for the in-browser version, we need to add a few extra controls. We need to make it possible for the user to install the application. The complete XAML can be found in the code bundle. The following code outlines the changes. We add a `StackPanel` called `InstallPanel`, in which the controls for the installation are placed. All other controls are placed in a `Grid` called `MainGrid`, for which the `Visibility` has been set to `Collapsed` initially. Both the `InstallPanel` and the `MainGrid` are now children of the `LayoutRoot` Grid.

```
<Grid x:Name="LayoutRoot">
  <StackPanel x:Name="InstallPanel"
              Orientation="Vertical"
              HorizontalAlignment="Center"
              Margin="10"
              VerticalAlignment="Top">
    <TextBlock x:Name="InstallTextBlock"
               Text="This application needs to be installed before
                  it can be used. Click the button below to
                  install."
```

```
                          Width="500"
                          TextWrapping="Wrap"
                          FontWeight="Bold"
                          FontSize="20">
              </TextBlock>
              <Button x:Name="InstallButton"
                      Click="InstallButton_Click"
                      Content="Install"
                      Width="100"
                      Height="35">
              </Button>
              <TextBlock x:Name="InstallErrorTextBlock"
                          Foreground="Red" >
              </TextBlock>
          </StackPanel>
          <Grid x:Name="MainGrid"
                 Visibility="Collapsed">
              <Grid.RowDefinitions>
                <RowDefinition Height="50"></RowDefinition>
                <RowDefinition Height="100"></RowDefinition>
                <RowDefinition Height="*"></RowDefinition>
              </Grid.RowDefinitions>
              . . .
          </Grid>
      </Grid>
```

2. On starting the application, we need to check if we're running the application inside the browser or as a stand-alone, trusted application. We can do so using the following code where the `Boolean IsRunningOfflineAndElevated` contains `true` if the conditions are met:

```
private bool IsRunningOfflineAndElevated = false;
public MainPage()
{
  InitializeComponent();
  CheckApplicationState();
}
private void CheckApplicationState()
{
  if (Application.Current.IsRunningOutOfBrowser &&
    Application.Current.HasElevatedPermissions)
    IsRunningOfflineAndElevated = true;
  else
    IsRunningOfflineAndElevated = false;
}
```

3. Based on the value of `IsRunningOfflineAndElevated`, we can change the UI. If it is `false`, meaning that we're still in the browser, we display the `InstallPanel`. If it is `true`, meaning that the application is running as a trusted application, the `InstallPanel` is hidden and the real application UI is shown. This check is done using the following code, which is called from the constructor as well:

```
private void ChangeUI()
{
  if (IsRunningOfflineAndElevated)
  {
    MainGrid.Visibility = System.Windows.Visibility.Visible;
    InstallPanel.Visibility = System.Windows.Visibility.Collapsed;
  }
  else
  {
    MainGrid.Visibility = System.Windows.Visibility.Collapsed;
    InstallPanel.Visibility = System.Windows.Visibility.Visible;
  }
}
```

4. If the application is not yet installed, we can perform the installation from code. To do so, we can add the following code in the `Click` event handler of the `InstallButton`, which will check the current state of the application and install it if needed:

```
private void InstallButton_Click(object sender, RoutedEventArgs e)
{
  if (Application.Current.InstallState ==
    InstallState.NotInstalled)
  {

    Application.Current.Install();
  }
  else if (Application.Current.InstallState ==
    InstallState.InstallFailed)
  {

    InstallErrorTextBlock.Text = "This application failed
      to install, please try again";
  }
  else if (Application.Current.InstallState ==
    InstallState.Installed)
  {

    InstallErrorTextBlock.Text = "Application is already
      installed. Please run offline.";
  }
}
```

5. To store the results coming from Twitter, we need the `TweetUpdate` class again. However, this class should now be in the Silverlight project. (In the previous recipe where we had an intermediate service layer, this class was part of the service project.) The code for this class is as follows:

```
public class TweetUpdate
{
  public string Message { get; set; }
  public string User { get; set; }
  public string Location { get; set; }
}
```

Note that the `DataContractAttribute` as well as the `DataMemberAttribute` are removed. Both these attributes were needed previously because instances of this class were used in communication with the intermediate service.

6. We're now ready to start the communication with Twitter. If the `IsRunningOfflineAndElevated` Boolean variable is `true`, we can perform a call to Twitter to load the public timeline. This call does not require authentication. Note that we're now writing almost the same code we were writing earlier in the service layer, but now inside the Silverlight application itself. The difference is that now the call to the service happens asynchronously. The code below performs the call to Twitter using a `WebClient` instance, uses LINQ-To-XML to parse the XML and create a `List<TweetUpdates>`:

```
public MainPage()
{
  InitializeComponent();
  CheckApplicationState();
  ChangeUI();
  if (IsRunningOfflineAndElevated)
    GetPublicTimeLine();
}
private List<TweetUpdate> publicTimelineTwitterData;
private void GetPublicTimeLine()
{
  string publicTimeLine =
    "http://twitter.com/statuses/public_timeline.xml";
  WebClient client = new WebClient();
  client.DownloadStringCompleted += new
    DownloadStringCompletedEventHandler
    (client_DownloadStringCompleted);
  client.DownloadStringAsync(new Uri(publicTimeLine,
    UriKind.Absolute));
}
void client_DownloadStringCompleted(object sender,
  DownloadStringCompletedEventArgs e)
{
  XDocument document = XDocument.Parse(e.Result);
```

```
publicTimelineTwitterData =
  (from status in document.Descendants("status")
  select new TweetUpdate
  {
    Message = status.Element("text").Value.Trim(),
    User = status.Element("user").Element("name").Value.Trim()
  }).ToList();
  PublicTimeLineListBox.ItemsSource = publicTimelineTwitterData;
}
```

7. The application also allows the user to log in. When logged in, the user timeline and friends timeline can be loaded. Both these methods of the Twitter API require that we **authorize**. With Silverlight 4, we can send credentials when using the `WebClient` class using its `Credentials` property. However, sending credentials is only possible when using the `ClientHttpStack` and not the default `BrowserHttpStack`. Making Silverlight use the `ClientHttpStack` is done by using the `WebRequest`. `RegisterPrefix` and passing in `http://`. This code makes sure that all requests over `http://` are now executed using the `ClientHttpStack`. The code below shows the code to retrieve the user timeline (the friends timeline is similar, the code for this can be found in the samples):

```
private void LoginButton_Click(object sender, RoutedEventArgs e)
{
  LoadAuthorizedContent();
}

private List<TweetUpdate> userTimelineTwitterData;
private void LoadAuthorizedContent()
{
  if (UserNameTextBox.Text != string.Empty &&
    PasswordTextBox.Password != string.Empty)
  {
    WebRequest.RegisterPrefix("http://",
      System.Net.Browser.WebRequestCreator.ClientHttp);
    string userTimeLine =
      "http://twitter.com/statuses/user_timeline/"
      + UserNameTextBox.Text + ".xml";
    WebClient client = new WebClient();
    client.Credentials = new NetworkCredential(
      UserNameTextBox.Text, PasswordTextBox.Password);
    client.UseDefaultCredentials = false;
    client.DownloadStringCompleted += new
      DownloadStringCompletedEventHandler
      (user_DownloadStringCompleted);
    client.DownloadStringAsync(new Uri(userTimeLine,
      UriKind.Absolute));
```

```
      }
    }
    void user_DownloadStringCompleted(object sender,
      DownloadStringCompletedEventArgs e)
    {
      XDocument document = XDocument.Parse(e.Result);
      userTimelineTwitterData =
        (from status in document.Descendants("status")
        select new TweetUpdate
        {
          Message = status.Element("text").Value.Trim(),
          User = status.Element("user").Element("name").Value.Trim()
        }).ToList();
      UserTimeLineListBox.ItemsSource = userTimelineTwitterData;
    }
```

8. To add a message to Twitter from our client, we need to post it using the HTTP POST method. We are using an `HttpWebRequest` for this and set its method to POST. To this `HttpWebRequest`, we also add the user-entered credentials because this service method requires authorization as well. Silverlight will then send the message to Twitter.

```
    private void AddTweetButton_Click(object sender,
      RoutedEventArgs e)
    {
      string uri = @"http://twitter.com/statuses/update.xml";
      try
      {
        string message = AddTweetTextBox.Text.Trim();
        string parameters = string.Format("status={0}&source={1}",
          HttpUtility.HtmlEncode(message), "Trusted SilverWitter");
        WebRequest.RegisterPrefix("http://",
          System.Net.Browser.WebRequestCreator.ClientHttp);
        HttpWebRequest request = (HttpWebRequest)
          WebRequestCreator.ClientHttp.Create
          (new Uri(uri, UriKind.Absolute));
        request.Method = "POST";
        request.Credentials = new
          NetworkCredential(UserNameTextBox.Text,
          PasswordTextBox.Password);
        request.ContentType = "application/x-www-form-urlencoded";
        request.BeginGetRequestStream(new AsyncCallback(result =>
          {
            using (StreamWriter writer =
              new StreamWriter(request.EndGetRequestStream(result)))
```

```
            {
                writer.Write(parameters);
            }
            request.BeginGetResponse(response =>
                {
                    try
                    {
                        WebResponse rs = request.EndGetResponse(response);
                        Dispatcher.BeginInvoke(LoadAuthorizedContent);
                    }
                    catch (WebException ex)
                    {
                        Dispatcher.BeginInvoke(() =>
                            HandleError(ex.Message));
                    }
                }, request);
            }),
            null);
    }
    catch (Exception ex)
    {
        Dispatcher.BeginInvoke(() => HandleError(ex.Message));
    }
    AddTweetTextBox.Text = string.Empty;
}
private void HandleError(string exceptionMessage)
{
    ErrorTextBlock.Text = "An error occurred: " + exceptionMessage;
}
```

9. The code is now ready. However, we still need to configure the application to allow it to run out-of-browser and with elevated permissions. To do so, right-click on the Silverlight project node in the **Solution Explorer** and select **Properties**. In the Silverlight tab of the **Properties** window, select the **Enable running application out of the browser** checkbox. Finally, click on the **Out-Of-Browser settings** button on the same tab and in the resulting dialog, select the **Require elevated trust when running outside the browser** checkbox.

With these steps completed, we have created a standalone Twitter client. Because it runs with elevated permissions, there's no need to add an intermediate service layer between the Silverlight client and Twitter. The running application can be seen in the following screenshot:

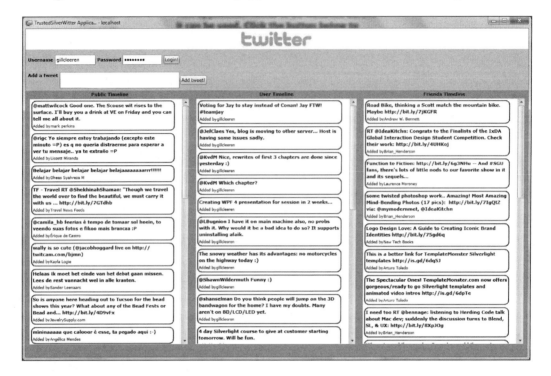

How it works...

To build this application, two major new features added to the platform with the release of Silverlight 4 were put to work: no more cross-domain restrictions when running with elevated permissions and passing credentials using the `ClientHttpStack`. Let's take a look at these in some more detail.

Let's go cross-domain!

In many recipes in this book, we talked about the cross-domain restrictions that Silverlight has in place. Basically, these come down to Silverlight not allowing us to make requests to services that are not in the same domain as the Silverlight application. Silverlight will make the request only if there's a cross-domain policy file in place that allows the request. Cross-domain restrictions are required for security reasons. We looked at cross-domain issues in depth in Chapter 6.

With Silverlight 3, it became possible to create out-of-browser Silverlight applications, allowing us to create standalone Silverlight applications, which do not require a browser to be open to run. However, they still run in the sandbox like in-browser applications, meaning these applications do not have extra permissions on the system. Silverlight 4 extends this model.

With version 4, it becomes possible to create **Trusted Silverlight applications**, which run with elevated permissions. As a result, they have more permissions on the system and can perform some tasks in a different manner. One of these is the ability for this type of applications to perform cross-domain calls without the need of a policy file.

For some applications, this is a big plus. Take, for example, our Twitter application. In the in-browser version, which we created in the previous recipe, we had to build a service layer that sits between the Silverlight client and Twitter itself. The reason is that Twitter does not expose a policy file, so Silverlight applications can't directly communicate with Twitter's API. With trusted Silverlight 4 applications, the fact that this file isn't there is no problem. When running with elevated permissions, Silverlight will not check for the existence of the file and will perform the service request anyhow.

Applying elevated permissions to Silverlight can be done through Visual Studio. In the **Project Properties**, under the **Out-Of-Browser settings**, we can check that the application should request to the user to run with these permissions. On installation, the user will not be prompted with the regular install screen. Instead, the following dialog box shown in that asks the user if he or she fully trusts the application:

Silverlight 4 also gives us the option to sign the XAP file, which results in a more relaxed installation screen being displayed when installing a trusted Silverlight application. The process of signing the XAP file is outside the scope of this book.

Pass me those credentials, will you?

Being able to access Twitter without cross-domain restrictions is one thing. We also need to be able to **pass credentials** to a service when it requires us to. In Silverlight 3, the WebClient class already had a Credentials property, but this property was not working properly. Silverlight 4 changed this and now allows us to pass credentials to a service. One thing that is required is that we use the ClientHttpStack.

Passing credentials is very simple and can be done using the following code:

```
WebRequest.RegisterPrefix("http://",
    System.Net.Browser.WebRequestCreator.ClientHttp);
WebClient client = new WebClient();
client.Credentials = new NetworkCredential(UserNameTextBox.Text,
    PasswordTextBox.Password);
```

We are specifying that we want the application to use the `ClientHttpStack` using the `WebRequest.Register` method: basically we're saying for all traffic that goes over `http://`, use the `ClientHttpStack`.

See also

In the *Working cross-domain from a trusted application* recipe in Chapter 6, we looked at working with trusted applications from Silverlight. Working with Twitter was the topic of the previous recipe.

9
Talking to WCF RIA Services

In this chapter, we will cover:

- ▸ Setting up a data solution to work with RIA Services
- ▸ Getting data on the client
- ▸ Sorting and filtering data
- ▸ Persisting data to the server
- ▸ Persisting a unit of work/changeset
- ▸ Working with concurrency and transactions
- ▸ Tracking a user's identity
- ▸ Controlling a user's access to a service and service methods
- ▸ Validating data using data annotations
- ▸ Validating data using shared code
- ▸ Using the DomainDataSource
- ▸ Using the DomainDataSource to page through data
- ▸ Sorting, filtering, and grouping data using the DomainDataSource

Introduction

Microsoft WCF RIA Services is a framework developed to simplify Line of Business RIA development. RIA Services addresses the complexity of building N-tier applications by providing a framework, controls, and services on both your server side (an ASP.NET application) and your client side (your Silverlight Application).

RIA Services makes it easy to get data from your services to your client. It does this by allowing you to write services linked to a data store (a database, your own classes, an Entity Model, and so on) on your server side, and then regenerates these entities on your client. It also generates the necessary context, methods, and operations on your client to easily talk to your services. So, in essence, WCF RIA Server is a server-side technology that projects code to a client using WCF as a means of communication between the server and the client. In addition, it makes it easy to add validation and authentication to your services and/or entities.

This chapter will teach you how to work with RIA Services, from building a simple service to query data to writing validation on authenticated service methods.

Setting up a data solution to work with RIA Services

When you want to start working with RIA Services, you'll have to install the SDK. Besides that, you'll have to think about a few things when starting a new solution to enable RIA Services for that solution. This recipe will guide you through the steps we need to complete to start using RIA Services. Along with that, it will explore some general concepts concerning RIA Services by explaining how we should structure our code.

Getting ready

Before you can use RIA Services, the correct SDK has to be installed. WCF RIA Services is distributed together with the Silverlight 4 SDK for use with Visual Studio 2010. You can download and install the Silverlight 4 SDK from `http://go.microsoft.com/fwlink/?LinkID=177428`. The completed solution can be found in the `Chapter09\Setting_Up_A_Solution_Completed` folder.

How to do it...

To set up a data solution to work with RIA Services, we'll start a new application called **WorkingWithRIAServices**. In order to do this, we'll need to complete the following steps:

1. Select **File | New | Project...**, choose a new Silverlight Project, and name the project as **WorkingWithRIAServices** as shown in the following screenshot:

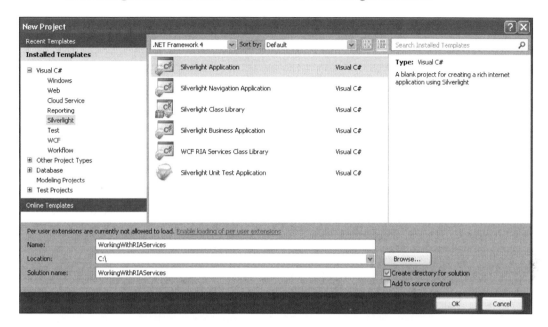

2. After we've done this, we'll be presented with a pop-up screen as shown in the following screenshot. In this screen, we'll need to select the **Enable WCF RIA Services** checkbox and click on the **OK** button. Our RIA Services-enabled solution will be generated for us.

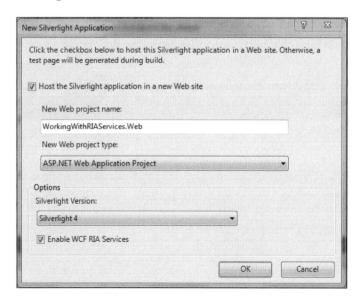

How it works...

The magic happens as we select the **Enable WCF RIA Services** checkbox. By doing this, we tell Visual Studio to form an association between our client (our Silverlight application) and server (our web application) project so that application logic can be shared between them. Visual Studio will automatically add references to the necessary assemblies—`System.ComponentModel.DataAnnotations` (used to enable dynamic, data-like annotations to your properties and methods) and `System.ServiceModel.DomainServices.Client`.

There's more...

Microsoft WCF RIA Services brings together the ASP.NET and Silverlight platforms, thus simplifying the traditional N-tier application pattern. We write our application logic (data access) in the mid-tier (typically in our server project), and we can share entities and application logic (data validation, custom methods, and so on) between the tiers easily. This means that we can share entities, code, and validation between our server project and our Silverlight project.

The WCF RIA Services Toolkit

Besides the WCF RIA Services SDK, which is included with Silverlight 4 SDK, a RIA Services Toolkit exists. This toolkit contains the classes and namespaces necessary to get RIA Services to work with LINQ to SQL. In our examples, we're using the Entity Framework as a datastore, so we don't need this toolkit. However, if you plan on using LINQ to SQL, you might want to install it. You can find it at `http://go.microsoft.com/fwlink/?LinkID=169408`.

See also

The other recipes in this chapter start from this basic recipe. Take a look at them to learn how to get data to your client, update data, sort data, and page data.

Getting data on the client

This recipe will explain what we have to do to design a service using RIA Services to get data from a (database) server to our client (our Silverlight application) through the service. It will explain how to create a data store, how to create our first RIA Service and Query Method, and how to call this method from our client. It will also explain how this works, thus giving you an insight into the strengths and ease of using RIA Services.

Getting ready

This recipe uses the AdventureWorks Lite database—a free database you can download from http://www.codeplex.com/MSFTDBProdSamples. To follow this recipe, you need to have this database installed on an SQL Server instance you can access from your machine.

We're starting from the solution completed in the previous recipe. You can find a starter solution located in the Chapter09\Getting_Data_Starter\ folder in the code bundle available on the Packt website. The completed solution can be found in the Chapter09\ Getting_Data_Completed\ folder.

How to do it...

To begin designing a service using RIA Services, we need to complete the following steps:

1. We first need to have some kind of data store from where we'll get our data. This can be a database, an XML file, or some simple static classes. In most scenarios, we'll get our data from a database. So, we'll use the AdventureWorks Lite database and we'll use the Entity Framework as ORM. Add a new ADO.NET Entity Data Model to the server application and name it as **AdventureWorksModel**. We'll need to choose **Generate from database** and make a new connection referring to our database location. We then need to select which tables to include in our model. For this recipe, add the **Product** table and click on the **Finish** button. We now have a datastore containing the products from the AdventureWorks Lite database.

2. Press *F5* to build the application. We now need to expose this table to the client application. We do this by adding a new class—a DomainService. Right-click on the server application, select **Add | New item...**, and select **Domain Service Class**. Name the class as ProductService and click on the **Add** button.

3. You'll see that a pop-up window appears. Select our DataContext in this pop-up window. In this example, these are the entities you just exposed through your Entity Model. Select **Product** and click on the **OK** button.

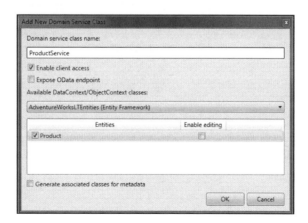

4. Build the solution once to ensure the necessary client-side classes are generated in our Silverlight-application. Add a `DataGrid` (or any other data-enabled control) to `MainPage.xaml` and name it as `myDataGrid`. This is the grid in which the products will be shown.

5. In the `MainPage.xaml.cs` file, add `using WorkingWithRIAServices.Web` and `using System.ServiceModel.DomainServices.Client` as well as our other `using` directives. In our `MainPage` class, add a new property of the `ProductContext` type and name it as `context`. Add the following code in our `MainPage` constructor:

```
context = new ProductContext();
LoadOperation<Product> lo =
    context.Load(context.GetProductsQuery());
myDataGrid.ItemsSource = lo.Entities;
```

6. We can now build and run the solution. You'll see that the grid gets filled with the products from the AdventureWorks Lite database. This can be seen in the following screenshot:

Working with WCF RIA Services

Color	DiscontinuedDate	ListPrice	ModifiedDate	Name	ProductCategor
Black		1431.5000	3/11/2004 10:01:36 AM	HL Road Frame - Black, 58	18
Red		1431.5000	3/11/2004 10:01:36 AM	HL Road Frame - Red, 58	18
Red		34.9900	3/11/2004 10:01:36 AM	Sport-100 Helmet, Red	35
Black		34.9900	3/11/2004 10:01:36 AM	Sport-100 Helmet, Black	35
White		9.5000	3/11/2004 10:01:36 AM	Mountain Bike Socks, M	27
White		9.5000	3/11/2004 10:01:36 AM	Mountain Bike Socks, L	27
Blue		34.9900	3/11/2004 10:01:36 AM	Sport-100 Helmet, Blue	35
Multi		8.9900	3/11/2004 10:01:36 AM	AWC Logo Cap	23
Multi		49.9900	3/11/2004 10:01:36 AM	Long-Sleeve Logo Jersey, S	25

How it works...

The `DomainService` class—`ProductService`—that we've added is the class that provides a public interface to the mid-tier data. When we add a `DomainService` class, code will be automatically generated:

```
[EnableClientAccess()]
public class ProductService : LinqToEntitiesDomainService
    <AdventureWorksLTEntities>
{
    public IQueryable<Product> GetProducts()
    {
```

```
        return this.ObjectContext.Products;
    }
}
```

When we added the `ProductService` class, we signalled that it should get its data from an Entity Model. Due to this, the `ProductService` class inherits from `LinqToEntitiesDomainService` (a built-in abstract class). We also chose to expose the `Product` entity. Hence, Visual Studio automatically generated a `GetProducts()` method for us that obtains data from the AdventureWorks Modelcontext.

This `DomainService` is typically the starting point for our application logic. In this service, we might want to add new methods, change the parameters or the body of existing methods, or include other application logic.

When we built our solution, a lot of things happened on the client as well. As the `ProductService` is marked with the `[EnableClientAccess()]` attribute, proxy code will be automatically generated in our Silverlight application on each build. When we click on the **Show All Files** icon in the **Solution Explorer**, we can see this code by opening the `WorkingWithRIAServies.Web.g.cs` file.

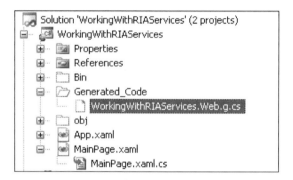

If we open the generated file, we'll see that a client-side version of our server-side entity— `Product`—has been generated (you'll also notice that it raises `INotifyPropertyChanged` notifications, so they are data-bindable). We'll also see that a class called `ProductContext`, which inherits from `DomainContext`, has been generated.

In this class, methods are generated to load the data from our database into the `DomainContext`. In this recipe, this method is called `GetProductsQuery` and it returns an `EntityQuery<Product>` object. Similar methods will be created for each query method. (A query method is typically a method on our Domain Service that returns a collection of entities, generally as `IEnumberable<T>` or `IQueryable<T>`.) These methods can be used as arguments on the `Load` method of our context. Passing one of these methods will execute the EntityQuery returned by it.

This class can be seen as the client-side representation of our server-side data.

Now, back to the constructor of our `MainPage`. To get data into our `DataGrid`, we initialized a new `ProductContext` named `context`. We also constructed a new `LoadOperation` of the `Product` type called `lo`, which is the result of a `context.Load` call. To that `Load` method, we passed the query we wanted to use to load `Entities` (in this case, `GetProductsQuery`). After that, we set the `DataGrid.ItemsSource` property to `lo.Entities`, which is the `Entities` of our `LoadOperation` that will effectively contain a list (`IEnumerable`) of `Product`.

When we pass a query to the `Load` method of our context, that query will be executed to fill the entities of the new `LoadOperation` object. The query we passed is an automatically generated method called `GetProductQuery`. This is shown in the following code:

```
public EntityQuery<Product> GetProductsQuery()
{
  this.ValidateMethod("GetProductsQuery", null);
  return base.CreateQuery<Product>("GetProducts", null, false, true);
}
```

This method will call the server-side `GetProduct` method, which will get the products from our database. Once these products are asynchronously loaded in the `Entities` collection of our `LoadOperation` object, our grid will be automatically filled with them as it's bound to that collection.

There's more...

As you've noticed, a lot of code gets automatically generated on our client when we use RIA Services. Working with RIA Services almost feels like we're not using services to get our data, seeing that we've got a client-side representation of all our entities and our context.

RIA Services automatically generates this client-side `EntityQuery`, returning methods for every query method that will have the same name as the server-side method, postfixed with `Query`. Server-side methods whose names are prefixed with `Get`, `Fetch`, `Find`, `Query`, `Retrieve`, or `Select`, and which return an `IEnumberable<T>` or `IQueryable<T>` (where `T` is an Entity type) are Query methods that will result in a client-side `EntityQuery` returning method. We can also mark these methods with the `[Query]` attribute to specifically tell the code generator that a method is a `Query` method.

An important fact to notice is that method overloading is not possible due to automatic generation of `Load` methods for our query methods.

See also

Once we've got data on our client, you might want to learn how to shape this data. Have a look at the next recipe to learn how to do this by writing a custom query method, or have a look at the *Sorting, filtering, and grouping data using the DomainDataSource* recipe to learn how to let the Silverlight `DomainDataSource` handle this for you.

Sorting and filtering data

In most applications, you'll want to give the user the ability to filter and/or sort the data they see on their screen. This recipe will show you one way of doing this: by using custom Query methods on your server project and accepting parameters to control the filtering/sorting you want to use.

Getting ready

This recipe uses the AdventureWorks Lite database—a free database you can download from `http://www.codeplex.com/MSFTDBProdSamples`. To follow this recipe, you need to have this database installed on an SQL Server instance you can access from your machine.

We're starting from the solution completed in the previous recipe. You can find a starter solution located in the `Chapter09\Sorting_And_Filtering_Starter\` folder in the code bundle available on the Packt website. The completed solution can be found in the `Chapter09\Sorting_And_Filtering_Completed\` folder.

How to do it...

To begin sorting and filtering our data, we'll need to follow step 1 to step 6 of the previous recipe to make sure that we have a `ProductService (DomainService)` that gets products from the AdventureWorks Lite database using the Entity Framework. On our client side, we should have a `DataGrid` displaying these products. Alternatively, the provided starter solution can be used. We'll need to complete the following steps:

1. Add a new class called `SortAndFilterOption` to our Silverlight project. This class is used for easy binding to our UI and contains the parameters we will want to pass to our service. Add a child class called `SortOption`. This class contains a `Key` property and a `Description` property. The `SortAndFilterOption` class has three properties: a `SortOptions` property (to bind to a combobox in your UI), a `SelectedSortOption` property (to bind to the `SelectedItem` property of that combobox), and a `Filter` property (to bind to a textbox in your UI). In the constructor, initialize the necessary values for an object of this type. This is shown in the following code:

```
public class SortAndFilterOption
{
  public class SortOption
  {
    public string Description { get; set; }
    public int Key { get; set; }
  }
  public List<SortOption> SortOptions { get; set; }
```

```
public SortOption SelectedSortOption { get; set; }
public string Filter { get; set; }
public SortAndFilterOption()
{
    Filter = "";
    SortOptions = new List<SortOption>();
    SortOptions.Add(new SortOption() { Description="Ascending",
        Key=1});
    SortOptions.Add(new SortOption() { Description="Descending",
        Key=2});
    SelectedSortOption = SortOptions[0];
}
}
```

2. In the `MainPage.xaml` file, add a `ComboBox` and bind it to the `SortOptions` list. Bind the `SelectedItem` property, with `TwoWay` binding to the `SelectedSortOption` property. Add a `TextBox` to our UI and bind its `Text` property to the `Filter` property using `TwoWay` binding. Also add a `Button` called `FilterAndSort` that will be used to actually execute the sort and filter operation. Surround these controls with a `Grid` for layout and name this `Grid` as `grdFilterAndSortOptions`.

3. In the `MainPage` class, add a property called `mySortAndFilterOptions` of the `SortAndFilterOption` type. Instantiate a new instance of it in our `MainPage` constructor and set it as the `DataContext` of `grdFilterAndSortOptions`.

4. On our `DomainService`, add a new `Query` method named `GetFilteredAndSortedProduct` that accepts two parameters. These parameters are a filter parameter and a parameter telling it to sort in an ascending or descending order. In the method body, filter and sort the `Product` collection of our Entity Model accordingly. This is shown in the following code:

```
public IQueryable<Product> GetFilteredAndSortedProduct(string
    filter, int ascendingordescending)
{
    var queryFilter = from p in this.ObjectContext.Products
                      where ((filter == "") ? filter == "" :
                          p.Name.ToLower().Contains(filter.ToLower()))
                      select p;
    if (ascendingordescending == 1)
    {
        return queryFilter.OrderBy(p => p.Name);
    }
    else
    {
        return queryFilter.OrderByDescending(p => p.Name);
    }
}
```

5. Build the solution. Now, add a property called `context` of the `ProductContext` type to `MainPage.cs` and instantiate it in its constructor. Create a `LoadOperation` of the `Product` type using the newly created query from the previous step and passing the `Filter` and `SelectedSortOption.Key` properties of `mySortAndFilterOptions` as parameters. After this, set the `ItemsSource` property of `myDataGrid` to the `Entities` collection of the newly created `LoadOperation`. This is shown in the following code:

```
public MainPage()
{
    InitializeComponent();
    mySortAndFilterOptions = new SortAndFilterOption();
    grdFilterAndSortOptions.DataContext = mySortAndFilterOptions;
    context = new ProductContext();
    LoadOperation<Product> loProduct = context.Load
        (context.GetFilteredAndSortedProductQuery
        (mySortAndFilterOptions.Filter,
        mySortAndFilterOptions.SelectedSortOption.Key));
    myDataGrid.ItemsSource = loProduct.Entities;
}
```

6. Add a `Click` handler to the button we created in step 2. In this `Click` handler, call the `FilteredAndSortedProductQuery` again using the `Filter` and `SelectedSortOption.Key` properties of `mySortAndFilterOptions`. Also set the `ItemsSource` property of our `DataGrid` to the `Entities` collection of our `LoadOperation`. This is shown in the following code:

```
LoadOperation<Product> loSortAndFilter = context.Load
    (context.GetFilteredAndSortedProductQuery
    (mySortAndFilterOptions.Filter,
    mySortAndFilterOptions.SelectedSortOption.Key));
myDataGrid.ItemsSource = loSortAndFilter.Entities;
```

7. Build and run the solution. We can now filter and sort our grid by using the filter controls we've created. This can be seen in the following screenshot:

Working with WCF RIA Services

Product name should contain: |t| and products are sorted | Ascending ▼ | | Filter and sort! |

Color	DiscontinuedDate	ListPrice	ModifiedDate	Name	ProductCategoryID	Product
		159.0000	3/11/2004 10:01:36 AM	All-Purpose Bike Stand	31	879
Blue		63.5000	3/11/2004 10:01:36 AM	Classic Vest, L	29	866
Blue		63.5000	3/11/2004 10:01:36 AM	Classic Vest, M	29	865
Blue		63.5000	3/11/2004 10:01:36 AM	Classic Vest, S	29	864
		21.9800	3/11/2004 10:01:36 AM	Fender Set - Mountain	34	878
Silver		106.5000	3/11/2004 10:01:36 AM	Front Brakes	10	948
Silver		91.4900	3/11/2004 10:01:36 AM	Front Derailleur	13	945
		34.9900	3/11/2004 10:01:36 AM	Headlights - Dual-Beam	37	847
		44.9900	3/11/2004 10:01:36 AM	Headlights - Weatherproof	37	848

How it works...

On our server side, we've created an extra query method—
GetFilteredAndSortedProducts—that accepts two parameters and returns a list
of Products depending on the parameters we pass to the method. As this method's
signature begins with Get and returns an IQueryable collection, a client-side method
is generated on our DomainContext. This means we can call this method from our client
by using a LoadOperation and by passing this method as a query method.

In our client application, we've created a SortAndFilterOption class that holds the
inputted parameters. With some simple data binding, we can make sure that the instance
of this class will always contain the inputted Filter and SortOption properties from
our UI.

Everything we need is now in place. In the Click handler of our FilterAndSort
button, we can now create a new LoadOperation on our DomainContext. When we
pass our new method with the parameters from our SortAndFilterOption instance,
the server-side method will be called. As we've set the ItemsSource of our DataGrid to
the resulting Entities of our LoadOperation, our DataGrid will be automatically filled
with a filtered and sorted list of products when the LoadOperation is complete.

See also

In this recipe, we've learned how to shape data by writing a custom query method. To learn
how to do this using the Silverlight DomainDataSource control, have a look at the *Sorting,
filtering, and grouping data using the DomainDataSource* recipe.

Persisting data to the server

When you're designing a Line of Business application, one of the typical requirements is
making sure that the user is able to save the changes they make back to their datastore.
This recipe will show you what you should do to persist data you've changed on your client's
DomainContext to your datastore.

Getting ready

This recipe uses the AdventureWorks Lite database—a free database you can download from
http://www.codeplex.com/MSFTDBProdSamples. To follow this recipe, you need to
have this database installed on an SQL Server instance you can access from your machine.

We're starting from the solution completed in the *Getting data on the Client* recipe. You can
find a starter solution located in the Chapter09\Persisting_Data_Starter\ folder in
the code bundle available on the Packt website. The completed solution can be found in the
Chapter09\Persisting_Data_Completed\ folder.

How to do it...

To begin persisting our data, we'll need to follow step 1 to step 6 of the *Getting data on the client* recipe to make sure that we have a `ProductService (DomainService)` that gets products from the AdventureWorks Lite database using the Entity Framework. On our client side, we should have a `DataGrid` displaying these products. In our `MainPage` class, we should have a `context` property that contains an instance of our `ProductContext` `DomainContext`. This property is created in the constructor of the `MainPage` class. It's this `context` property that will be used to persist changes. Alternatively, you can use the provided starter solution.

To get started, we need to complete the following steps:

1. When we create the **ProductService** class, select the **Enable editing** checkbox (this is already selected when using the starter solution).

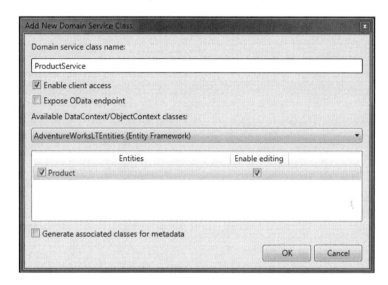

2. We're going to make sure that the changes we make to the data in our `DataGrid` are automatically persisted to our datastore (the AdventureWorksLiTe database) when we stop editing a row. Our `DataGrid` should be editable by default, so no changes have to be made to it. Now, add a handler to the `RowEditEnded` event of our `DataGrid` and call `SubmitChanges()` on our `ProductContext` in this handler. This is shown in the following code:

```
Private void myDataGrid_RowEditEnded(object sender,
  DataGridRowEditEndedEventArgs e)
{
  if (!context.IsSubmitting)
  {
```

```
        if (context.HasChanges)
          context.SubmitChanges();
    }
}
```

3. Build and run the solution. When we stop editing a row, changes will be saved to our database.

Working with WCF RIA Services

Color	DiscontinuedDate	ListPrice	ModifiedDate	Name	ProductCategoryID	ProductID
Black		1431.5000	3/11/2004 10:01:36 AM	HL Road Frame - Black, 58 Test	18	680
Red		1431.5000	3/11/2004 10:01:36 AM	HL Road Frame - Red, 58	18	706
Red		34.9900	3/11/2004 10:01:36 AM	Sport-100 Helmet, Red	35	707
Black		34.9900	3/11/2004 10:01:36 AM	Sport-100 Helmet, Black	35	708
White		9.5000	3/11/2004 10:01:36 AM	Mountain Bike Socks, M	27	709
White		9.5000	3/11/2004 10:01:36 AM	Mountain Bike Socks, L	27	710
Blue		34.9900	3/11/2004 10:01:36 AM	Sport-100 Helmet, Blue	35	711
Multi		8.9900	3/11/2004 10:01:36 AM	AWC Logo Cap	23	712
Multi		49.9900	3/11/2004 10:01:36 AM	Long-Sleeve Logo Jersey, S	25	713
Multi		49.9900	3/11/2004 10:01:36 AM	Long-Sleeve Logo Jersey, M	25	714
Multi		49.9900	3/11/2004 10:01:36 AM	Long-Sleeve Logo Jersey, L	25	715
Multi		49.9900	3/11/2004 10:01:36 AM	Long-Sleeve Logo Jersey, XL	25	716

How it works...

By selecting the **Enable editing** checkbox when we created the **ProductService** class on our server-side application, we made sure that `Insert`, `Update`, and `Delete` methods are created for that Entity. How they are created depends on the type of datastore we're using. In this case, we're using the Entity Framework. So, in the `Insert`, `Update`, and `Delete` methods, code is generated to persist changes using the Entity Framework.

Our `ProductContext` instance has an EntityContainer called `DomainContext.Entities`. This container manages a set of EntityLists (in this example there's only one list—a list of Products). So, the `DomainContext.Entities` EntityContainer will contain references to all Products in the `DomainContext.Products` list. Each Entity contained in any EntityList of our EntityContainer has an EntityState. It's this EntityState that is used for change tracking.

Now, when we call `SubmitChanges()` on our `context`, all entities in each EntityList of our EntityContainer will be inspected. If the EntityState of an Entity is different from "Unmodified", the appropriate method will be called on this Entity on our server (the `Insert`, `Update`, or `Delete` method) and our changes will be persisted to our datastore.

There's more...

If something goes wrong while updating (connection lost, invalid data), you would of course like to be notified of this. We can easily do that by adding a Callback method—SubmitOperation. This method will be called when the SubmitOperation is completed and will contain a list of Entities in error.

To do this, rewrite the previous code as follows:

```
private void myDataGrid_RowEditEnded(object sender,
  DataGridRowEditEndedEventArgs e)
{
  if (!context.IsSubmitting)
  {
    if (context.HasChanges)
      context.SubmitChanges(OnSubmitCompleted, null);
  }
}
private void OnSubmitCompleted(SubmitOperation so)
{
  if (so.HasError)
  {
    MessageBox.Show(so.Error.Message);
  }
}
```

Now, when something goes wrong, a MessageBox will pop up showing us the error. The SubmitOperation so used in OnSubmitCompleted contains a full list of all Entities in the error—so.EntitiesInError. When something goes wrong, we can find out exactly which Entity generated the error and what the error is by looking at this collection.

See also

In this recipe, we've learned the basics about persisting data to our server. To learn how to persist a bunch of changes at once, have a look at the next recipe. To learn about concurrency and transactions, have a look at the *Working with concurrency and transactions* recipe.

Persisting a Unit of Work/changeset

In various Line of Business applications, it's important that changes can be persisted to our datastore in one go. Imagine you have a `DataGrid` containing products and lines of detail for each product. In such a case, it's important that these entities are persisted together in one go as saving a detail line of a product when the product itself hasn't been saved will result in an error. In this recipe, we'll learn what we should do to persist the data we've changed on our `DomainContext` to our datastore. Instead of submitting a change to an Entity when it has been changed, this recipe will show you how to submit a Unit of Work/changeset, which can consist of multiple changed, added, or deleted entities.

Getting ready

This recipe uses the AdventureWorks Lite database—a free database you can download from `http://www.codeplex.com/MSFTDBProdSamples`. To follow this recipe, you need to have this database installed on an SQL Server instance you can access from your machine.

We're starting from the solution completed in the *Getting data on the Client* recipe. You can find a starter solution located in the `Chapter09\Persisting_Unit_of_Work_Starter\` folder in the code bundle available on the Packt website. The completed solution can be found in the `Chapter09\Persisting_Unit_of_Work_Completed\` folder.

How to do it...

In order to begin persisting data, we'll need to follow step 1 to step 3 of the previous recipe to make sure that we have a `ProductService` (`DomainService`) that gets products from the AdventureWorks Lite database using the Entity Framework and for which editing is enabled on Product entities. On our client side, we should have a DataGrid displaying these products. In our `MainPage` class, we should have a `context` property that contains an instance of our `ProductContext` `DomainContext`. This property is created in the constructor of the `MainPage` class. It's this `context` property that will be used to persist changes. Alternatively, you can use the provided starter solution.

To get started, we'll need to complete the following steps:

1. First, besides the `DataGrid`, add XAML for a `TextBlock` named `txtChanges` that will be used to track changes in the `DataGrid`. Also add two buttons—one to submit changes and the other to reject changes. This is shown in the following code:

```
<StackPanel Orientation="Vertical"
            Grid.Column="1"
            Margin="20">
    <TextBlock Text="Change tracking"
               FontSize="18"></TextBlock>
    <TextBlock x:Name="txtChanges"
               Margin="0,5,0,5"></TextBlock>
```

```
<StackPanel Orientation="Horizontal">
  <Button x:Name="btnSubmit"
          Click="btnSubmit_Click"
          Content="Submit changes"></Button>
  <Button x:Name="btnReject"
          Click="btnReject_Click"
          Content="Reject changes"></Button>
</StackPanel>
</StackPanel>
```

2. Add an event handler to the `RowEditEnded` event of our `DataGrid`, in which we'll update `txtChanges` to reflect the changes we've made. This is shown in the following code:

```
private void myDataGrid_RowEditEnded(object sender,
  DataGridRowEditEndedEventArgs e)
{
  UpdateChanges();
}
private void UpdateChanges()
{
  EntityChangeSet myChangeSet =
    context.EntityContainer.GetChanges();
  txtChanges.Text = myChangeSet.ToString();
}
```

3. Add event handlers to our buttons to submit and/or reject changes on our `DomainContext`. This can be seen in the following code:

```
private void btnSubmit_Click(object sender, RoutedEventArgs e)
{
  if (!context.IsSubmitting)
  {
    if (context.HasChanges)
    {
      context.SubmitChanges(OnSubmitCompleted, null);
    }
  }
}
private void OnSubmitCompleted(SubmitOperation so)
{
  UpdateChanges();
  if (so.HasError)
  {
    MessageBox.Show(so.Error.Message);
  }
}
private void btnReject_Click(object sender, RoutedEventArgs e)
{
  if (context.HasChanges)
  {
```

```
        context.RejectChanges();
        UpdateChanges();
    }
}
```

4. Build and run the solution. Changes will be submitted only when we click on the **Submit changes** button and a full changeset will be submitted at once. This can be seen in the following screenshot:

Working with WCF RIA Services							Change tracking
Color	DiscontinuedDate	ListPrice	ModifiedDate	Name	Product		
Black		1431.5000	3/11/2004 10:01:36 AM	HL Road Frame - Black, 58 Testing	18		{Added = 0, Modified = 2, Removed = 0}
Red		1431.5000	3/11/2004 10:01:36 AM	HL Road Frame - Red, 58	18		Submit changes | Reject changes
Red		34.9900	3/11/2004 10:01:36 AM	Sport-100 Helmet, Red Testing	35		
Black		34.9900	3/11/2004 10:01:36 AM	Sport-100 Helmet, Black	35		
White		9.5000	3/11/2004 10:01:36 AM	Mountain Bike Socks, M	27		
White		9.5000	3/11/2004 10:01:36 AM	Mountain Bike Socks, L	27		
Blue		34.9900	3/11/2004 10:01:36 AM	Sport-100 Helmet, Blue	35		
Multi		8.9900	3/11/2004 10:01:36 AM	AWC Logo Cap	23		
Multi		49.9900	3/11/2004 10:01:36 AM	Long-Sleeve Logo Jersey, S	25		
Multi		49.9900	3/11/2004 10:01:36 AM	Long-Sleeve Logo Jersey, M	25		
Multi		49.9900	3/11/2004 10:01:36 AM	Long-Sleeve Logo Jersey, L	25		
Multi		49.9900	3/11/2004 10:01:36 AM	Long-Sleeve Logo Jersey, XL	25		
Red		1431.5000	3/11/2004 10:01:36 AM	HL Road Frame - Red, 62	18		
Red		1431.5000	3/11/2004 10:01:36 AM	HL Road Frame - Red, 44	18		
Red		1431.5000	3/11/2004 10:01:36 AM	HL Road Frame - Red, 48	18		
Red		1431.5000	3/11/2004 10:01:36 AM	HL Road Frame - Red, 52	18		
Red		1431.5000	3/11/2004 10:01:36 AM	HL Road Frame - Red, 56	18		

How it works...

Changes to the entities in our `DomainContext` are tracked and locally persisted on our client-side `DomainContext` instance of the `ProductContext` type. These changes are persisted to our datastore when we explicitly call `SubmitChanges()` on this `context`. Hence, it's easy to work with Units of Work/changesets instead of persisting data on every change. The combination of all changes that have happened on our `context` and haven't been submitted or rejected is referred to as the not persisted changeset. When we submit the changes to our `DomainService`, the whole changeset (Unit of Work) is persisted. Each Entity will be looked at, its `EntityState` will be inspected, and if necessary, the correct `Update`, `Insert`, or `Delete` method of our `DomainService` will be called. On the server, all these methods are executed on the `ObjectContext` of the Entity Framework. After all the methods have been executed, the server-side `ObjectContext` is persisted.

As the `DomainContext` (`context`) has to have a collection of all changes on its entities, we can get this list of changes and visualize it. The `context.EntityContainer.GetChanges()` will return an `EntityChangeSet`—a list of all changes on the `EntityContainer` Entities.

There's more...

In this recipe, we've added code only to modify an Entity, but not to insert or delete an Entity. However, there is nothing special in implementing this. As long as we make sure that any code we write to remove or add an Entity is working on the same `DomainContext`, changes will be tracked and correctly submitted when we call `SubmitChanges()` on our `DomainContext`.

The following code will add a new product to our `DomainContext`:

```
private void AddProduct()
{
    context.Products.Add(new Product() {
    // set product properties here
    });
}
```

The following code can be used to remove a product from our `DomainContext`:

```
private void RemoveProduct()
{
    context.Products.Remove(context.Products[0]);
}
```

See also

When persisting data, it might be interesting to learn about handling concurrency and transactions. In order to achieve this, have a look at the next recipe.

Working with concurrency and transactions

When you're working in a multi-user environment, concurrency is something that needs to be taken into account. What happens when two or more users update the same row? Transactions are equally important. If you've got a bunch of Entities that need updating, should they be updated in one transaction, or should updates happen one by one? This recipe will explain the possibilities you get for managing your own concurrency and transaction behavior.

Getting ready

This recipe uses the AdventureWorks Lite database—a free database you can download from `http://www.codeplex.com/MSFTDBProdSamples`. To follow this recipe, you need to have this database installed on an SQL Server instance you can access from your machine.

We're starting from the solution completed in the *Getting data on the Client* recipe. You can find a starter solution located in the `Chapter09\Working_With_Concurrency_and_Transactions_Starter\` folder in the code bundle available on the Packt website. The completed solution can be found in the `Chapter09\Working_With_Concurrency_and_Transactions_Completed\` folder.

How to do it...

In order to begin working with concurrency and transactions, we'll need to follow step 1 to step 6 of the *Getting data on the Client* recipe to make sure that we have a `ProductService` (`DomainService`) that gets products from the AdventureWorks Lite database using the Entity Framework and for which editing is enabled on Product entities. On our client side, we should have a DataGrid displaying these products. In our `MainPage` class, we should have a `context` property that contains an instance of our `ProductContext DomainContext`. This property is created in the constructor of the `MainPage` class. It's this `context` property that will be used to persist changes. We should also create a button to submit the changes we make on the data in our `DataGrid`, which includes a callback method to catch any errors. Alternatively, you can use the provided starter solution.

To get started, we'll need to complete the following steps:

1. The Entity Framework implements an optimistic concurrency model by default. This means that no locks are held on our data and concurrency will not be checked when we submit changes to our database. Of course, this is not the scenario we always want, so we need to change this. We need to open our **Entity Model** and select the **Name** property of our Product Entity. Now, set its **Concurrency Mode** value to **Fixed**, instead of the default **None** value. This can be seen in the following screenshot:

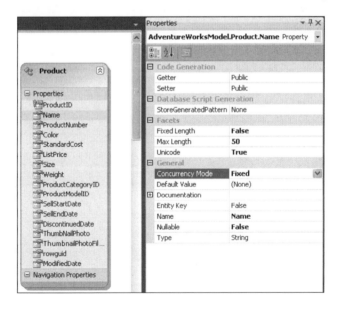

2. Start the solution twice and wait until both DataGrids are filled with products. Edit a product name in the first application instance and submit the changes. Now, edit the same product name in the other running application instance without reloading. We'll get a concurrency error on that Entity.

3. Transactions are not created by the RIA Services Framework itself. It just uses the default implementation used by the datastore we've chosen. However, we can still hook into the update processing pipeline to create our own transactions. To do this, we should override the `Submit` method on our `DomainService`. In this override, we can wrap the call to `base.Submit()` in our own transaction scope. So, add a reference to `System.Transaction` to our server project. Also add a `using` directive for `System.Transaction` to our `DomainService ProductService`. Now, add the following code to the `ProductService` class:

```
public override bool Submit(ChangeSet changeSet)
{
  bool returnValue;
  using (TransactionScope myTransactionScope = new
    TransactionScope(TransactionScopeOption.Required,
    new TransactionOptions { IsolationLevel =
    System.Transactions.IsolationLevel.ReadCommitted }))
  {
    returnValue = base.Submit(changeSet);
    myTransactionScope.Complete();
  }
  return returnValue;
}
```

4. Build and run the application. If we set a breakpoint on the `Submit` method we just created in our `DomainService`, you'll notice that this method gets called when `SubmitChanges()` on the `DomainContext` is executed. Also, the call is nicely wrapped into our own `TransactionScope`.

How it works...

Concurrency conflicts are returned to the client when they happen. We can then show a message to a user or handle them on the client (typically by refetching the most recent data, redoing the changes, and resubmitting).

As far as transactions are concerned, most methods on our (`LinqToEntities`) `DomainService` can be overridden, which means we can hook into them as we like. By manually creating a transaction with a certain scope, we make sure that all actions are executed in that transaction scope.

Tracking a user's identity

In quite a few applications, knowing which user is using your application is important. You might want to enable certain features if a certain user is logged in, or limit the data you're offering depending on the logged-in user's identity. In this recipe, you'll learn how easy it is to get to know which user is using your application. You'll learn how to verify and track a user's identity in your Silverlight application.

Getting ready

This recipe uses the AdventureWorks Lite database—a free database you can download from `http://www.codeplex.com/MSFTDBProdSamples`. To follow this recipe, you need to have this database installed on an SQL Server instance you can access from your machine.

We're starting from the solution completed in the *Getting data on the Client* recipe. You can find a starter solution located in the `Chapter09\Tracking_a_User_Starter\` folder in the code bundle available on the Packt website. The completed solution can be found in the `Chapter09\Tracking_a_User_Completed\` folder.

How to do it...

In order to track a user's identity in our Silverlight application, we need to have an RIA Services-enabled solution at hand. To make it easy for us, we'll follow step 1 to step 6 of the *Getting data on the Client* recipe to make sure that all references and links are correctly implemented. Alternatively, you can use the provided starter solution.

To track a user's identity, we'll need to complete the following steps:

1. We'll use Windows Authentication for this recipe. Check the `web.config` file on our server application and make sure that the `<authentication>` tag in `<system.web>` has its `mode` set to `Windows`, which is the default value.

2. Add a new `DomainService` to our server application. Use the **Authentication Domain Service** template for this and name it as **AuthenticationService**.

3. Build the solution. We can use the `WebContext` class to **access this Authentication Service & User on our client side**. Add an instance of `WebContext` to the application lifetime object collection in our application and add a `WindowsAuthentication` service to this instance by adding the following code to `App.xaml`:

    ```
    <Application
     xmlns="http://schemas.microsoft.com/winfx/2006/xaml/presentation"
     xmlns:x="http://schemas.microsoft.com/winfx/2006/xaml"
     x:Class="WorkingWithRIAServices.App"
     xmlns:local="clr-namespace:WorkingWithRIAServices"
     xmlns:authserv="clr-namespace:System.ServiceModel.DomainServices
      .Client.ApplicationServices;
    ```

```
    assembly=System.ServiceModel.DomainServices.Client.Web">
    <Application.ApplicationLifetimeObjects>
      <local:WebContext>
        <local:WebContext.Authentication>
          <authserv:WindowsAuthentication />
        </local:WebContext.Authentication>
      </local:WebContext>
    </Application.ApplicationLifetimeObjects>
  </Application>
```

4. Add the current `WebContext` to our application resources to make it available
    to XAML. Change the `Application.Startup` event in `App.xaml.cs` to the
    following code:

```
private void Application_Startup(object sender,
  StartupEventArgs e)
{
  this.Resources.Add("WebContext", WebContext.Current);
  this.RootVisual = new MainPage();
}
```

5. Add the following XAML code to the `MainPage.xaml` file to display user information
    from the `WebContext`:

```
<StackPanel Orientation="Vertical"
            DataContext="{StaticResource WebContext}"
            Margin="20">
  <TextBlock Text="User Identity"
             FontSize="18"></TextBlock>
  <StackPanel Orientation="Horizontal">
    <TextBlock Text="Username: "></TextBlock>
    <TextBlock Text="{Binding User.Name}"></TextBlock>
  </StackPanel>
  <StackPanel Orientation="Horizontal">
    <TextBlock Text="User being loaded: " ></TextBlock>
    <TextBlock Text="{Binding Authentication.IsLoadingUser}" >
    </TextBlock>
  </StackPanel>
</StackPanel>
```

6. Load the user in the `MainPage` constructor by adding the following line of code to
    `MainPage.xaml.cs`:

```
WebContext.Current.Authentication.LoadUser();
```

7. Build and run the application. You'll see the user information of the logged-in user on the screen. This can be seen in the following screenshot:

How it works...

When we tell our server application (through the `web.config` file) that it should provide a certain authentication mode (Windows), the identity of the user using that application is in line with what we enter in the authentication mode setting. An Authentication Domain Service provides easy access to the properties and methods we need for this. It defines a User (inheriting from `UserBase`) and a service (inheriting from `AuthenticationBase<User>`). Once we've added such a service, the necessary methods will be generated on our client, just as methods are generated when we add query methods on our server.

Whenever we tell our `WebContext` to access these methods, they are accessed through an instance of `WebContext`, for example, loading a user, login, logout. When client-side methods are executed, they call server-side methods that get the authenticated user and pass it back to the client, where it's easily accessible through the `WebContext` instance.

There's more...

In this recipe, we've learned how to achieve some basic tracking of our users' identities. Extra options exist for more advanced tracking.

If the default user information isn't enough, we can add custom fields to our users' profiles. To do this, RIA Services uses the profile manager in ASP .NET. In short, the following two steps need to be completed:

1. Enable profiles by adding `<profile enabled="true" />` to the `<system.web>` section in the `web.config` file.

2. Add custom fields to the `User` class in our `AuthenticationService.cs` file.

These custom fields are accessible on both our server and our client.

Another advanced option is User Roles. Again, RIA Services uses the Role Manager in ASP.NET for this. In short, the following two steps need to be performed:

1. Enable the Role Manager by adding `<roleManager enable="true" />` to the `<system.web>` section in the `web.config` file.

2. The `WebContext.Current.User.Roles` collection is now available and will contain the roles our authenticated user has.

See also

In this recipe, we've learned how to track a user's identity. To learn how to control a user's access, have a look at the next recipe.

Controlling a user's access to a service and service methods

In the previous recipe, we've learned how to track a user's identity. However, most applications that need a user's identity need it to do something with it, for example, restricting access to a certain service or a service method so that only an authenticated user can access it. This will make sure that our service can't be freely used by anyone. Only the users we allow in will be able to use it. In this recipe, you'll learn how to restrict access to a service or service method to authenticated users only.

Getting ready

This recipe uses the AdventureWorks Lite database—a free database you can download from `http://www.codeplex.com/MSFTDBProdSamples`. To follow this recipe, you need to have this database installed on an SQL Server instance you can access from your machine.

We're starting from the solution completed in the previous recipe. You can find a starter solution located in the `Chapter09\Controlling_Access_Starter\` folder in the code bundle available on the Packt website. The completed solution can be found in the `Chapter09\Controlling_Access_Completed\` folder.

How to do it...

We'll need to make sure that we have an RIA Services-enabled solution with authentication. To achieve this, we'll need to follow step 1 to step 7 of the previous recipe. Alternatively, you can use the provided starter solution.

Once we've got this, we'll need to complete the following steps to restrict the access to authenticated users:

1. Open the `ProductService.cs` file on the server. Locate the `GetProduct` method (which is used to fill the DataGrid with data) and annotate it with the `[RequiresAuthentication]` attribute.

2. Open the `web.config` file on our server, locate the `<authentication>` tag, and set its `mode` to `None`.

3. Build and run the solution. You'll notice that your DataGrid remains empty. This is because access to the `GetProduct` query is now restricted to authenticated users.

4. Open the `web.config` file on our server again and change the authentication mode to `Windows`.

5. Build and run the solution. You'll notice that our DataGrid is again filled with data. This is because the user is now authenticated through Windows Authentication.

6. To restrict access to the complete service instead of specific methods, annotate the `ProductService` class with the `[RequiresAuthentication]` attribute.

How it works...

The `[RequiresAuthentication]` attribute tells our service or service method that it can be executed only by an authenticated user. Users aren't authenticated if the authentication mode is set to `None`, and so access is restricted. However, when we set the authentication mode to `Windows` (or `Forms` and provide authentication logic for this), users using our server application are authenticated through Windows Authentication and can now execute these methods.

There's more...

Besides allowing access to methods/services to authenticated users, we can also allow access only to users that have a certain role. To do this, we need to set up our solution to use the Role Manager as well as applying the `[RequiresRoles("TheRequiredRole")]` attribute. This attribute will make sure that the annotated method or service can be accessed only by authenticated users having a certain role.

Validating data using data annotations

Validation of your data before persisting it is a requirement for almost every application. By using validation on your Entities, you make sure that no invalid data is persisted to your datastore. When you don't implement validation, there's a risk that a user will input wrongly formatted or plain incorrect data on the screen and even persist this data to your datastore. This is something you should definitely avoid. In this recipe, you'll learn how to validate data using data annotation attributes that you can use on your Entities.

Getting ready

This recipe uses the AdventureWorks Lite database—a free database you can download from `http://www.codeplex.com/MSFTDBProdSamples`. To follow this recipe, you need to have this database installed on an SQL Server instance you can access from your machine.

We're starting from the solution completed in the _Getting data on the Client_ recipe. You can find a starter solution located in the `Chapter09\Validating_Using_Data_Annotations_Starter\` folder in the code bundle available on the Packt website. The completed solution can be found in the `Chapter09\Validating_Using_Data_Annotations_Completed\` folder.

How to do it...

First of all, if you're using the solution of the previous recipe, you'll need to delete the `ProductService` class as we'll recreate it with an extra metadata file. If you're not using that solution, do make sure that you have a UI with a DataGrid that shows the Products from the AdventureWorks Lite database. Alternatively, you can use the provided starter solution.

In order to begin validating data using data annotations, we'll need to complete the following steps:

1. Add a new `DomainService` and name it as **ProductService**. When creating the service, make sure that you select the **Generate associated classes for metadata** checkbox. (If you're using the starter solution, you can skip this step.) This can be seen in the following screenshot:

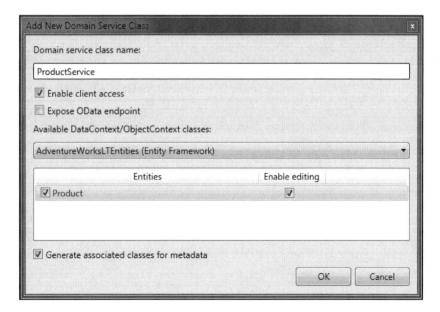

2. Open the generated `ProductService.metadata.cs` file and locate the internally sealed `ProductMetadata` class. In this class, annotate properties with attributes to enable validation. This is shown in the following code:

```
[Required]
[StringLength(50, MinimumLength=1, ErrorMessage="The product name
   must be between 1 and 50 chars")]
public string Name;
[Required]
[DataType(DataType.Currency)]
public Decimal StandardCost;
```

3. Build the solution and try to edit a row in your DataGrid. You'll notice that when you try to input invalid values for the properties we've annotated with validation attributes, the DataGrid shows you validation errors. This can be seen in the following screenshot:

DiscontinuedDate	ListPrice	ModifiedDate	Name	ProductCategoryID	Produ
	1432.5000	3/11/2004 9:01:36 AM		The Name field is required.	
	1431.5000	3/11/2004 9:01:36 AM	HL Road Frame - Red, 58	18	706
	34.9900	3/11/2004 9:01:36 AM	Sport-100 Helmet, Red	35	707
	34.9900	3/11/2004 9:01:36 AM	Sport-100 Helmet, Black	35	708
	9.5000	3/11/2004 9:01:36 AM	Mountain Bike Socks, M	27	709
	9.5000	3/11/2004 9:01:36 AM	Mountain Bike Socks, L	27	710
	34.9900	3/11/2004 9:01:36 AM	Sport-100 Helmet, Blue	35	711

How it works...

When we select the **Generate associated classes for metadata** checkbox, RIA Services generates an extra file for us (in this case `ProductService.metadata.cs`). This file contains metadata for all the entities we've selected (Product).

When we add validation attributes on the `ProductMetadata` properties, these attributes are propagated to their generated client-entity representation. These validation attributes will be evaluated at runtime in the `set` methods of these generated properties to ensure that the validation rules are upheld.

As a DataGrid (or DataForm) is automatically able to look for these validation rules, it will show validation errors if validation fails. This feature comes out of the box with a DataGrid or DataForm, without us having to do any work ourselves. Hence, we can easily enable validation on our entities by just using data annotations. As you might have noticed, we didn't write a single extra line of code on our client.

By using named parameters in the constructors of our attributes, we can further customize how the attributes should behave. For example, `ErrorMessage` enables us to customize the message shown when validation fails.

There's more...

In this recipe, we've used just a few of the possible data annotations. `DataTypeAttribute`, `RangeAttribute`, `RegularExpressionAttribute`, `RequiredAttribute`, `StringLengthAttribute`, and `CustomValidationAttribute` are all the data annotations at our disposal.

For all these attributes, named parameters are possible to further customize the way validation should occur. `ErrorMessage`, `ErrorMessageResourceName`, and `ErrorMessageResourceType` are available on all attributes, but many more are available depending on the attribute you use. We can check these named parameters by looking at the IntelliSense tooltip we get on the attribute constructor.

See also

Validating data using data annotations is just one interesting way of validating our entities. Another way of doing this is using shared code. Have a look at the next recipe to learn how to do this.

Validating data using shared code

Validation of your data before persisting it is a requirement for almost every application. By using validation on your Entities, you make sure that no invalid data is persisted to your datastore. When you don't implement validation, there's a risk that a user will input wrongly formatted or plain incorrect data on the screen and even persist this data to your datastore. This is something you should definitely avoid. In this recipe, you'll learn how to validate data on an entity level using code that is shared between your server application and your client application.

Getting ready

This recipe uses the AdventureWorks Lite database—a free database you can download from `http://www.codeplex.com/MSFTDBProdSamples`. To follow this recipe, you need to have this database installed on an SQL Server instance you can access from your machine.

We're starting from the solution completed in the Persisting Data to the Server recipe. You can find a starter solution located in the `Chapter09\Validating_Using_Shared_Code_Starter\` folder in the code bundle available on the Packt website. The completed solution can be found in the `Chapter09\ Validating_Using_Shared_Code_Completed\` folder.

How to do it...

If you're not using the solution from the previous recipe, make sure that you have a UI with a `DataGrid` that shows the Products from the AdventureWorks Lite database on your client. Also make sure that you have a `DomainService` with associated metadata on your server. Alternatively, you can use the provided starter solution.

In order to begin validating data using shared code, we'll need to complete the following steps:

1. Add a new class to our server application and name it as `WeightValidator. shared.cs`.

2. In this class, add a public static method named `IsWeightValid` that should return a `ValidationResult` and accept a `Product` and `ValidationContext` as parameters. In this method, check if the product's weight is between `1` and `1500` and return an error if it isn't:

```
public static ValidationResult IsWeightValid(Product product,
  ValidationContext context)
{
  bool valid = (product.Weight >= 1 && product.Weight <= 1500);
  if (!valid)
  {
    return new ValidationResult("The inputted weight isn't
      valid.");
  }
  return null;
}
```

3. Open the `ProductService.metadata.cs` file and locate the `Product` class. Add a `CustomValidation` attribute to this class and pass in our `WeightValidator` type and `IsWeightValid` as parameters:

```
[CustomValidation(typeof(WeightValidator), "IsWeightValid")]
[MetadataTypeAttribute(typeof(Product.ProductMetadata))]
public partial class Product
```

4. Build and run the application. Try inputting an invalid value for **Weight**. You'll notice that the DataGrid automatically generates a validation summary, telling you that the inputted value isn't valid. This can be seen in the following screenshot:

ate	SellStartDate	Size	StandardCost	ThumbNailPhoto	ThumbnailPhotoFileName	Weight
	5/31/1998 10:00:00 PM	58	1059.3100	System.Byte[]	no_image_available_small.gif	2000
	5/31/1998 10:00:00 PM	58	1059.3100	System.Byte[]	no_image_available_small.gif	1016.04
	6/30/2001 10:00:00 PM		13.0863	System.Byte[]	no_image_available_small.gif	
	6/30/2001 10:00:00 PM		13.0863	System.Byte[]	no_image_available_small.gif	
)2 10:00:00 PM	6/30/2001 10:00:00 PM	M	3.3963	System.Byte[]	no_image_available_small.gif	

❶ 1 Error

The inputted weight isn't valid.

How it works...

When we create a file having `shared` at the end of the filename filename, the classes in this file are copied to our client application. This means everything we write in it is accessible from the Silverlight application. We can check this by looking at the generated `Code` folder in our client project.

Now, by annotating the `Product` class in the metadata file with the `CustomValidation` attribute, by passing in the type of Validator to use and the method used for validation as a string, we tell the application that extra validation should occur on this entity. This is not the same as the attributes we use on entity properties. This validation is on the entity as a whole, which means we can use this to, for example, write validation that should be done by comparing different properties of our entity.

As a DataGrid (or DataForm) is automatically able to look for these validation rules, it will show validation errors if validation fails. This feature comes out of the box with a DataGrid or DataForm, without us having to do any work ourselves. As this is validation on the entity as a whole, the DataGrid automatically generates a validation summary. As you might have noticed, we didn't write a single extra line of code on our client.

So, when we input an invalid value, the DataGrid uses the client-side generated code from our shared file to validate the entity, based on the `CustomValidation` rule we added to the Product entity.

See also

Validating data using shared code is one way of validating our entities. To learn how to validate using data annotations, have a look at the *Validating data using data annotations* recipe.

Using the DomainDataSource

The `DomainDataSource` is a Silverlight control that makes it easy to interact with services written using RIA Services. This control makes it possible to write rich, data-bound, validating user controls with minimal code-behind. This recipe will show you how to use a `DomainDataSource` to transfer data from your server to your client.

Getting ready

This recipe uses the AdventureWorks Lite database—a free database you can download from `http://www.codeplex.com/MSFTDBProdSamples`. To follow this recipe, you need to have this database installed on an SQL Server instance you can access from your machine.

We're starting from the solution completed in the *Getting data on the Client* recipe. You can find a starter solution located in the `Chapter09\Using_DomainDataSource_Starter\` folder in the code bundle available on the Packt website. The completed solution can be found in the `Chapter09\Using_DomainDataSource_Completed\` folder.

How to do it...

If you're not using the solution from the previous recipe, make sure that you have a UI with a `DataGrid` that shows the Products from the AdventureWorks Lite database on your client. Alternatively, you can use the provided starter solution.

To get started, we'll need to complete the following steps:

1. Add references to `System.Windows.Controls.Data` and `System.Windows.Controls.DomainServices` to our Silverlight application.

2. Add the following XML namespace statements to `MainPage.xaml` if they aren't there already:

    ```
    xmlns:riaControls="clr-namespace:System.Windows.Controls;
        assembly=System.Windows.Controls.DomainServices"
    xmlns:domain="clr-namespace:WorkingWithRIAServices.Web"
    ```

3. Add the following XAML code to our `MainPage` to define the `DomainDataSource`, passing in the correct query and binding the result to our DataGrid:

    ```
    <riaControls:DomainDataSource x:Name="myDomainDataSource"
                                  QueryName="GetProductsQuery"
                                  AutoLoad="True">
      <riaControls:DomainDataSource.DomainContext>
        <domain:ProductContext />
      </riaControls:DomainDataSource.DomainContext>
    </riaControls:DomainDataSource>
    <my:DataGrid x:Name="myDataGrid"
    ```

```
            ItemsSource="{Binding Data,
                ElementName=myDomainDataSource}"
            Grid.Row="1">
    </my:DataGrid>
```

4. Build and run the application. You'll see that the grid will be loaded with products using the `DomainDataSource`. This can be seen in the following screenshot:

Working with WCF RIA Services

Color	DiscontinuedDate	ListPrice	ModifiedDate	Name	ProductCategoryID
Black		1431.5000	3/11/2004 10:01:36 AM	HL Road Frame - Black, 58	18
Red		1431.5000	3/11/2004 10:01:36 AM	HL Road Frame - Red, 58	18
Red		34.9900	3/11/2004 10:01:36 AM	Sport-100 Helmet, Red	35
Black		34.9900	3/11/2004 10:01:36 AM	Sport-100 Helmet, Black	35
White		9.5000	3/11/2004 10:01:36 AM	Mountain Bike Socks, M	27
White		9.5000	3/11/2004 10:01:36 AM	Mountain Bike Socks, L	27
Blue		34.9900	3/11/2004 10:01:36 AM	Sport-100 Helmet, Blue	35
Multi		8.9900	3/11/2004 10:01:36 AM	AWC Logo Cap	23
Multi		49.9900	3/11/2004 10:01:36 AM	Long-Sleeve Logo Jersey, S	25

How it works...

When we add a `DomainDataSource` XAML control, a new `DomainDataSource` is created behind the scenes and it gets access to an instance of our `DomainContext` (in this case the `ProductContext`). By specifying the `QueryName`, we tell the `DomainDataSource` which query to use to load data when our application starts. `AutoLoad = true` means that the `DomainDataSource` can reload data whenever the query changes. So, what happens is that when we launch our application, the query to get products is executed on the server.

By using `ElementBinding` to bind the `ItemsSource` of our `DataGrid` to the `Data` property of the `DomainDataSource`, our `DataGrid` is automatically populated with the results of that query. In fact, this is a replacement for writing a `LoadOperation` for that query in the code-behind.

There's more...

In this example, we've used a simple query to fetch data. Of course, sometimes we need to add parameters to a query method. Presuming we have a query method called `GetProductStartingWithQuery` that accepts a `strStartsWith` string and returns a list of products starting with the letters we enter, we can call it by changing our `DomainDataSource` to the following code:

```
<riaControls:DomainDataSource x:Name="myDomainDataSource"
                        QueryName="GetProductStartingWithQuery"
                        AutoLoad="True">
```

```
<riaControls:DomainDataSource.DomainContext>
  <domain:ProductContext />
</riaControls:DomainDataSource.DomainContext>
<riaControls:DomainDataSource.QueryParameters>
  <riaData:Parameter ParameterName="strStartsWith"
                     Value="A" />
</riaControls:DomainDataSource.QueryParameters>
</riaControls:DomainDataSource>
```

We can even take that step further: What if we want the parameters to contain a value a user can enter in our UI? Without using any code-behind, we can get this behavior using a `ControlParameter` on our `DomainDataSource` by presuming we have a textbox in our UI called `txtProductNameStartsWith`. This is shown in the following code:

```
<riaControls:DomainDataSource x:Name="myDomainDataSource"
                              QueryName="GetProductStartingWithQuery"
                              AutoLoad="True">
  <riaControls:DomainDataSource.DomainContext>
    <domain:ProductContext />
  </riaControls:DomainDataSource.DomainContext>
  <riaControls:DomainDataSource.QueryParameters>
    <riaData:ControlParameter ParameterName="strStartsWith"
                              ControlName="txtProductNameStartsWith"
                              PropertyName="Text"
                              RefreshEventName="TextChanged" />
  </riaControls:DomainDataSource.QueryParameters>
</riaControls:DomainDataSource>
```

See also

Now that we've learned how to use the `DomainDataSource`, you might want to know how to page through and shape your data using the `DomainDataSource`. Have a look at the *Using the DomainDataSource to page through data* and *Sorting, filtering, and grouping data using the DomainDataSource* recipes to learn how to do this.

Using the DomainDataSource to page through data

We can easily implement paging behavior using the `DomainDataSource`. Paging is important for two reasons: we typically don't want to have a list of hundreds of detail lines on one screen because this severely limits the user experience and slows down our application. Besides that, paging makes sure that we can fetch parts of data from our server instead of fetching everything at once. This makes sure that bandwidth use is limited and again makes working with the application faster and more user friendly. This recipe will show you how to do it.

Getting ready

This recipe uses the AdventureWorks Lite database—a free database you can download from `http://www.codeplex.com/MSFTDBProdSamples`. To follow this recipe, you need to have this database installed on an SQL Server instance you can access from your machine.

We're starting from the solution completed in the previous recipe. You can find a starter solution located in the `Chapter09\Using_DomainDataSource_Paging_Starter\` folder in the code bundle available on the Packt website. The completed solution can be found in the `Chapter09\Using_DomainDataSource_Paging_Completed\` folder.

How to do it...

If you're not using the solution from the previous recipe, make sure that you have an RIA-enabled solution with a service that returns the products from the AdventureWorks Lite database. On your client side, you should have a `DataGrid` to display these products. The products should be filled using a `DomainDataSource`, the result of which is bound to the `ItemsSource` property of your `DataGrid`. Alternatively, you can use the provided starter solution.

To begin paging using the `DomainDataSource`, we need to complete the following steps:

1. Add a `DataPager` control to `MainPage.xaml` and bind it to the `Data` property of our `DomainDataSource` as shown in the following code:

```
<data:DataPager Grid.Row="2"
                Source="{Binding Data,
                    ElementName=myDomainDataSource}" />
```

2. Locate our `DomainDataSource` and change it by adding the `PageSize` and `LoadSize` properties to it:

```
<riaControls:DomainDataSource x:Name="myDomainDataSource"
                              PageSize="20"
                              LoadSize="40"
                              QueryName="GetProductsQuery"
                              AutoLoad="True">
```

3. Locate the `GetProducts` query on our `DomainService` and change it as shown in the following code so that it returns an ordered collection. Paging works only with ordered collections.:

```
public IQueryable<Product> GetProducts()
{
    return this.ObjectContext.Product.OrderBy(p => p.Name);
}
```

4. Build and run the application. You can now page through the loaded products using the data pager. This can be seen in the following screenshot:

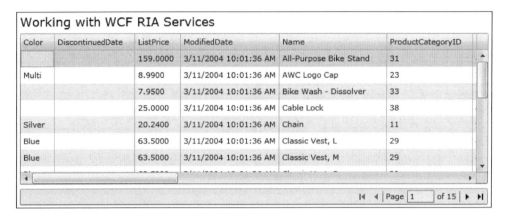

How it works...

When we use a `DomainDataSource`, Silverlight and RIA Services will automatically implement the paging behavior for us, depending on the values of `PageSize` and `LoadSize`. When executing the query method to get products, the `DomainDataSource` will limit the number of products downloaded at a time by dividing the entire query into pieces depending on the value we've set as `LoadSize`. It will also make sure that only the number of products we've defined in `PageSize` are shown at the same time.

When the UI requires data that wasn't requested, more data will be automatically requested. In this recipe, this means that more data will be requested once we page through to page 3.

The `DataPager` reacts to the `Data` property of the `DomainDataSource`. It's this `Data` property that is filled with data on demand, so that's the collection the `DataPager` will react to.

See also

Now that you've learned how to use the `DomainDataSource` to page data, you might want to know how to use it to shape your data. Have a look at the next recipe to learn how to do this.

Sorting, filtering, and grouping data using the DomainDataSource

Using the `DomainDataSource`, we can shape our data in XAML without writing any code in the code-behind. We can allow the users of our application to shape the data they see on screen by sorting, filtering, or grouping it. This increases the user friendliness of the software by making it easy to find what a user of the application is looking for. In this recipe, you'll learn how to shape your data by sorting, filtering, and grouping it with the `DomainDataSource`.

Getting ready

This recipe uses the AdventureWorks Lite database—a free database you can download from `http://www.codeplex.com/MSFTDBProdSamples`. To follow this recipe, you need to have this database installed on an SQL Server instance you can access from your machine.

We're starting from the solution completed in the *Using the DomainDataSource* recipe. You can find a starter solution located in the `Chapter09\Using_DomainDataSource_Sorting_Filtering_Grouping_Starter\` folder in the code bundle available on the Packt website. The completed solution can be found in the `Chapter09\Using_DomainDataSource_Sorting_Filtering_Grouping_Completed\` folder.

How to do it...

If you're not using the solution from the *Using the DomainDataSource* recipe, make sure that you have an RIA-enabled solution with a service that returns the products from the AdventureWorks Lite database. On your client side, you should have a `DataGrid` to display these products. The products should be filled using a `DomainDataSource`, the result of which is bound to the `ItemsSource` property of your `DataGrid`. Alternatively, you can use the provided starter solution.

To begin shaping our data, we'll need to complete the following steps:

1. Locate the `DomainDataSource` object in `MainPage.xaml`. Add a `SortDescriptor` to it, passing in `Name` as `PropertyPath` and `Ascending` as `Direction`. This is shown in the following code:

```
<riaControls:DomainDataSource.SortDescriptors>
  <riaData:SortDescriptor PropertyPath="Name"
                          Direction="Ascending" />
</riaControls:DomainDataSource.SortDescriptors>
```

2. In the same `DomainDataSource`, add a FilterDescriptorCollection with one `FilterDescriptor` setting the `PropertyPath` to `Name`, `Operator` to `Contains`, and `Value` to `A`. This is shown in the following code:

```
<riaControls:DomainDataSource.FilterDescriptors>
  <riaControls:FilterDescriptor PropertyPath="Name"
                                Operator="Contains"
                                Value="A" />
</riaControls:DomainDataSource.FilterDescriptors>
```

3. In the same `DomainDataSource`, add a `GroupDescriptor`, passing in `ProductCategoryID` as `PropertyPath`. This is shown in the following code:

```
<riaControls:DomainDataSource.GroupDescriptors>
  <riaControls:GroupDescriptor PropertyPath="ProductCategoryID" />
</riaControls:DomainDataSource.GroupDescriptors>
```

4. Build and run the application. You'll notice that our `DataGrid` is now sorted, filtered, and grouped based on what we defined in the previous steps.

Working with WCF RIA Services

Name ▲	ProductCategoryID	Color	DiscontinuedDate	ListPrice	ModifiedDate	P
▲ ProductCategoryID: 5 (32 items)						▲
Mountain-100 Black, 38	5	Black		3374.9900	3/11/2004 10:01:36 AM	7
Mountain-100 Black, 42	5	Black		3374.9900	3/11/2004 10:01:36 AM	7
Mountain-100 Black, 44	5	Black		3374.9900	3/11/2004 10:01:36 AM	7
Mountain-100 Black, 48	5	Black		3374.9900	3/11/2004 10:01:36 AM	7
Mountain-100 Silver, 38	5	Silver		3399.9900	3/11/2004 10:01:36 AM	7
Mountain-100 Silver, 42	5	Silver		3399.9900	3/11/2004 10:01:36 AM	7
Mountain-100 Silver, 44	5	Silver		3399.9900	3/11/2004 10:01:36 AM	7
Mountain-100 Silver, 48	5	Silver		3399.9900	3/11/2004 10:01:36 AM	7
Mountain-200 Black, 38	5	Black		2294.9900	3/11/2004 10:01:36 AM	7 ▼

How it works...

To add sorting to our `DomainDataSource`, all we have to do is add a `SortDescriptor`. In this object, we define a `PropertyPath` that specifies the property on which to sort, and the `Direction`. When we use `SortDescriptors`, the `DomainDataSource` will automatically use these descriptors to return sorted data. The query method we pass through is executed and the collection is correctly sorted before being returned to our Silverlight application.

If we now look at our `DataGrid`, we'll see sorted data. This is what's expected as our `DataGrid` is bound to the `Data` property of our `DomainDataSource`. However, you'll also notice that the `DataGrid` reflects the `SortDescriptors` in its column headers: you see in which direction the column has been sorted. Why is this? This is because the `Data` property is actually an `ICollectionView` interface. Our `DataGrid` automatically works with this interface, so it's able to manipulate the data as well. Actually, if we click on a column header on our `DataGrid`, the `DomainDataSource` will even reload its data using the sorting options we've just passed through by clicking the column header of our `DataGrid`.

The same logic applies for the `FilterDescriptors` and the `GroupDescripters`. Due to the `ICollectionView` interface, the `DataGrid` bound to the `DomainDataSource` automatically reacts to them.

There's more...

Of course, we can add multiple `SortDescriptors`, `GroupDescriptors`, and `FilterDescriptors`. However, there's something special about this last one. We might want to change something about the way the filters behave. Sometimes, we'd want our query to return the rows filtered by all the `FilterDescriptors` (an AND relation), and other times, we might want to get the rows filtered by any of the `FilterDescriptors` (an OR relation).

That's why we can set the `FilterOperator` property on `FilterDescriptors`, which allows us to define how filters relate to each other. We can get this behavior by using the following listed XAML code (this code will return all products that have an A or a B in their name):

```
<riaControls:DomainDataSource.FilterDescriptors FilterOperator="Or">
    <riaControls:FilterDescriptor PropertyPath="Name"
                                  Operator="Contains"
                                  Value="A" />
    <riaControls:FilterDescriptor PropertyPath="Name"
                                  Operator="Contains"
                                  Value="B" />
</riaControls:DomainDataSource.FilterDescriptors>
```

Besides that, we can also bind filters to UI elements that allow us to use—for example—a `TextBox` control, in which we let the user input a few values. The filter changes depending on the inputted values, thus allowing us to use changeable values instead of hard-coded ones for our filter. Assuming we have a `TextBox` named `txtFilter`, the following syntax will result in that behavior:

```
<riaControls:DomainDataSource.FilterDescriptors FilterOperator="Or">
    <riaControls:FilterDescriptor PropertyPath="Name"
                                  Operator="Contains"
                                  IgnoredValue=""
                                  Value="{Binding
                                      ElementName=txtFilter, Path=Text}">
    </riaControls:FilterDescriptor>
</riaControls:DomainDataSource.FilterDescriptors>
```

10
Converting Your Existing Applications to Use Silverlight

In this chapter, we will cover:

- ▶ Calling a stored procedure from Silverlight
- ▶ Working with LINQ to SQL from Silverlight
- ▶ Working with the Entity Framework from Silverlight
- ▶ Converting a Silverlight application to use WCF RIA Services
- ▶ Using ASP.NET authentication in Silverlight
- ▶ Using ASP.NET roles in Silverlight
- ▶ Using ASP.NET profiles in Silverlight

Introduction

Building new applications costs a lot of money. In many real-world cases, there won't be enough budget to cover a complete migration to a new platform. A sometimes more logical approach is a phased migration, where parts of the application are replaced. If we already have a web application in place, it's feasible to add Silverlight for specific functionalities within that application, while leaving others as they were.

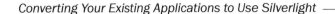

This chapter is all about techniques to leverage your existing knowledge, applications, and business requirements to Silverlight. A lot of the technical procedures that are used in this chapter are described in detail in the other chapters of this book. In this chapter, we'll focus on specifics concerning data and authentication/authorization scenarios, and not on how to construct the service calls you'll have to use.

We'll start with talking about how you can enable often-used database scenarios, such as calling a stored procedure or working with an ORM like LINQ to SQL or the Entity Framework.

In the previous chapter, we looked at working with **WCF RIA Services**. This chapter contains a recipe that shows how to enable WCF RIA Services for existing applications.

Integrating with an existing authentication system may also be something we encounter. Silverlight supports using the built-in ASP.NET Membership API through the use of **ASP.NET Application Services**.

Calling a stored procedure from Silverlight

In a lot of applications, **stored procedures** are used to perform CRUD operations or complicated calculations on your data. As Silverlight is a very good technology to create business applications with, sooner or later you'll probably have the need to call a stored procedure from a Silverlight application.

In this recipe, you'll learn how to do that.

Getting ready

We're starting from a starter solution that already includes the XAML markup for the UI, and a WCF service. If you want, you can use the starter solution located in the `Chapter 10\CallingAStoredProcedure_Starter` folder in the code bundle available on the Packt website. The completed solution can be found in the `Chapter 10\CallingAStoredProcedure_Completed` folder.

As well as this, you'll also need the **ContosoSales database** (running on SQL 2005, 2008, or an express version of either). You can find a database backup in the `Chapter 10` folder.

How to do it...

We're going to write standard ADO.NET code to call the `GetStore` stored procedure (which is already in the database and which accepts one parameter—`storeID`) and connect our Silverlight application to the WCF service containing a method to call that stored procedure. To achieve this, complete the following steps:

1. Open the web application project and add a new class file to it. Name it as `StoreDTO.cs` and add the following code to it:

```
[DataContract]
public class StoreDTO
{
    [DataMember]
    public int StoreID { get; set; }
    [DataMember]
    public string StoreImage { get; set; }
    [DataMember]
    public string City { get; set; }
    [DataMember]
    public string StateProvince { get; set; }
    [DataMember]
    public string StoreName { get; set; }

    public StoreDTO(int storeID, string storeImage, string city,
        string stateProvince, string storeName)
    {
        this.StoreID = StoreID;
        this.StoreImage = StoreImage;
        this.City = City;
        this.StateProvince = StateProvince;
        this.StoreName = StoreName;
    }

}
```

2. Open `DataService.svc` and add the following code to call the `GetStore` stored procedure, passing in a `StoreID` parameter (if applicable, change the connection string to match your server and database location):

```
[OperationContract]
public StoreDTO GetStore(int storeID)
{
    StoreDTO returnValue = null;

    SqlConnection conn = new SqlConnection("Data Source=.;Initial
        Catalog=ContosoSales;Integrated Security=True");

    SqlCommand cmd = new SqlCommand("GetStore", conn);
    cmd.CommandType = CommandType.StoredProcedure;
    cmd.Parameters.Add(new SqlParameter("@storeid", storeID));
```

```
conn.Open();
SqlDataReader drStore = cmd.ExecuteReader();

while (drStore.Read())
{
    returnValue = new StoreDTO(Convert.ToInt32(drStore.
GetValue(0))
                        , drStore.GetValue(1).ToString()
                        , drStore.GetValue(2).ToString()
                        , drStore.GetValue(3).ToString()
                        , drStore.GetValue(4).ToString());
}

drStore.Close();
conn.Close();

return returnValue;
}
```

3. Open the Silverlight application and add a service reference to `DataService.svc` to it by right-clicking on the project and selecting **Add Service Reference**. Name this reference as `DataServiceReference`.

4. Open `MainPage.xaml.cs` and add the following code to call the WCF Service method we've just created on the server side:

```
private void btnFetch_Click(object sender, RoutedEventArgs e)
{
    DataServiceClient client = new DataServiceClient();
    client.GetStoreCompleted += new
EventHandler<GetStoreCompletedEventArgs>(client_
GetStoreCompleted);
    client.GetStoreAsync(Convert.ToInt32(txtID.Text.Trim()));
}

void client_GetStoreCompleted(object sender,
GetStoreCompletedEventArgs e)
{
    if (e.Error == null)
    {
        this.DataContext = e.Result;
    }
    else
    {
        MessageBox.Show(e.Error.Message);
    }
}
```

5. You can now build and run your application. When you press the **Fetch store** button, the correct store will be fetched and shown through a stored procedure call:

How it works...

Most of the techniques we've used in this recipe are already written about in various other recipes in this book, and in any case, you're always working via some kind of service to access your database and stored procedure.

In the first step, we've created a class that will contain the object we're going to pass from the service to the Silverlight application. In the method we've created in step 2, the standard ADO.NET code is added to call the stored procedure: we open a connection to the database, create a command, and add a parameter to it to pass in the store ID. Next, a `DataReader` is initialized to put the data the stored procedure returns in a new instance of the `StoreDTO` object. Finally, the `DataReader` and connection are closed and the `StoreDTO` object is returned.

The other code you see in this recipe (communicating with WCF using data binding) has already been discussed in other recipes in much more detail. For data binding, have a look at Chapter 2, *An Introduction to Data Binding* and Chapter 3, *Advanced Data Binding*. For WCF, have a look at Chapter 7, *Talking to WCF and ASMX Services*.

See also

In this recipe, we've used standard ADO.NET to call the stored procedure. However, you can use other techniques to achieve this, such as the Entity Framework. Have a look at the *Working with the Entity Framework from Silverlight* recipe to learn how to access your database through EF from Silverlight.

Working with LINQ to SQL from Silverlight

LINQ TO SQL is one of the two Microsoft Object Relational Mapper products, typically aimed at somewhat simpler applications where using a one-on-one database to object mapping is all you need (the other one is the ADO .NET Entity Framework). This ORM can be used together with Silverlight. As getting data into a Silverlight application is typically a matter of using a service-oriented approach, the same applies here. In this recipe, you'll learn how to get data from a LINQ TO SQL model into your Silverlight application.

Getting ready

We're starting from a starter solution that already includes the XAML markup for the UI and a WCF service. If you want, you can use the starter solution located in the `Chapter 10\WorkingWithLinqToSQL_Starter` folder in the code bundle available on the Packt website. The completed solution can be found in the `Chapter 10\WorkingWithLinqToSQL_Completed` folder.

As well as this, you'll also need the **ContosoSales database** (running on SQL 2005, 2008, or an express version of either). You can find a database backup in the `Chapter 10` folder.

How to do it...

We're going to add LINQ TO SQL Data Classes to our application, write the necessary methods to fetch and update data, and connect our Silverlight application to the WCF service calling these methods. To achieve this, complete the following steps:

1. Add the LINQ to SQL Data Classes to the web application project. Do this by right-clicking, selecting **Add New Item**, and then selecting **LINQ TO SQL Classes**. When asked for a name, name it as `ContosoSales`. You'll be presented with a design surface for `ContosoSales.dbml`. From the **server explorer** pane, drag the Store table from your `ContosoSales` database to the design surface.

2. Add a reference to `System.Runtime.Serialization`.

3. Add a new class file to the web application project, name it `StoreDTO.cs`, and add the following code to it:

```
[DataContract]
public class StoreDTO
{
    [DataMember]
    public int StoreID { get; set; }
    [DataMember]
    public string StoreImage { get; set; }
    [DataMember]
    public string City { get; set; }
    [DataMember]
    public string StateProvince { get; set; }
    [DataMember]
    public string StoreName { get; set; }

    public StoreDTO(int StoreID, string StoreImage, string City,
string StateProvince, string StoreName)
    {
        this.StoreID = StoreID;
        this.StoreImage = StoreImage;
        this.City = City;
        this.StateProvince = StateProvince;
```

```
            this.StoreName = StoreName;
        }

    }
```

4. Open `DataService.svc` and add the following code to select the stores to transfer to the Silverlight application:

```
[OperationContract]
public List<StoreDTO> GetStores()
{
    using (var ctx = new ContosoSalesDataContext())
    {
        List<StoreDTO> storesToReturn = new List<StoreDTO>();

        foreach (var item in ctx.Stores.Where(s => s.StoreName.
StartsWith("A")))
        {
            storesToReturn.Add(new StoreDTO(item.StoreID, item.
StoreImage, item.City, item.StateProvince, item.StoreName));
        }
        return storesToReturn;
    }
}
```

5. In the same class, add the following method to update a changed entity:

```
[OperationContract]
public bool SaveStore(StoreDTO storeToSave)
{
    try
    {
        using (var ctx = new ContosoSalesDataContext())
        {
            Store currentStore = ctx.Stores.First<Store>(s =>
s.StoreID == storeToSave.StoreID);
            currentStore.StoreName = storeToSave.StoreName;
            ctx.SubmitChanges();
        }
        return true;
    }
    catch (Exception)
    {
        return false;
    }
}
```

6. Open the Silverlight application, and **add a service reference** to `DataService.svc` to it by right-clicking the project and selecting **Add Service Reference**. Name this reference `DataServiceReference`.

7. Open `MainPage.xaml.cs`, and add the following property to it:

```
public ObservableCollection<StoreDTO> Stores { get; set; }
```

8. Add a `LoadStores()` method to it and call this method from the constructor:

```
private void LoadStores()
{
    DataServiceClient client = new DataServiceClient();
    client.GetStoresCompleted += new EventHandler<GetStoresComplet
edEventArgs>(client_GetStoresCompleted);
    client.GetStoresAsync();
}

void client_GetStoresCompleted(object sender,
GetStoresCompletedEventArgs e)
{
    if (e.Error == null)
    {
        Stores = e.Result;
        lbStores.ItemsSource = Stores;
    }
}
```

9. Add the following code to make sure your changes are persisted on the click of the **Save changes** button:

```
private void btnSaveChanges_Click(object sender, RoutedEventArgs
e)
{
    DataServiceClient client = new DataServiceClient();
    client.SaveStoreCompleted += new EventHandler<SaveStoreComplet
edEventArgs>(client_SaveStoreCompleted);
        client.SaveStoreAsync((StoreDTO)((Button)sender).
DataContext);
}

void client_SaveStoreCompleted(object sender,
SaveStoreCompletedEventArgs e)
{
    if (e.Error == null)
    {
        if (e.Result)
        {
            MessageBox.Show("Changes succesfully saved!");
        }
        else
        {
            MessageBox.Show("An error occurred.");
```

```
        }
    }
    else
    {
        MessageBox.Show(e.Error.Message);
    }
}
```

10. You can now build and run your application. On load, it will fetch stores from the `ContosoSales` database, using the Entity Framework through a WCF Service. When you press the **Save changes** button, your changes will be persisted to that database:

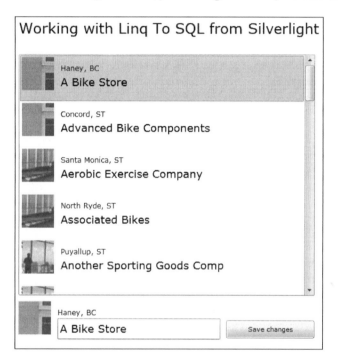

How it works...

Most of the techniques we've used in this recipe have already been discussed in various other recipes in this book, and in any case, you're always working via some kind of service to access your generated LINQ TO SQL entities.

The important thing to keep in mind when working with the LINQ TO SQL from Silverlight is that the generated entities cannot be serialized to Silverlight. If you try to add a service reference to a service that sends regular, generated entities over the wire, you'll notice that the proxy classes can't be created. This is because Silverlight doesn't contain the same set of namespaces (some of which are used by LINQ TO SQL) that you have in regular .NET.

Therefore, you have to create a **Data Transfer Object** (**DTO**). As well as the fact that it's a necessity in this case, using DTOs to transfer over the wire is regarded as a good strategy in general. You typically don't want to transfer the complete entity over the wire (keeping bandwidth and speed in mind), so it's always better to create DTOs and perform some kind of mapping to/from the entities.

So that's exactly what happens in this recipe. In step 2, we've created a DTO class, StoreDTO. It is objects of this type that are transferred—not the complete, generated Store entity itself. In steps 3 and 4, we perform some basic mapping from/to the Store entity.

The other code you see in this recipe (communicating with WCF using data binding) has already been described in other recipes in much more detail. For data binding, have a look at Chapter 2, *An Introduction to Data Binding* and Chapter 3, *Advanced Data Binding*. For WCF, have a look at Chapter 7, *Talking to WCF and ASMX Services*.

There's more...

In this recipe, we've used a WCF service. However, you can use virtually any kind of service you want to get your data across: have a look at other recipes in this book to decide which strategy is right for you. One option that's pretty interesting is using WCF RIA Services, as this makes it a lot easier to work with data in a service-oriented fashion—for one thing, you don't have to create your own DTO objects.

What is LINQ TO SQL?

LINQ TO SQL is often perceived as an **Object Relational Mapper**, which it kind of is, although it doesn't support a lot of features that its bigger brothers (ADO.NET Entity Framework, nHibernate) do support.

More correct would be stating that LINQ TO SQL is actually a provider for LINQ, which allows it to be used to query SQL Server databases. When using LINQ TO SQL, a regular LINQ query is converted to a SQL query to query the database, which in turn is made possible because LINQ TO SQL maps SQL Tables to classes, containing the table columns as data members. This means that, unlike when using the Entity Framework, you are bound to the provided one on one mapping. However, as it is very easy to set up and use, it is still suited for smaller scale applications. To learn more about LINQ TO SQL, have a look at the following URL: http://msdn.microsoft.com/en-us/library/bb425822.aspx.

See also

Related to this recipe, and very similar, is using the Entity Framework as an ORM instead of LINQ TO SQL. Have a look at the *Working with the Entity Framework from Silverlight* recipe for more details on this.

Working with the Entity Framework from Silverlight

One of the often-used **Object Relational Mappers** in a .NET environment is the Entity Framework. This ORM can be used together with Silverlight. As getting data into a Silverlight application is typically a matter of using a service-oriented approach, the same applies here.

In this recipe, you'll learn how to get data from an Entity Framework model into your Silverlight application. This recipe is very much like the previous one—the techniques are the same; the difference mainly lies in the way you create this model and in the queries you'll write to manipulate data.

Getting ready

We're starting from a starter solution that already includes the XAML markup for the UI and a WCF service. If you want, you can use the starter solution located in the `Chapter 10\WorkingWithEF_Starter` folder in the code bundle available on the Packt website. The completed solution can be found in the `Chapter 10\WorkingWithEF_Completed` folder.

As well as this, you'll also need the ContosoSales database (running on SQL 2005, 2008, or an express version of either). You can find a database backup in the `Chapter 10` folder.

How to do it...

We're going to add an **Entity Framework Model** to our application, write the necessary methods to fetch and update data, and connect our Silverlight application to the WCF service calling these methods. To achieve this, complete the following steps:

1. Add a new Entity Framework Model to the web application project. Do this by right-clicking, choosing **Add New Item**, and then choosing **ADO .NET Entity Framework Model**. When asked for a name, name it `ContosoSales`, and point it to the `ContosoSales` database on your SQL Server. When asked which entities to include, select the `Stores` table.

2. Add a new class file to the web application project, name it `StoreDTO.cs`, and add the following code to it:

```
[DataContract]
public class StoreDTO
{
    [DataMember]
    public int StoreID { get; set; }
    [DataMember]
    public string StoreImage { get; set; }
    [DataMember]
```

```
    public string City { get; set; }
    [DataMember]
    public string StateProvince { get; set; }
    [DataMember]
    public string StoreName { get; set; }

    public StoreDTO(int storeID, string storeImage, string city,
string stateProvince, string storeName)
    {
        this.StoreID = StoreID;
        this.StoreImage = StoreImage;
        this.City = City;
        this.StateProvince = StateProvince;
        this.StoreName = StoreName;
    }
}
```

3. Open `DataService.svc` and add the following code to select the stores to transfer to the Silverlight application:

```
[OperationContract]
public List<StoreDTO> GetStores()
{
    using (var ctx = new ContosoSalesEntities())
    {
        List<StoreDTO> storesToReturn = new List<StoreDTO>();

        foreach (var item in ctx.Store.Where(s => s.StoreName.
StartsWith("A")))
        {
            storesToReturn.Add(new StoreDTO(item.StoreID, item.
StoreImage, item.City, item.StateProvince, item.StoreName));
        }

        return storesToReturn;
    }
}
```

4. In the same class, add the following method to update a changed entity:

```
[OperationContract]
public bool SaveStore(StoreDTO storeToSave)
{
    try
```

```
    {
        using (var ctx = new ContosoSalesEntities())
        {
            Store currentStore = ctx.Store.First<Store>(s =>
s.StoreID == storeToSave.StoreID);
            currentStore.StoreName = storeToSave.StoreName;
            ctx.SaveChanges();
        }
        return true;
    }
    catch (Exception)
    {
        return false;
    }
}
```

5. Open the Silverlight application and add a service reference to `DataService.svc` to it by right-clicking on the project and selecting **Add Service Reference**. Name this reference `DataServiceReference`.

6. Open `MainPage.xaml.cs` and add the following property to it:

```
public ObservableCollection<StoreDTO> Stores { get; set; }
```

7. Add a `LoadStores()` method to it and call this method from the constructor:

```
private void LoadStores()
{
    DataServiceClient client = new DataServiceClient();
    client.GetStoresCompleted += new EventHandler<GetStoresComplet
edEventArgs>(client_GetStoresCompleted);
    client.GetStoresAsync();
}


void client_GetStoresCompleted(object sender,
GetStoresCompletedEventArgs e)
{
    if (e.Error == null)
    {
        Stores = e.Result;
        lbStores.ItemsSource = Stores;
    }
}
```

8. Add the following code to make sure your changes are persisted on the click event of the **Save changes** button:

```
private void btnSaveChanges_Click(object sender, RoutedEventArgs
e)
{
    DataServiceClient client = new DataServiceClient();
    client.SaveStoreCompleted += new EventHandler<SaveStoreComplet
edEventArgs>(client_SaveStoreCompleted);
        client.SaveStoreAsync((StoreDTO)((Button)sender).
DataContext);
}


void client_SaveStoreCompleted(object sender,
SaveStoreCompletedEventArgs e)
{
    if (e.Error == null)
    {
        if (e.Result)
        {
            MessageBox.Show("Changes succesfully saved!");
        }
        else
        {
            MessageBox.Show("An error occurred.");
        }
    }
    else
    {
        MessageBox.Show(e.Error.Message);
    }
}
```

9. You can now build and run your application. On load, it will fetch stores from the `ContosoSales` database using the Entity Framework through a WCF Service. When you click on the **Save changes** button, your changes will be persisted to that database.

How it works...

Most of the techniques you see in this recipe have already been described in various other recipes in this book, and in any case, you're always working via some kind of service to access your Entity Framework model/entities.

The important thing to keep in mind when working with the Entity Framework from Silverlight is that the generated entities cannot be serialized to Silverlight: if you try to add a service reference to a service that sends regular, generated entities over the wire, you'll notice the proxy classes can't be created. This is because Silverlight doesn't contain the same set of namespaces (some of which are used by the Entity Framework) that you have in regular .NET.

Therefore, you have to create a **Data Transfer Object** (**DTO**). As well as the fact that it's a necessity in this case, using DTOs to transfer over the wire is regarded as a good strategy in general—you typically don't want to transfer the complete entity over the wire (keeping bandwidth and speed in mind), so it's always better to create DTOs and perform some kind of mapping to/from the entities.

So that's exactly what happens in this recipe. In step 2, we created a DTO class, `StoreDTO`. It is objects of this type that are transferred, and not the complete, generated Store entity itself. In steps 3 and 4, we performed some basic mapping from/to the Store entity.

The other code you see in this recipe (communicating with WCF using data binding) has already been discussed in other recipes in much more detail. For data binding, have a look at Chapter 2, *An Introduction to Data Binding* and Chapter 3, *Advanced Data Binding*. For WCF, have a look at Chapter 7, *Talking to WCF and ASMX Services*.

There's more...

In this recipe, we've used a WCF service. However, you can use virtually any kind of service you want to get your data across. Have a look at other recipes in this book to decide which strategy is right for you. One option that's pretty interesting is using WCF RIA Services, as this makes it a lot easier to work with data in a service-oriented fashion—for one thing, you don't have to create your own DTO objects.

What is the Entity Framework?

The Entity Framework is an Object Relational Mapper, currently at version 4 (included with .NET 4). Its main purpose is abstracting the relational schema of the data stored in the database, and presenting the data as a conceptual schema to the application or developer (comparable to LINQ TO SQL).

Typically, it generates a one-to-one mapping between the tables in your database and the classes in your Entity Model, but you aren't limited to this (as you are when using LINQ TO SQL); and in more advanced applications, you wouldn't want to use the default one-to-one mappings. Using a technology like the Entity Framework allows developers to access their databases through the Entity Model instead of through writing SQL queries and calling stored procedures (although you can do this when needed), thus providing a more concise way of programming in relation to your other code. If you want more information on the Entity Framework, have a look at the following URL: http://msdn.microsoft.com/en-us/library/aa697427 (VS.80) .aspx.

See also

Related to this recipe, and very much alike, is using LINQ TO SQL as an ORM instead of the Entity Framework. Have a look at the *Working with LINQ TO SQL from Silverlight* recipe for more details on this.

Converting a Silverlight application to use WCF RIA Services

At a certain time in a project's lifecycle, you might come across a requirement that's very easy to solve with WCF RIA Services, or you might decide to change the project to start using WCF RIA Services. However, you typically don't want to start from a new solution if you already have some code in place.

This recipe will show you how to enable an existing Silverlight solution to start using WCF RIA Services.

Getting ready

Make sure you have installed the **WCF RIA Services SDK**. This is included in the Silverlight 4 SDK, which you can download at http://www.silverlight.net/.

We're starting from a simple, empty, and existing Silverlight application. No starter solution has been included. A completed solution can be found in the Chapter 10\ EnablingWCFRIAServices_Completed folder.

How to do it...

We're going to enable WCF RIA Services for an existing Silverlight application. To achieve this, complete the following steps:

1. Create a new Silverlight solution and name it **EnablingWCFRIAServices**. Do NOT select **Enable RIA Services** when creating this solution.

2. You'll end up with two projects: the Silverlight project and the hosting web application project. Open the **Project Properties** of the Silverlight project and navigate to the **Silverlight** tab.

3. On this tab, locate the **.NET RIA Services Link** combobox and point this to **EnablingWCFRIAServices.Web**.

4. You can now build and run your application. From this moment on, you can add your DomainServices to the web application.

How it works...

Enabling WCF RIA Services for an existing Silverlight project is actually quite a simple process. By setting the **.NET RIA Services link** property in the Silverlight project properties, Visual Studio will automatically add all the necessary references to both the Silverlight project and the web project you've selected.

From now on, you can start adding DomainServices as described in Chapter 9, *Talking to WCF RIA Services*.

See also

Have a look at Chapter 9, *Talking to WCF RIA Services* to learn more about WCF RIA Services.

Using ASP.NET Authentication in Silverlight

When creating ASP.NET web applications, we often have to authenticate visitors. Not every user has the permission to see just any information contained in the website. For example, only paying subscribers have access to read all articles or perform searches on the site. Also, an administrator should be able to log in to the application and make changes such as changing the content or adding an article.

This typical behavior is supported by some authentication mechanism. ASP.NET 2.0 introduced the ASP.NET Membership API, a built-in authentication system in ASP.NET that supports user authentication, role management, profile management and so on. Through ASP.NET Application Services, added with ASP.NET 3.5, this system is exposed for client-side use. Technologies such as ASP.NET AJAX and Silverlight can use these services to authenticate a user from a client-side application on the server side.

In this sample, we'll look at how Silverlight applications can integrate with an (existing) authentication system built with ASP.NET Membership.

Getting ready

This recipe requires that SQL Server or SQL Server Express is installed on your machine, since the code we are creating is talking to a database.

To follow along with this recipe, you can use a starter solution located in the `Chapter10/ UserAuthentication_Starter` folder in the code bundle available on the Packt website. The completed code for this recipe can be found in the `Chapter10/ UserAuthentication_Completed` folder.

How to do it...

For this recipe, we'll build an application where a user can log in. If the authentication succeeds, he or she can view the employee information. Should he or she fail to provide correct authentication information, the employee data will not be accessible for that user. All the authentication data (usernames and passwords) is contained in a database and is managed by the ASP.NET Membership API, and thus lives at the server side. However, we will allow the user to log in from the client-side Silverlight application. Let's take a look at the steps we need to follow to support ASP.NET Authentication from Silverlight:

1. We'll build this example from scratch. Create a new Silverlight application and name it **UserAuthentication**. The solution contains a Silverlight application and an ASP.NET website.

2. To kick things off, we should first do some work on that website. We'll start by adding a database that contains the user information. For this sample, we'll use the default `ASPNETDB.MDF` database, but all that is explained here can be added to any existing database. To have Visual Studio create this default database for us, select any file in the website in the **Solution Explorer** and then go to **Project | ASP.NET Configuration**. An administration website called **ASP.NET Web Site Administration Tool** will appear, as shown in the following screenshot. Make sure that the SQL Server service is running for the next steps to succeed.

3. In this tool, head over to the **Security** tab. On this page, we must start by changing the authentication type, which is by default set to **Windows Authentication**. Click on the **Select Authentication Type** link and in the page that appears next, select **From the internet**. Confirm by clicking on **Done**.

4. We are now sent back to the **Security** page. We can now add some users using this tool. Click on the **Create user** link and add the details for a user. For the sample, we use the username **normaljoe** and the password **normal?**.

5. At this point, we are ready to start exposing the **ASP.NET Membership** information. We can do so by creating a **service**. We'll want this service to expose the possibility to **authenticate a user** from the client side by verifying his or her username and password combination. However, this functionality is already available in ASP.NET in the form of the ASP.NET Application Services. We thus only need to create a **service endpoint** and **enable the service** (it is disabled by default). Let's start with the service endpoint. Since we don't need to write any functionality for this service, we can add an empty text file and rename it to have the `.svc` extension. Name the newly added file as `AuthService.svc`.

6. In this file, we should now only add a line of code that will link the code already available in ASP.NET with our service endpoint. Add the following line of code:

```
<%@ ServiceHost Language="C#"
  Service="System.Web.ApplicationServices.AuthenticationService" %>
```

7. Next, we need to configure this service as if it were a regular WCF service. As we did not add the service as a service but as a text file, Visual Studio did not add any configuration code to the `web.config` file as it usually does. The following code needs to be added between the `<configuration></configuration>` tags in the `web.config` file. Note the `basicHttpBinding` that is used as binding type for the communication between Silverlight and the ASP.NET Application service.

```
<system.serviceModel>
  <services>
    <service
       name="System.Web.ApplicationServices.AuthenticationService"
       behaviorConfiguration="AuthenticationServiceBehaviors">
      <endpoint
    contract="System.Web.ApplicationServices.AuthenticationService"
       binding="basicHttpBinding" />
    </service>
  </services>
  <serviceHostingEnvironment aspNetCompatibilityEnabled="true"/>
  <behaviors>
    <serviceBehaviors>
      <behavior name="AuthenticationServiceBehaviors">
        <serviceMetadata httpGetEnabled="true"/>
      </behavior>
    </serviceBehaviors>
  </behaviors>
</system.serviceModel>
```

8. As already mentioned, the application services' functionality is not enabled by default; we need to enable it using configuration code. Again in the `web.config` file, add the following code between the `<configuration></configuration>` tags:

```
<system.web.extensions>
  <scripting>
    <webServices>
      <authenticationService enabled="true"
                             requireSSL="false"/>
    </webServices>
  </scripting>
</system.web.extensions>
```

9. Finally, let's check that the authentication mode is set to `Forms` (it should be fine already since we set this using the **ASP.NET Web Site Administration Tool)**.

```
<authentication mode="Forms" />
```

10. We're done what concerns the server side. Let's turn our attention to the client side. We'll start by adding a service reference. Adding this reference is nothing different from any other service reference we have already added. Right-click on the Silverlight project and select the **Add service reference** node. In the dialog box, click on the **Discover** button and the service should be located. Set the service namespace to `AuthenticationService`.

11. The Silverlight application contains two screens. The first screen, the main window, contains some `Button` instances and a `DataGrid`, which shows employee data. No data is shown by default; the user has to click on the **View Users** button. However, this button is only enabled after the user has authenticated. Authentication can be done using the second screen, a `ChildWindow` called `LoginWindow` that contains fields to enter username and password. Both screens can be seen at the end of this recipe and the XAML code can be found in the code bundle.

12. The application checks at startup if the user is already authenticated. It will do so using the operations exposed by the authentication service, namely the `IsLoggedIn` method. We create an instance of the `AuthenticationServiceClient` (the proxy class) and call the `IsLoggedInAsync` method on it. An event handler is attached on the `IsLoggedInCompleted` event.

```
private void UserControl_Loaded(object sender, RoutedEventArgs e)
{
    AuthenticationService.AuthenticationServiceClient proxy = new
      UserAuthentication.AuthenticationService.
        AuthenticationServiceClient();
    proxy.IsLoggedInCompleted += new EventHandler<UserAuthentication
      .AuthenticationService.IsLoggedInCompletedEventArgs>
      (proxy_IsLoggedInCompleted);
    proxy.IsLoggedInAsync();
}
```

13. In the callback method, we can check the result of the service call. If the result is false, the user is asked to enter his or her credentials in the `LoginWindow`, an instance of a Silverlight `ChildWindow`. If it is true, we enable the `ViewUsersButton` as well as the `LogoutButton`. The following code performs the check of the result:

```
void proxy_IsLoggedInCompleted(object sender, UserAuthentication
  .AuthenticationService.IsLoggedInCompletedEventArgs e)
{
    if (e.Result)
    {
        ViewUsersButton.IsEnabled = true;
        LogoutButton.IsEnabled = true;
    }
    else
    {
```

```
    var loginWindow = new LoginWindow();
    loginWindow.Closed += new EventHandler(loginWindow_Closed);
    loginWindow.Show();
  }
}
```

14. To actually log in the user in the `LoginWindow`, we can use the `Login` method. This method is called when the user clicks on the `OKButton`. When the call is completed, in the callback method, the `DialogResult` property of the `ChildWindow` class is evaluated and set to `True` if the login attempt was successful. This can be seen in the following lines of code:

```
private void OKButton_Click(object sender, RoutedEventArgs e)
{
  AuthenticationService.AuthenticationServiceClient proxy = new
    UserAuthentication.AuthenticationService.
  AuthenticationServiceClient();
  proxy.LoginCompleted += new EventHandler<UserAuthentication
    .AuthenticationService.LoginCompletedEventArgs>
    (proxy_LoginCompleted);
  proxy.LoginAsync(UserNameTextBox.Text, UserPasswordBox.Password,
    "", true);
}
void proxy_LoginCompleted(object sender,
  UserAuthentication.AuthenticationService.LoginCompletedEventArgs
  e)
{
  if (e.Error != null)
    StatusTextBlock.Text = e.Error.ToString();
  else
  {
    this.DialogResult = true;
  }
}
```

15. The `MainPage` can now react according to the result of the login attempt in the child window. In step 13, we added an event handler to the `Closed` event of the `LoginWindow` instance. In this method, we can check what the `DialogResult` property contains. If it is `True`, we enable the `ViewUsersButton`. This is shown in the following code snippet:

```
void loginWindow_Closed(object sender, EventArgs e)
{
  LoginWindow loginWindow = (LoginWindow)sender;
  bool? result = loginWindow.DialogResult;
  if (result.HasValue && result.Value)
```

```
  {
    ViewUsersButton.IsEnabled = true;
  }
}
```

16. When the user wants to leave the application, he or she can use the `LogoutButton`. The following code logs the user out of the application:

```
private void LogoutButton_Click(object sender, RoutedEventArgs e)
{
  AuthenticationService.AuthenticationServiceClient proxy = new
    UserAuthentication.AuthenticationService.
  AuthenticationServiceClient();
  proxy.LogoutCompleted += new EventHandler
    <System.ComponentModel.AsyncCompletedEventArgs>
    (proxy_LogoutCompleted);
  proxy.LogoutAsync();
}
void proxy_LogoutCompleted(object sender,
  System.ComponentModel.AsyncCompletedEventArgs e)
{
  if (e.Error == null)
  {
    LogoutButton.IsEnabled = false;
    ViewUsersButton.IsEnabled = false;
  }
}
```

We have now created a Silverlight application that uses the ASP.NET Membership API, more specifically ASP.NET authentication, to authenticate users. The following screenshot shows the **LoginWindow** being displayed because the user is not logged in.

How it works...

When we want to add a Silverlight application to an already existing ASP.NET application that uses ASP.NET Membership, we can easily reuse the authentication system. Since version 3.5, ASP.NET has contained the so-called Application Services, which expose some functionality of the server-side API to use by client-side platforms such as Silverlight.

ASP.NET Membership uses cookies to validate a user request. When we use the API from Silverlight, it creates the same cookies on the client side. When we are thus authenticated in the Silverlight application, we are also authenticated for the ASP.NET application; the cookies are identical.

The functionality for the Application Services is already contained in the ASP.NET platform. Therefore, we don't have to write any code: we only need to create an endpoint (*.svc file), which links the endpoint with the code of ASP.NET. We do need to configure the service; we need to add configuration code similar to a normal WCF service. Also, we need to enable the Application Services using configuration code.

A Silverlight application works with this service just in the same way as it would with any other service: Visual Studio creates a proxy when we add a service reference. This proxy class can be instantiated to use the exposed methods. The service contains methods to check if the user is already logged in and log the user in and out.

See also

In the next recipe, *Using ASP.NET Roles in Silverlight*, we will extend this application so it will check for roles to which the user account was added. In the *Using ASP.NET Profiles in Silverlight* recipe, we will look at how we can extend even further by adding the option to use ASP.NET Profiles.

Using ASP.NET Roles in Silverlight

Very often, user accounts are grouped into **roles**. Roles are then appended **rights** in the application and all users in a specific role inherit the rights of the role. Users can be part of more than one role. The ASP.NET Membership API contains an implementation for roles as well. Using the Application Services we already explored in the previous recipe, we can expose role functionality as well so it can be used in a Silverlight application.

In this recipe, we'll extend the application so we can check if users are in a specific role.

Getting ready

This recipe requires that SQL Server or SQL Server Express is installed on your machine, as the code we are creating talks to a database.

To follow along with this recipe, you can continue to use your code created with the previous recipe. Alternatively, you can also use the starter solution located in the `Chapter10/Roles_Starter` folder in the code bundle available on the Packt website. The completed code for this recipe can be found in the `Chapter10/Roles_Completed` folder.

How to do it...

In this recipe, we will create a few roles to which users can belong. The application we built in the previous example will now get some extra functionalities. The users belonging the `administrator` role will be able to add an employee and users belonging to the `superuser` role can also delete users. Let's take a look at the steps we need to follow to enable the use of ASP.NET roles in Silverlight:

1. We'll continue with the application created in the previous recipe. In the **ASP.NET Web Site Administration Tool**, we should start by enabling roles. To do so, click on the **Enable Roles** link on the **Security** tab. Once enabled, we can add roles. Add the following roles:

   ❑ `users`

   ❑ `admin`

   ❑ `superusers`

2. Create a few extra user accounts using the tool (the process to do so is explained in the previous recipe) and add them to roles as shown in the following table:

Username	Password	Member of
normaljoe	normal?	Users
adminjoe	admin??	Admin, users
superjoe	super??	Superusers, admin, users

3. We can now enable the use of the ASP.NET roles and the accompanying **Application Service**. First, let's add the service endpoint. Add an empty text file and set its name to `RoleService.svc`. The following code should be added to this file. It refers to the code in ASP.NET containing the functionality for the service.

   ```
   <%@ ServiceHost Language="C#"
       Service="System.Web.ApplicationServices.RoleService" %>
   ```

4. With the service endpoint added, we can add the configuration code. In the `web.config` file, in the `<system.serviceModel>` element, we should add the role service to configure the service itself as shown next:

```
<system.serviceModel>
  <services>
    <service
        name="System.Web.ApplicationServices.AuthenticationService"
        behaviorConfiguration="AuthenticationServiceBehaviors">
      <endpoint
    contract="System.Web.ApplicationServices.AuthenticationService"
    binding="basicHttpBinding" />
    </service>
    <service name="System.Web.ApplicationServices.RoleService"
            behaviorConfiguration="RoleServiceBehaviors">
      <endpoint
            contract="System.Web.ApplicationServices.RoleService"
            binding="basicHttpBinding" />
    </service>
  </services>
  <serviceHostingEnvironment aspNetCompatibilityEnabled="true"/>
  <behaviors>
    <serviceBehaviors>
      <behavior name="AuthenticationServiceBehaviors">
        <serviceMetadata httpGetEnabled="true"/>
      </behavior>
      <behavior name="RoleServiceBehaviors">
        <serviceMetadata httpGetEnabled="true"/>
      </behavior>
    </serviceBehaviors>
  </behaviors>
</system.serviceModel>
```

5. As this service is also not enabled by default, we should change the `<system.web.extensions>` as shown in the following code:

```
<system.web.extensions>
  <scripting>
    <webServices>
      <authenticationService enabled="true"
                            requireSSL="false"/>
      <roleService enabled="true"/>
    </webServices>
  </scripting>
</system.web.extensions>
```

6. With that, the server side is ready. We can now look at the Silverlight application. Add a service reference to the newly added service and set its namespace to `RoleService`.

7. To check the roles to which a user belongs, we can use the `GetRolesForCurrentUser` method from the service. This requires that we have first authenticated the user. The following code, which should be added in the `MainPage.xaml.cs` file, retrieves all the roles to which the user belongs after a successful login attempt in the `LoginWindow` screen:

```
void loginWindow_Closed(object sender, EventArgs e)
{
    LoginWindow loginWindow = (LoginWindow)sender;
    bool? result = loginWindow.DialogResult;
    if (result.HasValue && result.Value)
    {
        ViewUsersButton.IsEnabled = true;
        RoleService.RoleServiceClient roleProxy = new
            UserAuthentication.RoleService.RoleServiceClient();
        roleProxy.GetRolesForCurrentUserCompleted += new
            EventHandler<UserAuthentication.RoleService
            .GetRolesForCurrentUserCompletedEventArgs>
            (roleProxy_GetRolesForCurrentUserCompleted);
        roleProxy.GetRolesForCurrentUserAsync();
    }
}
```

8. In the completed event, we get all the roles in an `ObservableCollection<string>`. We can search this collection to see if a user belongs to a specific role and enable or disable specific buttons, as shown next:

```
void roleProxy_GetRolesForCurrentUserCompleted(object sender,
    UserAuthentication.RoleService.GetRolesForCurrentUserCompleted
    EventArgs e)
{
    if (e.Result.Contains("admin"))
    {
        AddUserButton.IsEnabled = true;
    }
    if (e.Result.Contains("superusers"))
    {
        DeleteUserButton.IsEnabled = true;
    }
}
```

We have now successfully integrated Silverlight and ASP.NET Roles. Try logging in with the account in both the `admin` and the `superuser` roles. Based on the role, different functionalities now become available in the application in the form of `Button` controls becoming enabled.

How it works...

Using the ASP.NET Application Services, we can do more than just authenticate a user. The role information contained in the ASP.NET Roles is also exposed and can, therefore, be integrated in a client-side platform. The way to connect and work with this service is similar to the authentication service, which was discussed in the previous recipe.

See also

In the previous recipe, *Using ASP.NET Authentication in Silverlight*, we looked at connecting with ASP.NET Authentication, which is similar to connecting with the roles mechanism. In the next recipe, *Using ASP.NET Profiles in Silverlight*, we'll look at how we can extend further by allowing storing profile information.

Using ASP.NET Profiles in Silverlight

With the ASP.NET Membership API, **profiles** were also introduced. Using profiles, we can easily enable personalization for an application: they enable us to store user preferences between visits, such as preferred colors and so on. Just like authentication and roles, profile information is exposed over an Application Service of ASP.NET. This can be connected with to store and fetch profile information.

In this recipe, we will look at how we can use the information stored in ASP.NET profiles inside a Silverlight application.

Getting ready

This recipe requires that SQL Server or SQL Server Express is installed on your machine, as the code we are creating talks to a database.

To follow along with this recipe, you can continue to use your code created with the previous recipe. Alternatively, you can also use the starter solution located in the `Chapter10/Profiles_Starter` folder in the code bundle available on the Packt website. The completed code for this recipe can be found in the `Chapter10/Profiles_Completed` folder.

How to do it...

In the previous two recipes, we created an application where a user can authenticate with his or her credentials. Based on these, the application will retrieve the roles to which the user belongs and based on this, apply rights within the application. In this part, we'll extend the existing application so that the user can change the background color based on his or her preference. This information will be stored in the profile tables in the ASP.NET-managed database using ASP. NET profiles. Let's take a look at the steps we need to follow to enable this:

1. We'll continue where we left off with the previous recipe. The first thing we'll do is, similarly to the previous recipes, adding the service endpoint. To do so, we'll add an empty text file and set its name to `ProfileService.svc`. The contents of this file is shown next. It refers to the code inside ASP.NET.

```
<%@ ServiceHost Language="C#"
Service="System.Web.ApplicationServices.Profile Service" %>
```

2. Next, we'll configure the service so it can be connected to from the Silverlight application. Change the `<system.serviceModel>` element like this:

```
<system.serviceModel>
  <services>
    <service
      name="System.Web.ApplicationServices.AuthenticationService"
      behaviorConfiguration="AuthenticationServiceBehaviors">
      <endpoint
    contract="System.Web.ApplicationServices.AuthenticationService"
    binding="basicHttpBinding" />
    </service>
    <service name="System.Web.ApplicationServices.RoleService"
            behaviorConfiguration="RoleServiceBehaviors">
      <endpoint
        contract="System.Web.ApplicationServices.RoleService"
        binding="basicHttpBinding" />
    </service>
    <service
      name="System.Web.ApplicationServices.ProfileService"
      behaviorConfiguration="ProfileServiceBehaviors">
      <endpoint
        contract="System.Web.ApplicationServices.ProfileService"
        binding="basicHttpBinding" />
    </service>
  </services>
  <serviceHostingEnvironment aspNetCompatibilityEnabled="true"/>
  <behaviors>
```

```
<serviceBehaviors>
  <behavior name="AuthenticationServiceBehaviors">
    <serviceMetadata httpGetEnabled="true"/>
  </behavior>
  <behavior name="RoleServiceBehaviors">
    <serviceMetadata httpGetEnabled="true"/>
  </behavior>
  <behavior name="ProfileServiceBehaviors">
    <serviceMetadata httpGetEnabled="true"/>
  </behavior>
</serviceBehaviors>
</behaviors>
</system.serviceModel>
```

3. ASP.NET Profiling needs some extra configuration inside the `web.config` file in the `profile` element between the `<system.web></system.web>` tags. Inside this element, we can specify which properties we want profiling to monitor. Here we are specifying that we want to store a property called `Background` of type `string`. The default value is set to `LightGray`. We can store just about any information in here:

```
<profile>
  <properties>
    <add name="Background"
         type="string"
         defaultValue="LightGray" />
  </properties>
</profile>
```

4. The profile application service is not enabled by default, just like the other Application Services. We need to change the `<system.web.extensions>` in the `web.config` to enable it. It can be done as shown next:

```
<system.web.extensions>
  <scripting>
    <webServices>
      <authenticationService enabled="true"
                             requireSSL="false"/>
      <roleService enabled="true"/>
      <profileService enabled="true"
                      readAccessProperties="Background"
                      writeAccessProperties="Background"/>
    </webServices>
  </scripting>
</system.web.extensions>
```

5. With that, the service is configured. We can start using it from the Silverlight application. On the client side, add a service reference and set the namespace to `ProfileService`.

6. The application's user interface is changed slightly. It now contains a few extra `Button` controls allowing to the user to select his or her favorite background color. This information is then stored in the profile of the user. After a user has logged in, we can use the `GetAllPropertiesForCurrentUser` method to retrieve the information already stored for the user. If nothing is stored yet, we will retrieve the default color from the profile service. The following code retrieves this information:

```
private void GetProfileInformation()
{
    ProfileService.ProfileServiceClient profileProxy = new
            UserAuthentication.ProfileService.ProfileServiceClient();
    profileProxy.GetAllPropertiesForCurrentUserCompleted +=
    new EventHandler<UserAuthentication.ProfileService.GetAll
    PropertiesForCurrentUserCompletedEventArgs>(profileProxy_
    GetAllPropertiesForCurrentUserCompleted);

    profileProxy.GetAllPropertiesForCurrentUserAsync(true);
}
```

7. In the `GetAllPropertiesForCurrentUserCompleted` event handler, we have access to *all profile properties*. These results are returned as a `Dictionary<string, object>`. This means that based on a key, we can retrieve the related object. The key in our case is the `Background` and the value is the color stored as a string. In the following code, we are searching the `Dictionary` and changing the `Background` property of the `LayoutRoot Grid` accordingly:

```
void profileProxy_GetAllPropertiesForCurrentUserCompleted(object
    sender, UserAuthentication.ProfileService.GetAllProperties
    ForCurrentUserCompletedEventArgs e)
{
    if (e.Error == null)
    {
        string selectedColor = e.Result["Background"].ToString();
        switch (selectedColor)
        {
            case "LightGray": LayoutRoot.Background =
                                    new SolidColorBrush(Colors.LightGray);
            break;
            case "Blue": LayoutRoot.Background =
                                new SolidColorBrush(Colors.Blue);
            break;
            case "Red": LayoutRoot.Background =
```

```
                          new SolidColorBrush(Colors.Red);
        break;
        case "Green": LayoutRoot.Background =
                          new SolidColorBrush(Colors.Green);
        break;
        default: LayoutRoot.Background =
                    new SolidColorBrush(Colors.LightGray);
        break;
      }
    }
  }
}
```

8. When we click on a `Button`, we want to store the new favorite color in the profile information of ASP.NET. To do so, we start by creating a new `Dictionary<string, object>` in which we add our key and value pair (Background and selected color respectively). Using the `SetPropertiesForCurrentUser` method, exposed by the profile service, we can store this information, as shown next:

```
private void ChangeColorForUser(string selectedColor)
{
  ProfileService.ProfileServiceClient profileProxy = new
    ProfileService.ProfileServiceClient();
  Dictionary<string, object> profileInfos = new
    Dictionary<string, object>();
  profileInfos.Add("Background", selectedColor);
  profileProxy.SetPropertiesForCurrentUserAsync(profileInfos,
    false, profileInfos);
  profileProxy.SetPropertiesForCurrentUserCompleted += new
    EventHandler<UserAuthentication.ProfileService.SetProperties
    ForCurrentUserCompletedEventArgs>
    (profileProxy_SetPropertiesForCurrentUserCompleted);
}
private void LightGrayButton_Click(object sender,
  RoutedEventArgs e)
{
  ChangeColorForUser("LightGray");
}
private void BlueButton_Click(object sender, RoutedEventArgs e)
{
  ChangeColorForUser("Blue");
}
private void RedButton_Click(object sender, RoutedEventArgs e)
{
  ChangeColorForUser("Red");
```

```
}
private void GreenButton_Click(object sender, RoutedEventArgs e)
{
  ChangeColorForUser("Green");
}
```

10. In the `SetPropertiesForCurrentUserCompleted` event handler, we can
    perform a call to the `GetProfileInformation` method (shown earlier) again
    so that the new information is retrieved again:

```
void profileProxy_SetPropertiesForCurrentUserCompleted(object
  sender, UserAuthentication.ProfileService.SetProperties
  ForCurrentUserCompletedEventArgs e)
{
  GetProfileInformation();
}
```

We have now stored and retrieved information from the ASP.NET profile service using its application service. All the information stored and used by the Silverlight application is also accessible by the ASP.NET application and vice-versa.

How it works...

Similarly to both authentication and roles, ASP.NET profiles are exposed using an ASP.NET application service. The code for this service lives inside the ASP.NET platform; we thus don't need to write any code for the service itself, we only have to write some configuration code.

Profiling allows us to store any type of object. Here, we used a simple string to store the background color. We need to specify which properties will be used in the configuration code.

See also

In this chapter, we have already looked at two other ASP.NET Application services. In *Using ASP.NET Authentication in Silverlight*, we looked at using its authentication ability. In the previous recipe, *Using ASP.NET Roles in Silverlight*, we looked at using ASP.NET roles from a Silverlight perspective.

Appendix

Creating a REST service from WCF

Using WCF Services, it is possible to expose a REST endpoint. This way, we can easily create a WCF services project in which some services have a SOAP endpoint while others have a REST endpoint.

In .NET 4.0, there are several ways to create REST services. In this example, we'll use a manual approach based on the `WebHttpBinding`. This process is quite simple: we need to make a configuration change to the configuration code of the service and apply an attribute on the service methods.

We'll create a small sample service project and expose the service as a REST endpoint. To do so, create a new empty ASP.NET web application in Visual Studio 2010 and name it `OfficeSupplies`. Within the created web application, add a new WCF service called `TonerService`. This triggers the creation of both the service interface, `ITonerService.cs`, and the service implementation, `TonerService.cs`.

To allow our service to communicate using REST, we'll first create a REST endpoint. In the `web.config` file, we'll start by adding the `webHttp` behavior:

```
<system.serviceModel>
  <behaviors>
  ...
    <endpointBehaviors>
      <behavior name="webBehavior">
        <webHttp/>
      </behavior>
    </endpointBehaviors>
  </behaviors>
</system.serviceModel>
```

Next, we can add a new endpoint that uses this behavior:

```
<services>
  <service name="OfficeSupplies.TonerService">
    <endpoint
      address=""
      behaviorConfiguration="webBehavior"
      binding="webHttpBinding"
      bindingConfiguration=""
      contract="OfficeSupplies.ITonerService"/>
  </service>
</services>
</system.serviceModel>
```

Finally, we have to apply an attribute, `WebGetAttribute`, on the service methods we want to expose over REST. Using the `UriTemplate` on this attribute, we can use the same endpoint for several service methods. In the following sample code snippet, we can see that `IsTonerAvailable` has its `UriTemplate` set to Toner:

```
[OperationContract]
[WebGet(UriTemplate = "toner",
  BodyStyle = WebMessageBodyStyle.Bare,
  RequestFormat = WebMessageFormat.Xml)]
bool IsTonerAvailable();
```

This service method can thus be accessed using `http://localhost:123/TonerService.svc/Toner`.

If we want to pass in a parameter, we can do so using a query expression. If we want to check the toner for a specific color, we can pass the color in using the following method:

```
[OperationContract]
[WebGet(UriTemplate = "toner/{color}",
  BodyStyle = WebMessageBodyStyle.Bare,
  RequestFormat = WebMessageFormat.Xml)]
bool IsColorAvailable(string color);
```

To invoke this service, we can perform a call to `http://localhost:123/TonerService.svc/Toner/Red`.

Installing a SQL Server database

In some samples of the book, we use a SQL Server database. To install a SQL Server database, we can either attach the SQL Server MDF file to SQL Server or execute a SQL query file that contains the commands to create the database, its tables, and its columns.

Attaching an MDF file

The simplest way to install a database is attaching the database into the SQL Server instance. To do so, follow the given steps:

1. Open SQL Server Management Studio and connect to the database engine (most of the time, this instance is called localhost).

2. Within the **Object Explorer**, right-click on the **Databases** node and select **Attach**.

3. In the **Attach Databases** dialog, click on the **Add** button and browse to the location of the MDF file that contains the database. Click **OK**; SQL Server will now attach the database to the SQL Server instance.

The database can now be consulted from within SQL Server Management Studio and it can also be used in our own applications.

Executing a query file

If attaching the database is not an option (for example, on an externally hosted database server), we can use a query file that contains all the commands needed to recreate the database and its tables. To do so, follow the next steps:

1. Open SQL Server Management Studio and connect to the database engine (usually localhost).

2. Within Management Studio, select **File | Open File** and select the query file (`*.sql`) containing the SQL commands.

3. Click on **Execute.**

Management Studio will now execute the commands, resulting in the database being created.

Working with Fiddler

Fiddler is a web debugging proxy tool. Being a proxy, it redirects all traffic going from your computer to the internet. This way, we can inspect the contents of the packages being sent over the wire. Fiddler also works for inspecting traffic to the local web server (ASP.NET Development Server or local IIS).

While developing with Silverlight in combination with services, Fiddler is a valuable tool. Without a debugging proxy, it's not possible to see what data Silverlight is sending to the service or to see the response coming back from the service. In this book, we show the usage of Fiddler several times. In your daily development life, Fiddler can help you track bugs when building Silverlight applications that work with services.

Setting up Fiddler is easy. To install it, download a free copy at `http://www.fiddler2.com/fiddler2/`. Once installed, if you're using Internet Explorer, you can start it by selecting **Tools | Fiddler2**.

Fiddler will open its main window, showing all the traffic going in and out from your machine.

Local traffic

By default, Fiddler will not capture local traffic (traffic going to your ASP.NET Development Server or local IIS) because Internet Explorer and .NET in general don't send requests for `http://localhost` through any proxy. It is however, important to be able to do so, mainly in development stages.

There are several ways to work around this problem. The easiest solution is replacing `http://localhost` in your request to `http://<ComputerName>` (for example `http://Dev01` where `Dev01` is the name of your computer). Another solution is replacing `http://localhost` with `http://ipv4.fiddler` (for IPv4 requests) or `http://ipv6.fiddler` (for IPv6 requests). If your request contains a port number (for example. `http://localhost:123/MyService.svc`), this port number should remain in the changed URL (for example. `http://ipv4.fiddler:123/MyService.svc`).

Working with the Silverlight control toolkit

The Silverlight Control Toolkit is a collection of controls and utilities that is not part of the default installation of Silverlight. It's hosted on CodePlex (Microsoft's open source hosting website: `http://www.codeplex.com`) as a project owned by Microsoft itself and managed by the Silverlight product team. It has an out-of-band release cycle (meaning that releases of the toolkit are not necessarily synchronized with releases of Silverlight). Being hosted on CodePlex also means that you get all the source code for the controls, including many unit tests.

To download the toolkit, go to `http://www.codeplex.com/Silverlight` where you can find the latest release. After installation, the new controls are added to the **Toolbox** in Visual Studio.

Once installed, the controls can be used just like regular controls. On adding one of these controls to your XAML, Visual Studio will add an XML namespace mapping (`xmlns:controlsToolkit="clr-namespace:System.Windows.Controls; assembly=System.Windows.Controls.Toolkit"`) within the XAML and create a reference to the toolkit assembly, `System.Windows.Control.Toolkit`.

Index

Thank you for buying
Microsoft Silverlight 4 Data and Services Cookbook

About Packt Publishing

Packt, pronounced 'packed', published its first book "*Mastering phpMyAdmin for Effective MySQL Management*" in April 2004 and subsequently continued to specialize in publishing highly focused books on specific technologies and solutions.

Our books and publications share the experiences of your fellow IT professionals in adapting and customizing today's systems, applications, and frameworks. Our solution-based books give you the knowledge and power to customize the software and technologies you're using to get the job done. Packt books are more specific and less general than the IT books you have seen in the past. Our unique business model allows us to bring you more focused information, giving you more of what you need to know, and less of what you don't.

Packt is a modern, yet unique publishing company, which focuses on producing quality, cutting-edge books for communities of developers, administrators, and newbies alike. For more information, please visit our website: www.PacktPub.com.

About Packt Enterprise

In 2010, Packt launched two new brands, Packt Enterprise and Packt Open Source, in order to continue its focus on specialization. This book is part of the Packt Enterprise brand, home to books published on enterprise software – software created by major vendors, including (but not limited to) IBM, Microsoft and Oracle, often for use in other corporations. Its titles will offer information relevant to a range of users of this software, including administrators, developers, architects, and end users.

Writing for Packt

We welcome all inquiries from people who are interested in authoring. Book proposals should be sent to author@packtpub.com. If your book idea is still at an early stage and you would like to discuss it first before writing a formal book proposal, contact us; one of our commissioning editors will get in touch with you.

We're not just looking for published authors; if you have strong technical skills but no writing experience, our experienced editors can help you develop a writing career, or simply get some additional reward for your expertise.

3D Game Development with Microsoft Silverlight 3

ISBN: 978-1-847198-92-1   Paperback: 452 pages

A practical guide to creating real-time responsive online 3D games in Silverlight 3 using C#, XBAP WPF, XAML, Balder, and Farseer Physics Engine

1. Develop online interactive 3D games and scenes in Microsoft Silverlight 3 and XBAP WPF

2. Integrate Balder 3D engine 1.0, Farseer Physics Engine 2.1, and advanced object-oriented techniques to simplify the game development process

3. Enhance development with animated 3D characters, sounds, music, physics, stages, gauges, and backgrounds

Plone 3 Multimedia

ISBN: 978-1-847197-66-5   Paperback: 315 pages

Embed, display, and manage multimedia content in your Plone website

1. Build a modern full-featured multimedia CMS with Plone and add-on products

2. Use and extend specialized multimedia content-types for images, audio, video, and Flash

3. Set up a custom multimedia CMS by collaborating with external resources such as YouTube, Google videos, and so on

4. Follow a step-by-step tutorial to create a feature-packed media-rich Plone site

Please check **www.PacktPub.com** for information on our titles

JavaFX 1.2 Application Development Cookbook

ISBN: 978-1-847198-94-5   Paperback: 360 pages

Over 60 recipes to create rich Internet applications with many exciting features

1. Easily develop feature-rich internet applications to interact with the user using various built-in components of JavaFX

2. Make your application visually appealing by using various JavaFX classes—ListView, Slider, ProgressBar—to display your content and enhance its look with the help of CSS styling

3. Enhance the look and feel of your application by embedding multimedia components such as images, audio, and video

Microsoft Silverlight 4 Business Application Development

ISBN: 978-1-847199-76-8   Paperback: 446 pages

Build enterprise-ready business applications with Silverlight

1. An introduction to building enterprise-ready business applications with Silverlight quickly.

2. Get hold of the basic tools and skills needed to get started in Silverlight application development

3. Integrate different media types, taking the RIA experience further with Silverlight, and much more!

4. Rapidly manage business focused controls, data, and business logic connectivity.

Please check **www.PacktPub.com** for information on our titles

Printed in Great Britain by
Amazon.co.uk, Ltd.,
Marston Gate.